PRAISE FOR *BULLETS OVER HOLLYWOOD*

——— roughly reviews a century of bad guys, tough broads, and blood-
d conflict."

—Variety

——— mplete . . . a study of the form as has seen print. A fine and welcome
ration of a classic genre."

—The Hollywood Reporter

——— than just a recap of great films; it doubles as a social history of
can organized crime."

—New York Post

——— ts Over Hollywood hits its target."

—Louisville Courier-Journal

Weaves in . . . stories of bootleggers, corrupt cops, dirty politicians and
gsters such as Al Capone [to] give a sense of where the facts ended and
celluloid myth began."

—Albany Times Union

"Fascinating and copiously informative history of the 'mob movie.'"

—Midwest Book Review

"Exhaustive history of the gangster film . . . drawing attention to the
forgotten gems."

—Philadelphia News-Gleaner

"Conveys the appeal of . . . such icons as Humphrey Bogart, Edward G.
Robinson and James Cagney, through concise analyses of key crime films
and well-drawn personal histories."

Publishers Weekly

"You will find lots of neat nuggets . . . but, even more, you will find a rich vein of cinematic history, well mined and analyzed."

—*Chicago Sun-Times*

"The section on women in [gangster] films—'Molls, Twists, Babes, and B Girls'—is particularly well done."

—*Denver Post*

"At its best discussing recurring themes in gangster films from the silent era into the 1950s . . . through [to] today."

—*CNN.com*

"[Has] all my favorites, including White Heat, High Sierra, and The Godfather. Rat-tat-a-tat!"

—Jim's Picks, *The Michael Dresser Show*

"A lively history of gangsters in American film."

—*AmericanMafia.com*

"A kaleidoscopic and entertaining look at the gangster genre from the silents to 2004 . . . fascinating."

—*Edmonton (Alberta) Journal*

"Packed with behind-the-scenes anecdotes and info about real-life hoods and their cinematic alter egos."

—*The A-List*

BULLETS
OVER
HOLLYWOOD

BULLETS OVER HOLLYWOOD

The American Gangster Picture
from the Silents to "The Sopranos"

John McCarty

DA CAPO PRESS
A Member of the Perseus Books Group

Many of the designations used by manufacturers and sellers to distinguish their products are claimed as trademarks. Where those designations appear in this book and Da Capo Press was aware of a trademark claim, those designations have been printed with initial capital letters.

Copyright © 2004 by John McCarty

Designed by Reginald R. Thompson
Set in 12 point ITC Clearface by The Perseus Books Group

Cataloging-in-Publication data for this book is available from the Library of Congress.

First Da Capo Press edition 2004
First Da Capo Press paperback edition 2005
ISBN 0-306-81429-3 (pbk.)

Published by Da Capo Press
A Member of the Perseus Books Group
http://www.dacapopress.com

Da Capo Press books are available at special discounts for bulk purchases in the U.S. by corporations, institutions, and other organizations. For more information, please contact the Special Markets Department at the Perseus Books Group, 11 Cambridge Center, Cambridge, MA 02142, or call (800) 255-1514 or (617) 252-5298, or e-mail special.markets@perseusbooks.com.

1 2 3 4 5 6 7 8 9—09 08 07 06 05

For those young people who
fall in love with film like I did
at an early age—and who are
eager to know what came before.

And for "Bugs"—my best pal.

Contents

x CONTENTS

"He will steal, Sir, an egg out of a cloister."
—William Shakespeare,
All's Well That Ends Well

Prologue:
Gunslingers to Gangsters

"There are enough killings herein to fill the
quota for an old time cowboy-Indian thriller."
—Variety on Little Caesar, January 1, 1931

HEIR TO THE WESTERN

F OR MOST OF THE TWENTIETH CENTURY, the era the film medium
came into its own, the morality plays of the so-called "cowboy
picture," or Western genre, were a staple of American movies and
television, as popular abroad as at home. Without a doubt, the degree of
the Western's popularity with the public waxed and waned, but the genre
was so quintessentially American that the American moviegoer and TV
watcher's affection for it remained constant, and their devotion to it
almost patriotic—until the form was called out into the street for a
shootout by its ambitious heir apparent: the gangster movie.

Sent to Boot Hill, the Western became the victim not only of the gangster movie's superior firepower but also of the greater relevance the
gangster movie's morality plays had to audiences moving quickly into
another millennium.

The gangster, like his forebear in American history and culture, the
gunslinger, is a classic character—and the gangster movie, like the Western, one of the American cinema's staple film genres. In many ways, the
two genres are strikingly similar. Gunplay and the violent struggle for
power and territory are the thematic linchpins that hold both of them

1

together. In the archetypal Western, however, the focus is typically on the hero—the strong, silent cowpoke, reticent about using his guns, but who is ultimately forced into a showdown with the bad guys who are victimizing the helpless townsfolk.

The archetypal gangster film offers basically the same ingredients, transposed to a modern, usually urban, setting. But then it turns the tables on audience expectations by often casting its spotlight not on the good guy cleaning up the town but on the bad guy, grappling for power and position. This link and others (as well as other distinctions) between the Western and the gangster film are not just superficial, for the gangster film is not simply an offshoot of the Western. It is the heir to it in our popular culture. It is the modern continuation of America's story reflected on film—a story the Western had grown too old to tell.

CROSSBREEDS AND RETREADS

During the transitional period of the 1930s to the 1950s, when the Western peaked in quantity and the upstart gangster film came on like, well, gangbusters, the Western and the gangster film sometimes merged when such stalwart B Western heroes as Roy Rogers, Gene Autry, Hopalong Cassidy, Tex Ritter, Tim McCoy, and many others found themselves going up against modern-day gangsters rather than Indians and outlaws. This cycle of films even had a name—the "cowboys versus modern gangsters" picture. Some of these crossbreeds were even set in traditional Old West period circa the 1880s, yet they still gave the bad guys the contemporary moniker of "gangsters," as in 1944's *Gangsters of the Frontier*, for example.

Even earlier, such veteran silent-era Western movie stars as William S. Hart saw the handwriting taking shape on the wall. As early as 1920, Hart made a full-fledged gangster movie himself, *The Cradle of Courage,* in which he played a petty crook who returns from the battlefields of World War I a changed man with a sense of honor and rectitude he never had before. Thus, he becomes a cop dedicated to cleaning up the crime-ridden streets of San Francisco.

This theme of the vet who returns from the war a changed man—albeit one who, unlike Hart, would often turn to a life of crime rather than away from it as a result of his wartime experiences and the economic and psychological pressures he faces at home—would become a fixture of many gangster movies, particularly those belonging to the subcategory of crime film known as film noir.

Like William S. Hart, virtually every other major actor associated with the Western put away his six-gun from time to time, took up a "gat," a "roscoe," or a "police special," and made a gangster movie or two—including the Western's greatest icon: John Wayne. Of Wayne's last four films, two were gangster movies[1]: *McQ* (1974) cast the Duke as an aging but still tough San Francisco cop in the Dirty Harry mold who brings down a crime lord (Al Lettieri) for killing his partner; and in *Brannigan* (1975), the Duke plays a gruff Chicago cop turned fish out of water when sent to London to bring an extradited drug kingpin (John Vernon) back to America for trial.

Because the ingredients of the Western and the gangster movie are fundamentally the same, the studios could often get more bang for their project development buck by taking the same story and making or remaking it in both genres. In this way, Warner Brothers could recycle a hit gangster film like *High Sierra* (1941) as a Western, *Colorado Territory* (1949), scoring another box office hit, then recycle it back to its gangster movie roots, this time in color and CinemaScope, under a brand-new title—*I Died a Thousand Times* (1955). Likewise, MGM could turn its gangster/heist classic *The Asphalt Jungle* (1950) into a Western—*The Badlanders*(1959)—then update it as a "blaxploitation" gangster movie, *Cool Breeze* (1972). Another studio, Twentieth Century Fox, could repackage a suspense-filled gangster movie about hostage-taking like *Show Them No Mercy!* (1935) into a suspense-filled noir Western about hostage-taking called *Rawhide* (1951). Or the same studio could cost-effectively repackage a potent drama about a dysfunctional family of ambitious, and shady, financiers like *House of Strangers* (1949) into a potent dysfunctional family-on-the-plains drama about powerful land barons and their sons called *Broken Lance* (1955).

Back-and-forth reshufflings, switcheroos, and retreads such as these were facilitated not only because the two genres easily assimilated each other's story ingredients but also because, although set in different time periods, the two genres are fundamentally about the same thing: the American odyssey.

CHANGING LANDSCAPE

The Western outlaw, like his opposite number the Western hero, was a product of America's epic nineteenth-century saga—the rugged, often violent settling of the frontier. Likewise, the gangster and his nemesis the T-man (or G-man) emerged with urban America in the twentieth century as part of our transformation from a wild frontier society to an industrialized one in which the ethnic groups pouring into America's great, growing cities had to struggle, sometimes viciously, to claim their share of the New World pie.

Even though America's nineteenth-century outlaws such as Jesse James, Butch Cassidy, and Billy the Kid sometimes ran in gangs, they were basically loners. They were also fairly young—in their teens or early twenties. Their lawless exploits reflected what might be called America's "adolescence"—that period during which America grew from volatile teenhood to early adulthood. As the country's maturing process continued into the next century, these outlaws, reflecting America's changing cultural (and geographic) landscape, morphed into something new and equally mythic: organized gangs whose individual members became popularly known as "gangsters."

In an effort not just to survive but to come to grips with one another, America's urban enclaves saw the rise of numerous ethnic gangs and/or strong-arm political affiliations with such colorful names as the True Blood Americans, the Bowery Boys, the Shirt Tails, the American Guards, the Hell's Kitchen Gang, the Gas House Gang, the Gophers, the Dead Rabbits, the Sydney Ducks, the Whyos, the Bloody Tubs, the Roach Guards, the Potato Pealers, the Plug Uglies, the Vampires, and the Tongs—groups that frequently clashed head-to-head with one another, and with the law, to achieve economic, political, and social power.

Police forces, buoyed by strong public support, swelled to combat the mounting problem of escalating street violence and the corruption of public officials by these warring gangs, problems that remained fairly localized and manageable until Prohibition.

THE TOMMY GUN AND THE POISONED CUP

Of the nation's failed experiment to get Americans off booze, historian Herbert Asbury noted: "The American people had expected to be greeted, when the great day came, by a covey of angels bearing gifts of peace, happiness, prosperity and salvation, which they had been assured would be theirs when the demon rum had been scotched. Instead, they were met by a horde of bootleggers, moonshiners, rumrunners, hijackers, gangsters, racketeers, trigger men, venal judges, corrupt police, crooked politicians, and speakeasy operators, all bearing the twin symbols of the Eighteenth Amendment—the Tommy Gun and the poisoned cup."[2]

When Prohibition arrived on America's doorstep to deny Americans even a cold glass of beer, the larger and more powerful of America's urban gangs were beginning to lose ground, crumbling under the weight of public pressure for law and order. But Prohibition enabled them to reorganize and develop even stronger muscle by engaging in illegal bootlegging to America's thirsty citizens. Thus, the likes of gang leaders such as Al Capone, heretofore looked upon by the public as lowlife thugs and menaces to society, became heroes to that same public because of their flouting of the Eighteenth Amendment.

Reaping huge financial profits from their bootlegging activities, Capone's gang and other gangs flourished and ultimately grew into a powerful national syndicate that moved into a host of illegal and equally profitable activities after Prohibition was abolished. The mob's power began to wane during the crackdown of the late 1930s. But the mob got a new lease on life when the government called upon the "patriotism" of important mob chieftains—such as Meyer Lansky and the deported Lucky Luciano—to assist the Allied war effort by using their muscle to ensure that industries and ports vital to the success of the war effort, at home and abroad, did not fall prey to strikers and saboteurs. As a result, the power of the mob not only revived during World War II but also got stronger than ever.

Because of Prohibition, the Great Depression, and World War II, gangsters assumed the mantle of yesteryear's gunslingers and outlaws, and the story of America's gangsters replaced the Western as America's quintessential narrative. It told the story of *modern* America. And, almost from its inception more than a century ago, the silver screen has been telling that story, and fostering the myth of the gangster as antihero in the process.

THE KINGS OF THE UNDERWORLD

Particularly during the golden age of the studio system in the 1930s and 1940s, when each of the major studios was cranking out hundreds of films every year—many of them gangster movies—virtually every major male star in Hollywood played a gangster at some point: Gary Cooper,

Clark Gable, Spencer Tracy, Paul Muni, Robert Taylor, Burt Lancaster, Kirk Douglas, John Garfield—the list goes on and on. Most would not become associated with and therefore not be typecast by their bad guy roles. Others, such as George Raft, would succumb to such typecasting. Only three major stars stand out for not only having become associated with gangster roles, but also possessing the versatility to transcend their genre identification and avoid typecasting in such roles: Edward G. Robinson, James Cagney, and Humphrey Bogart.

Individually, these three made more gangster movies in their careers than anyone before or since. For example, of the almost ninety films Edward G. Robinson appeared in during his film career of six decades, almost a third of them were crime and gangster movies. Cagney, whose film career also spanned six decades, made more than sixty films—a third of them in the gangster/crime genre. As for Bogart, his total is thirty-two gangster and crime pictures out of a total of almost eighty films.

More remarkable still is that whereas many of the gangster and crime films they made (quite a few for the same studio, Warner Brothers) may seem similar and tend to overlap in our minds, the *type* of character etched by these actors and developed from film to film was quite distinct. In other words, although the plots of the films may have been interchangeable, the personae these actors created in them were not. The murderously covetous Robinson gangster is as different from the psychopathic gangster hooked on violence personified by Cagney as the doomed loner inescapably trapped in his own skin fashioned by Bogart is from each of them. To some degree, every movie and TV crook, gangster, or public enemy played by anybody ever since—from Marlon Brando, Walter Matthau, Peter Falk, and Warren Beatty to Al Pacino, James Caan, Tom Hanks, and James Gandolfini is a variation to some degree on one (or all three) of the gangland types immortalized by these influential kings of the cinematic underworld. In his bravura turn as mob boss Tony Soprano in the dynamic HBO teleseries *The Sopranos*, James Gandolfini cleverly manages to embody all three types—sometimes at once!

THE GANGSTER OUTLAWS

Many of history's most notorious gangsters were also outlaws in the traditional Old West meaning of the term. They were descendants in spirit if not actual blood from Old West forbears like Jesse James, Billy the Kid, and the Younger Gang. In many cases, the only difference between these descendants and their nineteenth-century forbears was their method of getaway . . . horsepower rather than horseflesh.

It was the economic downturn of the Great Depression, coming on the heels of Prohibition, that contributed to the growing fascination in the country and in the movies with this old/new breed of outlaw gangster. As heartland Americans lost their jobs or saw their farms foreclosed on by that once-admired symbol of the Establishment, the banking system, rural gangs rose up to assault that system, becoming mythic figures to a society whose fear of such gangs had begun to give way to admiration.

Largely because of the tabloid newspapers of the day and the movies that drew inspiration from the blood and thunder headlines in them, the exploits of these heartland outlaw gangsters have taken on the characteristics of myth as strongly as their big-city counterparts, and their colorful names are as famous today as when they lived, killed, and died. Names such as John Dillinger, Bonnie Parker and Clyde Barrow, Ma Barker and her boys, Baby Face Nelson, Pretty Boy Floyd, Machine Gun Kelly, and many, many more resonate still. All had at least one movie made about them, most more than one.

THEY WENT THAT-A-WAY

As America comes to grips with its transformation from an industrialized nation to a high-tech, skill-oriented, primarily service-based society, gangster films continue, and even grow, in popularity. There are several reasons for this, I believe.

One reason is the anarchic appeal of the genre itself, which viewers find liberating, especially as the rules, regulations, and restrictions imposed by contemporary society increase. The antihero gangster—like his counterpart hero or villain in the Western—is not bound by fences. He goes where he wants, does what he wants, and takes no bull from anybody. "It's probably wishful thinking on some level," says writer-director David Chase in explaining the extraordinary impact on the public of gangster movies in general and his hit TV show about the mob, *The Sopranos*, in particular. "People want to think that they could be powerful enough and demand enough respect and fear that they could get whatever they want. That's a fantasy. I walk into a restaurant; they'll kick the guy out of the table he's sitting at so I can sit down. Tony Soprano doesn't have to come home at night; his wife puts up with it. People are scared of him and nobody messes with him—that's a big wish fulfillment. [Also], our lives have become so enmeshed with bureaucracy and nations and large things, that the tribal nature of human life is becoming erased. We are, at base, a tribal species. And we like stories about tribal conflict, tribal loyalty, and along with that is . . . the notion that people who betray really pay."[3]

Another reason is that in times of great turmoil or change, people tend to look back to the way things were. In terms of entertainment, that means opting for the recognizable and familiar—genre forms that may be as old as time but are still relevant, and thus reassuring.

Westerns peaked in popularity during the first half of the twentieth century primarily for that reason: they allowed Americans in the midst of great social, political, and economic change to find comfort in the familiar iconography of a less troubled time—at a time when that iconography still connected with much of the population.

Today, the characters, the landscapes, and the mythologies of the Western no longer provide the comforting familiarity or the degree of reassurance that they once did because our western past is now *too* remote. It is no longer relevant to an American population that is now too young to feel much sense of connection with the past, the epoch the Western conjures up.

Except for such anomalies as 1990's *Dances with Wolves,* actor-director Kevin Costner's politically correct picture postcard of the American Indian's frontier experience, and the occasional Clint Eastwood Western, such as 1992's *Unforgiven*—films that are more about past Westerns than our western past—the made-in-America Western is today as moribund as its epoch. The best Westerns—the classics of the genre—and those that transcended genre pigeonholing to become classics of world cinema have all gone that-a-way. One has to journey back to 1969 to rediscover the last one—and a very late contribution to the genre it was: *The Wild Bunch*, Sam Peckinpah's violent masterpiece about the passing of the West and, implicitly, the Western genre as well.

European filmmakers sought for a time to keep the Western alive by making so-called "spaghetti" or "Euro" Westerns, films that reflected their love of the Western by mimicking it. Shot on European locales resembling the American West, such as Almería, Spain, many of these films may *look* like authentic Westerns, but no matter how hard they try, they don't *feel* like the real thing—because the Old West *experience* is unique to America.

Not so the phenomenon of gangsterism. Virtually every country on the planet has had—and continues to have—its own problems with native gangsters. And so the gangster genre travels well. So as not to make this book the size of a doorstop, however, *Bullets Over Hollywood* focuses solely on the *American* gangster picture.

THE SAGA CONTINUES

The almost century-old American gangster film already boasts a substantial list of drama, comedy, and even musical classics, such as *Regeneration* (1915), *Scarface* (1932), *The Roaring Twenties* (1939), *White Heat* (1949), *Gun Crazy* (1949), *Bonnie and Clyde* (1967), *The Godfather* and *The Godfather Part II* (1972, 1974), *Once Upon a Time in America* (1984), *GoodFellas* (1990), *The Little Giant* (1933), *A Slight Case of Murder* (1938), *Brother Orchid* (1940), *Lights of New York* (1928), *Love Me or Leave Me* (1955), and *It's Always Fair Weather* (1955). But the best is not all behind us. Bold, even innovative, new contributions to the genre keep popping up on the big screen (as well as the small, in the form of *The Sopranos*, a cultural phenomenon)—such as *Carlito's Way* (1993), *The Last Seduction* (1993), *Donnie Brasco* (1997), *Road to Perdition* (2002), *Gangs of New York* (2002), and *Chicago* (2002), a groundbreaking movie musical set in the milieu of roaring 1920s gangland.

The cinema's fascination with modern day outlawry and modern day outlaws—a.k.a., gangsters—flickers on unabated. The themes, characters, landscapes, and stories of the gangster genre continue to prove enduring and resilient enough to be updated, reshaped, and expanded upon to connect with even today's teenagers and young adults.

Bullets Over Hollywood is this intersection of the movies and that dark corner of the American landscape the movies have been exploring, exploiting, and mythologizing for more than a century. A celluloid landscape of:

Bootleggers and bootlickers
Cutthroats and crooked politicians
Drug dealers and deadbeats
Flappers and feds
Heroes and hoods
Mean streets and meaner folks

Mobsters and molls

Roscoes and rackets

Tommy guns and T-men

A landscape of corpses where bullets are always flying, which, if it were a theme park, would go by the name "Underworld."

PART ONE
THE DEVIL'S TRIANGLE

"Poverty is the parent of revolution and crime."
—Aristotle, philosopher, (384–322 BC)

1

Mean Streets

"Crime is but a left-handed form of human endeavor."
—W. R. Burnett, The Asphalt Jungle (1949)

FATHER OF FILM

BLAME IT ON DAVID WARK GRIFFITH.
D. W., as this pioneer American filmmaker is more familiarly known, was born in Kentucky a decade after the end of the Civil War in which his father Jacob had fought as a colonel for the army of the Confederate States of America. Nicknamed "Roaring Jake," the elder Griffith became an alcoholic and somewhat of a ne'er-do-well after the war. When not drunk or idling, he would regale his son with tales of the south's bitter defeat in the "War of Northern Aggression." Many of these tales (apocryphal and otherwise) later found their way into his son's inflammatory Civil War epic *The Birth of a Nation* (1915), a film that remains as controversial today for its negative stereotyping of blacks and its celebration of the Ku Klux Klan as when it was made.

A landmark in the art of motion picture storytelling, but with a decidedly racist slant, this groundbreaking film continues to tarnish Griffith's reputation as much as enhance it.[1] Ironically, in terms of its racism, *The Birth of a Nation* remains somewhat of an anomaly in Griffith's career as he had not made a film (that survives, anyway) before *The Birth* that was anywhere near so racist, nor did he make another after. Quite the contrary: he tended to preach peace, understanding, and brotherhood in his

13

work, such as the epic *Intolerance* (1916), which he made on the heels of *The Birth of a Nation.*

After his father died, the young Griffith was compelled to leave high school to help support the family. He found work in Louisville, where he was introduced to the theater and decided this was the career for him. He set out to become an actor and a playwright. Though mostly unsuccessful at the latter, he worked steadily as an actor in road company productions, which led him east, where he landed a role in *Rescued from the Eagle's Nest* (1908) for the Thomas A. Edison Company in the new medium of the "flickers."

Other film roles followed at Edison and for another company, American Biograph, which that same year offered Griffith his first shot at directing. The result was *The Adventures of Dollie,* a one-reel (approximately ten-minute) short, which launched a career that changed the medium of film and ultimately led to the creation of an entertainment megalopolis called "Hollywood."

Griffith is often credited with innovating every technique and narrative device used in the cinema, from the close-up to the moving camera shot. In fact, neither Griffith nor any of his fellow directors at the Edison and Biograph companies innovated much of anything except, perhaps, in the handling of actors. Typically, the cameraman lit the set, laid out the shots, and determined the camera angles in these early films, coming up with innovations along the way, often by accident. What Griffith did—and it is visible in nascent form even in his first short film—was to coalesce these innovations into a dynamic whole, which his most celebrated leading lady, Lillian Gish, called "the grammar of film." In other words, D. W. Griffith gave the cinema its syntax, and in so doing evolved a new role for the director (the most talented and creatively ambitious ones, anyway) as the person chiefly responsible for "shaping" the finished product. He also developed the technique of "crosscutting" (shifting back and forth between parallel actions in shorter and shorter bursts to heighten tension and build to a powerful dramatic payoff) into an art form all his own.

CROSSCUTTING AND DARK DOINGS

The signature "Griffith Touch" of crosscutting is used extensively throughout the 1912 two-reeler *The Musketeers of Pig Alley*, the film that is alleged to be "the first [American] gangster film of any importance to survive,"[2] in which many of the characteristics of the gangster film genre as it would evolve begin to come together. The film even presents a prototype of one of the genre's fixture gangland characters—the smart-aleck, violence-loving punk, a type James Cagney would personify in the talkies of the 1930s—in the form of Elmer Booth's pugnacious, chain-smoking "The Snapper Kid."

To modern sensibilities, *The Musketeers of Pig Alley* may appear pure melodramatic hokum—of a type characteristic of many silent-era films made by Griffith and everybody else. But looks can be deceiving. Lillian Gish plays the archetypal silent screen waif—here, a child of the New York City slums. She is married to a poor musician (Walter Miller) who heads uptown to scare up some work so they can lead a better life, leaving her on her own. When he returns from a gig with his wallet stuffed with cash, he runs into the aforementioned Snapper Kid (the only character in the film who is referred to on-screen by name), who knocks him unconscious and steals the dough.

Later at the "Gangsters' Ball," a dance sponsored by the local mob, Gish captures the eye of the Kid and a rival gang leader (Alfred Paget). The latter slips her a Mickey—ostensibly to get her into bed, as our modern eyes would perceive it. But at the time the film was made, this action conveyed a very different meaning to audiences, as one of the most widespread underworld activities engaged in by New York City mobsters was the "white slave" racket, wherein young girls living on the street or on their own would be drugged and sold into prostitution. This unsavory gambit, not sex (or at least not sex alone), is what the Kid and his rival are up to.

Passions and plot complications mount—with Griffith crosscutting between them faster and faster in shorter and shorter shots as he builds to a powerful climax just as Francis Ford Coppola would do sixty years later at the conclusion of one of the most influential of all modern gangster films, *The Godfather,* as the new Don, Michael Corleone (Al Pacino), takes care of "all family business" in a baptism by fire that shifts back and forth between shots of the christening of Michael's godson and the bloody execution, one by one, of the Corleone family's underworld enemies.

Gish's musician husband revives and goes on the lookout for the Kid to reclaim his stolen money. Gish gets progressively more lightheaded from being drugged as the Kid and his rival step up their rivalry. The mob's "Big Boss" steps in, ordering the two rivals to settle their "feudal war" once and for all, and urban mayhem breaks out. As the rival gangsters and their henchmen stalk each other through streets and alleys like modern day Earps and Clantons in the O.K. Corral, they slither past doorways and around corners, their bodies hugging the walls for cover, until gunfire erupts everywhere.

Gish's husband spots the Kid in the melee and takes advantage of the gun smoke and confusion to get his money back. The cops arrive, busting things up and putting the warring factions under arrest. But the Kid manages to escape and hides out in Gish's apartment building, where he discovers, much to his consternation, not only to whom she is married, but also that she actually prefers the poor but honest musician to himself! Honorably, however, he backs off, and, believing that one good turn deserves another, the tearfully reunited musician and his wife back up the Kid's alibi when the cops try to arrest him for taking part in the gang war by saying that he was with them when the shooting started. The cops and the lovers depart, leaving the Kid alone and apparently broke, as suddenly the outstretched hand of someone we never see enters the frame and brightens the gangster's day by slipping him some cash—probably "protection money."

In its brief, barely seventeen-minute, running time, *The Musketeers of Pig Alley* established most of the basic ground rules of the American gangster film, from trading in sex (a rare commodity in the Western for most of that genre's history) as well as violence to exploiting material ripped "straight from the day's headlines" to casting, if not a completely sympathetic eye, at least an empathetic one on its lead gangster character, the Snapper Kid.

In contrast to the victimized musician, who is ostensibly the film's good guy with whom we are meant to identify, Elmer Booth's Snapper Kid is presented as being, and emerges, the more charismatic, complex, and thus more fascinating character, the prototype, in fact, of what would become a fixture of the gangster movie—the antihero. Like James Cagney's on-screen punks in the talkie era, Elmer Booth's swaggering, snappy dressing, bantam-sized Snapper Kid moves with the cocksure grace of a dancer—and is drawn to the world of violence like a moth to a flame. Anticipating anti-hero public enemies and mob kingpins of the 1970s gangster film like Steve McQueen's Doc McCoy in *The Getaway* (1972) and Al Pacino's Michael Corleone in *The Godfather*, the Snapper Kid even eludes capture at the end and escapes judicial punishment for his crimes.

Based on the strength of his performance and the persona he created in *The Musketeers of Pig Alley*, it is not inconceivable that Elmer Booth could have become the American cinema's first gangster movie star as the industry turned to making feature-length[3] films just a few years later. For example, the same year he made *Musketeers*, he starred for Griffith in another crime drama called *The Narrow Road* in which he plays an ex-con determined to go straight who almost succumbs to falling in with a gang of counterfeiters, but resists temptation at the last minute and stays the honorable course. Mirroring the film's title, the decision is a close one, though. After a hard day's work on a tough construction job, the character looks with exhaustion at his sore, aching hands, and we can almost hear his thoughts speaking the gangster's creed: "There's got to be a better, easier way to make dough than this."

Although his character ultimately chooses to abide by the law in *The Narrow Road* rather than continue to flout it as in *The Musketeers of Pig Alley,* Booth's persona of the street-smart, scrappy hot head is identical in both films, but not similar to characters he played in other films for Griffith, such as *The Unseen Enemy* (1912). This is further evidence that Booth (perhaps with Griffith's guidance) was evolving a powerful screen persona, one that would potentially have made him a natural to star in the bigger, splashier gangster movies yet to come. But, alas, this was not to be. Elmer Booth and another Griffith regular, character actor George A. Seigmann, were killed in an automobile accident just three years later in 1915 on the eve of the release of what is arguably America's first feature-length gangster film, *Regeneration,* for which Booth would have been ideal as the protagonist—a swaggering gangland tough who turns his life around and goes straight. Booth was thirty-three when he died.

Ironically, the driver of the car in which Booth and Seigmann were killed was another member of the Griffith stock company, Tod Browning, the future director of a number of influential silent-era gangster films featuring the actor who *would* become the American cinema's first gangster movie star (see Chapter 3).

"THE GANGSTER EVIL"

Anticipating the Italian neorealist cinema of the post–World War II period and the French New Wave of the 1960s, *The Musketeers of Pig Alley* employed another ingredient that would become a hallmark of the gangster genre and of many crime films to come. It was shot not on studio sets but on authentic locales—here, the crime-ridden streets, tenements, dance halls, and saloons of New York's Lower East Side slums. This gives the film a stark, almost documentary "this-is-happening-before-your-eyes" sense of realistic detail and un-prettified truth—even though, in fact, every shot in the film is staged.

Also like the Italian neorealists and French New Wave filmmakers, Griffith populated his cast with nonprofessionals as extras. The Biograph Company even proclaimed in its publicity bulletins that Griffith had hired actual gangsters with such colorful names as "Kid" Brood and "Harlem Tom" Evans to play background parts and serve as "technical advisers" to enhance the film's realism. Although this sounds like pure hype, it is by no means an impossible claim as there are a few rough-featured "actors" in the film who have the unmistakable look of real-life mugs.

Because of its topicality and strong sense of time and place, qualities that alone make it one of the classic early gangster movies, *The Musketeers of Pig Alley* struck an immediate and responsive chord with audiences, who turned it into one of Biograph's, and Griffith's, biggest box-office performers of the year. At the time of the film, many of New York's warring gangs (*Musketeers'* appear to be mostly Irish) were starting to encroach on each other's turf until no neighborhood seemed safe from gangland activity. Griffith capitalized on these headlines to build his story, although star Lillian Gish often claimed in her later years that he had based his scenario on contemporary accounts of the murder of a gambler named Herman Rosenthal in a string of gangland shootings to which members of New York City's vice squad had turned a blind eye because they were on the take. Her claim is not substantiated by the film, however, as the plot of *The Musketeers of Pig Alley*, as we have seen, bears no resemblance whatsoever to the events she describes.

Griffith flirted with the themes of police corruption and the need for reform, however, in another 1912 two-reeler called *One Is Business, The Other Crime*, which contrasts the stories of a poor blue-collar youth who turns to robbery when he can't find work, risking jail time if caught, and a white-collar youth who accepts a political bribe, risking no jail time at all if caught. The worlds of the two youths collide when the former robs the latter and is caught red-handed. But when the white-collar youth guilty of taking the bribe threatens to turn his blue-collar alter ego over to the police, the heroine intervenes; she orders her beau (the white-collar youth) to let the other off the hook because, she says, "he is no worse than you," a reform-minded social commentary that would become a fixture of many gangster movies of the sound era.

D. W. Griffith's contribution to the burgeoning art of the gangster and crime film, like his contribution to the art of film storytelling itself, is not to be minimized, no matter how strong the movement toward "political correctness" in all things, including film history, becomes. *The Musketeers of Pig Alley* illustrates the nature and style of that contribution in a nutshell. Griffith did not invent the gangster film's sense of naturalism, its use of real locations to communicate a sense of "you-are-there" authenticity. He and other filmmakers had been shooting on location since the day the movies were born. Nor were all the plot ingredients of *Musketeers* that would become generic to the gangster film brand new with that film. Griffith and other filmmakers had used practically all of them before in other films and would add new wrinkles to them in subsequent films as their careers progressed. In fact, as the prodigious Griffith closed out 1912—during which he astonishingly made almost sixty films for the Biograph Company—he shot another two-reeler about urban crime called *The Burglar's Dilemma*, which prominently featured (and may even have introduced) another archetype of the gangster and crime film: the "good cop/bad cop" interrogation scene.

Mirroring his contribution to film itself, what Griffith did in *The Musketeers of Pig Alley* was to bring together the various elements of the evolving crime film (thus far) to create what might be called the "grammar of the gangster film." As a result, *The Musketeers of Pig Alley* remains a cinematic touchstone. As a "depiction of the gangster evil" (as ballyhooed by Biograph's publicity machine), it boasts an atmosphere of undeniable authenticity, captured in stark black-and-white images that are still sharp. And with conviction and a still considerable amount of power, Griffith persuasively drives home what would become a prominent message of the gangster film—that "poverty breeds crime."

On the Bowery

Poverty, wretchedness, and vice are rife. This is the place, these narrow ways, diverging to the right and left, and reeking everywhere with dirt and filth. The coarse and bloated faces at the doors have counterparts at home, and all the wide world over. Debauchery has made the very houses prematurely old. See how the rotten beams are tumbling down, and how the patched and broken windows seem to scowl dimly, like eyes that have been hurt in drunken frays.[4]

This is how novelist Charles Dickens described the notorious Bowery and the Five Points section of lower Manhattan in his walking tour of New York City's slum districts in the decades leading up to the Civil War. These districts were breeding grounds for crime and corruption rivaling the slums of London's East End. As the decades wore on, the skid rows of the Bowery and Five Points got even worse, evolving into a garden of evil where, eventually, the seeds of the American Mafia would take root (see Chapter 12).

It was into this less-than-hospitable environment of dance halls and wall-to-wall saloons, rat-infested tenements, alleys, and streets awash in mud as the Civil War ground to a halt that a now-forgotten American writer named Owen Frawley Kildare was born. In 1915, his inspirational saga would become the source material for the first feature-length gangster movie made in America.[5]

Orphaned at an early age, Kildare survived on the streets of the Bowery, where he grew up to become a thief and small-time gang leader destined for a bad end until he turned his life around with the help of a dedicated young social worker and teacher named Marie R. Deering. Deering, whom Kildare gave the Bowery nickname of "Mamie Rose," taught him how to read and write. He blossomed into a successful chronicler of life in the slums from which he sprang in short stories with such descriptive titles as "A Limb of the Law," "The Level of the Sodden," "The Burden of the Many," and "The Hard Life," published in such popular magazines of the day as *Pearson's* and the enduring *Saturday Evening Post*. Through his stories, he drew public attention to the plight of those living and dying in the slums, earning himself the nickname the "Kipling of the Bowery" and spurring the cause of reform.

Kildare and Deering fell in love and were married, but she died suddenly of pneumonia; he dedicated his 1903 autobiography detailing his transformation from an illiterate (to age thirty) child of the Bowery who, by age thirty-eight, had become a professional writer, to her memory, calling it *My Mamie Rose: The Story of My Regeneration*.

Kildare's uplifting memoir was so popular that Broadway producers Liebler and Company approached him to turn it into a play. Written by Kildare in collaboration with playwright Walter Hackett, the drama, titled *The Regeneration*, premiered at Wallack's Theatre on September 1, 1908, and ran for a less-than-stellar thirty performances despite many favorable reviews.

Kildare's autobiography continued to be a popular seller, however, appealing to a mass thirst (as strong then as it is now) for tales of fact and fiction about people who are dealt a bad hand by life yet who triumph in the end, winning success and personal redemption. This popular theme made Kildare's autobiography a natural, therefore, for the new mass medium of the movies. Kildare did not live to see this happen, however. He died in 1911, the year before D. W. Griffith evoked contemporary Bowery life on the screen in *The Musketeers of Pig Alley*. But in 1915, producer William Fox acquired the rights to Kildare's autobiography for his Fox Film Corporation (the seeds of what would become Twentieth Century Fox) and hired a young protégé of Griffith's—Raoul Walsh—to adapt the book to the screen with scenario writer Carl Harbaugh (who also plays the role of the district attorney in the film) and to direct the picture, simply titled *Regeneration*.

TRUST THE TALE

Like many of his fellow pioneers, the roughneck Raoul Walsh, who was born in New York City in 1887, lived almost as many lives as a cat—boxer, bronco buster, sailor—before he found his calling in motion pictures. To the end of his life in 1981, Walsh said that everything he knew about filmmaking he had learned at the feet of his mentor, D. W. Griffith, for whom he had worked as an assistant on some of Griffith's Biograph shorts—and, most memorably, as an actor in Griffith's *The Birth of a Nation,* where the dead ringer Walsh played John Wilkes Booth in the Lincoln assassination sequence.

Walsh described adapting Kildare's story this way: "Heroine is running a mission in the Bowery for the city's needy. Hero . . . laughs at her for being a do-gooder. Although he is a gangster, she falls in love with him. *From there, play it by ear*" [italics mine].[6] This sort of flip remark is typical of pioneers such as Walsh, John Ford, and others whose public persona was that filmmaking—even if the film turned out to be masterpiece, as many of theirs did—was "no big deal" but "just a job of work." They would rather have been struck dead by lightning, it seems, than to have revealed their "feminine side" openly by discussing such things as artistic motives, aesthetic sensibilities, or recurring themes in their films. They preferred to let their work speak for itself, or they would regale interviewers and listeners with stories about working with certain stars and studio heads and amusing anecdotes about production problems on their films. [Many young filmmakers today who talk a good game about the art of filmmaking while getting little of that game on the screen might be wise to take heed.]

Whether it was due to the passage of time and the failing memory of the storyteller, or maybe just a lifelong tendency on the part of the early film pioneers like Walsh to exaggerate, their reminiscences seldom allowed facts to get in the way of a good story. For example, there is an impressive set piece in *Regeneration* involving a fire that breaks out on an excursion barge on the Hudson River. As the barge is consumed in flames and starts sinking, many of the passengers jump over the side into the water to save themselves. In his autobiography, Walsh recounts shooting the scene: "When the women jumped, their skirts ballooned up, and I was almost sure that some of them were not wearing anything underneath," he writes. "However, they were falling so fast that one body shut out another and I could not be certain . . . Two days after we finished shooting, the rushes were run in Fox's private projection room . . . To my horror, what I had suspected was the truth. At least a dozen of the females were naked as jaybirds under their long dresses . . . If we cut that part of the sequence, the whole thing would be ruined. If we ran the picture as it was, we'd all go up the river for a long, long time."[7]

To salvage things, Walsh said, he hired an optical man to come in to literally paint underwear on the women right on the celluloid film, frame by frame. The optical man's work is so seamless that it is completely undetectable on screen. On the other hand, the footage of people jumping from the ship is filmed in long shot from such a distance that even when viewed on the big screen it is difficult to pick out such details, or, for that matter, to distinguish the male jumpers from the females! One suspects that Walsh might have been stretching things a bit so that he could add that the studio was so impressed with his ingenuity that it rewarded him with a bonus and a new car, which is how he caps off his story.

Walsh's description of adapting Kildare's memoir to the screen is no less suspect. For one thing, the heroine does not *run* the mission in the Bowery. She does volunteer work there, teaching the illiterate how to read and write. Second, the hero does not laugh at her early on for being a do-gooder. On the contrary, he takes to her right away as she brings out the gentleman in him. And last, while the hero is indeed a gangster, it is clear that only as he begins to rehabilitate himself does Marie fall in love with him. Perhaps, Walsh's memory was just playing tricks on him. After all, he was summing up the first of what would be scores of feature films he would make over his long career, and he was doing so almost sixty years after the fact. So, let's give him the benefit of the doubt. Nevertheless, this is why with artists of any kind (but especially the roughneck, nononsense film pioneers of the silent era and the golden age of the Hollywood studio system in the 1930s and '40s) the wisest course is put your trust in the tale—in other words the evidence, or the film itself—not the teller. With that in mind, let's throw *Regeneration* on the projector and give it a look.

Preserved today by the Library of Congress and listed in the National Registry of important American movies, Raoul Walsh's *Regeneration* makes his mentor D. W. Griffith's evocation of urban squalor and gang life in *Musketeers* look almost pleasant by comparison. The atmosphere of grinding poverty is so strongly conveyed in the film that it is easy to see one reason why the main character (whose name is changed from Kildare to Conway in the largely fictionalized screen adaptation) is drawn to the world of gangsters; they've got decent clothes.

As the film opens, ten-year-old Owen (John McCann) sits alone by a window in the squalid one-room apartment where he was born watching the box containing his deceased mother being loaded into a hearse. The boy's look of bereavement and confusion mirrors Walsh's emotional description in his autobiography of his own feelings over the untimely loss of his mother as he watched her being lowered into her grave in a "dismal box."[8]

The orphaned lad is taken in by the childless Conroys (Maggie Weston and James Marcus) across the hall, and he is put to work doing chores for Mrs. Conroy and sent to fetch pots (called "growlers") of beer from the local saloon by her drunken idler of a husband. In spite of having a roof over his head, the boy eventually sees living on the street as the more preferable alternative. His surrogate "parents" argue constantly, with the boy always caught between them, his head moving back and forth from one to the other as if watching a tennis match. As this happens, Walsh masterfully dollies then irises the camera in on the anguished lad watching them spar with one another, creating an image that potently conveys the character's feelings of isolation and entrapment.

After another beating by his drunken "dad," Owen takes to the street for good and grows into a strapping youth (H. McCoy) who demonstrates leadership and brawn, as well as compassion, by rescuing a hunchbacked youth from bullying by Skinny (William Sheer), a rival street tough (whose screen character was inspired by a known gangster and adversary of Kildare's of the period named "Skinny" McCarthy).

Following this vignette, we next see Owen at age twenty-five; he is now the leader of his own Bowery gang consisting of the hunchback, Skinny, and other members, which is targeted by the district attorney, who has vowed to "sweep the city clean." From this point on, the part of Owen is played by Rockliffe Fellowes, a Canadian actor from Ottawa who was thirty-two at the time. Fellowes's insolent demeanor and proletarian rather than conventional leading-man looks uncannily anticipate the young Marlon Brando of *On the Waterfront* (1954). In fact, Fellowes resembles Brando both physically and in his acting style.[9]

The district attorney brings social-minded socialite Marie Deering (Anna Q. Nilsson[10]) to the Bowery to see the gangster class up close. A fight breaks out between some thugs, and when Marie fears that someone will be killed, Owen steps in and breaks up the fight. From the experience, Marie finds her true calling and goes to work at a local settlement house. At first, Owen steers clear of the place. But when the settlement house hosts an excursion on the Hudson, and Marie extends the invitation to others in the Bowery, Owen goes along, accompanied by his cronies Skinny and the hunchback.

When the barge goes up in flames as the result of a cigarette carelessly tossed away by Skinny, Owen saves two children from drowning, one of them belonging to a useless, drunken lout of a father. Owen is reminded of himself at that age and, perhaps stirred by the memory, takes his first steps toward transforming his life at the settlement house, where Marie teaches him to read and write, and their relationship blossoms into romance as they come to know, understand, and love each other in the same tentative manner that uneducated dockworker Terry Malloy (Marlon Brando) and the refined sister (Eva Marie Saint) of a dead co-worker fall in love in *Regeneration*'s gangster film ancestor, *On the Waterfront*, almost forty years later.

Owen drifts away from his gang. Appointed the new leader, Skinny knifes a cop in a fight and, having once helped Owen out of a similar scrape, turns to Owen to hide him out. Honoring the gangster code (if not always a time-honored one) of "Never rat on your friends and always keep your mouth shut" enshrined almost eighty years later in Martin Scorsese's modern take on the scenario of the wayward youth who grows up to become a gangster, *GoodFellas*, Owen does as Skinny asks. Square now, he orders Skinny to stay clear of him from then on.

By helping Skinny, however, Owen appears to Marie to have slipped back into his old ways, a conclusion reinforced by the DA who insists that Owen is "beyond saving." Nevertheless, she seeks Owen out, but runs into Skinny instead, who takes her captive, fearful that she will persuade Owen to turn him over to the cops. Owen gets wind of what's happened and confronts Skinny. In the melee that ensues, Marie is hit with a bullet fired by Skinny and dies in Owen's arms, urging him to foreswear vengeance, a promise he almost breaks when he gets hold of Skinny again and tries to strangle him until he sees a vision of Marie imploring him not to. Like a rat coming out of its hole, Skinny escapes through a window onto a clothesline stretching from one tenement to the next and, while trying to make it across, is shot and killed by the hunchback whom Owen once saved from Skinny's abuse. The film ends with Owen's heartfelt words that "She [Marie] made of my life a changed thing, and never can it be the same again."

Given the potential for mawkishness in its "saved from the ashes by the love and support of a good woman" story line, Walsh could easily have piled on the schmaltz, as his mentor Griffith was often guilty of doing with similar material (but restrained from doing in *Musketeers of Pig Alley*). But Walsh, along with Howard Hawks, was among the least sentimental (off-screen as well as on) of America's pioneer moviemakers. Only the scene where the gentle nature of Marie's character is telegraphed by showing her snuggling a kitten to her breast is over-the-top mush. It is the kind of character symbolism that seems more at home in a Griffith film than a Walsh one.

Griffith's influence on *Regeneration* is considerably stronger in Walsh's use—and honing—of the technique of crosscutting. The barge scene where Walsh's camera cuts with increasing rapidity from shots of the smoke and flames to lifeboats lowering to Owen's rescuing the two children to people jumping overboard is just one example of Walsh's skillful use of this technique in the film. Another, less spectacular, but arguably more powerful example of its use is the finale, when Owen rescues Marie from the villainous Skinny, only to be dealt the harsh blow of losing his beloved "Mamie Rose" in the end to a stray bullet meant for him.

2
Archetypes

"The appearance of the law must be
upheld, especially when it's being broken."
**—Boss Tweed (Jim Broadbent),
Gangs of New York (2002)**

BACK ALLEY BOYS

THE KIPLING OF THE BOWERY'S tale of regeneration and redemption
from a life of brutality and criminality proved durable enough, as
well as malleable enough, to be retold again and again to cinema
audiences over the years in various forms. It remains the prototype of
every boy-to-man/rags-to-riches/redeemed-or-destroyed gangster movie
story filmed ever since, from *The Public Enemy* (1931) to *Once Upon a
Time in America* (1984) to *Gangs of New York* (2002).

Based on a yarn[1] about of the beginnings of the Big Brother (later Big
Brother–Big Sister) movement by Rex Beach (author of the oft-filmed
Western tale "The Spoilers," notable for its set piece saloon brawl), *Big
Brother* (1923) provided a significant variation on Kildare's theme. It told
of a tough-as-nails gang leader, "Gentleman" Jim Donovan (Tom Moore),
whose heart is softened and who is ultimately redeemed not by the love
and support of a good woman but by the responsibility he places on himself to take care of the orphaned boy (Mickey Bennett) of a dead gang
member. The film's director, Allan Dwan (1885–1981), was another important pioneer in American film—and, next to D. W. Griffith, perhaps

the American cinema's most prolific director, and certainly its longest working.

Dwan was born in Canada but schooled in the United States, where he graduated from Notre Dame University with the goal of becoming an electrical engineer. His technical savvy brought him into contact with the burgeoning American film industry, and after selling some story ideas to Chicago's Essanay Studios, he went to work for a production company as a scenario editor. He made his directorial debut in 1911, three years after Griffith (for whom Dwan would later work), when the assigned director didn't show up, and he was thrust into the job.

Dwan proved as much at ease, and as adroit, helming super spectacles—such as the gargantuan 1922 production of *Robin Hood* starring Douglas Fairbanks, the popular star-producer of swashbucklers who considered Dwan his best director—as he was making light comedies, such as the Gloria Swanson vehicle *Manhandled* (1924), and social dramas like the gangster film *Big Brother*. If anything, it was Dwan's versatility—he loved the medium so much that he just wanted to make films, *any film*— that, perhaps, has diminished his reputation, and name recognition, as a pioneer. Unlike a Raoul Walsh, for example, who identified himself with the action picture even though he made many other types of films as well; a John Ford, who made all kinds of pictures but associated himself most closely with the Western; or an Alfred Hitchcock, who specialized in suspense films, Dwan's choice of material was so eclectic (fundamentally, he accepted whatever came his way) that, from the point of view of critics and even audiences, his cinematic footprints were invisible. He never lacked for work, though. His career spanned the silent era and the sound. He directed his last film, the low-budget crime-cum–science fiction thriller *The Most Dangerous Man Alive* for Columbia Pictures in 1958 (it was not released until 1961), then retired, leaving behind a body of work of more than 400 titles!

Big Brother, which he made for Paramount at about the midpoint in his long career, was among Dwan's personal favorites. Unfortunately, the studio failed to preserve the film's negative or any prints, so unless an errant print turns up sometime, somewhere in the world, it is a lost film.[2]

Shot on New York's Lower East Side, and employing real gangsters as extras just as D. W. Griffith and Raoul Walsh were alleged to have done in *The Musketeers of Pig Alley* and *Regeneration, Big Brother* was apparently so authentic in its portrayal of urban gangsterism and slum life (even including a doped-up "cokie" played by Raymond Hatton) that some reviewers took to describing it almost as a documentary. As *The New York Times* noted in its December 23 review: "Mr. Dwan shows trains on the elevated railroad, above and below, the Queensborough Bridge, street after street of hopelessly squalid dwellings and line after line of freshly laundered flannel and linen hanging on roofs and in open spaces." Many years later, Dwan described how he'd insisted on shooting on location in order to achieve the film's documentary-like atmosphere: "The basic thing was that we worked in real environments," he said.

> We didn't build sets. There were two gangs who were bitter enemies—the Hudson Dusters and the Gas House Gang—and, through diplomacy and some money, we got them both to bring their girls up to a big famous dance hall at the edge of Harlem. And we laid it on the line with the two gangleaders, and asked them, since they were being paid, to do exactly what we asked and nothing else. And they agreed—shook hands on it. But the police department—just in case—sent up their famous hard-arm squad—the toughest gang of policemen you'll ever know. They were standing by. Just as we were ready to start a big dance number, my cameraman [Hal Rosson] decided he needed more light, so to his electricians and grips he called out loudly, "Take the silks [scrims] off the broads [klieg lights]." Well, in gangland, "silks" are dresses and "broads" are girls, so they heard this command, thought it was an order, and started to [undress the girls]. Well, the girls revolted and ran for their lives, the guys got tangled up with each other and the fight was on. Somebody blew the whistle and the hard-arm squad came in and started to lay their clubs down, and we photographed it all. Nearly took all the police ambulances in New York to take these guys away to get patched up. It was the most vivid gang fight I've ever seen. And I had to go back and write it into the picture. But we got a very seedy, very authentic background for the picture and it was a real heartbreaker with fine characterizations.[3]

In the wake of *Big Brother*, Owen Kildare's sad but uplifting saga of his regeneration with the help of his ill-fated "Mamie Rose" was remade, as *Fools' Highway* (Universal Pictures, 1924), directed by Irving Cummings. The remake starred Mary Philbin—who would play Christine, the object of the title character's affections, opposite Lon Chaney in *The Phantom of the Opera* a year later—as Mamie Rose and Pat O' Malley as the gangster who is inspired and reformed by her love. Here, the character's actual surname Kildare is restored by screenwriters Lenore J. Coffee, Emil Forst, and Harvey Gates, but he is given the fictional first name of Mike.

Fools' Highway took even more license with Kildare's story than Walsh's version, for in it Mamie Rose was neither socialite nor social worker, but a mender in a Bowery clothing shop. She befriends the hoodlum Kildare and the two fall in love. Over the protests of Kildare's fellow gang members, she persuades him not just to give up his criminal ways but also to join the police force!

Despite, or perhaps because of, its almost complete fictionalization of Kildare's autobiography (capped off by what was to become the stereotypical Hollywood happy ending of the two lovers going off into the sunset, figuratively, and sometimes *literally*), *Fools' Highway*, another lost film, failed to repeat the success of *Regeneration* with critics.

Raoul Walsh himself reworked the formula he'd created with his next and last underworld film of the silent era, *Me, Gangster*, released by Fox Film Corporation in 1928. It was not a remake of *Regeneration*, but drawn from like-minded material—in this case, the fiction-based-on-fact story of another slum kid who'd grown up to be a hoodlum, then turned his life around, like Owen Kildare, to become a noted writer and reformer—Charles Francis Coe.

A prolific author—mainly of magazine articles and short fiction but of some novels as well, dealing primarily with the milieu of gangsters and racketeers—Coe (1890–1956) first spun his thinly veiled life story in a series of seven installments published in the *Saturday Evening Post* under the umbrella title "Me—Gangster" from August through September 1927. The same year, the series was published in book form by Grosset & Dunlap to tie in with the upcoming movie version filming on the West Coast at Fox Studios.

Written by Coe in collaboration with director Walsh, the screen adaptation bears striking similarities to the earlier Walsh gangster film, but marked differences too. Like *Regeneration,* it quickly takes us through the early years of its gangster protagonist, here named Jimmy Williams, a slum youth with no formal education who becomes a petty thief, then advances to armed robbery as an adult (Don Terry) when he becomes leader of his own gang. But then, Walsh follows him as he plans and executes a payroll robbery on his own, stashes the loot in a hiding place (the home he shares with his mother), and gets arrested. Refusing to tell where he's hidden the money, he's convicted and sent up the river.

During his incarceration, his mother dies in poverty. From this and the influence of a young woman (June Collyer) from the streets who is in love with him and urges him to go straight, he undergoes a spiritual transformation in jail, wins an early parole for good behavior, and decides to give the stolen payroll money back. But the members of his old gang have a hankering to get their mitts on the dough too; when he retrieves it, Collyer, similar to *Regeneration*'s Marie Deering, is kidnapped but in this instance held hostage in exchange for the loot, prompting her lover to leap into action like *Regeneration*'s Owen Conway and rescue her from his former cronies—although in *Me, Gangster*, she survives.

While Raoul Walsh may have been humbly dismissive of *Regeneration* in his autobiography, he ignores *Me, Gangster* altogether; he doesn't even mention it. Perhaps because gangster pictures had become common by 1928, and the screen story of the hoodlum regenerated by love and responsibility was already becoming a cliché, reviewers were up and down about it. For example, in its October review coinciding with the film's opening, *The New York Times* called the picture "an absorbing chronicle that points a moral in a subdued and sane fashion [although] toward the end there are pardonable periods of gun-play and general excitement." Contrarily, the *Variety* trade paper argued that same month: "Raoul Walsh had full opportunities for a crook epic, but whether it is the fault of the director or Coe's own transmutation, the yarn read better than it screens. Walsh has striven hard to inject little niceties. One such is the prison visiting room with a fellow inmate deterred from passing a chocolate bar to his baby, brought in by the convict's wife, because of a placard warning against the exchange of articles between visitors and prisoners. The guard comes over when signaled and passes the harmless confection to the baby, creating one of the all too few heart-throb moments which a frank morality theme such as that in *Me, Gangster* should possess."

The scene the critic describes is probably another of Walsh's attempts to tug at the viewer's heartstrings in the manner of Griffith, moments that Griffith usually pulled off successfully but Walsh seldom did and, for the most part, wisely eschewed in favor of a tough, largely unsentimental approach. This approach, already evident in the prototypical *Regeneration*, and sustained in *Me, Gangster* with its prison scenes, looks forward to his gangster and action pictures of the talkie era—most of them made for Warner Brothers. It is an approach that would reach its zenith in Walsh's swansong to the genre, the apocalyptic *White Heat* (1949), a brutal portrait of the modern gangster and the lawmen arrayed against him that is so absent of "heart-throb moments" it's like a punch in the gut. Perhaps with *Me, Gangster*, Walsh wasn't so much behind the times or just keeping pace with the times as laying the groundwork for his future work in the genre.

MOB RULE

As city police forces swelled to enforce the Prohibition statutes set forth in the 1919 Volstead Act, judgeships increased to handle the ballooning caseload, and America's gangsters, rolling in dough as never before, were able also to increase their power and influence as never before by buying off cops and politicians. This image of collusion between the devil's triangle of the mob, crooked politicians, and cops on the take was present in gangster movies as early as 1915.

Released just two months after Walsh's *Regeneration*, Frank Lloyd's *The Gentleman from Indiana,* which was distributed by Paramount and now seems to be a lost film, was an early take on the subject of government corruption by the mob; it also featured what would soon become another staple of gangster cinema: the character of the crusading newspaperman who goes up against mob rule.

In such gangster films, which Hollywood would continue cranking out for another forty years or more, this archetypal character is almost always a former hero—here of the sports field, where leading man Dustin Farnum is a former college football hero turned newspaper publisher. He launches a campaign to rid his city of mobsters and corrupt politicians, a call for reform he pushes all the way to Washington by winning a congressional seat.

Released by Universal the same month, Otis Johnson's *The Frame-Up* went this premise one better—by reversing it, and giving us another archetype of gangster cinema in the process: the upright, idealistic young politician who refuses to be compromised or bought off. This character would make a comfortable transition to gangster movies of the talkie era in such films as *Washington Merry-Go-Round* (1932), where Lee Tracy plays a freshman congressman who goes against the tide by refusing to accept gangland bribes like some of his fellow representatives. This type of character would subsequently become enshrined in the persona of James Stewart's "Mr. Smith" in Frank Capra's once-controversial exposé of political corruption in the U.S. Senate, *Mr. Smith Goes to Washington* (1939), a non-gangster film.

Regrettably *The Frame-Up* is a lost film, too. Based on a short story by the celebrated journalist, war correspondent, and prolific short story writer Richard Harding Davis, it exposed, in fictional form, the efforts of a big-city crime boss (Harry Carter) to buy a mayoral race. He goes about this by getting a young former city alderman (no doubt a heroic one) played by George Fawcett elected mayor so that he can bend the newly elected official to his will. The new mayor won't play ball, however, so the mobster sets him up on a false murder charge to get him out of the way, but the frame-up fails.

Perhaps fearing the scissors of the state's censorship board, the filmmakers apparently didn't ascribe a name to the city and state in which the film is set, not even a fictional one. Davis's original story, however, references such famous New York City restaurants as Delmonico's and such upstate cities as Albany and Utica, indicating the story's location as the Big Apple.

By the middle of the 1920s when Prohibition was in full swing and stories about mob influence over many city and local governments were running in newspapers practically on a weekly basis, the link between crime and political corruption had become a fixture of the gangster-film story. However, the mob's infiltration of society's Thin Blue Line separating law and order from anarchy—i.e., the police—was more often implied than explicitly stated.

One of the earliest gangster films to make the case that the mob could buy off cops as well as politicians was the aforementioned *Exclusive Rights*, produced in 1926 by J. G. Bachmann for the independent company Preferred Pictures run by B. P. Schulberg,[4] who would later honcho production at Paramount.

Exclusive Rights was based on a story by actor-writer Jerome M. Wilson that dealt in fictional form with the topic of an invisible government ruled by the mob. The story was adapted into a screenplay for director Frank O'Connor by the prolific silent-era scenario writer Eve Unsell, whose screenwriting career would extend into the talkie era, albeit briefly—she died in 1937.

The film focuses on a former war hero turned politician (in this case governor), played by Gayne Williams, who seeks to bring down a powerful mob boss (Charles Hill Mailes) by exposing the mobster's tentacles in state government. When Bikel (Sheldon Lewis), a member of the mobster's gang, is convicted of murder and sentenced to death, the governor sees his chance; he offers Bikel a deal. In exchange for turning state's evidence against the mob, he agrees to overturn Bikel's death sentence.

The mob boss' mother didn't raise any stupid gangsters, however; he's already one step ahead of the governor. Anticipating that Bikel will probably spill his guts as the date with "Ole Sparky" gets nearer, the wily mob boss, with the help of the governor's do-gooder fiancée (Lillian Rich), muscles a bill for abolishing capital punishment through the state legislature. When the bill reaches his desk, however, the governor refuses to sign it. In response, the mob boss frames a wartime buddy (Raymond McKee) of the governor's for murder, and the man is convicted and sentenced to death.

The governor finds himself torn between loyalty to his convictions and loyalty to a friend. Convictions win out in more ways than one as he still refuses to sign the bill, prompting his fiancée to break off their engagement. The governor proves just as wily as his adversary, however. He tricks the condemned Bikel and the mob boss into believing that he allowed his wartime buddy's execution to be carried out, and Bikel, realizing that the governor means business, breaks at last and signs a statement revealing the full range of the mob's activities, including the corruption of cops and government officials.

Newspaper and magazine reviewers were impressed by the film and, especially, its melodramatic but effective death row climax, although they questioned whether the brutality of the subject matter would revolt or attract audiences. It apparently attracted, for the low-budget *Exclusive Rights* was a critical and commercial success that opened the door for more gangster pictures, including major studio productions, dealing with the three elements without which mob rule in real-life can't occur— mobsters, dirty cops, and crooked pols. These characters are also the linchpins that hold the genre together.

The flip side of the incorruptible newsman who crusades against mob rule is the crusading newsman who is himself corrupted by mob rule—as typified by Richard Barthelmess's eager-beaver young reporter in Warner Brothers's *The Finger Points* (1931). Using a letter of recommendation from his old boss at the hometown Savannah newspaper where he came from, the ambitious Barthelmess gets a job at "The Press," a prestigious big-city newspaper. As gang warfare breaks out on the streets of the unnamed city (probably New York or Chicago), the editor of the paper calls for a journalistic crusade against mob rule and assigns every reporter to the task.

A story of Barthelmess's about an illegal casino results in the establishment's being raided and shut down and its gangster owner jailed. In reprisal, a couple of hoods tail Barthelmess and rough him up. His hospital convalescence results in mounting medical bills, but the paper refuses to pay them for him because he cannot prove with certainty that the beating he took was for writing the story and thus incurred while "on the job."

Bitter and broke, Barthelmess accepts a proposal from a mobster big shot (played by a pre-MGM, lower-billed Clark Gable) to go into the hush-money business. Gable feeds Barthelmess information about rival gang activities, which the reporter threatens to expose in "The Press" unless paid off for his silence; he and Gable then split the hush money. Soon, the reporter is living high on the hog in a plush apartment and wearing fancy clothes—much to the bafflement of his coworkers and girl (Fay Wray) at the newspaper, who can't figure out how he does it earning roughly the same amount they do, about $35 a week.

The corrupt reporter pushes things too far, however, when he usurps Gable's position with the city's top crime boss, known only as #1. Despite Gable's stated belief that the mob can kill anyone and get away with it except a reporter—a belief Barthelmess subscribes to as well—Gable changes his mind when an exposé of his murderous activities he'd expected to be suppressed suddenly appears in "The Press," and he's convinced Barthelmess has double-crossed him (in fact, it is a colleague of Barthelmess who submits the story). He puts the finger on Barthelmess to be rubbed out. The hit—the first ever of a newspaperman by the mob—gets national attention; in death, the corrupt Barthelmess becomes a martyr to the cause of freedom of the press and journalistic integrity. The city cracks down on mob rule, and Gable and his minions are rounded up and sent to prison.

Although compelling in spots, *The Finger Points* lacks the overall power it might have had because of the wishy-washy approach it takes toward the Barthelmess character, whom it presents as bad—but not *that* bad; as corrupt, but maybe not all *that* corrupt, at least not deep down. As an indictment of mob rule on the media, it might have been stronger if writers W. R. Burnett, John Monk Saunders, and Robert Lord had adhered more closely to the true story on which their script is loosely based—the 1930 mob slaying of *Chicago Tribune* reporter Jake Lingle.

Unlike Barthelmess's is-he-corrupt-or-faking-it reporter, Lingle was so connected to the Chicago mob, and so "in-the-know" about the dirty cops on the mob's payroll and the mob's illegal activities, that he extorted hundreds of thousands of dollars from them for keeping their names and activities out of the news. He had the mob in such a vise that he bragged of being the real power who fixed the price of (illegal) beer in town.

Lingle's braggadocio inevitably led to his undoing when the Chicago mob decided that, his being a reporter or not, it had had enough of him and ordered his execution—the first mob hit of a reporter in the history of organized crime in America. As in the film, an official crackdown and journalistic crusade ensued that led to several arrests.

The Finger Points suspensefully evokes the paranoia of its Lingle character's final moments when the camera follows him along a deserted street (except for a milk truck), darting from doorway to doorway, constantly looking over his shoulder, and, giving us a scare worthy of a horror film, suddenly colliding with another pedestrian, who turns out to be a priest![5] He catches his breath and moves on, the camera with him, and is machine-gunned from above shortly thereafter, bullets spraying the wall of the building behind him as he frenziedly runs back and forth in a fruitless effort to escape the raining gunfire, all of which is captured by the camera in a single, stunning take.

From an overall standpoint, though, the film is more successful in its portrait of the Clark Gable character (a composite of several hoods involved in the Lingle case, among them the redoubtable Al Capone); as written and, especially, acted, Gable's gangland tough Louie Blanco is more charismatic, more persuasive, more empathetic, and truer than the Barthelmess character. It's no surprise that after *The Finger Points* Gable found himself with a fat new contract at MGM and a star-making breakout role in that studio's Academy Award–nominated gangster film *A Free Soul* (1931), playing a very similar part.

The threat of mob rule is not restricted to the big city. It can occur anywhere. In Richard Fleischer's *Violent Saturday* (1955), gangsters descend on a small Arizona mining town to pull a payroll heist, and they turn the town upside down over a long, bloody weekend that leaves a number of citizens dead until the gangsters are finally brought down by a courageous cop (Victor Mature) and an Amish farmer (Ernest Borgnine).

In one startling scene, gangster J. Carrol Naish takes a shotgun blast that realistically knocks him off his feet and catapults him several yards backward into the dirt. In another shocker, Ernest Borgnine's Amish farmer is forced to stab Lee Marvin's sadistic, decongestant-sniffing thug in the back with a pitchfork in order to save Mature's life. Fleischer expected to take a lot of flak over these graphic scenes, which were years away from becoming commonplace in movies, but to his surprise he received none. "Frankly, I thought there might be some from the Amish at least. But I guess the Amish don't go to enough movies, or *any* movies for that matter," he reported. "The dilemma of the Borgnine character in that scene was one of the elements I brought to the script: Should he resort to violence to prevent a good man from being killed? Killing is against everything he stands for, and it becomes a very difficult choice for him to go against his religious conscience. That element was not in the script [by Sidney Boehm] at first."[6]

Taking a moral stand against mob rule is the core element of *The Phenix City Story* released by Allied Artists the same year. If Chicago of the Roaring Twenties is the prototype in our nation's history and popular culture of the rule of lawlessness in a big-city environment, the border town on the Alabama-Georgia state line of Phenix City is surely the template of a more "down-home" kind of mob rule.

Phenix City, Alabama, was known variously as the "wickedest city in America" and as "Sin City" because gambling, prostitution, loan sharking, and a host of other illegal activities once flourished there, completely out in the open; everyone from the cops, the city legislature, and the courts to the board of elections was in the pocket of local racketeers. The tide began to turn, however, when Albert Patterson, the newly elected state attorney general, who had run on a platform of vowing to clean up "Sin City" once and for all, was assassinated on a public street by the Phenix City mob as an object lesson in intimidation.

The lesson had the reverse effect, however. Fed up with having their civil rights violated by rigged elections, sick of having their children subjected to lawlessness and sleaze, and now feeling the assassinated official's blood on their hands from their own inaction, the good citizens of Phenix City turned Patterson's murder into their own St. Valentine's Day Massacre and rose up with indignation, forcing the governor to institute martial law and send in troops to bust up the rackets and put away the racketeers.

This wild shoot-em-up tale of mobsters on Main Street sounds like something straight out of the late nineteenth century or the Old West. But it took place in the modern south of 1954. And the following year, it became the subject of *The Phenix City Story* (1955), a hard-hitting gangster picture directed in semi-documentary style by Chicago-born Phil Karlson (1908–1985).

The film was shot on location in Phenix City where the events unfolded, using locals as consultants, as extras, and in speaking roles along with professional actors. It opens with a full reel of interviews with eyewitnesses to the still-fresh events that tee viewers up to the fact that the dramatization we are about to see is no flight of Hollywood fantasy. (Many prints in circulation today of the seldom-shown film eliminate this prologue of interviews.)

The film synthesizes the true story's various heroes and villains into a few individual figures for us to follow, such as the vice club owner full of Southern smarm, played by veteran character actor Edward Arnold, who holds the entire city by the throat and is behind all the graft and murder. Another veteran character actor of the day, John McIntire, plays the ill-fated attorney general, and Richard Kiley plays his son, John Patterson, the film's hero and the archetypal fixture of so many gangster movies about mob rule: the returning vet who finds the freedom from fear and intimidation he'd been fighting for abroad has been lost to his fellow citizens at home. Here, this character is a lawyer, as well, whose job in the army was to prosecute Nazi war criminals at the Nuremberg trials. For this reason, he takes special umbrage at the corruption and injustice he finds all around him in mob-controlled Phenix City. When his father is elected attorney general and then killed, Kiley himself picks up the banner and carries it to victory against the murderous Arnold and his racketeer minions.

Although some of the film's brutal scenes of gangland violence may have lost their edge due to our exposure to even greater brutality on the screen over the years, and the impact of other scenes are diluted from appearing too telegraphed (for example, we just *know* McIntire will buy the farm when he insists on going it alone to his office), *The Phenix City Story* is nevertheless a powerful and gripping movie, one that is surprising in its boldness, especially for its time. It seldom hedges and pulls very few punches. In what may be the film's strongest scene, the body of a little black girl is tossed on the lawn of Kiley's home in front of his kids, a note attached to the murdered child's dress warning Kiley that his kids are next if he doesn't back off. In the den of iniquity that is Phenix City, the bodies of murdered blacks are useful not only for intimidating other blacks, but also for sending messages to unruly whites as well.

As the events of *The Phenix City Story* take place before the civil rights movement, the issue of racial prejudice is not one that is directly confronted by the film, except as part of a big picture that shows the city's racketeers to be equal-opportunity oppressors. It is one of the real-life ironies of the case, therefore, that after he had helped to smash the mob in Phenix City and to restore human rights to all its citizens, the real John Patterson was a staunch segregationist when he went on to become governor of Alabama, where he served several terms, even earning the endorsement of the Ku Klux Klan.

But that aspect of the story was in the future. Karlson's film exposes Phenix City's gangland past, and he and screenwriters Crane Wilbur and Daniel Mainwaring confront this subject matter forthrightly with no holds barred. *The Phenix City Story* deals with what happens when bad people take over and good people sit on their hands and do nothing about it—until the prospect of nothing is all that is left if they don't act. In that sense, this little B picture—one that has influenced a whole generation of filmmakers, including Martin Scorsese—is not only a tale of mob rule; it is a mirror of World War II, the Holocaust, and the communist witchhunt era of McCarthyism in America when it was made.

Given today's freedom of the screen to portray graphic vice and violence, combined with the ongoing popularity of sensational Americana and the gangster genre, *The Phenix City Story* would seem ripe for remake treatment. Even though a big-budget, R-rated color remake could certainly be grittier and more outspoken, it would inevitably lack the you-are-there feel of the original, which was filmed literally on the spot as the mean streets of Phenix City were being swept clean.

A year after the release of *The Phenix City Story*, co-screenwriter Daniel Mainwaring penned another powerful script about a small town under siege where no one knows whom to trust and citizen is set against citizen—the science-fiction classic *Invasion of the Body Snatchers* (1956), directed by Don Siegel. Meanwhile, Phil Karlson went on to make the feature-length pilot for the TV series *The Untouchables* that was released to theaters overseas as *The Scarface Mob* (1959), and the engaging thriller *Key Witness* (1960) about a family terrorized by a gang of punks against whom the father (Jeffrey Hunter) is to testify in court.

In 1973, Karlson returned to the theme of mob rule over a small town with *Walking Tall*. Like *The Phenix City Story*, it too is based on a true story—and a very similar one—about a newly elected county sheriff, Buford Pusser (Joe Don Baker), whose jurisdiction on the Tennessee-Mississippi border is overrun by gamblers, prostitutes, loan sharks, and other lawbreakers. Pusser is determined to take his county back from the racketeers, especially after they kill his wife in reprisal. He goes after them with his only weapon, a huge baseball bat, and in the process of cleaning up the country scum becomes a rural, then national, legend.

Walking Tall was one of the biggest hits Karlson ever had, spawning two sequels and a TV series, none of which he was connected with. Although it is as brutal as *The Phenix City Story*, and considerably more graphic, *Walking Tall* is a much less powerful and disturbing movie than its predecessor, and not as convincing nor as haunting in its scary message that "This could happen where *you* live."

MOUTHPIECES

Unless or until it is found, another treasure of the silent-era gangster film that is presumed lost is Paramount's *The City Gone Wild*, directed by James Cruze. Although not especially well reviewed on its release in 1927, it remains a major early gangster picture for the portrait it offered of another archetypal figure of the genre: the gangland "mouthpiece," or defense lawyer, who lines his pockets getting mobster clients off the hook.

Thomas Meighan, a popular leading man of the time, plays the mouthpiece, whose closest friend, and professional adversary, is the district attorney. Both men are in love with the same girl (Marietta Millner), who, like the district attorney, is unaware that her wealthy father (Charles Hill Mailes again) is the brain behind the mob that is turning the city into a gangland battleground.

On the verge of marrying Meighan, but disapproving of his clients, Millner urges him to give up his practice or risk losing her. She makes up his mind for him after he gets another hood off on a technicality by spurning him and accepting a marriage proposal from his pal, the district attorney, instead.

When the DA discovers that his fiancée's father is behind the crime wave and refuses to keep silent, he is murdered. Out of loyalty to his dead friend, Meighan sets out to get revenge. He closes up his practice, has himself elected district attorney, and rounds up all the gangsters he'd once helped free, including the DA's killer (Fred Kohler), in order to bring them to justice. Kohler's moll (not-yet-legendary silent screen siren Louise Brooks) threatens to expose Millner's father publicly unless Meighan lets Kohler go. Still in love with Millner, the former mouthpiece agrees, but suffers a crisis of conscience in the process that pushes him to consider resigning as DA.

All ends happily, though, when Brooks experiences a change of heart. She tips Millner to the truth about her corrupt father so that Meighan won't have to hold back. Meighan and Millner get back together, and he is able to carry on his crusade against his former mob paymasters.

After *The City Gone Wild,* the quick-witted, fast-talking legal "mouthpiece" would become a fixture in movie stories about the underworld, just as in real life. Indeed, when New York's "Dapper Don," John Gotti, went on trial in the 1980s, he and his defense counsel, Bruce Cutler, were so joined at the hip, they seemed like characters in a mob movie.

The tale of the corrupt-turned-honest "mouthpiece" à la Thomas Meighan in *The City Gone Wild* would become especially prevalent in gangster movies of the talkie era due to the sound film's ability to exploit verbal as well as visual courtroom theatrics. For example, in David O. Selznick's 1932 production of *State's Attorney,* directed by George Archainbaud from a screenplay by Rowland Brown and noted crime reporter Gene Fowler, John Barrymore hams it up deliciously in the title role, a corrupt "mouthpiece" for mob boss William "Stage" Boyd.[7] Barrymore maneuvers himself into the district attorney's chair to help his mob employer out, then sets his sights on the governorship. But good girl Helen Twelvetrees awakens Barrymore to his sense of public duty, and he throws away his chances of becoming governor by exposing Boyd and his own unsavory past in the courtroom. The film was effectively remade in 1937 as *Criminal Lawyer* with motor-mouthed Lee Tracy in the Barrymore role.

Perhaps definitive of this type of underworld saga was Warner Brothers's *The Mouthpiece* released the same year. In it, Warren William plays a defense counsel to the mob whose courtroom histrionics are, if possible, even more flamboyant than the scenery-chewing Barrymore's. At one point he swallows an alleged vial of poison—the state's only incriminating evidence in a murder charge against his client—to ensure an acquittal. When the jury sees the lawyer suffers no ill effects from the liquid, acquittal follows. Only after the courtroom has cleared does William rush to a waiting private ambulance, where he has the deadly poison pumped from his stomach just in time.[8]

Like Thomas Meighan and John Barrymore, Warren William's "mouthpiece" too is spurred by love and a crisis of conscience to turn on the mob and send its chieftain to jail. Unlike them, however, he pays with his life when the mobster's loyal lieutenants rub him out for going against them.

The Mouthpiece is a tough, exciting morality tale in the fast-paced Warner Brothers style. It was remade twice by the same studio, as *The Man Who Talked Too Much* (1940), starring George Brent, and again in 1955 as *Illegal* with Edward G. Robinson in the William role.

Although a minor B picture, and barely feature length, Warner Brothers's 1936 *The Law in Her Hands* is that rarity among gangster films to offer a female in the male-dominated mouthpiece role. Played by the attractive Margaret Lindsay, she's a "smart dame with plenty of moxie" whom the city's top mobster (Lyle Talbot) recruits to keep himself out of jail and his protection rackets from being put out of business by the crime-fighting assistant district attorney (Warren Hull).

Initially, Lindsay's ethics make her reluctant to take the job, but her practice is going down the tubes, so what the hell! Eventually, however, like most male mouthpieces on the screen before her and after, conscience gets the better of her, she experiences pangs of guilt, and she opts out. Her mobster boss still calls the shots, however; labeling her a "cheap shyster" like every other mouthpiece on his payroll, he manipulates her into staying on board. When the mobster kills a material witness to one of his crimes and gets called up on a murder charge, it is Lindsay who defends him. But at the last second, she turns the tables on him in the courtroom and gets him sent to the slammer.

What is fascinating about *The Law in Her Hands* is not so much the boldness of its gender switch but—as a film made in the conservative wake of the anything-goes, pre-censorship years before the Motion Picture Production Code came into effect (approximately 1930–1934) when female characters on the screen could say, do, and be whatever they wanted—the reactionary stance it finally takes toward that switch. The film's theme emerges in the end not as the triumph of good versus evil or conscience over corruption but the old-fashioned virtue that a woman's place is in the home.

In love with the not even subtly chauvinist assistant DA, who urges her to give up her practice and marry him because " the law is no place for a woman," Lindsay pulls a fast one on her crooked client and sends him up the river because she finally buys into her lover's argument hook, line, and sinker. Agreeably—in fact, even jubilantly—she then files for disbarment proceedings against herself for violating her oath of office. Free of her ambition for a law career once and for all, she can now be the stay-at-home wife baking cookies that she'd always longed to be!

In Abraham Polonsky's hard-hitting mouthpiece movie *Force of Evil* (1948), based on the sprawling underworld novel *Tucker's People* by leftist writer Ira Wolfert, the hero (John Garfield) is a corrupt lawyer masterminding the mob's strong-arm consolidation of New York City's numbers rackets into a single combine—a corporate business, or legal lottery. Like *The Musketeers of Pig Alley*'s Snapper Kid, *Regeneration*'s Owen Conway, *Me, Gangster*'s Jimmy Williams, and all the other wild boys of the streets in gangster movies before him, Garfield's character is stuck in a trap of his own making. "I wasn't strong enough to avoid corruption, but I was strong enough to grab a piece of it," he cynically tells his girlfriend (Beatrice Pearson) in one of the film's many quotable lines.

When the brother (Thomas Gomez) who put Garfield through law school opts to get out of his small-time numbers racket rather than become swept up in big-time gangsterism, Garfield's character faces a moral choice. As symbolized by his brother, about whom he cares deeply but whom he seldom looks up, Garfield must confront his own conscience at last and see if he has the strength to get out.

Anticipating the ends-justify-the-means philosophy of the family of hoodlums in *The Godfather* movies decades later, who view their worst violence as "not personal, just business," the gangsters in *Force of Evil* don't see themselves as evil and corrupt but rather as normal financiers. "What do you mean gangsters? It's business!" Garfield responds indignantly to repeated accusations of being tied to mob activities.

In the view of writer-director Polonsky, and also that of novelist Ira Wolfert, who cowrote the film's script with Polonsky, telescoping its focus on the Garfield character, who is just one of many in the book, the subject of *Force of Evil* is the dark side of capitalism—greed run amuck. And its theme is that you don't have to be a gangster to be a gangster. You can, for example, be a mouthpiece lawyer (or a corporate executive). Polonsky encapsulates the moral choice faced by Garfield in a single, compelling shot as the character, on the run from the mob (and implicitly from himself), heads up a narrow side street in the direction of Trinity Church, which seems squashed on each side by the tall skyscrapers of Wall Street.

Garfield's character eventually does the right thing and joins the office of the district attorney's crusade against the numbers racket, becoming that which the filmmakers hold in highest esteem—a person of honor, guided by conscience.

For this "subversive" view, Polonsky, a former Communist Party member and committed leftist, was hauled before the House Un-American

Activities Committee (HUAC)—along with many others connected with *Force of Evil*, including Ira Wolfert and John Garfield—not long after the film was released (and failed at the box office). Refusing to name names, he was blacklisted by the industry and did not direct another film for almost twenty years.

Poetically written and spoken, *Force of Evil* has since achieved cult status as one of the most potent gangster films of the post–World War II period, and arguably the best mouthpiece movie ever. One future director profoundly influenced by the film was Martin Scorsese, whose 1973 *Mean Streets* puts its lead character, played by Harvey Keitel, in a similar dilemma as Garfield where he has to face a similar moral choice for similar reasons.

The character of the mouthpiece in gangster or crime films also provided former leading men—or screen heart-throbs—entering the September of their careers the opportunity to make a graceful transition to colorful character roles by revealing their acting chops in parts where they have to be the good guy and the bad guy at once, like John Barrymore in *State's Attorney*. One time matinee idol Robert Taylor, whose screen career as a pretty boy playing love scenes with Hollywood's top female stars like Greta Garbo and Lana Turner throughout the 1930s and '40s was winding down in the '50s as he approached fifty, would notably do this as well in MGM's candy-striped gangster film about Prohibition-era Chicago, *Party Girl* (1958).

In fact, Taylor was really pushing the envelope with his career at this time. He'd already played a policeman on the take from the mob in MGM's *Rogue Cop* (1954), although he is still that film's hero, and a psychopathic buffalo killer in the same studio's *The Last Hunt* (1956), where he was clearly the bad guy. In *Party Girl,* he takes the already clichéd role of the cynical defense attorney who puts his considerable legal talents to work manipulating the law to keep his mobster employers out of jail. But Taylor's character is even more cynical about the law than Warren William's in *The Mouthpiece*, albeit for different reasons, none of them remotely involved with the vagaries of justice. William's mouthpiece subverted the legal system on behalf of his (mostly) guilty clients because he'd once been a prosecutor and sent an innocent man to the chair. Taylor's mouthpiece, on the other hand, is just plain ruthlessly ambitious, as compensation for having been born with a clubfoot, and so he debases himself by working the wrong side of the law as mobster Lee J. Cobb's highly paid puppet. Reportedly, Taylor threw himself into the role with the zeal of a young Method actor by researching the deformity with doctors who specialized in treating it and scrutinizing X-rays to get the sense and feel of having to walk with a clubfoot.

Taylor's cynical outlook changes, however, when he falls reluctantly in love with a beautiful dancer (Cyd Charisse) who performs at Cobb's mob galas, giving her an inside look at Cobb's underworld activities that eventually puts her life in danger. When Cobb targets her to be rubbed out, Taylor protects her by finally going straight. He turns state's evidence against his former employer to put him out of business, and even guns the mobster down in a final duel.

Party Girl has become a cult film over the years, largely due to the vaunted reputation of its director, Nicholas Ray, as a Hollywood maverick, although the film itself is clearly a product of the MGM glitz factory that manufactured it. Even Ray, although satisfied that he had done the best he could, considered the picture compromised, a job he'd taken "for the money" only.

George Wells's final script (to which seven additional, unnamed screenwriters had contributed as well) offers the full catalogue of Roaring Twenties gangster-film ingredients, from shoot-outs to show-stopping numbers. Having been born in the Midwest and having grown up knowing Prohibition-era Chicago, Ray wanted to give the film as much of a sense of time and place as possible by shooting on location, but MGM restricted him to filming most of *Party Girl* on its Culver City sound stages. So, Ray opted instead to give the film's studio-bound look as much visual razzmatazz as possible. The colorful result is stunning. This may be another reason why *Party Girl*, a film that seems more typical of MGM's musical extravaganzas of the 1950s than its gangster films of any period, has become a cult favorite to fans of the "Mouthpiece School" of mob movies.

"I am through walkin' the wild side. I been cured. Born again. Like the Watergaters." So declares Carlito Brigante (Al Pacino) in Brian De Palma's *Carlito's Way* (1993), a superior mob movie that puts an interesting twist on the traditional corrupt-mouthpiece-who-turns-honest scenario. Here it is the gangster, a New York City hoodlum of Puerto Rican descent who formerly ran drugs and a host of other rackets, who wants out. After getting his thirty-year stretch in prison tossed on a technicality after serving five, Pacino recognizes the break he's gotten and decides to go straight. Meanwhile, his close friend and mouthpiece (Sean Penn), whose mega-buck practice consists of representing mob scum referred to him over the years by Pacino, is getting involved deeper and deeper in illegal activities of his own and keeps pulling the reluctant, but obligated, Pacino back in with him.

All of this leads to one of De Palma's best Hitchcock-like set pieces as Pacino, having learned "there ain't no friends in this shit business," settles scores with the unscrupulous Penn and escapes to Grand Central Station, where he has to outrun a gauntlet of hitmen assigned to kill him, to rendezvous with his girlfriend (Penelope Ann Miller) in time to catch the train to Miami and safety. Does he make it? I won't tell.

Gritty and realistic with a strong performance by Pacino and a great one by Penn, *Carlito's Way* rings true in its fatalistic sense of irony about the "damned if you don't, damned if you do" milieu it authentically captures. It also boasts a lot of memorable lines, arguably the most unforgettable of which (because of its repetition and unsettling importance in the plot) is John Leguizamo's banal "I'm Benny Blanco from the Bronx."

3
The Mobster of a Thousand Faces

"Don't step on it! It may be Lon Chaney!"
—Popular 1920s phrase

A LTHOUGH HE MAY BE MORE FAMOUS TODAY for his classic portrayals of Quasimodo in *The Hunchback of Notre Dame* (1923), the title character in *The Phantom of the Opera* (1925), and many other grotesques, legendary screen star Lon Chaney played far more crooks, underworld types, and outright gangsters during his seventeen-year reign as one of the silent era's most versatile, esteemed, and highest-paid film stars.

A GENIUS FOR MAKEUP

Chaney was christened Leonidas Frank Chaney on April 1, 1883, in Colorado Springs, Colorado. The second of four children (three boys, one of whom died in infancy, and one girl) born to Frank, a barber, and Emma Chaney, he went by the nickname "Lon" since childhood.

Both of Lon Chaney's parents were deaf—his father because of a childhood illness, his mother from birth. Chaney's biographers and others who have written about the screen legend assert that the actor's penchant for playing characters with disabilities or deformities—or who are marked as outsiders by society for other reasons, such as being a minority, or a gangster—likely stemmed from seeing his parents branded as "different," even by polite society, and cruelly taunted as "dummies" by neighborhood children. I'm sure there is some truth to this, but I have a feeling it may be overstated.

Chaney did not pursue a show business career playing such characters. He was a song and dance man on the musical stage. Not until he went west to seek work in the movies did his persona as "the man of a thousand faces" come into being, and it seems to have been motivated as much by economic as by psychological interests. Quite simply, the actor may have realized that by being able to "look the part" in a wider range of roles, he'd get more work. So, he applied his genius for makeup effects, and his acrobatic skills, to achieving just that. Eventually his talent for disappearing physically into his "outsider" characters, and humanizing even the most bizarre and twisted among them, became a highly exploitable—and profitable—gimmick. It led to Chaney's carving out a niche for himself in the industry (and film history) that is unique to this day.

At the time of his death of throat cancer in 1930, Chaney ranked alongside Swedish import Greta Garbo as MGM's most popular star; had he lived, it is possible his star power would have endured, for unlike many actors of the silent screen, the stage-trained Chaney had no fear of the microphone.

As an article in the June 22, 1930, edition of *The New York Times* reported, Chaney had welcomed the chance to expand upon his persona as the cinema's "Man of Mystery" in the new medium of the talkies. "[Chaney] realized the microphone would prevent him from indulging in the make-ups which had won him the sobriquet of the 'man of a thousand faces,'" the *Times* wrote on the eve of Chaney's talkie debut in the underworld drama *The Unholy Three*, a remake of one of his biggest silent successes. "He had secured most of his facial distortions by holding foreign substances of divers [*sic*] shapes and sizes in his mouth. However, Chaney had made up his mind that if he couldn't indulge the genius for make-up which had earned him his unusual position in the cinema world, he would develop a new talent, that of voice disguises for talking pictures."

Commented Chaney in the same article: "Even as a prop boy, I used to watch [stage actors] Richard Mansfield and Robert Mantell and others. Those old actors never showed the audience themselves, but really donned the personality of the character they were playing. From the beginning of my acting career, I always strove to bury my own personality in my part. That is my idea of acting. And there is no question that talking pictures are bringing back the old style of acting. I want to talk in at least two voices, or dialects, in each picture."

In *The Unholy Three*, he kept his word, using not just two more voices, but four—those of an old woman, a ventriloquist's dummy, a talking parrot, and a young woman in the courtroom gallery where the film's climax takes place—in addition to his own (one assumes) as the gang leader of the unsavory trio of jewel robbers that calls itself "the unholy three."

It is easy to imagine that if he had not died prematurely and had lived well into the sound era, he might have gone on to become the first great gangster movie star of the talkies. His rough-edged, blue-collar looks and bulldog demeanor as the silent film era's first full-fledged gangster anti-hero would have made him a natural choice to play Rico Bandello (Edward G. Robinson) in *Little Caesar* (1930); the part of Tony Camonte (Paul Muni), the underworld antihero of *Scarface* (1932); or even some of Humphrey Bogart's gangster roles, especially that of the doomed Roy Earle in *High Sierra* (1941). Perhaps only the gangsters played by the more youthful and pugnacious James Cagney[1] (who, like Chaney, began his career as a stage hoofer) may have eluded him—although Chaney does strike a very Cagney-like pose in *Outside the Law* (1921), one of his earliest gangster film successes.

THE PENALTY

The Samuel Goldwyn production of *The Penalty* (1920) presented Lon Chaney in one of genre's earliest, meatiest mobster roles, and he used the opportunity to create an indelible portrait of the traditional gangster film figure of the victimized youth who turns to crime for revenge, becoming the city's top gang boss.

A violent, psychotic "lord and master of the underworld," *The Penalty*'s protagonist, called Blizzard, is a Little Caesar and Phantom of the Opera rolled into one. An inexperienced doctor unnecessarily amputated his legs when he was a boy, filling him with a desire for vengeance against the doctor specifically and society at large. Now grown, he has become a megalomaniac who, in a moment of frenzied grandiosity, calls himself "a modern Caesar." But he is also an accomplished pianist, who soars into flights of romantic rapture on the ivories, as one of his molls, perversely stationed beneath him, works the pedals for him with her hands. It's no wonder Universal Pictures considered no one but Chaney for the part of the Phantom when it came time to cast the picture a few years later; in these scenes, Chaney's performance seems almost like a warm-up for his most famous role.

Not all of Chaney's contemporaries were enamored of the man's abilities. The acerbic director Josef von Sternberg, who would contribute as much to the gangster genre as Chaney with his groundbreaking 1927 film, *Underworld*, called him "a man who poisons wells," in other words, a performer "who confused makeup with acting" and indulged in "extravagant histrionics."[2] It's true that many of Chaney's vehicles were contrived and full of inconsistencies and improbabilities and are not great films. Typically, his roles were rooted in some kind of gimmick that enabled him to appear in a different disguise each time, thereby cementing his reputation and box-office appeal, and making the phrase "Don't step on it; it may be Lon Chaney" one of the most popular of the day. But Sternberg's criticism that Chaney was a man who confused makeup with acting is unfair, for however mediocre many of Chaney's films may have been, his performances—particularly in gangster roles—in them are as subtle and believable as they are "extravagantly histrionic."

The Penalty is a good example. The plot, as most reviewers noted even at the time, is wildly implausible, its final twist stretching our suspension of disbelief beyond the limit. But Chaney delivers a powerful, multi-shaded performance that's much more than bravura "stunt" work. Commented one reviewer: "When Chaney appears with both his legs sawed off above the knees, some will exclaim, 'How in the world can he do that?,' but after they have followed his acting for awhile, and felt the force of his presence on the screen, they will take it as just a part of his role that his legs are missing."

It's true that as audiences we can't help but gape in wonder at Chaney's physical prowess and endurance, as the actor, his limbs trussed tightly behind him and concealed beneath a long coat, hops about on crutches, jumps to the floor from platforms (landing on his knees), walks up stairs, slides down poles, and hoists himself up a pegged wall hand by hand to spy into an adjoining room. But such gymnastics are not all there is to his performance. He's equally impressive in the less flamboyant scenes, when the camera is focusing only on his expressive face—his features grim but eyes twinkling—as he wrestles with the rising evil in himself, aware that his urges are sick, yet eager to surrender to them at the same time. We see his pain when he spurns with barely concealed horror and distaste the advances of the woman who loves him—because her actions remind him that the woman *he* loves looks upon him as a freak. And when he fantasizes about his grand scheme to bring the city to *its* knees, he reveals the full measure of his wounded pride, a revelation that shocks even his closest underling.[3]

Even the risible conclusion—the doctor who crippled him operates on Chaney's brain, removing the "contusion at the base of the skull" that has driven the inherently good man to evil—still manages to pack a punch due to Chaney's skill and firm grasp of the character. A reformed man, he sits at his beloved piano with his wife by his side, fantasizing about how he will dismantle the criminal empire he created. But a quivering drug addict named Frisco Pete, whom Chaney had reduced to subservience by threatening to withhold the man's dope supply, shoots Chaney in the back because he's afraid the reformed criminal will "snitch" on the gang. As his killer escapes, Chaney calmly realizes he's paying the penalty for his past misdeeds. "Don't grieve, dear," he tells his tearful wife. "Death interests me."

It's a remarkable performance that lifts what is otherwise an uneven albeit slickly made early gangster film to near-classic status.

THE CHANEY-BROWNING GANG

Chaney followed *The Penalty* with another strong, but very different, gangster role for Universal in Tod Browning's *Outside the Law*. Chaney had worked with Browning before, in the 1919 crime picture *The Wicked Darling*, in which Chaney had a supporting role as a crooked tough guy named "Stoop Collins," a member of a small-time gang of thieves led by the bad/good girl of the title, played by Priscilla Dean.[4]

Chaney's association with Browning—a director as "obsessed" in his choice of subject matter as the actor was in his selection of and commitment to his roles—formed a perfect match between star and filmmaker. It would extend to eight more collaborations in the coming decade, four of them gangster or quasi-gangster films: the already mentioned *The Unholy Three* (1925), *The Blackbird* (1926), *The Road to Mandalay* (1926), and *The Big City* (1928).

A son of the south like his mentor in the movies, D. W. Griffith, Charles Albert "Tod" Browning was born in Louisville, Kentucky, on July

12, 1880. He left home at the age of sixteen to join a traveling carnival as a roustabout and occasional barker. He later turned to performing, first as a clown, then as a contortionist and illusionist with an act called "The Living Hypnotic Corpse" that he performed on riverboats along the Mississippi. After that he went into vaudeville, where he performed the same acts on stage, as well as some comedy, song, and dance routines.

Browning met Griffith through a mutual acquaintance in 1913 and recognized the opportunity for steady employment—and unlimited audience-generating potential—offered by the infant medium in which Griffith was fast gaining a reputation. Browning eagerly joined Griffith's company as an actor, stuntman, and assistant director. When Griffith went west to make pictures, Browning went with him, and it was there that he directed his own first films, a series of two-reelers with such exploitable titles as *The Living Head* (1915), *The Burned Hand* (1915), and *Everybody's Doing It* (1916). Browning codirected his first feature-length film, the Civil War drama *Jim Bludso*, in 1917. That same year, he moved to Metro (which had not yet evolved into Goldwyn-Mayer) Pictures, where he directed such tasty sounding vehicles as *The Jury of Fate* (1917), *The Legion of Death* (1918), *Revenge* (1918), and *The Eyes of Mystery* (1918), the latter a haunted house melodrama foreshadowing his work in the horror film genre with such pictures as *Dracula* (1931), his most famous film.

In 1919, Browning contracted with Universal to direct the aforementioned *The Wicked Darling*, where he met Lon Chaney. The two men shared similar showbiz backgrounds and were about the same age, so they became friends. Chaney was carving a niche for himself in the industry with his genius for pantomime and his versatility. With, and sometimes even without, the aid of makeup, he was adept at playing almost any type of role, a highly promotable gimmick. Tod Browning was a writer-director eager to exploit that gimmick in ever more sensational ways.

In *Outside the Law*, for example, Chaney plays two parts, the first a vicious, Cagney-esque gangster in bow tie and fedora named Black Mike Sylva.[5] The second is Ah Wing, the Asian servant of a reformer assisting the film's main leads (Priscilla Dean and Wheeler Oakman) in going straight. Chaney's dual characters—particularly Ah Wing—get little screen time because the film's primary focus is the relationship between Dean and Oakman and their rehabilitation from a life of crime. Black Mike and Ah Wing are really just supporting roles. They only take center stage during the gun-blazing finale, when Black Mike and his gang try to get even with the lovers for a double cross. As Chaney's Black Mike attempts to throttle the life out of Oakman, his Ah Wing pumps a bullet into Black Mike's black heart, and the villain crashes through a railing, falls from a balcony (a stunt Chaney appears to have performed himself), and expires from his wounds. With the aid of clever cutting, Browning gives us the chance to watch one Lon Chaney kill another.

Critics termed this lightweight but fast-paced and efficient little potboiler "Real underworld stuff [that] begins with action and ends with action, and carries a strong moral: that virtue or honesty has its reward"—a message typical of the crime films of the period. Browning later made a talkie version of *Outside the Law* (1930) that neither begins with action nor ends with it. Despite a fair amount of camera movement (itself unusual for Browning), the film is extremely stagy and, even though only eighty-two minutes long, seems to go on for a couple of hours. The youthful cast moves the same way, shuffling along like geriatrics—one can almost hear a technician ordering Browning to slow the actors' movements to a crawl because the cumbersome sound equipment wasn't picking up their footsteps—and speak their lines in the halting manner people usually reserve for foreigners or the hard-of-hearing.

Set in San Francisco like the original, the remake features Edward G. Robinson in Chaney's fashion-plate gangster role, although his character is renamed Cobra Collins. Ah Wing was dropped, as were many other characters, but an attempt was made to retain the Asian angle by turning Robinson into a Chinese-American. As Robinson wears not the slightest daub of makeup to indicate his character's ethnicity, this revelation, which comes when he introduces an Asian woman as his mother, is so astonishingly improbable that we can't help but wonder if our leg is being pulled. Our incredulity persists to such a degree that at the conclusion of the film, when Robinson is killed and the hero (Owen Moore) calls out to the cops "There's a half million bucks and a dead Chinaman waitin' for you up here," we wonder who the hell he's talking about. Whatever the reason for the character's totally Western appearance, it wasn't because of any aversion on Robinson's part to being made up as an Asian if the role called for it (as it certainly does here). He'd already played a Japanese on Broadway, and for his next film, the comedy *East Is West* (1930), he would put on Asian makeup to play a character called Charlie Yong, the "chop suey king of San Francisco's Chinatown." And he would do so again in a later gangster film, *The Hatchet Man* (1932), where he plays a Tong assassin. Moore and Mary Nolan[6] are much more convincing as the young crooks who are reformed by the love of a child and decide to seek a new life on the straight and narrow as soon as they put in a one- to five-year stretch in the pen for bank robbery.

GANGLAND SOUP

Chaney followed his back-to-back successes as a gangster in *The Penalty* and *Outside the Law* with other "crook roles" in *Flesh and Blood* (1922), directed by Irving Cummings, and another underworld drama for Samuel Goldwyn and director Wallace Worsley called *Voices in the City* (1921), in which he plays a corrupt political boss in control of the mob. *Variety* called the film, which is now lost, an "interesting underworld melodrama with intricate plotting and counter-plotting" in which "Lon Chaney, as always, gets the utmost out of the role of a powerful leader of lawbreakers."

Rounding out Chaney's gangster films of 1922 was *The Light in the Dark*, an early directorial effort of Clarence Brown, who in a few short years would begin his MGM reign as Greta Garbo's favorite director, his career lasting well beyond hers into the 1950s. *The Light in the Dark*'s combination of gritty realism—the film vividly captures the oppressive atmosphere of tenement life on New York's Lower East Side, where it was shot on location—and uplifting theme of love, honor, faith, and redemption made it ideal for inspirational showings around the country at schools and churches, which circulated it for years in a shortened version under the title *The Light of Faith*. Chaney plays a tough mug who proves to have a heart of gold when he nurses a young girl (Hope Hampton[7]) back to health with the aid (he thinks) of a chalice he's stolen that he is convinced is the magical Holy Grail of legend. He falls in love with the girl, who is grateful to him but unable to return his affections because she's still in love with the rich cad (E. K. Lincoln) who had rejected her after discovering she was from the wrong side of the tracks. The rich cad sees the error of his ways, however. He comes after the girl to win her over, and Chaney steps nobly aside to allow true love to take its course, while his own goes unrequited—the fate suffered by many of his screen characters in and out of the gangster genre, and typical of the antihero at large on the screen until the 1970s.

In 1923's *The Shock*, directed by Lambert Hillyer, Chaney played a cripple in the employ of Christine Mayo's "Queen of the San Francisco

Underworld." Mayo uses him to exact revenge against a banker (William Welsh) who caused her to be sent up the river for a time. But her villainous underling refuses to carry out his mission when he falls in unrequited love with the banker's daughter (Virginia Valli) and undergoes a spiritual transformation. Not to be outfoxed, the vengeful Mayo lures Valli to San Francisco in the hope of sullying her reputation. But the Great San Francisco Earthquake intervenes to thwart Mayo's plans, and Valli, if not the city, is saved from "ruination." In one of the most improbable of all happy endings, the "Shock" also cures Chaney of his deformity so that he can at last satisfy his love for Valli.

VIOLENCE AND VENTRILOQUISM

Chaney reunited with Tod Browning for the first version of *The Unholy Three* (1925), the most successful collaboration, critically and commercially, of their careers. Although not as deliriously perverse as some of his later films with and without Chaney, *The Unholy Three* is nevertheless quintessential Tod Browning. Based on a tale by the British writer Clarence "Tod" Robbins, who also provided the source for Browning's classic chiller *Freaks* (1932), the film begins in typical Browning territory—a carnival sideshow populated with tattooed ladies, Siamese twins, sword swallowers, and other assorted human oddities. As the crowds surge to gawk, Chaney, a sideshow ventriloquist, has his accomplice (Mae Busch) move among them, picking their pockets.

Tired of petty hauls—a watch here, a wallet there—Chaney forms an unholy alliance with a midget and a strongman and opens an exotic bird shop to be used as a front for luring wealthy patrons. Disguising himself as a kindly gray-haired grandmother, Chaney uses his skills as a ventriloquist to convince customers the birds can speak. (As this is a silent film, director Browning cleverly shows the birds "speaking" using comic-strip word balloons superimposed over the birds' heads.) When delivery is made to the customers' homes, Chaney and his cohorts use the opportunity to case the surroundings for expensive jewels and other valuables, returning later to rob the houses.

To make the shop appear as innocent and aboveboard as possible, the strongman poses as "Granny Chaney's" son-in-law and chief delivery boy, while the midget convincingly disguises himself as her infant grandson, dressed in swaddling clothes. Pretending to be Granny's daughter, Busch works as a clerk in the shop, assisted by the dim but honest Hector (Matt Moore), who is completely ignorant of the group's illegal activities and falls for the girl. When she falls for Moore in return, Chaney grows jealous—for he's in love with Busch as well—and the successful operation shows its first signs of cracking.

When a customer rings up to complain that the parrot he'd bought no longer talks, Chaney and the midget pay a friendly house call, where Chaney uses his ventriloquist skills again to give the parrot a voice. He also witnesses the delivery of a valuable ruby necklace. The unholy three make plans to steal the necklace on Christmas Eve, but Chaney's unease at the prospect of leaving Busch and Moore alone for the evening decorating the shop Christmas tree prompts him to postpone the burglary for several hours. Impatient to get his hands on the necklace, the greedy midget manipulates the strongman into pulling the job without Chaney; during the course of the robbery, the owner of the necklace is murdered.

Chaney berates the pair for the killing but is pleased with their haul and stashes the necklace in a toy elephant for safekeeping until the heat is off. In the film's most suspenseful scene, a detective almost stumbles upon the necklace until the strongman grabs the toy elephant away from him and, upbraiding the detective for "teasing the baby," returns it to the wailing midget's outstretched hands.

This close shave with the cops prompts Chaney to shut down operations and disappear to the gang's mountain hideout. Before skipping, however, he orders the midget to plant the necklace in Moore's apartment, and the young man is later arrested. When Busch threatens to blow the whistle to save her lover, the unholy three tie her up and take her along.

At the mountain hideout, Busch offers to marry Chaney if he'll get Moore off the hook. Posing once more as Granny, Chaney attends the trial and slips Moore a note urging him to take the stand in his own defense but to say nothing, just silently to mumble the Lord's Prayer. Meanwhile, Chaney throws his voice into Moore' mouth, revealing the details of the bird shop scam, the theft of the necklace, and the murder. The ploy backfires, however, and when it looks like Moore will be convicted anyway, Chaney keeps his promise to Busch by standing up and making a full confession, naming the midget and the strongman as the genuine culprits.

At the cabin, the midget and the strongman have a falling out and are killed (the latter by Chaney's pet gorilla), and Busch escapes. She rejoins Chaney, intending to keep her part of the bargain, but the reformed gang leader has a change of heart and allows her to go to the exonerated Moore instead. Chaney then returns to his former job as a sideshow ventrilo-quist—apparently with the blessing of the authorities, who've chosen to forgive him for all the other crimes in which he *did* take part.

Perhaps because it was one of the more bizarre gangster dramas turned out by Hollywood during what one contemporary reviewer prematurely labeled "the golden age of underworld stories," the film inspired more acclaim than it seems to merit today. It boasts some unusual images: the vision of Chaney whipping off his Granny wig and transforming into his gangster self—forgetting that Granny's earrings are still dangling from his lobes—and of the midget relaxing in his crib with a cigar stuck in his mouth. But structurally the film isn't very well worked out, and at times it seems almost disdainful of the audience.

The ape that kills the strongman isn't introduced to the viewer until the moment it's unleashed. Coming out of nowhere, it seems hardly more than a contrivance thrown in by Browning to give the audience a last-minute frisson while getting the strongman out of the way. Similarly, little is made of the fascinating relationship Browning sets up between "the greedy bit of flesh" midget and the strongman, his beefy but cowardly protector. The film intriguingly hints at a homosexual under-current—particularly in the scenes where the midget and Mae Busch reveal a mutual "loathing" for one another.

The conclusion, where Chaney confesses all and is let off scot-free, is not only implausible but seems only to serve the design of leaving audiences with a happy ending. Although cleverly rendered through title cards and pantomime, Chaney's ventriloquism scenes don't really work in a silent-film format. They cry out for sound, which is why the story became such an ideal vehicle for Chaney's talkie debut.

The talkie remake, directed by Jack Conway, is superior to the silent version in every respect, although one would not think so judging from the very different critical reaction the two versions received. *Variety* called the silent version "a wow of a story [in which] Lon Chaney stands out like a million dollars." And yet five years later, it said of the remake: "[The] weakness is that the story doesn't adapt well to the talkie tech-nique. Skill in make-up permitted Chaney to get away with the imperson-ation of the old woman before, but his handling of dialog destroys all plausibility."

Conway's talkie follows Browning's silent fairly closely, even recreat-ing whole scenes from the earlier film shot for shot. But the talkie fleshes out the story and characters more, and the medium of sound allows the characters to engage in some hilarious repartee. At one point, Elliott Nugent's Hector (who is still sappy, but nowhere near as stupid as Matt Moore) marvels to his girl (Lila Lee), "It's wonderful the way your grandma can make those birds talk!" To which Lee caustically responds, "Hector, she could make Coolidge talk!"

Contemporary reviewers felt that Lee wasn't "nearly as convincing as Mae Busch was in the silent picture," but Lila Lee breathes more sparkle and personality into the role, giving the character of Rosie a hard-edged yet vulnerable quality similar to the later bad/good–girl roles of Glenda Farrell, Joan Blondell, Claire Trevor, and, of course, Bette Davis. The writers also make more of the implied undercurrents in the midget and strongman's relationship; in a priceless exchange, the midget disdainfully says, "You're the one that shoulda been the old woman"; the strongman replies, "I'm not that kind of guy."

Variety to the contrary, Chaney's handling of his dialogue and vocal impersonations is not only convincing but quite impressive; no one voice sounds like another, and yet they all belong to Chaney. Believing audiences might be skeptical of this, the actor even made out a legal document testifying that the voices were his, a deposition widely circulated prior to the film's release. Witnessed by a prominent Los Angeles notary public, the statement contended: "I, Lon Chaney, being duly sworn, depose and say: In the photoplay entitled *The Unholy Three*, produced by Metro-Goldwyn-Mayer Corporation, all voice reproductions which purport to be reproductions of my voice, to wit the ventriloquist's, the old woman's, the dummy's, the parrot's, and the girl's [a member of the sideshow audience], are actual reproductions of my own, and in no place in said photoplay, or in any other of the various characters played by me in said photoplay, was a 'double' or substitute used for my voice."

The remake also lays the groundwork for the strongman's murder by Chaney's pet gorilla by introducing the creature to us in the opening carnival sideshow scenes. Fearful of the strongman's strength and the possibility that he may someday turn against him, Chaney cages the beast (which the strongman took joy in mistreating) and keeps it in the back of the bird shop throughout the film—and later takes it to the mountain hideout—"just in case."

Also much improved is the courtroom denouement. The remake throws out the contrived ventriloquism scene and has Chaney, in his Granny disguise, take the stand in Nugent's defense. As the DA bears down on the old woman's assertion that the midget and the strongman committed the robbery and murder, Chaney gets flustered, lapses into his real voice, and is unmasked. Chaney nobly lets Lee out of her bargain just as he did Busch in the silent version, but rather than going back to his old life as a sideshow ventriloquist, he's more realistically sent to prison and promises to "send Lee a card now and then."

LIMEHOUSE BLUES

The Chaney-Browning Gang followed the silent *The Unholy Three* with *The Blackbird* (1926), in which Chaney plays an even more intriguing dual role. The film in this writer's opinion stands up better today than the more acclaimed silent version of *The Unholy Three*, and may be Browning's best picture. It too would have made an excellent vehicle for Chaney's talkie debut, for its plot also centers on the gangster protagonist's ability to disguise both his appearance and his voice.

The film is set in London's seedy Limehouse District. Chaney takes two challenging roles: the villainous, morally crippled gang leader and thief, the Blackbird, and his kindly, crippled brother, the Bishop, beloved by all in Limehouse for his work on behalf of the poor. In reality, they're the same person.

Whenever the cops put on the heat, the Blackbird pulls a fast fade, dons the Bishop's clothes and crutches, throws his hip and arm out of joint, and assumes the identity of the Bishop. The Blackbird further cements the masquerade by assuming two voices, conducting frequent loud altercations with the Bishop behind the locked doors of the bishop's room in the district's mission house.

The Blackbird and his high-society partner in crime, dapper West End Bertie (Owen Moore), ply their trade by robbing wealthy Londoners who visit Limehouse for an occasional lowlife night on the town. The operation begins to fall apart, however, when the Blackbird and Bertie fall in love with the same girl, an attractive French lass named Fifi (Renee Adoree), who does a puppet show in one of the slum's dingy cabarets. When it becomes clear that Fifi has eyes only for Bertie, the jealous Blackbird dons his kindly Bishop guise and counsels the young woman to forget the criminal. But Bertie decides to go straight, so she agrees to marry him. Furious, the Blackbird frames Bertie for the murder of a policeman. Believing in Bertie's innocence, Fifi turns again for help to the Bishop, who hides Bertie out. When he and Bertie are alone, however, the Bishop manipulates Bertie into believing that Fifi and the Blackbird are carrying on an affair.

Jealous to get her man back (even if he gets a stretch in prison), the Blackbird's ex-wife (Doris Lloyd) tells Scotland Yard that the Blackbird is guilty of the policeman's murder. Fifi and Bertie are reunited when she convinces him of her genuine devotion, and the police let the man go. Informed that the Blackbird is hiding out in the Bishop's digs, the cops attempt to break down the door. The Blackbird fakes a shouting match and a fight between himself and the Bishop, tossing furniture about the room and making it sound as if he's giving the Bishop a terrible beating.

Simultaneously, he struggles into the Bishop's clothes, and then tosses open a window to convince the police the Blackbird has flown. Throwing his hip and leg out of joint to complete the disguise, he hobbles to the door to let the police in, but just as he gets there, they burst inside and he's accidentally knocked to the floor, landing at an awkward angle and breaking his back.

The ex-wife arrives as the police go for a doctor. Not knowing how bad his wounds are, the Blackbird/Bishop clues the startled woman in on his dual identity and, to avoid being unmasked during the doctor's physical examination, persuades her to stall the doctor long enough for him to regain his strength and get back on his feet. She suggests that he pretend to be asleep and resting comfortably so that the doctor will put off disturbing him. While going along with this, he slips into unconsciousness and expires from his injuries with the tearful woman by his side, whispering, "You fooled 'em to the end."

Although it was only a moderate box office success, *The Blackbird* reveals the Chaney-Browning Gang at peak form. Chaney is not only physically and temperamentally convincing as the brother opposites, he is astonishing at times in his ability, with only minimal use of makeup, to make even the facial features of the Blackbird and the Bishop appear dissimilar.

Atmospherically photographed by Percy Hilburn, beautifully designed by Cedric Gibbons and A. Arnold Gillespie, and sharply edited by Errol Taggart, *The Blackbird* is one of Browning's most striking productions. The pictorial qualities of the film alone make it worth seeing; the surviving prints have been well preserved and are still gorgeous to behold. And for a Browning film, the plot is not only well worked out and plausible but credibly sustained throughout. And it ends, unlike the two versions of

The Unholy Three, with a twist that is genuinely surprising, grimly satis-fying, and emotionally powerful.

Like most early gangster films, *The Blackbird* offers the familiar moral that crime doesn't pay. But it also looks forward to the later, more anar-chic underworld films of the 1930s, particularly those made by Warner Brothers, by offering viewers a gangster who is not only unrepentant of his violent and crooked ways but who keeps to those ways right to the bitter end.

CHANEY UNMASKED

The year 1926 also saw the release of another Browning/Chaney quasi-gangster film, *The Road to Mandalay*. With an Asian setting, the film is part underworld story and part domestic drama, with the emphasis on the latter. Chaney plays a scarfaced gang leader and smuggler named Singapore Joe, whose shop clerk daughter (Lois Moran) is not only unaware that he's her father, but is repelled by the man's grotesque appearance and unsavory reputation. When the innocent young woman falls for one of Chaney's criminal associates (Owen Moore), and the two plan to marry, Chaney's paternal instincts kick in, and he sets out to disrupt the wedding. Diverted from his criminal activities, he finds his criminal empire threatened by a brutal rival (Sojin) and must fight to hold on to his kingpin status. Sojin puts the moves on Chaney's daughter, he tries to rape her, and Chaney is killed in a knife fight saving her virtue and her life. Only then does she learn who Chaney really is and how much he obviously loved her.

Coming right after the superlative *The Blackbird, The Road to Man-dalay* is something of a letdown. Events unfold rapidly, but often without motivation; the entire construction of the film seems haphazard. But this assessment may be unfair because the only surviving print of the film is an abridgment of the original seven-reel release.

Browning and Chaney's last gangster film together, *The Big City* (1928), returned the duo to the landscape of their earlier underworld successes—the streets of modern-day America. Its merits—and position in the Browning/Chaney gangster film pantheon—cannot be adequately judged, however, because the film is on MGM's "lost list." Over the years, MGM managed to preserve most of the films Chaney made for them; their track record is certainly superior to that of any other studio. Of the eighteen silent films Chaney made for MGM, only three are presumed lost: *The Tower of Lies* (1925), *London After Midnight* (1927), and *The Big City* (1928).

All we have to go on today in assessing *The Big City* are a few surviving stills and the opinions of some reviewers, which don't always stand the test of time. Sporting no makeup, Chaney again played a flashily dressed big-city crime boss (a figure fast becoming a staple in Hollywood gangster films of the period) who finds that his successful jewel robbery operation is being undermined by gang rivals. With the help of his girlfriend (Betty Compson) and a loyal lieutenant (James Murray), Chaney turns the tables on his rivals, then he and his two cohorts decide to go straight.

One reviewer wrote: "*The Big City* begins at a swift gallop and ends at a lazy lope. The first half is filled with ingenious ideas, with surprise following surprise, but when Mr. Browning attacks the reformation of the leading gangster he permits the pace of his story to slacken until it becomes slightly tedious." *Variety* concluded: "The heavy publicity should be placed on Chaney as himself, without disguise, just to see the difference. For the picture itself, the best that may be said of it is that it ends with a laugh. When the chief crook reforms and tells his girl he's going to marry her, she's overwhelmed. Rushing toward him for a pleasurable hug, he repulses her, saying: 'Listen! I ain't going to buy you nothing. I'm just going to marry you.'"

Although its only known prints are missing an entire reel and are marred by print decomposition, Chaney's last silent gangster film, Jack Conway's *While the City Sleeps* (1928), remains one of his best. Again wearing no makeup (except, perhaps, for a hairpiece designed to make him appear a little thin on top), he delivers one of his most sensitive and moving performances as a veteran Irish cop in New York City's plainclothes division who suffers from chronically sore feet and, despite his gruff exterior, a sentimental and lonely heart.

Known throughout the city for his dedication to duty and his ability to turn youthful offenders onto the straight and narrow, he falls for a girl twenty years his junior when he assigns himself to protect her from a mob hit.

While she is hiding out in his cluttered bachelor apartment, Chaney gradually reveals his feelings toward her. Out of gratitude for all he's doing, she agrees to marry him, despite being in love with a younger man (Carroll Nye), small-time hood Chaney had given a break to in exchange for promising to move to another city and into an honest line of work.

Nye mends his ways and returns to New York to marry the girl. When he finds her living in Chaney's apartment, he flies into a jealous rage, hurls her to the floor, and accuses her of two-timing him with the older man. Once she explains things, he apologizes for his ugly behavior and agrees to stand aside because he, too, is in Chaney's debt. He encounters Chaney on the stairs, admits that he'd asked the girl to marry him, and then lies that she turned him down because "she really loves you." Over-joyed, Chaney goes up to the room and realizes the truth when he hears the girl weeping inconsolably.

After tracking the gang leader targeting the girl (she witnessed his killing of a policeman) to his lair and running him to the ground in an exciting rooftop shoot-out, Chaney reunites the two young lovers, con-vincing them that his marriage proposal was a sham designed to keep the girl out of harm's reach until the gang leader was captured or killed. The joyful couple goes off together arm in arm; the film's moving final shot shows the tough detective standing beside his adoring landlady (Lydia Yeamans Titus) waving good-bye. As Chaney's arm circles the woman's shoulder, the young lovers look back and happily conclude that their aging friend and benefactor has at last found love of his own, but the barely concealed longing on Chaney's expressive face as he gazes at the younger woman tells all.

Even though it drew only a mixed reception at the time, *While the City Sleeps* holds up today, even in its truncated form, as a really cracker-jack gangster picture of the silent era. It is full of wild fights, furious gun-play (like Raoul Walsh's *Me, Gangster,* released the same month, it was distributed to theaters with a synchronized effects track so that audiences could hear all the "popping of bullets"), exciting chases, and underworld ambience. But it's the humanness of Chaney's performance that gives the film its texture and its punch.

THE GANGSTER DEFINED

As styles in filmmaking, and in America's social climate, changed over the years, the motives and behavior of the movie gangster would also change. But not substantially, for the early silent-era gangster pictures, Chaney's especially, had defined the character's basic flaws.

He is an undisciplined child, fascinated with the forbidden, who never grows up and still bitterly resents the "parental" authority of the police because of the control it represents over him.

A violent Peter Pan who justifies his every antisocial act, even murder, as debts owed to him.

An innate loner, no matter how much company he keeps, and a grandiose schemer determined to acquire wealth and power by the shortest route possible—who invariably sees that route through the barrel of a gun.

4
A Landscape of Night and Shade

"Who's Attila? The head of some wop gang?"
—Bull Weed (George Bancroft),
Underworld (1927)

THE SUN NEVER RISES

ERHAPS BECAUSE OF ITS ENCOMPASSING TITLE, Paramount's 1927 production of *Underworld* is often assumed to be the American cinema's first gangster movie, an erroneous assumption as we have seen. Even the film's director, Josef von Sternberg,[1] contributed to this false assumption by writing in his autobiography that the subject matter of *Underworld* "was untried material, as no films had as yet been made of this deplorable phase of our culture."[2]

Hugely popular with critics and audiences upon its release, *Underworld* was clearly not the first gangster movie but the first film about gangsters to marshal many of the burgeoning genre's disparate elements into a collective model for other filmmakers to emulate. Although corrupt politicians and the specter of mob rule over society may be absent from *Underworld,* virtually every other convention of the time then established is present: the antihero mobster with a personal code of honor; the gaudy atmosphere of nightclubs and speakeasies (the gangster film equivalent of the Western saloon); secret hideouts; gang rivalries; speeding roadsters and pursuing cops on motorcycles; and the requisite flapper heroine who also has a code, and who typically forsakes her hoodlum sugar daddy for the upright and decent hero.

Just as important as the marshaling of the genre's many ingredients, however, was the aesthetic achievement of the film, which Sternberg described as an "experiment in photographic violence and montage."[3] Befitting the film's title—and anticipating the subgenre of the crime picture called film noir that would come into its own in the years of the Second World War—Sternberg's underworld is different from the milieu of most other gangster films of the era. It's a forbidding landscape of night and shade, always shrouded in darkness. From first frame to last, daylight never intrudes.

SALVATION HUNTER

Josef von Sternberg was born Jonas (or "Jo" as he was called) Sternberg in Vienna, Austria, in 1894. He was seven when his family immigrated to America, and he spent the next decade shuttling back and forth between continents, soaking up knowledge of his European roots and roots in the new world simultaneously.

Sternberg got his start in the film industry as a teenager working in the cutting rooms of the World Film Company in Fort Lee, New Jersey. When the United States entered World War I, he found himself stationed in our nation's capital getting more film experience making training pictures for the Army Signal Corps. After the war, he apprenticed with some of the leading film directors of the silent era, including Wallace Worsley, director of Lon Chaney's *The Hunchback of Notre Dame* and *The Penalty*, and Irishman Roy William Neill; it was on the credits of one of the latter's pictures (*By Divine Right*, 1923) that Sternberg began adding the European nobility–sounding "von" to his name, having already changed his first name to Josef, perhaps for the same reason.

In 1925, the now "Josef von" Sternberg directed his first feature, a gritty portrait in the poetic manner of Germany's so-called "street films" of derelict life on the docks of California's San Pedro Bay called *The Salvation Hunters*, a title that sums up the central theme of most Sternberg films and the hopes and dreams of their characters. A succès d'estime but not a money-maker, *The Salvation Hunters* earned a spot on many critics' "ten best" lists and brought Sternberg to the attention of Hollywood, where such influential producer/stars as Mary Pickford and

Charles Chaplin, who considered the film to be a masterpiece, offered him work.

Already the stereotypical image of the autocratic, "art or bust," silent-era movie director complete with boots and riding crop, Sternberg made what might be called a hash of his good fortune. He turned his back on the opportunity to direct a vehicle for Pickford—perhaps because it was to be a vehicle for her, and not for him. And the film he made for Chaplin's company, *The Sea Gull* (no relation to the play by Chekhov), was never released because of artistic differences between Sternberg and his equally autocratic producer, Chaplin himself.

Fast developing a reputation as too much of a maverick behind the camera like another Hollywood black sheep with a "von" added to his name (Erich von Stroheim), Sternberg found himself out of work but, fortunately for him, not ultimately unemployable as a director like Stroheim. Paramount gave him a job as an assistant director, and in that capacity he rescued a troubled production directed by Frank Lloyd called *Children of Divorce* (1927) from ultimately having to be scrapped by writing and directing new scenes to make the film play better with audiences.

The grateful studio rescued Sternberg as a reward by giving him a feature of his own to direct—although not an important one, just in case he messed up: a quickie gangster picture called *Underworld*.

"SHAKESPEARE OF THE MOVIES"

Underworld derived from a story written for the studio by reporter-turned-novelist-playwright-screenwriter Ben Hecht. It was adapted into a scenario by Sternberg, Hecht, Arthur Rosson, Charles Furthman (the only collaborator to get screen credit for the adaptation), his brother Jules, and director Howard Hawks, a friend of Rosson's and the Furthmans.

Sternberg maintained in his autobiography that when he came on to the picture, he scrapped most of Hecht's story and set the film in a fictional (but typically Sternbergian) world of light, shade, smoke, and mist referred to only as "a great city." Allegedly when Hecht saw the completed film, he requested that Paramount remove his name from the credits because Sternberg had "softened" his original intent. (Hecht would later rectify this with his take-no-prisoners script for the 1932 *Scarface*, a film that no one, even today, can accuse of being "soft.") Paramount obviously denied the request, as Hecht's name remains on the screen—fortunately for him, as he went on to win the 1927–1928 award for Best Original Story given out by the newly created Academy of Motion Picture Arts and Sciences, launching a screen career as one of Hollywood's most prolific, versatile, and honored screenwriters that would earn him the industry nickname "the Shakespeare of the movies."

Ben Hecht was born in New York City in 1893 but grew up in the Midwest when his family moved to Wisconsin. Always a prodigious reader and writer, he pursued a career as a reporter at the *Chicago Journal* and was writing about the crime beat and every other beat in the Windy City when barely out of his teens. He later published his columns as a book titled *101 Afternoons in Chicago* (1922), which won him a national reputation.

Hecht quickly expanded his writing activities into other areas, including novels and plays. In collaboration with another Chicago reporter-turned-playwright, Charles MacArthur, he wrote his first Broadway hit, the archetypal big-city newsroom comedy-drama *The Front Page* (1928), which opened at the Times Square Theatre on August 14, 1928, and ran for 276 performances. With its cynical and abrasive wit and rapid-fire dialogue, *The Front Page* was made for the talkies, and the first film version[4] arrived in 1930. It was directed by Lewis Milestone and starred Adolphe Menjou and Pat O'Brien, respectively, as Hecht-MacArthur's prototypical battling adversaries of the city room, ultra-manipulative managing editor Walter Burns and his insubordinate ace reporter Hildy Johnson.[5]

Although Hecht would rise to the top of the heap as one of Hollywood's premier Oscar-winning screenwriters and would work with all the American cinema's great directors—from John Ford, Alfred Hitchcock, and Howard Hawks to George Stevens and William Wyler—he despised Hollywood and the business, if not the art, of filmmaking. Nevertheless, when barely into his twenties, he had started trying to break into the movie business writing treatments (lengthy story outlines) for possible films, and he boldly sold one he'd adapted from a novel called *Double Trouble* by Herbert Quick to the already established playwright-scenarist Anita Loos. Loos expanded it into a full-length scenario that was filmed in 1915 starring Douglas Fairbanks and directed by Christy Cabanne. Hecht received no screen credit, however.[6] That came with *Underworld*, for which Hecht drew inspiration from events he'd witnessed covering stories in the Midwest crime mecca of Chicago.

Most reviewers credited Ben Hecht for the film's in-the-streets realism; wrote *Variety*: "*Underworld*, without mentioning Chicago as the scene of the ensuing machine gun warfare between crooks and the cops, evidently is a page out of Ben Hecht's underworld acquaintance with the Cicero and South Side[7] gun mob. The 'hanging by the neck' death sentence is another tip-off that New York [where electrocution was the method of choice], at least, is whitewashed, and it makes one wonder how Illinois and other Midwestern censors will feel about some of the niceties of highway robbery, foot-padding,[8] double-crossing, and martial warfare with the authorities, and other fine points of underworld behavior."

The film's ending, where the gangster protagonist is trapped in his hideout with his mistrusted lover as the police cordon off the streets and riddle the place with bullets, is clearly Hecht's contribution, as the identical scene, with only slight variation, climaxes the 1932 *Scarface* that Hecht also wrote.

Although he would go on to write only one more excellent gangster picture, the 1947 film noir *Ride the Pink Horse* starring and directed by Robert Montgomery, it is with *Underworld* and *Scarface* that Ben Hecht earned his pantheon status in the gangster movie hall of fame. "Soft" or not, *Underworld* was a home-run hit out of the park for Hecht—and the ultra-violent, ultra-perverse *Scarface* would be another. Visually, however, *Underworld* is a Sternberg picture through and through.

A GALA OF BOOZE AND BROADS

Seen today, *Underworld* inevitably disappoints—not so much because we as audiences have changed and grown jaded, and the film now strikes us as naïve, as because so little in the genre itself has changed with us. Over the years, virtually everything in Sternberg's film has been done to death on the screen, and often still is.

As *Underworld* opens, a has-been lawyer turned derelict (Clive Brook) witnesses a bank job pulled off by the city's blustering crime kingpin "Bull" Weed (George Bancroft). Instead of rubbing out the only witness to his crime, however, the criminal takes a liking to the affable young man, whom he nicknames "Rolls Royce" on account of the man's courtly manners and gift of gab.

Bancroft gets Brook a job sweeping the floor of a local nightclub, the Dreamland Café, where Brook is immediately attracted to Bancroft's flapper girlfriend, Feathers (Evelyn Brent). He also encounters Bancroft's gangland rival, Buck Mulligan (Fred Kohler), who taunts the recovering drunk by offering him money for a drink, then contemptuously tosses the money into a spittoon for Brook to fetch (a scene *Scarface* director Howard Hawks would borrow for his 1959 Western *Rio Bravo*, which co-starred Angie Dickinson as a gambler whose name "Feathers" he borrowed from *Underworld* as well).

An appropriately named bull of a man who can bend silver dollars with his bare hands, Bancroft easily intimidates the rival Kohler into backing off, and the vengeful thug vows to get even with both Bancroft and Brook. Bancroft draws first blood, however, by framing the mobster for a jewel robbery, although the charges are subsequently dismissed for lack of evidence.

Bancroft buys Brook a new set of clothes and sets him up in business as his mouthpiece. As the trio of Bancroft, Brook, and Brent spend more time together, however, Brook and Brent find themselves falling in love. Out of loyalty to Bancroft, though, they hold their amour in check.

During a gala of "booze and broads" where the gangsters vote for their favorite flapper as Queen of the Ball, Brook and Brent dance together. Bancroft becomes jealous and ostracizes his former pal. Meanwhile, rival gangster Kohler makes a drunken pass at Brent, prompting the jealous Bancroft to follow him to his office and shoot him in cold blood.

Bancroft is arrested for Kohler's murder, tried, convicted, and receives a sentence of death. While Bancroft languishes in prison waiting for his date with the executioner, Brook and Brent give in to their feelings for each other. Rumors of their open affair drift back to Bancroft, and he vows vengeance on the pair for their disloyalty. The lovers opt to move to a different city for a fresh start, but at the last moment realize that they can't turn their backs on Bancroft because, they say, "We owe him everything." So, they enlist several members of Bancroft's gang in a daring plan to spring him from prison. The plan goes awry, however, but Bancroft manages to break out on his own and holes up in his bulletproof, steel-enforced hideout. Brent shows up as the police surround the place. The gangster accuses her of leading the cops to him and roughs her up, then attempts to flee through a back door. Finding it locked and knowing his ex-pal Brook has the keys, he figures he's been set up by the duo.

The police evacuate the adjoining buildings, rain gunfire and tear gas on Bancroft's hideout, and a real battle ensues. Brook arrives and is shot as he unlocks the hideout's back door and slips inside. Bancroft attacks the badly wounded man for being a no-good double-crosser and vows that the three of them will go down together. The girl insists that she and her lover had only been trying to help the gangster escape. Seeing that Brook had put his own life in danger—and indeed had been shot—coming to the gangster's aid, Bancroft is finally persuaded of the duo's loyalty and friendship. Realizing how wrong he'd been, he mounts an escape plan, and when the two are safely away, locks the door behind them and walks out the front of his hideout, giving himself up to police.

As the cops lead Bancroft away to his delayed date with the executioner, one of them remarks that the only thing the former kingpin succeeded in doing by breaking out of prison was winning one more hour of freedom. "There was something I had to find out," the gangster replies. "And that hour was worth more to me than my whole life."

A low-budget film, which the studio had dismissed as an unimportant B picture until it started doing A-picture business at the box office, *Underworld* is not in a class artistically with Sternberg's two masterpieces of the silent era film, *The Last Command* and *The Docks of New York* (both 1928). Nevertheless, it does share many of their qualities: resplendent lighting and cinematography (by Bert Glennon, who also shot *The Last Command* for Sternberg); vivid use of montage (editing) not only in action sequences but in dialogue scenes as well, presenting information and conveying meaning with as few intertitles as possible; and strong, believable performances by all concerned, most notably George Bancroft (a fixture of many Sternberg films of the silent and early sound era) as the coarse, brutal, jovial, ignorant, conceited, generous, loving, pathetic, and, in the end, regenerated tough guy whom Clive Brook's Rolls Royce admiringly, but also sadly, likens to "Attila the Hun at the gates of Rome." ("Who's Attila? The head of some wop gang?" the gangster amusingly responds.) Evelyn Brent makes a saucy, attractive, vulnerable, and ultimately endearing Feathers. And as Rolls Royce, Clive Brook matches Bancroft and Brent at every turn; his is arguably the film's most challenging role in terms of maintaining audience sympathy.

The film's unanimously favorable reviews reflected its surging popularity with audiences. "A WHALE OF A FILM YARN!" headlined *Variety*. "A film of integrity on the part of director, scenario writer, actors and cameraman, done with back-bone," echoed the *National Board of Review*. "Best of all, at least for those looking for cinema growth on our native screen, it is a film made in America, with an actor and a director who need take off their hats to none."[9]

THE DRAGNET

Underworld was such an unexpected hit for the studio that, according to Sternberg, Paramount gratefully bestowed a $10,000 bonus on him. More importantly to the director, the studio requested from him a follow-up film in the gangster genre in the hopes of striking box office lightning twice. That film was *The Dragnet*, released by Paramount the following year, and starring George Bancroft and Evelyn Brent.

Written by Sternberg (uncredited) and the screenwriting duo of Charles and Jules Furthman from a story by Oliver H.P. Garrett, *The Dragnet* featured Bancroft as a cop this time, named Two-Gun Nolan. A big-city captain of detectives, Nolan hits the bottle after accidentally killing his partner (Leslie Fenton), an erudite sleuth nicknamed "Shakespeare," in a shootout. In fact, he's not the one responsible at all; the guilty party is gang boss Dapper Dan Trent (William Powell). When Powell's moll, an alluring flapper known as "The Magpie" (Brent), after numerous verbal skirmishes with Bancroft, finds herself falling victim to an opposites-attract romantic scenario, she spills the beans about Powell's duplicity to the big lug, and Bancroft swears off the booze, then sets out to bring Powell and his gang to justice.

How well *The Dragnet* stacks up against the more acclaimed *Underworld* is now all but impossible to say, as it is yet another lost film of the silent era. Sternberg apparently didn't think much of it, as he makes no reference to it in his autobiography. Likewise, his biographer, the film historian Herman G. Weinberg, says little about it, either, other than to make note that "For the second time, Sternberg inserted a ballroom scene with frenetic flying confetti and paper streamers (previously seen in *Underworld*), which was to become a favorite pictorial element with him."[10]

As with so many lost films, all we have left to go on are some surviving still photos of scenes from the film and what contemporary reviewers had to say about it. The latter may not always be discerning as to a film's long-term merits because tastes and perceptions change with time, but at least they can be instructive from an eyewitness' perspective as to the basic tone and content of the film. A portion of *The New York Times*'s June 1928 review is worth repeating in that regard:

"Mr. Von Sternberg has a number of weird ideas in this film," noted the unnamed critic. "He depicts the stunning girl, known to her entourage of murderers and burglars as the Magpie, on more than one occasion trying to outdo Two-Gun Nolan in volleys of epithets. With evident relish, a crook's banquet is pictured. The guests are all arrayed in faultless black and white, and when one of two of them are called upon to address the gathering it is quite obvious they would sooner face a policeman's pistol. Dapper Dan Trent, the big boss of the underworld, decides before the dessert that indiscreet chatter is a capital offense and he forthwith puts a bullet through one of his pals, who looks as if he rather enjoyed his summary dismissal from this mundane sphere."

And in another review in the same paper written (presumably) by a different unnamed critic, the author concludes: *"The Drag Net* [sic] is one of those pictures for which one is at least grateful that it has not been produced with sound. When the time comes for making a 'Drag Net' with sound accompaniment it will be like the Rough Riders and the Indians let loose in the Battle of Summit Springs." He (or she) would not have long to wait.

You Ain't Heard Nothin' Yet

When singer-actor Al Jolson blurted "I'd walk a million miles for one of my Mammy's smiles" and "You ain't heard nothin' yet" from the screen in the 1927 Warner Brothers production of *The Jazz Singer*, a silent film with synchronized sequences of song and dialogue, the arrival of the talkies (or "talkers" as they were then called) was announced, and the movie industry, if not the movies themselves, would never be the same again.

A year later, Warner Brothers released the "First 100 Percent All-Talking Picture" (ballyhooed the ads). And guess what that first 100 percent all-talking picture was, quiz-show fans? A *gangster picture*, that's what: *Lights of New York*.

A tale of bootleggers, gunmen, cops, and mugs—the latter a couple of simpletons (played by Eugene Palette and Cullen Landis) who fall for a pair of big-city con men on the lookout for investors to front a speakeasy, *Lights of New York*, although certainly a pioneer given its status as that first "100 Percent All-Talking Picture," was also "100 percent crude," agreed most reviewers. Critics savaged *Lights of New York* and caustically cautioned exhibitors to put off wiring their theaters for sound if "this was the best the 'Talkers' had to offer." It was, and is, the kind of picture that, were it not for its pulling power as a novelty, would likely not even be remembered, except as the picture that killed off sound pictures if the "talkers" hadn't gotten better, fast.

Certainly *Lights of New York* suggests nothing of the rat-a-tat style of Warner Brothers's gangster pictures, Paramount's gangster pictures, or any other studio's gangster pictures as the Roaring Twenties gave way to the Turbulent Thirties. Frankly, in terms of excitement and realistic acting, it shows little kinship with most silent-era gangster films, either. It is crude by any standard, but in addition to its major claim to fame as the first all-talkie in any genre, it does offer another first: the audible utterance of the mob's foreboding command (delivered here in hilarious slow motion so that the microphone would pick up every syllable) by actor Wheeler Oakman as the big boss to "Take . . . them . . . for . . . a . . . ride."

Sternberg made his first talkie a year later, the gangster film *Thunderbolt*, released by Paramount in 1929. It would be the final installment in Sternberg's unofficial "gangster trilogy." Sternberg developed the scenario from a story by the Furthman brothers. It starred Sternberg regular George Bancroft as the title character, whose nickname refers to his powerful right fist, which is capable of flattening an adversary like a thunderbolt.

Bancroft's moll Ritzy (Fay Wray) decides she's had enough of the underworld life and opts to go straight, dumping him for an upstanding young man who works in a bank, played by Richard Arlen. The jealous and possessive Bancroft, however, refuses to be dumped and threatens Arlen's life. As Bancroft creeps into Arlen's apartment to rub him out, a neighborhood dog follows him inside, and its sudden bark rouses Arlen, saving his life. Then the cops (whom Fay Wray had alerted to Bancroft's plan) turn up and arrest the mobster, who is already wanted on charges of robbery and murder in eleven states!

Tried and convicted as quickly as Bull Weed in *Underworld*, Bancroft is sent to prison to await death, this time in the electric chair. Meanwhile, Wray and Arlen, like Evelyn Brent and Clive Brook before them, make plans to marry while her former sugar daddy is safely imprisoned. But the nuptials are stalled when Arlen is framed for robbing his own bank and for murder. Tried, convicted, and sentenced to death as well, the innocent man lands in the cell opposite Bancroft's. Wray and Arlen's mother

(Eugenie Besserer) try to persuade Bancroft into confessing that he engineered the frame-up from behind prison walls. He emphatically denies his culpability, however, and Arlen's sentence stands.

As their respective appointments in the hot seat draw near, Bancroft befriends Arlen for the purpose of lowering the man's guard so that he can kill Arlen with a single blow from his thunderbolt fist as they bid goodbye through the bars when walking the last mile. At the last moment, however, Arlen reveals that it was actually the gangster who had stolen Wray from him—the two were sweethearts before she picked up with Bancroft—and the basically decent Bancroft lets Arlen off the hook by confessing his responsibility for the man's frame-up to authorities.

Sternberg scholar Herman G. Weinberg has likened *Thunderbolt* to *Underworld* by calling it "a work of realism, unprettified in the slightest degree."[11] But that description no more fits *Thunderbolt* than it does *Lights of New York*, although Sternberg's first talkie cannot be equated to the latter in any other regard. Even though only a year apart in production and release, it is light years ahead of *Lights of New York* in every capacity.

Yes, Sternberg's stylish black-and-white photography (courtesy of cameraman Henry W. Gerrard, although Sternberg closely supervised the lighting of his pictures himself) is starkly pretty indeed. And despite some dollops of suspense here and there, and an occasional eruption of violence, the film is more surreal than realistic. Laced with gallows humor and the kind of snappy repartee that would become the hallmark of 1930s screwball comedies, it subscribes to no known definition of the word "realism" that I know of. For example, when Bancroft arrives on death row, he's asked by one of the other condemned if he can sing tenor, as the convicts have a death-house quartet whose tenor recently walked the last mile, leaving a vacancy. Bancroft is also allowed to keep a dog (the same one that had earlier given him away) in his cell.

With only a few minutes left before Bancroft is to fry, the frazzled warden (Tully Marshall) realizes the condemned man hasn't been granted his favorite last meal, and quickly offers him anything he wishes. But Bancroft turns the offer down, maintaining that gulping a full-course meal in such a short amount of time will only give him indigestion "later on." He opts for some liquor instead, but the warden must deny the request: "I can't, unless you're sick. You are sick, aren't you?" To which Bancroft kicks back with a grin, and remarks, "Warden, I feel like I'm going to die." When the anxiety-ridden warden extends the shot glass nervously through the bars with a twitching hand, Bancroft pushes it right back to him with a "I think you need this more than I do." Finally, as Bancroft is led to the execution chamber, the prison chaplain (Robert Elliott), whose spiritual services Bancroft had always declined, stands idle, not knowing what to do, until the big gorilla gives him a "Come on, Chaplain, I'll give you a break too." I would hardly call any of this "unprettified realism."

Despite the noirish (an adjective that hadn't yet been invented) look of the film, the unserious nature of *Thunderbolt* is due, I think, to Sternberg's having decided that he'd already taken the gangster movie—his type of gangster movie, anyway—as far as he wanted to go, and he opted instead to poke fun at what he felt were fast becoming the genre's grimmer clichés. Nevertheless, the fledgling Academy of Motion Picture Arts and Sciences took the film seriously enough to nominate Bancroft as best actor for 1928/29—although he lost to Warner Baxter in the first "100 percent All-Talking Western," *In Old Arizona,* codirected by Irving Cummings and the ubiquitous Raoul Walsh.

Like *Underworld, Thunderbolt* was a substantial critical and commercial hit for Paramount and for Sternberg, who nevertheless from then on eschewed the genre to which he'd contributed so much in favor of turning actress Marlene Dietrich into an icon in a string of increasingly Baroque works of exotic exotica such as *Morocco* (1930), *Dishonored* (1931), and *Shanghai Express* (1932).

A deftly made and amusing gangster film, *Thunderbolt* is not without its flaws, however. For example, Fay Wray, then only a few years away from being memorably groped by the cinema's biggest male chauvinist ape, *King Kong* (1933), is awfully delicate and waif-like for a moll, even a reformed one. And Richard Arlen is a total lunkhead as the framed boyfriend. Hero or antihero, condemned or not, she should have stuck with the more colorful Bancroft.

5
Molls, Twists, Babes, and B Girls

"They don't think they're tough or desperate
They know the law always wins
They've been shot at before, but they do not ignore
That death is the wages of sin."

—Bonnie Parker,
"The Story of Bonnie and Clyde," 1934

LADIES OF THE PAVEMENT

LIKE THE WESTERN, THE GANGSTER MOVIE has been a male-dominated genre for most of its existence, much like the underworld society it depicts. That doesn't mean Hollywood has ignored the distaff side of gangland altogether, of course. Far from it. A modern variation on the dance hall girls and frontier prostitutes of old, molls, twists, babes, and B girls have been served up as adornments—sometimes even more than that—in gangster movies from the beginning.

William A. Wellman's *Ladies of the Mob* and Irving Cummings's *Romance of the Underworld* (both 1928) were among the earliest feature-length films to thrust the ladies into the limelight. The Wellman film, which is presumed lost, starred "It" girl Clara Bow, one of the most popular romantic comedy stars of her day, in an atypically dramatic role—that of a young woman whose gangster father is sent to the chair for murder. Embittered against society, Bow's mother raises the girl to become a master crook. Bow partners with youthful offender Richard Arlen and other, more hardened crooks to pull off a bank raid. But when she and Arlen fall in love, she undergoes a moral transformation. To prevent Arlen from going down the same road as her father, and herself from suffering the same fate as her mother, Bow steers Arlen clear of the robbery, and the two decide to go straight thereafter. *Ladies of the Mob* was a big hit for the studio (Paramount) and for Clara Bow; nonetheless, she returned to making romantic comedies, and never appeared in a film quite like it again.

Based on a popular 1911 play by triple-threat Broadway writer-producer-director Paul Armstrong, *A Romance of the Underworld*[1] picked up on the same themes of poverty, crime, and redemption characteristic of the earliest mob movies (themes that emerged again in *Ladies of the Mob*). Mary Astor stars as a poor country girl who goes to work as a "hostess" (we all know what that means) in a seedy dance hall and speakeasy frequented by gangsters and other lowlifes. When the place is raided and she's almost jailed, she seizes the opportunity to improve her life by working as a laundress and waitress to support herself while taking courses in stenography to become a secretary.

She lucks out and lands a job as personal secretary to John Boles as an up-and-coming businessman from a well-to-do family who knows nothing of her past. They fall in love and plan to marry, but her past comes back to haunt her when one of the gangsters she'd known during her "hostess" days, played by Ben Bard, threatens to expose her unless she pays him off. She finds herself at another moral crossroads. Should she give in to Bard's blackmail, probably be bled dry, and likely be exposed by him anyway? Or should she continue on her path toward redemption by turning Bard in to the police detective (Robert Elliott) who'd shown compassion for her during the speakeasy raid, even though this course of action too will likely lead to exposure of her past?

Although not in the same hard-hitting league as many of the gangster morality plays of the era that focused on the guys—such as *Regeneration*, *Big Brother*, and some of the gangster pictures of Lon Chaney—*A Romance of the Underworld*, like *Ladies of the Mob*, gave audiences of the time the opportunity to see the underworld from the less familiar female point of view. Befitting the technical and artistic sophistication of silent-era films by 1928, this William A. Fox presentation is slickly directed by Cummings, who made the equally fine *Dressed to Kill* for Fox the same year. It is beautifully photographed (by Conrad Wells), boasting many subtle camera moves, and deftly edited (by Frank Hall). Furthermore, it is earnestly and realistically acted by all—but most importantly by Mary Astor, who is luminous as the wayward girl regenerated.

Luminous too as a gal-gone-wrong who wants to go right is Loretta Young in Wellman's dynamic moll melodrama of the early talkie pre-Code years, *Midnight Mary* (1933), written by Anita Loos. The film unfolds in a compelling series of flashbacks as Young, on trial for the murder of a gangster who had threatened to kill her lover (Franchot Tone), recounts the sordid details that brought her from an environment of poverty to this midnight moment of truth in her life.

If *Midnight Mary* echoes the familiar themes of Wellman's own *Ladies of the Mob*, director Ray Enright's *Blondie Johnson* (1933) seems almost to be a loose remake. The title character, played by the vivacious, wisecracking Joan Blondell, quits her job over sexual harassment, is unable to find work, and runs out of luck with nowhere to live. So, she hooks up with a young racketeer (Chester Morris) and gets involved in the protection game, where she quickly rises to the top because of her moxie and smarts. She and Morris even fall for each other, but she puts the brakes on the romance to concentrate on building a bankroll; like *Gone With the Wind*'s Scarlett O'Hara, she's determined never to go hungry again.

Complications arise when infighting breaks out among the racketeers in Blondie's organization. The successful enterprise she's built up begins to go down the tubes as the law closes in—and she realizes how much she's sacrificed, including the chance for love, because of the wrong choices she's made in life from her fixation, born of her past, with grabbing money and power.

Of course, not all molls, twists, babes, and B girls have felt the same pangs of guilt and remorse over their criminal deeds. The Midnight Marys and Blondie Johnsons may generally be the rule in gangster movies, but as always, there are notable exceptions.

THEIR KIND OF TOWN

> *"No woman can love a man enough to kill him.*
> *They aren't worth it, because there are always plenty more."*
> —*Belva Gaertner, Inmate,*
> *Cook County Jail, 1924*

"This trial . . . the whole world . . . it's all . . . show business!"
    —Billy Flynn (Richard Gere),
    Chicago (2002)

Director-choreographer Rob Marshall's dazzling, Oscar-winning musical film *Chicago* (2002) is imbued with the spirit of in-your-face lawlessness and corruption characteristic of gangland during its golden age of the 1920s—even though there are no actual gangsters in sight. What we think of as the traditional lawbreakers of the era make just a fleeting appearance; the name Al Capone is heard in a mock newsreel, and one of the "starlets" on Murderess Row reveals her showbiz dream of headlining at a nightclub owned by South Side mob kingpin "Big Jim" Colosimo (to whom Capone at first was an underling). Here the twisted heart of criminality belongs to all, from chorines and cops, prison guards and prosecutors, to mouthpieces and the media. That's the Chicago way.

Marshall's film is that rare commodity, a picture about the aura of gangland—expressed in musical form, no less—that crackles with a gritty truth beneath its veneer of playfulness, fantasy, and parody. Perhaps this truthfulness is because the story is inspired by a real incident, one that, embarrassingly enough, is of a kind that is even more common today in our era of instant news cycles, twenty-four-hour news networks, and mainstream turned tabloid journalism. This gives *Chicago* a contemporary relevance that is characteristic of the best films in the gangster genre.

The incident in question occurred in the Windy City in the 1920s. It involved the month-apart arrest of two women for the same type of crime—shooting their lovers. The murders landed them on Murderess Row, a special section of Chicago's Cook County jail reserved for ladies awaiting trial for bumping off hubbies and boyfriends.

Belva Gaertner was an attractive chorus girl in her mid-thirties who had blown away her lover. Beulah Annan, who had shot her lover too, was a married laundress in her twenties with a yen for the good life that her humble garage mechanic husband couldn't provide. Respectively dubbed the "classiest" and the "prettiest" women on Murderess Row, Belva and Beulah were perfect fodder for the sob-sister press looking for a human interest story, and they soon found themselves competing with each other for the public's affection in the media circus that ensued. Beulah trumped Belva by claiming to be pregnant (it went unnoticed that she never had the baby), but there was enough newspaper space and airtime on the radio to go around; they each got off scot-free when fact surrendered to hoopla and farce in and out of the courtroom.

Released to an obscurity they hadn't envisioned as the media and public quickly lost interest in them following their acquittal, Beulah divorced her long-suffering husband and died several years later in a mental asylum, whereas Belva married a wealthy industrialist and moved to Europe.

Both murderesses may have faded from the limelight, but they were not forgotten—especially by the sob sister whose stories in the *Chicago Tribune* had done so much to create a media storm around the duo and to stir up the sympathy for them that ultimately led to their getting off: Maurine Dallas Watkins (1896–1969).

Not long after the trial, Watkins, perhaps as an act of contrition for her part in helping to spring the deadly duo, gave up "journalism" altogether and went to Yale to study playwrighting. There, she turned the Gaertner-Annan fiasco into a satiric comedy titled *Chicago,* the story of a pretty but fundamentally untalented wannabe singer named Roxie Hart who shoots her lover dead because he's been faking his starmaking showbiz connections just to get into her pants. Claiming the deceased was a burglar and that she had acted in self-defense, she winds up on Murderess Row to await trial. The flamboyant Billy Flynn, a criminal lawyer who has never lost a case due to his knack for stretching the truth whichever way he wants, represents her. Thrust into the media spotlight, Roxie soaks up every bit of the attention and sympathy lavished upon her by the press, becoming the star she has longed to be as the jailhouse rocks and the courthouse rolls from the ensuing circus that turns the criminal justice system into another form of mass entertainment. Roxie even has her spotlight challenged, albeit briefly, by another murdering chorine, Velma Kelly, a minor character in the play whose starpower is quickly dimmed by Roxie's moxie. In the end, the all-male jury acquits Roxie, and she subsequently returns to the quiet life with her sap of a husband Amos, who has stood by her side all along.

Watkins scored a home run her first time at bat when legendary producer Sam H. Harris brought her play to Broadway. Directed by the equally legendary George Abbott, *Chicago* premiered at the Music Box Theatre on December 30, 1926, with Francine Larrimore as Roxie, Edward Ellis as Billy Flynn, and Juliette Crosby in the bit part of Velma. Almost a year to the day later, in December 1927, a film version appeared starring silent-screen siren Phyllis Haver as Roxie, Robert Edeson as

Flynn, and Julia Taye as Velma. Curiously, the film version directed unofficially by producer Cecil B. DeMille, who gave the director credit to his assistant, Frank Urson, got cold feet when it came to the Roxie-Amos relationship. In the film, Amos (Victor Varconi) gives the two-timing, publicity mad Roxie the boot. Notes *Variety*'s review of December 28, 1927: "[On stage] Amos was very much of a sap. In the picture he is transformed into a dynamic husband, who steals to pay counsel fees, finally tells the wife to take the air with the finishing inference that he will wed the young housemaid who has admired him from afar since reel one."

Twentieth Century Fox's sound remake *Roxie Hart* (1942) took the relationship a conservative step farther by making Amos (George Chandler) the killer. Knowing he'd probably get the chair, she takes the rap for him believing she stands a better chance of getting off. After her acquittal, though, she divorces him so that she can marry the reporter (George Montgomery) whose stories helped free her and can settle down to have a (large) family.

Briskly directed by gangster movie stalwart William A. Wellman, *Roxie Hart* is primarily a vehicle for its star, Ginger Rogers, who had won an Oscar in 1940 for her performance as another title character, Kitty Foyle, and was hoping to do so again this time in a much flashier title role. Alas, she went un-nominated, even though she has a great time playing the peroxide publicity hound. Adolphe Menjou is even better, though; in fact, he is hilarious as the proudly unscrupulous Billy Flynn. Helene Reynolds's Velma is even more of a walk-on role than it was in the play and the first film version, however.

Roxie Hart does retain the play's satiric portrait of a legal system turned into entertainment—and may even be more cynical in its portrait than the original play—but it makes no effort to evoke the Roaring Twenties in which the story is set nor to capture the aura of gambling, guzzling, grifting, and gangland that is at the heart of Watkins's *Chicago*. This fell to Chicago-born director-choreographer Bob Fosse (1927–1987), who, together with lyricist Fred Ebb and composer John Kander, fashioned the musical play *Chicago* out of Watkins's old warhorse upon which the Oscar-winning 2002 film is based.

Fosse and Ebb, who also collaborated on the musical play's book together, expanded the role of Velma into that of a superstar on Murderess Row who is upstaged by Roxie, a former fan of the jailed torch singer who usurps Velma's fame (and dressing room) in the manner of Anne Baxter's character in the classic Joseph L. Mankiewicz film about showbiz, *All About Eve* (1950).

Fosse's *Chicago*—a biting, highly stylized satire told in sexy song and slinky dance about today's cult of celebrity as mirrored in the case of these two 1920s murderesses—hit Broadway's 46th Street Theatre on June 30, 1975, starring Fosse's wife Gwen Verdon (for whom he had developed the project) as Roxie, Chita Rivera as Velma, and Jerry Orbach as Billy Flynn. It ran for two successful years, and was revived in 1996 on Broadway. (Rivera has a cameo in the movie version playing a character named Nicole, perhaps as an homage to Fosse, whose daughter with Gwen Verdon is also named Nicole.)

Fosse, who was also an Oscar-winning film director (for *Cabaret*, 1972), had long sought to bring his *pièce de résistance* to the screen himself. But the task of translating so uniquely theatrical an experience into a script that worked in another, very different medium eluded him to his death. A quarter of a century later, long after the movie musical had been declared an extinct species, Rob Marshall and screenwriter Bill Condon found the Rosetta Stone and spectacularly realized Fosse's dream. (The film is dedicated to the memories of the late Bob Fosse, Gwen Verdon, and Robert Fryer, one of the producers of the original Broadway musical.) Together with a surprising but impeccable cast— Catherine Zeta-Jones as Velma, Richard Gere as Billy Flynn, and the hugely talented Renee Zellweger as Roxie—Marshall (whose direction and choreography are much in the style of Bob Fosse), Condon, and company created a movie that captures the theatrical essence of its source yet is wildly cinematic at the same time. And that breathtakingly evokes the spirit of corruption, spin, and sin of Big Jim Colosimo and Al Capone's Chicago during gangland's golden age better than any gang- land film without gangsters ever made.

Welsh-born actress Catherine Zeta-Jones picked up a best support- ing actress Oscar for her performance as the sexy, conniving Velma, a role she had warmed up for nicely with her subtler—and arguably more challenging—turn as another sexy but non-singing conniver in Steven Soderbergh's *Traffic* (2000).

The film is based on a 1989 British miniseries called *Traffik*, which dealt with the perils of the modern-day drug trade on both sides of the law. Soderbegh's film locates the story in the United States and Mexico, whereas the British miniseries spread from Europe to the poppy fields of Afghanistan. Zeta-Jones's role as the wife of a jailed Mexican drug kingpin played by Steven Bauer is even more of a supporting one here than Velma in *Chicago* (which for all intents and purposes is a costarring role); nevertheless, her character is arguably the most memorable in *Traffic* because of the deft manner in which she turns that character, and our expectations of her, on its ear.

Ignorant of her gangster husband's business affairs when he's arrested, pregnant with their child, and not knowing how she's going to get by when he's sent up the river, she seizes control of the business and slickly uses her dormant wiles as a sultry dragon lady-in-waiting not only to keep the business going, but also to build it up better in the end than her macho mate in the calabozo ever did.

LOVE AND BULLETS

Even before the movies got hold of the story of these two legendary gangster outlaws, the relationship between gun moll Bonnie Parker and bank robber Clyde Barrow was already being romanticized by Bonnie herself in the poems she wrote about their life on the run and the pictures they took of themselves that were published in the press. But there remains considerable speculation as to how romantic their confusing affair actually was. Some accounts say Clyde was a homosexual who recruited other males in the gang to service him as well as the allegedly sexually voracious Bonnie. Others say he was bisexual, or perhaps impotent. In any case, their relationship was distinctly unusual.

Bonnie was nineteen and married (her husband was in prison) when she met Clyde; he was twenty-one and just out of prison. He was arrested shortly thereafter for burglary and car theft and sent back to the slammer for another stretch. Bonnie, who told friends she'd been "bored crapless" before meeting Clyde, smuggled him a gun, and he escaped. But he was recaptured pulling another robbery and given fourteen years. While in prison, he chopped off two of his toes to get off a work detail and was paroled early. He rejoined Bonnie in 1932 a hardened criminal. The pair formed the Barrow Gang and went on a spree of robberies, kidnappings, and murder throughout the Southwest that landed them on the government's Most Wanted list.

On and off, the gang consisted of an escaped convict and gunman named Ray Hamilton; a filling station attendant named William Daniel Jones, whom the pair kidnapped then persuaded to join them; and a petty thief named Henry Methvin, whose recruitment would ultimately spell doom to the pair. But the most lasting recruit was Clyde's brother Ivan, nicknamed "Buck," who had also done time in prison, and Buck's wife Blanche, a preacher's daughter, who went along, she later told police, because it was "a wife's duty to stay with her husband."

Tracked by police to a tourist camp in Missouri, the gang was surrounded and sprayed with machine-gun fire. Buck was severely wounded and Blanche partially blinded in one eye, but Bonnie and Clyde were unhurt and the gang managed to elude capture once again, escaping across the border into Iowa. There, a posse descended on the gang's hideout in the woods and opened fire from every direction. Buck was hit again, and he and Blanche were captured. Bonnie, Clyde, and gang member Jones were wounded as well but got away once more in a stolen car.

After licking their wounds, the remains of the Barrow Gang stepped up its campaign of robberies, kidnappings, and murder throughout Louisiana and Texas. Jones was eventually caught; Bonnie and Clyde then recruited Henry Methvin to take his place. Wanted on robbery charges in both states, Methvin made a deal with the law to escape prosecution by helping to set a trap for the duo. The year was 1934.

Methvin scheduled a rendezvous with the pair on a secluded country road near the Louisiana-Texas border. But the Texas Highway Authority, under the command of former Texas Ranger Frank Hamer, met them instead. The lawmen hid in the bushes alongside the road, and when Bonnie and Clyde pulled up in their white Ford V–8 sedan, the lawmen opened fire. Hundreds of rounds were fired at the car and its trapped occupants, killing Bonnie and Clyde straight away. In one of the ironies of the case, Clyde's body was reportedly riddled with twenty-five rounds, Bonnie's with twenty-three. If true, the rounds equaled their exact ages at the time of their deaths.

Bonnie had imagined the pair's finish in a heavily romantic but also remarkably clear-eyed and insightful poem she'd sent to the newspapers just prior to the ambush. Titled "The Story of Bonnie and Clyde," it prophetically served as their epitaph, its concluding lines reading:

Someday they'll go down together
And they'll bury them side by side
To few it'll be grief, to the law a relief
But it's death for Bonnie and Clyde.

Three years after their deaths, the story of gangland's most famous moll and her frog-like Prince Charming received the first of its many screen treatments in producer Walter Wangers's *You Only Live Once* (1937), the second American film by expatriate director Fritz Lang. Lang had made several underworld dramas in his native Germany before fleeing the Nazis in 1933 and escaping to France, then the United States—notably his quasi-gangster film series about the master criminal Dr. Mabuse and the classic *M* (1931),[2] the story of a serial killer (Peter Lorre) who is hunted down and tried for his inhuman crimes by Berlin's gangsters and underworlders when the cops' far-reaching manhunt threatens their own criminal activities. Lang's first American film, *Fury* (1936), was a crime drama as well, but with an overtone of warning about the looming specter in America of mob violence, which was then raging through Europe.

In *You Only Live Once*, Eddie Taylor (Henry Fonda), a so-called "three-time loser" (the film's original title), attempts to go straight but is railroaded back to prison for a crime he didn't commit and is sentenced to death. The focus, however, is on the response of his wife (Sylvia Sidney) to these events, and how they challenge her belief system (a theme that runs through Lang's work both in Germany and America). As Fonda's date with the executioner draws near, she smuggles him a gun, and he breaks out of prison, accidentally killing the prison chaplain during the escape. He and Sidney flee to Canada, the newspapers filled with sensational accounts of Fonda's daring escape and the pair's subsequent crimes—most of them apocryphal. They manage to cross the Canadian border to "freedom," only to be trapped and cut down on the other side.

Apart from its "young lovers on the run" angle, there is little of the Bonnie and Clyde story (fact *or* fiction) in this Bonnie and Clyde–inspired film. Unlike the hard case Clyde Barrow, Fonda's Eddie Taylor is an inherently decent fellow who—unlike the Bogart gangster, for example—seems condemned to living a life of crime less by his own choice than because of the callousness of others and an implacable fate. As Sidney's sister (Jean Dixon) in the film, who is actually named Bonnie, says of Fonda's doomed character: "Eddie Taylor's been pounding on the door of the execution chamber since he was born."

Sylvia Sidney's character, on the other hand, is a complete innocent—at least when the film begins—who believes in the fairness of society's judicial institutions and in the good fellowship of others to give her husband a square deal. That belief system is sorely put to the test and ultimately completely shattered when she's driven to become a criminal herself.

What *You Only Live Once* may lack as a factual recounting of the Bonnie and Clyde saga, it more than makes up in excitement and atmosphere. Lang's staging of the bank robbery for which Fonda is framed is especially taut, as well as ominous of Fonda's fate. Portions of the sequence were later used as a stock footage for a bank robbery scene in the low-budget 1945 biopic *Dillinger* (see Chapter 8). Ironically, Dillinger, who followed Bonnie and Clyde in death in 1934 as well, had reportedly said of the pair: "They were kill-crazy punks and clodhoppers, bad news to decent bank robbers. They gave us a bad name."

Although not as artful as Lang's heavily fictionalized take on the Bonnie and Clyde saga, the 1939 *Persons in Hiding* inched much nearer to the truth of it. J. Carrol Naish plays the Clyde character, a petty thief who graduates to bigger crimes when he meets and falls for the attractive and ambitious Patricia Morison. A scheming parcel of greedy goods in the soon-to-come film noir tradition, Morison pushes the no-brain hoodlum into a spree of robberies, kidnappings, and, ultimately, murder that lands the duo on the FBI's Most Wanted list. G-Man Lynne Overman picks up the pair's bloody trail and at one point gets captured. He manages to turn the tables, though, and brings the bandits down.

Unlike the Lang film (and many other films to come inspired by the Bonnie and Clyde story), *Persons in Hiding* doesn't portray the deadly couple as innocents or as victims of an indifferent society. They're venal and brutal, and they get what they deserve—from the law, and from each other. This is especially true of Morison's "Bonnie," who is named Dorothy in the film. She makes no attempt to ingratiate herself and win our sympathy. From the moment she appears on the screen to the moment she leaves it, she's all business.

A gritty, fast-paced, and worthy little B movie (it runs barely over an hour), *Persons in Hiding* was adapted from a book of the same name by FBI chief J. Edgar Hoover (ghosted for him by female crime, mystery, and movie writer Courtney Ryley Cooper, who was found hanged in her apartment in 1940, the victim of an—*ahem*—apparent suicide). A calculated attempt by the self-aggrandizing Hoover to promote the image of the Bureau by chronicling its greatest successes for the public, the book became a best-seller. Paramount bought the screen rights and put several writers and directors to work translating the episodic Bureau press kit into a series of quickie feature films. Combining elements of the Bonnie and Clyde saga, whom the FBI hadn't brought down, with stories in the book about other killer couples the FBI had, *Persons in Hiding,* directed by Louis King, was easily the best of the series,[3] largely because of Patricia Morison's ice-cold gun moll.

Often confused with *You Only Live Once* is Nicholas Ray's *They Live by Night* (1949), another reworking of the Bonnie and Clyde tale, based on the book *Thieves Like Us* by yet another crime reporter turned novelist, Edward Anderson. The book was published the same year the Lang film was released. And like the earlier film, the focus of Anderson's Depression-era Bonnie and Clyde story, as well as Ray's film version of it, is doomed innocence.

Two hardened criminals (Jay C. Flippen and Howard De Silva) and one youthful offender (Farley Granger) break out of a southern prison and kidnap a farmer and his battered Model T to make their getaway. The two hard cases coerce Granger into helping them pull off several crimes that trigger a large-scale police manhunt. While hiding out with Flippen's no-good brother (Will Wright) and sister-in-law (Helen Craig), Granger meets a young girl (Cathy O'Donnell), and the two fall in love. But their passionate affair proves short-lived when Craig tips the cops to the gang's whereabouts in exchange for her husband's immunity from prosecution. As the cops close in, one of the gang is killed, the other recaptured. The young lovers manage to escape. They're hunted down and, determined to stay together even in death, perish in each other's arms like Henry Fonda and Sylvia Sidney at the conclusion of *You Only Live Once.*

As with the Lang film, *They Live by Night* connects with the true story of Bonnie and Clyde mostly in terms of its period setting and premise of two young lovers on the run from the law. But the connection is there. Impressively staged by Nicholas Ray (formerly a stage director making his film directing debut) and movingly acted by Granger and especially O'Donnell—although the impending doom of their backwoods romance is a bit oversentimentalized at times—*They Live by Night* has a strong, almost documentary sense of place (even though most of it was shot in Hollywood and environs), and still packs an emotional punch. Filmed in 1946 under the working title *Thieves Like Us,* the finished film was shelved for two years when Howard Hughes took control of the studio (RKO). Seeing little commercial potential in the picture, he unceremoniously dumped it into a few theaters on the bottom half of a double bill under the meaningless new title *They Live by Night.* Reviews were few and far between, but good; nevertheless, there was no word-of-mouth, so, to the chagrin but not the surprise of Nicholas Ray and the film's producer, John Houseman, the picture died in the end like Farley Granger and Cathy O'Donnell's doomed lovers. Time has restored the balance, however, and today *They Live by Night* is considered a classic noir gangster film of the 1940s.

Obviously, there is something in this type of story that appeals to maverick filmmakers. Lang and Ray were both well known for locking horns with their Hollywood paymasters, as is Robert Altman, who turned his own hand to the Bonnie and Clyde saga in a 1974 remake of *They Live by Night* under the source novel's original title, *Thieves Like Us*. Filmed away from Hollywood in Mississippi, the film stars Altman regulars John Schuck and Bert Remsen in the Jay C. Flippen and Howard de Silva roles, respectively, and Keith Carradine and Shelly Duvall as a much less glamorous and much less sentimentalized version of the young lovers, Bowie and Keechie. Louise Fletcher made her film debut as the woman who turns the gang in and triggers the young lovers' doom. Unlike Anderson's novel and the first film made from it, however, Duvall's character Keechie survives at the conclusion of the Altman film. Explained Altman biographer Patrick McGilligan: "Altman felt that if Keechie died the ending would be too much like [Arthur Penn's 1967 film] *Bonnie and Clyde*. [He] felt very strongly that if you wanted to make a statement at all, it was that that kind of lady survived, that the Matties [Fletcher's character] survived, that the Keechies survived. Keechie turned into Mattie. The boys got shot down, but that kind of hard, put-upon woman survived and sired a lot of us."[4]

Director Joseph H. Lewis's take on the Bonnie and Clyde story, *Gun Crazy* (a.k.a., *Deadly Is the Female*, 1949)[5] removes some of the blame for their criminal lifestyle from society's shoulders and puts it squarely on theirs. Based on a *Saturday Evening Post* story by novelist MacKinlay Kantor and adapted to the screen by the blacklisted Dalton Trumbo (the screenplay is credited to Kantor and Millard Kauffman, Trumbo's "front"), Lewis's cult classic portrays its doomed lovers on the run from the law— Bart Tare (John Dall) and Annie Laurie Starr (Peggy Cummins)—as being victims too, but of themselves. The film doesn't let society completely off the hook, though; its opening scenes paint a disturbing picture of America's tolerance and even love of guns, a theme no other Bonnie and Clyde film or few other gangster films before it have addressed so head-on.

The film begins with the young Bart (Rusty Tamblyn) coveting a gun in a hardware store window, then breaking the glass and snatching it. He's caught and brought before the local judge (Morris Carnovsky), who is presented with character testimony from Bart's sister, his two closest friends, and his schoolteacher to consider before passing sentence. They all describe Bart as a boy who enjoys handling and firing guns, but only for sport; he can't bring himself even to kill wild game. Bart confirms this, telling the judge that he likes to shoot because it makes him "feel good." The disturbing nature of this response is that it hints at a darker need the firing of guns satisfies in the orphaned boy to which even he isn't privy. The judge sentences Bart to reform school where he'll get the guidance to help him outgrow the obsession with guns or at least learn how to control it.

After reform school, Bart (Dall) joins the army and serves as a weapons instructor. His stint over, he returns to his hometown and takes a job with the Remington Firearms Company. During a night on the town with his two boyhood pals—one of them now a cop, the other a newspaperman—he encounters Cummins, a sexy blonde sharpshooter in a carnival sideshow, and accepts the barker's (Barry Kroger) challenge to test his marksmanship against hers on stage. Dall wins the match, he joins the act, and he and Cummins become lovers. Following a violent confrontation with the jealous Kroger, the two get the boot. Out of work, out of money, and down on their luck, Cummins suggests pulling off a robbery or two for some quick cash, and Dall agrees, "just so long as no one is killed," he says. One robbery leads to another, however, and before long the lovers are being hunted in several states. They decide to pull one last job that will net them enough cash to skip the country, but in the course of the robbery, Cummins kills two people.

The manhunt intensified, they flee to the mountains where they're trapped in fog. As the law surrounds them and Dall's childhood pals call out for him and Cummins to give up, Cummins draws her gun and says she'll shoot if anyone comes nearer. The figures of Dall's childhood pals emerge from the fog, and she goes to fire, compelling Dall to shoot her—the only living thing he kills in the film—to save his friends' lives. His shot is mistaken for an attack, and Dall himself is killed in a hail of police bullets.

Gun Crazy is an uneven film that veers from being a small masterpiece to an average, low-budget crime picture, back to small masterpiece again. Parts of it are banal and slow moving, whereas others—the opening sequence featuring the young Bart, the major robbery sequences (which boast an amazing on-the-spot realism and real-time tension due to Lewis's method of capturing the action in a single shot from an eye-witness point of view), and the final showdown in the fog—are absolutely brilliant.

The leads are good too—especially Cummins, whose sexy, manipulative, fundamentally sociopathic Laurie makes *Persons in Hiding*'s Patricia Morison seem almost a dainty flower by comparison. Her character is the key to the film's mystery, for as the judge suspects early on, Bart's obsession with guns suggests that there is something missing in the boy (parental guidance and love, maybe) that renders him less than whole. This missing piece, the judge rightly fears, might be filled by something dark and deadly someday. As Dall says to Cummins at one point: "We go together, Laurie, I don't know why. Like guns and ammunition go together."

On the lighter side, although perhaps not intentionally, is *Guns Don't Argue* (1957), a cheap exploitation picture culled from episodes of a television series called *Gangbusters* that was inspired by a long-running radio show with the same title. The TV series ran on NBC for ten months in 1952 and was later syndicated under the title *Captured*. Each episode featured an FBI agent (played by an actor) narrating the "true story" of how the Bureau tracked down a particular public enemy of the 1930s and brought an end to his or her criminal career.

To avoid the expense of a lot of costly period costumes and cars, producer William Faris updated the stories to the early 1950s and shot them in and around Los Angeles. This cheapskate approach, coupled with the slipshod manner in which the episodes were put together, resulted in some wonderful gaffes, as in an episode about the notorious Ma Barker that is supposed to be set in Sioux Falls, Iowa, but the street signs read BEVERLY BLVD and WILSHIRE.

When the TV series went off the air, Faris stitched together several episodes and repackaged them as feature films, the first of which, *Gangbusters,* was released in 1955. It was followed two years later by the aforementioned *Guns Don't Argue*, which included segments on Ma Barker[6] as well as the FBI's most wanted moll and her man, Bonnie and Clyde. The film telescopes the career of the Barrow Gang into a tight fifteen-plus action-packed—and howlingly funny—minutes.

An FBI agent (played by Jim Davis) is assigned to the case after the Barrow Gang robs a music store and kills the owner. Gang member Ray Hamilton is captured by police and sent to a prison farm. Clyde (Baynes Baron) and Bonnie (Tamar Cooper), who wears a black beret all the time and is constantly puffing on a stogie (the real Bonnie had once posed for a Barrow Gang snapshot with these items), break Hamilton out, machine-gunning everyone in sight. "This ruthless massacre of guards and convicts alike horrified even hardened criminals," intones the narrator. It's also pretty damn pointless because Hamilton, after being broken out of prison, mysteriously disappears from the story, making the viewer wonder why Bonnie and Clyde risked their lives springing him in the first place.

The FBI closes in with the help of a farmer who'd once aided the dynamic duo but now is repulsed by their barbarity (if not their stupidity). Together, they've set up an ambush. In a scene that comes remarkably close to depicting the event as it occurred, and serves as a template for the 1967 *Bonnie and Clyde*, the farmer pulls his rattletrap truck off the road to change a tire. Bonnie and Clyde drive up, and Clyde gets out to lend a helping hand. In a classic example of screen acting at its nadir, Bonnie does a goofy, wide-eyed double take when she hears the bushes move across the street (unable to get enough of a bad thing, this double-take is a repeat of the same shot used several other times throughout the film), and whips out her tommy gun as the concealed feds open fire. Clyde also goes for his gun, but the duo doesn't stand a chance. As FBI bullets rain upon the car (leaving not a scratch, hole, or dent), Clyde drops to the road like a sack of potatoes, and Bonnie slumps dead in the car window, her ever-present stogie dangling, then slipping from her lips. For all the wrong reasons, this is one moll movie that should not be missed!

Infinitely more professionally made, but nowhere near as funny, and perhaps even more of a stage-setter for Warner Brothers's *Bonnie and Clyde* a decade later, is American-International's *The Bonnie Parker Story* (1958), featuring platinum blonde Dorothy Provine in the title role. (In keeping with Peggy Cummins's deadly moll with the blond tresses in *Gun Crazy* and *The Bonnie Parker Story*, the 1967 version to come would cast Bonnie [Faye Dunaway] as a blonde as well. Actually, Dunaway is a brunette; the real Bonnie Parker was a strawberry blonde, whose hair often came across as dark in black-and-white photographs.)

Set in the proper Depression-era period, *The Bonnie Parker Story* generally plays it straight with the facts, although for some reason all of the characters' names are changed except for Bonnie herself. Clyde Barrow is renamed Guy Darrow in the film; his brother Buck is renamed Chuck, and so on.

An innocent Texas teenager as the film opens, Bonnie marries Duke (Richard Bakalyan), a hometown boy, unaware that he makes his money robbing banks. Her dreams of marital bliss dampened when he's arrested and imprisoned for life, the frustrated and embittered young woman allows herself to be picked up by a drifter at the local greasy spoon where she works, and the drifter, Clyde Darrow (Jack Hogan), rescues her from her boring, poverty-stricken existence by introducing her to a life of crime that she finds increasingly alluring. She joins Darrow's gang, which is led by his brother Chuck (Joseph Turkel) and, like Blondie Johnson, is so skilled at what she does that she takes over as leader without a word of protest from her impotent and none-too-swift paramour Clyde when Chuck is killed.

More reminiscent of *Gun Crazy*'s Peggy Cummins, perhaps, than earlier screen Bonnies, Provine's tough-talking, cigar-smoking, pistol-packing blonde bombshell is clearly the deadlier member of the Bonnie and Clyde team. She's attractive and feminine on the outside, but a hardened killer just like the men on the inside.

The Bonnie Parker Story is an exciting, fast-paced little B with a nice, hard edge. Released on a double bill with AIP's even better *Machine Gun Kelly*, directed by Roger Corman, the film earned some decent reviews, a rarity for AIP products. *Variety,* for example, called it "obviously an exploitation item, but capably constructed and intelligently carried out." However, it was up to the Warren Beatty–produced/Arthur Penn–directed *Bonnie and Clyde* to score as the most famous and influential film about the exploits of the notorious couple—and also the most controversial.

Youthful audiences of the antiestablishment 1960s took to the movie like moths to a flame, turning the film into a counterculture hit that helped to tear down the last barriers remaining of the old-fashioned Code with respect to scenes of explicit violence and carnage on the screen.

Contemporary critics were of two minds about *Bonnie and Clyde*, which is par for the course for most groundbreaking films. Many embraced it right away as a daring and original work, despite its well-worn topic; others attacked it as a senseless bloodbath aimed at the yahoo trade. Still others attacked it, *then* embraced it. *Newsweek* critic Joseph Morgenstern, for example, at first gave *Bonnie and Clyde* a scathing notice, calling it an ugly film in which "some of the most gruesome carnage since Verdun is accompanied by some of the most gleeful off-screen fiddling since the Grand Old Opry." A week later, he posted a second review in the same magazine recanting his earlier opinion, calling his initial response "grossly unfair and regrettably inaccurate." Even more surprisingly, when three-decade *New York Times* film critic Bosley Crowther, who had also written a review condemning the film, failed to make a similar turnabout, he was let go as the paper's first-string film critic for being too out of touch with contemporary tastes. Producer Warren Beatty even had to fight with studio chief Jack L. Warner to get behind the film at Warner Brothers, the only major studio where Beatty could get the film made—and the only one where it *should* have been made given the studio's trendsetting history with the genre. Eventually, the film earned Oscar nominations in all the major categories, and scored two wins (see Appendix I).

The script for *Bonnie and Clyde* was kicking around Hollywood for years. Even its eventual director, Arthur Penn, had seen and passed on it at one time. Novice screenwriters David Newman and Robert Benton had turned their frustrated sights overseas and tried to interest French director Jean-Luc Godard in making the film. Godard's New Wave gangster picture about two young criminals in love and on the run, *A Bout de Soufflé* (*Breathless*, 1959), was itself inspired by Hollywood gangster films, and had strongly influenced the avant-garde style of Newman and Benton's script. François Truffaut, who had provided Godard with the idea for *A Bout de Soufflé*, was approached as well. Both directors were interested but were committed elsewhere, and the script fell into limbo again. It finally landed on the desk of Warren Beatty, a young and successful actor who wanted to produce his own projects. He bought the property; having worked with Arthur Penn on an earlier avant-garde gangster film, *Mickey One* (1965), he approached the director, and this time Penn signed on.

Primarily a director of Broadway plays (*The Miracle Worker, Wait Until Dark*) and live TV drama (*Studio One, Playhouse 90*), the East Coast–bred Penn might have seemed an odd choice for such a violent, action-filled tale of rural romance and robbery. But his work has always focused on characters that have great difficulty communicating or connecting with each other or with society except through outbursts of passion and violent physicality. Furthermore, his first Hollywood film, *The Left-Handed Gun* (1958), bears striking similarities to *Bonnie and Clyde* in other ways. Both are about historically famous young guns on the run (Billy the Kid in the earlier film) who suffer from feelings of inadequacy, are motivated to violence as a way of overcoming those feelings, and fall into a life of outlawry. They also share a perception of themselves that is pure romantic fantasy—a fantasy that ultimately leads to their deaths. Both films contain several scenes that are remarkably similar, as well as the use of slow motion[7] to heighten the drama and horror of some violent set pieces.

Bonnie and Clyde has often been accused of stretching the facts in order to glamorize the deadly duo and turn them into romantic, even heroic figures. For the most part, the film accurately recounts the saga, supported by a great deal of authentic period detail. The assault in the woods following the auto camp ambush that results in the death of Buck Barrow (Gene Hackman) is staged to look remarkably close to actual photos of the crime scene that still exist, which the filmmakers undoubtedly consulted. It is true that the real Bonnie and Clyde were far from glamorous. They were rather drab in appearance—although many contemporary accounts refer to Bonnie as looking "sexy" and "cute"—they did not at all resemble movie stars like Warren Beatty and Faye Dunaway. However, that is exactly how they saw *themselves*—not as movie stars, perhaps, but as media stars most certainly, who kept the Kodak close by to snap pictures of themselves with their guns that they could send to the newspapers to feed their growing legend.

So, if *Bonnie and Clyde* romanticizes the notorious couple (which it does), this is because the tale is told from their own self-absorbed point of view. The film's bold use of graphic carnage illustrates this: it is only when acts of violence draw close to the pair, or reach right into the ranks of the Barrow Gang, that it turns ugly and painful. The self-absorbed couple sees everything, even death, only as it relates *to them*. A cop blown away at a distance is just a bloodless rag doll. But when one of *them* takes a bullet, reality crashes in and things get up close and personal. The film makes this point repeatedly: when Bonnie pays a visit to her mother for what will be the last time, the scene takes on a nostalgic hue that reflects Bonnie's sentimental delusions. She and Clyde act like distant relatives who have come by for a family reunion, not like desperate criminals hunted by the law. Says Clyde to Bonnie's mother, "Bonnie and I were just talking the other day, Mother Parker, about how she wants to settle down and live no more than three miles from her precious mother." Mama's grasp on things is a lot firmer: "I don't know, Clyde Barrow. She lives three miles from me, and she won't live very long." Bonnie's face pales, as if she's just glimpsed her own ghost, and she and Clyde quickly return to their fantasy world of love and bullets, where, self-absorbed and self-destructive to the last, they meet their end. Typically, Bonnie romanticizes even that moment in her final poem, "The Story of Bonnie Clyde," that she sends to the newspapers to cement their legend. Significantly their death is the most graphic scene in the film; it wrenches the ugly truth from their romantic illusion, as their bodies are shot to bloody pieces in a barrage of gunfire.[8]

Myths and legends act out the anarchic fantasies we may share but cannot act upon ourselves. In the case of the real Bonnie and Clyde, the public took to them as folk heroes because they robbed the robbers—the hated banks of Depression-era America that were taking away the family farms and foreclosing on friends and neighbors. And they killed the killers, the police that were backing up the reposessors. The youth of the '60s took to *Bonnie and Clyde* because its theme of young lovers on the run from authority seemed to buy into the antiestablishment feelings of the youth movement. Capturing this mood also, but focusing on a very different type of moll on the run, is Roger Corman's *Bloody Mama* (1970), one of a slew of Depression-era rural shoot-em-ups to follow in the wake of *Bonnie and Clyde*'s enormous cultural impact.

The protagonist of the film is another notorious bank robbing legend: Kate "Ma" Barker, who, with her strapping brood tied to her apron strings, plagued banks across the South and the West in the 1930s. The murderous matriarch and her boys had earlier been portrayed on screen in one of the series of films based on the J. Edgar Hoover book *Persons in Hiding* made in the 1930s and '40s. Titled *Queen of the Mob*, it offers a mostly fictionalized account of the career of Ma Barker, featuring veteran actress Blanche Yurka as Ma Barker (renamed Ma Webster in the film) and Paul Kelly, William Henry, Richard Denning, and James Seay as the sons who form her gang. *Guns Don't Argue* and *Ma Barker's Killer Brood* also tackled the story in their own historically fractured and aesthetically ridiculous way. More recently Theresa Russell had a go at the character of bloody Kate in the barely released *Public Enemies* (1996), another example (like *Bonnie and Clyde* and scores of Westerns about Jesse James, Billy the Kid, and you-name-it) where a next generation of filmmakers has felt compelled to dust off the old legends and take another look at them through the prism of "today." Befitting today's keen interest in the female criminal and whether she springs from nature or nurture, more screen time than ever before in a Ma Barker film is given over in *Public Enemies* to the upbringing of young Kate. Notwithstanding this, it is still Roger Corman's *Bloody Mama*, uneven though it is, that remains the most interesting treatment of the tale, if only for one memorably New Wave, even surrealistic, scene where Ma and her boys are surrounded in a cabin by federal agents—and the locals set up bleachers across the road to cheer and jeer the ensuing shoot-out as if watching a hometown football game.

NOIR BABES

If there is a definitive noir babe it may well be Kathy Moffat (Jane Greer) in the 1947 gangster film *Out of the Past*. The sexy, duplicitous dame was already a fixture in noir gangster and crime films before *Out of the Past*, of course. But none of them—not even *The Maltese Falcon*'s lying conniver Brigid O'Shaughnessy (Mary Astor) was a match for Jane Greer's beautiful but deadly manipulator.

Typical of films noir, the hero of the film played by Robert Mitchum is not a gangster himself. He's a private eye to whom money doesn't smell, no matter where it comes from. He hires out to a gangster (Kirk Douglas), and then finds himself up to his chin in a noir world of double-dealing, double-crosses, and multiple murder that endangers him morally and physically.

To escape his sordid past, Mitchum takes an alias and sets himself up as the owner of a garage in a sleepy northern California town. There, he falls for a local girl (Virginia Huston); she knows nothing of his past, but her parents suspect there is something a bit too world-wise about him for their taste.

Mitchum's past catches up with him when one of Douglas's gangsters (Paul Valentine) locates him and suggests a meeting with Douglas for old time's sake. Mitchum agrees; on a date with Huston that night, he tells her he must go away for a while to straighten some things out and he comes clean with her about his past:

Several years earlier Douglas hired him to find the gangster's mistress (Jane Greer), who disappeared to Mexico with $40,000 of the gangster's money after pumping several bullets into him. Mitchum located the woman, who denied stealing any money, and he fell for her. Rather than turn her over to Douglas, he disappeared with her. But they were found by Mitchum's money-hungry partner (Steve Brodie), who demanded a share of the loot Greer allegedly stole in exchange for his silence. Greer killed him and Mitchum hid the body, subsequently discovering a bank statement showing a deposit of $40,000 to an account in her name. Realizing she had strung him along and that he was now an accomplice to murder, he had taken a powder to rebuild his life under an alias.

Back in the present, Huston tells Mitchum she loves him no matter what he's done, that she has faith in him, and that she will marry him as soon as his dealings with Douglas are finished. Mitchum meets with Douglas and finds that Greer, having long since run out of the $40,000 she had stolen, has come back to the gangster as well. He also finds that his longing for her has not cooled. She plays on his feelings, and their love affair picks up where it left off.

Douglas feels Mitchum owes him one and assigns him a job to settle accounts. Mitchum is to put the squeeze on a crooked accountant who saved the gangster a bundle on a tax case and is now bleeding him to keep quiet. When the accountant is murdered, Mitchum realizes he's been set up for a frame—a frame soon compounded when the conniving Greer kills Douglas and threatens to pin the blame on Mitchum for that murder too unless he helps her cover her tracks and get away. Filled with self-contempt because he has allowed himself to be used by her once more, but unable to turn his back on her a second time (a dilemma pulp writer James M. Cain described as "the love rack"), he surrenders to her will (or appears to), as their fates intertwine.

Sublimely directed by Jacques Tourneur, one of the cinema's most underappreciated stylists, and crackling with noirish cynicism and witty non sequiturs, this moody masterpiece of what has been labeled "the annihilating melodrama" influenced countless other noir gangster and crime films of the late 1940s and early 1950s, and continues to cast a spell over the neo-noir crime films of today. For example, Lawrence Kasdan's steamy *Body Heat* (1981), featuring Kathleen Turner as a more explicitly carnal version of Greer's Kathy Moffat, is an outright homage to *Out of the Past* but without the gangster elements. Taylor Hackford's subsequent *Against All Odds* (1984) is more than that; it's a remake. And it even has Jane Greer in a cameo, playing the mother of her character in the original. Australian actress Rachel Ward plays Kathy (renamed Jessie). While sexy enough, she nonetheless lacks the air of the siren that Greer's ethereal Kathy effortlessly exudes.

Marie Windsor's babes in such noir gangster films as *The Narrow Margin* (1952) and *The Killing* (1956) are a study in contrast to Greer's sly schemer because they are completely on the surface and in your face. They're out for the dough, or for whatever luxuries the saps they've taken up with can offer, and they make no bones about it; they don't even attempt to hide their disdain of these saps for being such dumb palookas. For example, in Stanley Kubrick's heist film *The Killing*, when Windsor's milquetoast husband (Elisha Cook Jr.)—whom she expects to shower her with wealth with his share of the heist so she can scram—asks her what's for dinner, she tells it like it is: "Steak. If you can't smell it cooking, it's because it's still down at the supermarket."

Born Emily Bertleson, Marie Windsor (1922–2001) is the perfect noir babe: sexy and smart, with no trace of the vulnerability of, say, a Gloria Grahame, whose noir babes are more often good-bad than bad-bad. Windsor's molls, twists, babes, and B girls are as bad-bad as they come, or at least persuasive that they are. It is ironic, therefore, that in a screen career that spanned more than thirty years, Windsor appeared in so few bona fide gangster and crime film classics. *The Narrow Margin* and *The Killing* are among those few.

The Narrow Margin belongs—or should belong—on every movie fan's short list of the best B pictures, gangster or otherwise, ever made. Directed by veteran filmmaker Richard Fleischer, who made a number of small but impressive B gangster and crime films before moving to A pictures and superproductions like Walt Disney's *20,000 Leagues Under the Sea* (1954), *The Narrow Margin* is a testament to the power of the B movie. Working on B pictures may have denied filmmakers ample budgets but compensated them by giving them the freedom to exercise their imaginations and skills without having the studio suits standing over their shoulders watching every move they made. Often, the results were outstanding, as is the case with *The Narrow Margin*.

"I was under contract as a B picture director at RKO," Richard Fleischer described.

> As was the custom in those days, they just handed me a treatment or a script and said, 'This is your next assignment.' I would then work on the script, rewrite it somewhat. I always worked on the screenplays of my films. I was very lucky that way because most B picture directors didn't have that opportunity. The head of my unit, Sid Rogell, always gave me the best assignments and let me work on them right from the beginning, as was the case with *The Narrow Margin*. It started out as an original story by Martin Goldsmith and Jack Leonard, which I then developed into a screenplay with Earl Felton, who also wrote the scripts for two other B pictures of mine, *Trapped* (1949) and *Armored Car Robbery* (1950). The

original story was very good—so good, in fact, that it was nominated for an Academy Award, which was quite a thing for a B picture. I had a really wonderful producer, Stanley Rubin, so it was a prime situation given the constraints of budget and time. I shot the picture in 13 days at a cost of $200,000. You spend more than that on costumes on an A picture.[9]

By the time he came to make *The Narrow Margin*, Fleischer's entire philosophy toward film directing as well as his technique had changed.

I had become very proficient at making these small B pictures cheaply and efficiently. One day I screened a film I'd just finished called *The Clay Pigeon* (1949), and I was suddenly overwhelmed by the fact that it was done in the most conventional way possible—long shot, two over-the-shoulder shots, two close-ups, and bang the scene was done. I suddenly realized that if I continued with that technique, I would never progress beyond that point. I got very depressed. Then I vowed that if I got the chance to make another picture, I'd break all my previous rules about how a picture should be shot, and not just do it for the budget and the schedule.

The pressures of getting a picture done on time, on budget and doing it in the most efficient way possible are always there. But efficiency can become an illusion. Because you can be very efficient and cut the proper corners to get the film done on time and on budget and still get a very handsome, very interesting looking picture. But I didn't realize that until it dawned on my when I saw *The Clay Pigeon* and said, "My God, the cameraman or the assistant director could have made this! There's nothing about it that says it's *my* picture!"

Another thing that contributed to my falling into this trap was the people I worked with at RKO, particularly the cameramen. They worked very, very efficiently, and since I didn't know much about camera setups when I first started, I'd always rely on what the cameraman told me. If I said, "Can we make an angle from here?" and the cameraman said "No, I don't have a rubber lens, it doesn't stretch that far, the shot will be out of focus," I would accept that. Then I realized I didn't have to accept it. On *Trapped* I got a cameraman [Guy Roe] who said, "Sure you can have that angle. It'll take a little more time, but, of course, you can have it." That was a revelation to me. He did *Armored Car Robbery* with me, too. Then on *The Narrow Margin*, I got George E. Diskant, a wonderful cameraman, who was not only very efficient but was also willing to try anything.

Shot entirely on the studio's soundstages, virtually the whole picture takes place on a train, in small compartments, creating an almost palpable sense of claustrophobia. There isn't even a background music score to help transport the viewer out of the feeling of being confined on the endlessly moving locomotive. "It was a daring thing to do," Fleischer said. "I wanted the sound effects of the train to serve as music in heightening the suspense, and it took a lot of convincing to get the studio to back me in that decision."

Anthony Mann's Civil War spy movie *The Tall Target* for MGM also takes place on a moving train and eschews a music score. It beat *The Narrow Margin* to theaters by a year (it was released in 1951), but not because it was produced first. *The Narrow Margin* was held up from distribution for more than a year after it was in the can by studio head Howard Hughes. "It was his practice to hold onto a lot of finished pictures in his projection room, where he'd run them over and over again, trying to decide what he wanted to do with them, if anything," explained Fleischer. "Mostly he would wind up changing the endings, which prompted us to call him an 'anal-erotic.' He particularly liked *The Narrow Margin* and held onto it for a year because he was toying with the idea of remaking it into an A picture with big stars. But he finally decided not to and released the original as it stood. And the picture did really well, getting a spread in *Time* magazine, earning an Oscar nomination for its story, and so on. But by the time it came out, I had left the studio for greener pastures, as they say."

Veteran gravel-voiced tough guy Charles McGraw plays the lead, a cop assigned to transport a gangster's tough-talking widow (Marie Windsor) to the West Coast, where she is to testify before a grand jury about the mob's activities. The bulk of the action is restricted to the interior of the moving train as McGraw plays cat and mouse with several mob hit men to prevent the woman (whom the mobsters have never seen) from being killed. The film plays on our expectations of the genre with several ingenious twists, the biggest of which involves Windsor, who is at her acerbic best as the sexy, hard-as-nails moll who seems fully capable of protecting herself without help from any man, including McGraw—albeit for reasons I shall not reveal here.

Almost forty years later, this low-budget gem finally did get the A-budget treatment Howard Hughes had been considering when it was remade by director Peter Hyams as *Narrow Margin* (1990). The remake features Gene Hackman in the Charles McGraw role and Ann Archer as the woman in jeopardy, whom Hackman bumblingly tries to protect. Again, the bulk of the action is set aboard a speeding train, but Hyams takes a very different approach from Fleischer by focusing on wild stunts and over-the-top action and thrills rather than on tension and suspense. Fleischer saw the remake and felt it was well made but basically just an ordinary run-of-the-mill action picture about the mob. "They made a lot of mistakes—at least I saw them as mistakes," he said.

> For one thing, most of the character twists were left out. In our film, *nobody* is what he or she appears to be. Everybody has a double identity, or assumes one for a time. You think they're one thing, and they turn out to be another. Another thing they left out of the remake was the feeling of claustrophobia. There are only a few places you can hide on a train, and that became the game to keep the suspense going: where would McGraw hide Windsor next so she wouldn't be found by the mob's hitmen? You don't open the picture up, as they did in the remake, and stage action on the roof of the train, or go outside with all those chases through the woods, or you wind up with a very different kind of picture.

I'll say. There's no Marie Windsor!

Windsor etched her most memorable portrait of a noir babe, however, in *The Killing* as the two-timing sexpot who wittingly turns her milquetoast husband's life upside down and unwittingly brings her lover (Vince Edwards) to ruin.

The third feature film of the young Stanley Kubrick (1928–1999), and his second straight gangster movie after the poverty row *Killer's Kiss* (1955), *The Killing* combines elements of John Huston's classic heist film *The Asphalt Jungle* with *Rififi* (1955), another classic heist film made in France by the blacklisted American director Jules Dassin. Kubrick's film has the same star (Sterling Hayden) as Huston's, playing a roughly similar role (although he's the heist's ringleader this time around, not just a strong-arm functionary), whose assessment of his colleague's motives ("None of these guys are criminals in the usual sense . . . they've just got a little larceny in 'em") is echoed in the Huston film by the worldview expressed by the heist's financier that "crime is nothing more than a left-handed form of human endeavor." Many of Kubrick's character types are similar—notably Colleen Gray as Hayden's girlfriend, who is a virtual clone of the Hayden character's girlfriend in *The Asphalt Jungle* played by

Jean Hagen. Windsor's closest counterpart in *Asphalt* is Marilyn Monroe's "sometime niece" to sugar daddy lawyer Louis Calhern. But she's really just a sweet young thing—even though Calhern pays dearly for trying to keep her in style. Windsor, however, is a Lorelei who crashes men on the rocks even when trying to steer them straight.

Both the Huston film and the Kubrick film share a subtext involving horse racing as well. The title *The Killing* refers not only to the gang's big score (the killing it hopes to make) but also to the robbery's centerpiece, the diversionary killing of a racehorse. The title also hints at the bloodbath that climaxes the film.

Similar to *Rififi*, Kubrick makes the robbery sequence the focal point and suspense showpiece of *The Killing*. But his approach to creating suspense is very different from Jules Dassin's. In *Rififi*, we hold our collective breath in anticipation that a slip of the men's tools as they burrow into the jewelry store they intend to rob will trigger the store's expensive alarm system any second. In *The Killing*, Kubrick creates suspense by establishing a rigid timetable for each stage of the robbery and by using a narrator and repeated shots of the betting room clock to keep us aware of and thinking about that timetable every step of the way. The narrator also keeps the linear progression of the robbery straight in our minds while Kubrick's camera shifts back and forth in time during the heist to show each gang member carrying out his concurrent task. Kubrick's experimental "time and motion study" may not be as intense as its counterpart robbery sequence in the Dassin film, but it is an equally bravura piece of filmmaking.

Bravura too is Marie Windsor in her last great (but not last) noir babe role. Transformed from a sexy brunette into a bombshell platinum blonde for *The Killing*, she's like a well scrubbed (but still junker) used car, dissing her mouse of a husband—until the mouse makes with a .45 caliber squeak.

Marie Windsor's noir babe Sherry Peatty in *The Killing* needs a man to pull off the heist and another man to grab the stolen loot so she can get free of the former. This was, after all, the 1950s. In our post-feminist age, however, the noir babe needs the opposite sex for the occasional roll in the hay, as a foil, or as a prop to help her reach her goal. Otherwise, she can do it all herself. She has become not just a more active participant in the noir world of deceit and betrayal, but a big-time player, as well. And Linda Fiorentino's Bridget Gregory in *The Last Seduction* (1994) is her role model.

Sexy, beautiful, smart, and totally ruthless ("Anyone check you for a heartbeat lately?" asks her lawyer played by J. T. Walsh), she not only rocks but rules. When her drug dealer husband (Bill Pullman) loses his cool and releases his tension on her after a drug deal that almost went south, she takes the $700,000 he scored and skips out on him. Then she holes up in a safe, small, totally nondescript upstate New York town off the beaten track to plan a foolproof getaway.

With her looks, brazen sexuality, and totally upfront attitude about what she wants, expects, and is willing to give in return, she stands out like Helen of Troy at a barn dance. To Peter Berg's small-town hick with big-city dreams and a yen for settling down, she is a goddess. And so Berg eagerly takes on the role she's cast him in—that of her next, and last, seduction, the one aimed at putting Pullman, his mob connections, and private investigators off her trail for good.

The screenplay by Steve Barancik, under the direction of John Dahl, is full of twists, turns, plot complications, and red herrings in the best tradition of gangster films noir and neo-noir. It is a tradition that *The Last Seduction* not just emulates, but also revolutionizes. Fiorentino's brilliant performance as the self-loving Bridget Gregory takes the noir babe's greatest quality—the will to win—and runs with it, compelling us to *want* her to win, as well.

PANDORA'S BOX

> Dr. Soberin: "You should have been called Pandora.
> She had a curiosity about a box and opened it
> and let loose all the evil in the world."
> Lily Carver: "Never mind about evil. What's in it?"
> **—Kiss Me Deadly (1955)**

Arguably the most literally explosive moll, twist, babe, or B girl in the movies also has the distinction of having made her Hollywood film debut in such a role as well as her swansong to a screen career in the same movie. She is Gaby Rodgers. And the film is Robert Aldrich's *Kiss Me Deadly*.

Born Gaby Rosenberg, she and her family fled Nazi Germany and eventually settled in America, where she was raised. She got her start on the New York stage and worked steadily on TV during the golden age of live television drama during the 1950s. After winning the role of the effortlessly sexy Lily Carver in *Kiss Me Deadly*, she completely retired from the big and small screen for the domestic roles of wife and mother. Today she lives on Long Island where she occasionally dabbles in stage work as a director.

In one respect, Rodgers's withdrawal from the screen after her memorable turn in *Kiss Me Deadly* is disappointing. It makes us wonder what other screen performances might have been. On the other hand, she is so one-of-a-kind in *Kiss Me Deadly* that we almost don't want the illusion spoiled by seeing her in anything else. So, in an odd way, maybe it's good for gangster movie fans, and fans of this movie in particular, that she did retire from the screen.

At the time, no one noticed, however, because *Kiss Me Deadly* was far from a critical and commercial hit. It had its greatest success with critics and audiences in Europe, especially France, where up-and-coming young filmmakers like Claude Chabrol, Jean-Luc Godard, and François Truffaut—who hoped to challenge the classical style of their native cinema—looked upon Aldrich's subversive exercise in genre bending and low-budget, almost guerrilla-type, on-location filmmaking as their bible.

The film is based on a 1952 novel by Mickey Spillane, featuring Spillane's recurring post-noir thug of a private eye, Mike Hammer. According to Aldrich, in adapting the book to the screen, he and screenwriter A. I. Bezzerides kept little of Spillane's material except for the book's title and some of his characters. This is mostly true. For example, the villains in the novel belong to the Mafia. There are gangsters in the film, too, but the real villains are Cold War-ish and more obscure in pedigree.

Fundamentally, the plot is a reworking of *The Maltese Falcon*. It turns on a group of conniving, unscrupulous characters—one of them the gumshoe "hero"—trying to locate a missing black box rather than a missing black bird that is so valuable it is worth killing, and dying, for. Rather than the stuff that dreams are made of, however, the elusive prize proves to be the stuff of nightmares—apocalyptic nightmares at that.

As the film opens, sleazeball private eye Mike Hammer (Ralph Meeker) picks up a half-naked hitchhiker (Cloris Leachman) who says she's running away from an asylum where she was being held against her will. Almost immediately, her shadowy pursuers catch up with the duo. Hammer is knocked out. Leachman is tortured for information as to the box's location, but she takes the secret to her grave. She and the unconscious Meeker are put in his car, which is pushed off a cliff. He survives, however, and wants the scoop as well as a chance to get even. A cop pal (Wesley Addy) tells him the FBI is on the case and to stay out of it, but this only piques Meeker's interest more; he realizes he's onto something big and potentially lucrative, and he wants in. He pursues the case on his own, and the trail of death leads to the mysterious doctor Soberin (Albert Dekker), the sexy blonde Lily Carver (Gaby Rodgers), and ultimately to the black box itself. What's in the box is never explicitly spelled out. It just gives off a glow when the box is opened a crack, suggesting a radioactive surge.[10]

Reportedly, Aldrich gave little in the way of direction to Rodgers except to imply that the character she plays is a lesbian—thus the dressy black top with the white lapels suggestive of a man's sport coat that she wears in the film. Everything else about her, though—and everything Rodgers exudes—is alluringly feminine, and effortlessly capable of drawing any man. With her sexy trace of some indefinable foreign accent, her dreamy way of talking (a hint that the character is on drugs), her mixture of strength and vulnerability, and her "help me" eyes to her perfectly shaped mouth and scarlet lips, she radiates "bombshell"—in the literal meaning of the word. When she finally gets her greedy hands on the black box and opens it against all warning to see what it is that she does have her hands on, she triggers a radioactive explosion. In her way, she's as mad as Cody Jarrett—and for many of the same reasons—as well as prescient of our age of terror today. She goes Jarrett (and his like) an apocalyptic step better, though. He lights up an oil refinery. But she takes out all of Malibu, and possibly much of southern California with the fallout.

For many years, prints of *Kiss Me Deadly* that were circulating on television and in revival houses concluded with Rodgers's immolation and the explosion of the beach house, leaving the viewer to think that Hammer and his secretary Velda (Maxine Cooper), who are trapped in the beach house with Rodgers, perish too. In fact, Hammer and Velda do get away to safety and survive, as the restored version of *Kiss Me Deadly* on television and available on home video now show. The cut version adds a nihilistic kicker to the film's other (intentionally) subversive twists by appearing to kill off the hero and heroine along with the evildoers. Aldrich was not above doing such extreme things in his films, but *Kiss Me Deadly* was not one of them. The director once observed that holding *yourself* in esteem no matter what others may think about you, or the odds you may face finding and holding onto your self-esteem, is what his movies are *really* about.[11]

Bearing this in mind, Hammer and Velda *must* make it out in order for Hammer (who is, after all, the film's protagonist) to achieve esteem in his own eyes, as well as ours, by turning his back on the potential rewards the black box may offer because of its greater potential for danger, and by saving Velda at the risk of his own life.

Even so, what we will always take away most from *Kiss Me Deadly* is not its restored ending. It is the image of Gaby Rodgers's modern Pandora—winsome yet wanton, delectable but deadly.

PART TWO
THE HOODS

"Gangsters have this thing about flowers. They think that whoever sends the biggest arrangement cares the most."
—A Bronx Tale *(1993)*

6
The Shame
of a Nation

"You can go a long way with a smile.
You can go a lot farther with a smile and a gun."
—Alphonso Capone, gangster, 1899–1947

Boss of Bosses

A T THE HEIGHT OF HIS CAREER as the Chicago underworld's king-pin, Alphonso Capone was the most famous gangster in America. And as a classic symbol of the American gangster, his figure looms large in film history and culture.

Although the movies have certainly done their part in mythologizing Capone's life and exploits, Capone played no small role in that himself. For example, he always said he'd been born in Italy and that his family migrated to the United States shortly after his birth. In fact, he was born the youngest of four brothers in Brooklyn, New York, in 1899. The infamous slash on his cheek, which earned him the fearsome nickname "Scarface," he claimed he'd received from a German bayonet on a World War I battlefield, whereas the only combat Capone ever saw up close and personal took place on the streets and in the back alleys of New York and Chicago. The scar came from a knife fight with a hoodlum rival over a girl.

Capone began his career as a mobster in the traditional way. He started out as a delinquent street tough and gradually moved up the ladder. Feared for his violent temper and sadistic brutality, he quickly rose to prominence as one of the top killers in New York's Five Points Gang, the city's last great pre-Prohibition terrorist mob. Another member of the gang was Johnny Torrio. When Torrio moved to Chicago to assist his uncle, Big Jim Colosimo, one of the city's top crime bosses, he took Capone along as bodyguard.

Soon Colosimo was being challenged by Torrio, who wanted to expand profits from his uncle's lucrative South Side prostitution, gambling, and bootlegging activities to the even more lucrative North Side, the off-limits turf of the city's other top gangster, Irishman Dion O'Banion. Uninterested in a gang war he felt would be bad for business, Colosimo ordered Torrio to put the brakes on his greed. Torrio responded by orchestrating his uncle's murder with the help of pal Capone and seizing control of South Side operations himself. Then he and Capone engineered the murder of rival O'Banion, who was gunned down in the flower shop that served as his headquarters, and moved against O'Banion's North Side associates.

Gang war broke out. The streets of Chicago erupted in gunfire and carnage that, as the late Big Jim Colosimo predicted, proved bad for business. After being severely wounded in an assassination attempt by the North Siders, Torrio decided he'd had enough. He handed control of business over to Capone and went back to New York, where he lived in wealthy retirement until his death in 1957.

A wily businessman and strong arm organizer, as well as a degenerate killer, Capone also became the underworld's first equal-opportunity employer by opening up his organization to Irish, Jewish, Polish, black, and other ethnic gang members. The result was not only a growing operation but also a stronger one poised to take over the North Side, now the dominion of O'Banion associate George "Bugs" Moran.

Repeatedly frustrated in his efforts to kill Moran, Capone finally made the costliest mistake of his criminal career by setting the wheels in motion for an all-out assault on the North Side mob's leadership. Capone missed his primary target, Moran, but the slaughter of seven members of Moran's gang on February 14, 1929—the notorious "St. Valentine's Day Massacre"—drew headlines from coast to coast, leading to a chorus of public outrage and an official crackdown (by federal agent Eliot Ness and his "Untouchables," among many other lawmen) on the Capone mob's activities.

Fearing that two of the murderers—John Scalise and Alberto Anselmi—might knuckle under to police pressure and reveal who was behind the massacre, Capone personally beat them to death with a baseball bat and had their bodies, now all but unrecognizable as human, dumped in an Indiana cornfield as a warning to others in his organization who might be considering turning state's evidence. As a result, federal agents were unable to pin the massacre on Capone, and no one was ever brought to trial for the crime.

Capone never did get Moran, who died of cancer in 1957, his power in the underworld long gone. But the feds finally did get Capone, who was convicted on a tax-evasion charge in 1931 and given an eleven-year sentence. Although the powerful organization he'd built up remained intact while he was in prison, Capone's power over it evaporated. Released in 1939, he retired to his private estate in Florida, where he died in 1947 from the ravages of syphilis, a disease he'd contracted many years earlier in a New York City brothel.

THE RACKET

Although the character of the mob chieftain was already a gangster-movie staple by the coming of the talkies, very few such screen characters were boldly patterned on, or suggestive of, the real Capone. Even George Bancroft's Bull Weed in *Underworld* is not a particularly Capone-like figure except in the broadest sense (his burliness and love of fancy clothes), although the underworld milieu Weed inhabits is clearly modeled on Capone's Chicago. There is, however, a veiled reference to the Capone-ordered hit of Dion O'Banion in Ben Hecht's scenario in the scene where Weed tracks down and shoots his rival, Irish mobster Buck Mulligan, in Mulligan's flower shop.[1]

The first gangster film to base its mobster villain on the legendary Capone was *The Racket* (1928), produced by aviator/businessman-turned–movie mogul Howard Hughes. The film is based on a sensational play by ex-newspaperman Bartlett Cormack, who had been a society columnist and crime reporter in the Windy City before heading to New York, then Hollywood, having set his sights on a career as a playwright and screenwriter. The play premiered at New York's Ambassador Theatre on November 22, 1927, and ran for 119 performances. Future gangster movie icon Edward G. Robinson played the Capone-like figure on stage, a character whose name, Nick Scarsi, boldly echoed Capone's nickname of "Scarface." Although Robinson had appeared in minor parts in several movies already, and even looked like Capone to a degree, he was passed over for the film version in favor of actor Louis Wolheim, who more resembled central casting's idea of a brutish-looking gangster.[2]

Even bolder was the play's uncompromising portrait of a city completely under siege by the mob, a city where politicians and judges are in the pocket of gangsters, where cops are on the take, and where even federal agents assigned to enforce the Prohibition statutes have their fingers in the cookie jar. Unlike Hecht and Sternberg, Cormack didn't even try to disguise the milieu of his cynical underworld drama. The play names Chicago and even refers to such real-life cronies of Capone's as corrupt mayor Big Bill Thompson. As a result, the play was prohibited from being performed in Chicago when it went on the tour after its Broadway run—a ban that stayed in place for almost two decades.

The film version was less forthright about the Chicago connection, but it proved no less controversial because of its inflammatory content. The story pits tough, incorruptible cop Captain McQuigg (played by Thomas Meighan of *The City Gone Wild*) against Wolheim's Scarsi, a big-city bootlegger and gang leader who rides in high-powered cars and dresses in gaudy suits and overcoats. Scarsi uses his ties with the city's most powerful politician, nicknamed the "Old Man" (Burr McIntosh), to get McQuigg transferred to traffic duty. When Scarsi's younger brother (George Stone, a fixture of gangster movies in supporting roles throughout the 1930s as George E. Stone) falls for a torch singer (Marie Prevost) whose kind Scarsi loathes, the gangster tries to bust up the relationship, incurring the singer's wrath. When Stone is picked up by one of McQuigg's patrolmen on a hit-and-run charge, McQuigg sees an opportunity to bring Scarsi down.

Because she was with Stone the night the accident occurred, the singer is held as a material witness. Scarsi pays a visit to the precinct where she's being held, runs up against the patrolman who arrested his brother, and kills him in a fight. McQuigg arrests Scarsi for murder. Scarsi threatens to blow the whistle on the "Old Man" and every other crooked politician in the city unless the corrupt district attorney gets him off. The DA, however, is under orders from the "Old Man" to silence the gangster permanently, which he pulls off by manipulating Scarsi into making a break for it with an unloaded gun so that the gangster is shot down while trying to escape. Thereafter, all goes back to a corrupt "normal," and the mob's covert rule over the city is sustained.

To achieve a sense of authenticity, director Lewis Milestone followed the leads of D. W. Griffith, Raoul Walsh, and Allan Dwan before him; he hired real bootleggers and gangsters to serve as "technical consultants" and extras. They apparently shared so many details about the workings of the underworld that when the film was released, Milestone's "consultants" subsequently reneged on the deal and tried to stop the picture from being shown. They even issued death threats against stars Meighan and Wolheim, producer Hughes, and director Milestone. Recorded silent film historian Kevin Brownlow: "Nothing happened. After all, once the picture was out, there was little point in shooting the men who made it—that would merely arouse the newspapers to give it massive publicity. The only sensible course was to get it banned via the politicians."[3]

Like the stage play, the film was banned in Chicago. Meanwhile, in Capone's native New York, the State Education Department's Motion Picture Division—to which each new release had to be submitted for review in order to be granted a license for exhibition in the state—demanded more than twenty cuts and alterations in the film on the grounds that the picture tended to incite crime and corrupt the morals of the viewing public. Among the changes demanded (and giving us a good idea of what the picture contained) were the following:

- The alteration of one of the subtitles (also called inter-titles) suggesting that a judge knowingly signed a bogus writ of habeas corpus.
- The elimination of all scenes showing reporters drinking inside police headquarters.
- The elimination of the following subtitle suggesting mob rule: "[Scarsi] will have you thrown off the [police] force if you don't."
- The elimination of a shot showing the Nick Scarsi character offering a policeman a roll of bills as a bribe.
- The elimination of a subtitle with Scarsi's line: "Did you imagine I'd let any lousy policeman that'd knock his own Mother over for a vote tell me what to do?"
- The elimination of the subtitle: "So that government of the professionals—by the professionals—and for the professionals—shall not perish from the earth."

Howard Hughes and representatives of the studio protested the changes demanded by the state's censor board in the New York press, declaring these changes to be arbitrary, censorious, and against the principles of free speech. But he gave in to them quickly. In a horse trade with the state's licensing division, Hughes and the studio managed to get two or three of the required changes dropped from the list, but made all the rest. Each print of the 8-reel feature was then resubmitted to the state to ensure the revisions had been made, and a license for exhibition was granted to each print accordingly.

These alterations, although satisfying the state, did little to satisfy groups in some of the state's localities, however. For example, in a letter to the director of the state's Motion Picture Division after *The Racket* was shown in Far Rockaway, New York, the president of that area's Parents & Teachers Association railed that, "A film such as this can only serve to create in the minds of our youth contempt for our courts and prosecutors, and disgust for and disappointment in a government where crime and criminals can run rampant, in open defiance of law and order."

In his dissection of the film's various malfeasances, the author of the above letter gives a blow-by-blow account of the experience of seeing this important—indeed watershed—early gangster film for the first time.

> The action consists of a shooting at a police captain by gangsters from roof tops, a beer running pitched gun fight in the heart of the city, an attempted pistol battle between rival gangs in a wide open speak easy operated with the full and intimate knowledge of the police, the release from arrest of a gang leader by service of a writ of habeas corpus on the police captain in the station house before he had the time to book the prisoner, the cowardly shooting in the back of a policeman in a suburban police station by the same gang leader, the subsequent arrest of the murderer, his attempted escape from the police upon the orders of "the old man," supposedly in control of judges and prosecutor, and the actual carrying out of the plan by the district attorney himself.

The author concluded by asking the state's Motion Picture Division to reconsider its decision and to bar the picture from being shown in New York State entirely. The Division didn't.

Despite the hullabaloo over *The Racket*'s jaundiced view of law, order, and the legal system—or, perhaps, because of them—the picture was enthusiastically embraced by critics. Wrote *Variety* (July 11, 1928): "*The*

Racket, like all great pictures, started with a great yarn and a director alive to its possibilities. It grips your interest from the first shot." Hollywood honored *The Racket* with a Best Picture nomination at the first (1927–1928) Academy Awards ceremony, but it lost to William A. Wellman's spectacular World War I aerial adventure, *Wings*.

Almost a quarter of a century later, millions of Americans were glued to the new medium of television in their living rooms, in bars and restaurants, even in doctors' waiting rooms and blood banks watching the real-life drama unfold of Chairman Estes Kefauver's special committee hearings on organized crime in the United States. For many citizens, the revelation of an invisible or shadow government run by the mob and crooked officials came as a shock—heretofore the stuff of such movies as *The Racket*. Always the savvy businessman, Howard Hughes, who was then running his own studio, RKO, took notice of the huge audience the televised hearings were getting, pulled *The Racket* out of mothballs, dusted the script off, and updated and remade it to capitalize on the notoriety of the televised hearings by grabbing some of their audience. He cast Robert Mitchum as Captain McQuigg and Robert Ryan as McQuigg's mobster nemesis, whose surname is changed in the remake from the Caponian Scarsi to the more ethnically ambiguous Scanlon. In most respects, however, the remake follows the plot of the original fairly closely.

With the help of the "Old Man" (who is referred to but never seen) and other corrupt officials, Scanlon gets McQuigg bounced from one precinct to another. As before, McQuigg finally gets to Scanlon through the gangster's kid brother when a cop belonging to McQuigg's elite squad of Untouchables-like crime fighters nails the kid on a grand larceny charge, to which the kid's singer girlfriend (film noir femme fatale Lizabeth Scott) was a witness. Scanlon visits the jailhouse to get at the girl, encounters the cop who arrested his kid brother, and shoots him. The incident is witnessed by a cub reporter, and McQuigg arrests Scanlon on a murder charge. A mob henchman in line for an important judgeship and a corrupt member of the police force's special investigations team arrive on the scene, and when the belligerent Scanlon says he'll sing if they don't get him out of this mess, they manipulate him into trying to escape and gun him down. The more upbeat ending of the 1951 version of *The Racket*, however, has a special commission put the screws to the men who murdered Scanlon, the implication being that they themselves will probably sing, and that the

"Old Man" and all the other racketeers in the city will quickly be brought to justice.

It has been suggested that the director of the remake, John Cromwell, a former actor who had actually appeared in a small role in the original 1927 production of *The Racket* on Broadway, undertook the project without enthusiasm simply to fulfill a contractual obligation to Hughes. He left the film as soon as shooting was finished. Not satisfied with the results, Hughes brought in directors Nicholas Ray and Tay Garnett to shoot some additional scenes, then had the film's editor, Sherman Todd, shoot a few more after they moved on. Regardless of all the creative input, this *Racket* is a somewhat listless and stagy affair. Robert Mitchum's performance as the firebrand McQuigg is so laid-back (even for Mitchum) that the character comes across not as incorruptible but as uninvolved. Robert Ryan, on the other hand, gives a charismatic, albeit sometimes overwrought, performance as Scanlon, a character described by others in the film as an old-time mob boss (despite his youthful looks) who refuses to subscribe to the syndicate's new methods of political chicanery in place of deadly violence and who has to be gotten out of the way. Where the original apparently captured audience attention through its controversial subject matter and authentic if somewhat veiled portrait of Capone, the remake seems leadenly familiar—like a dish that, even in 1951, has been served up one too many times.

LITTLE CAESAR

While the character of Nick Scarsi in the silent-era film *The Racket* was more openly patterned on the real life gangster Al Capone, and, a year later, Universal's gangster musical *Broadway* (1929) would feature a supporting character nicknamed "Scar" played by Leslie Fenton, it was not until Warner Brothers's *Little Caesar* (1930), based on a popular novel by a young writer named W. R. Burnett published by Dial Press the year before, that the screen would tackle the brutal story of Chicago's most infamous gangster head-on.

Some revisionists have claimed that Edward G. Robinson was not director Mervyn LeRoy's first and only choice to play Capone figure Caesar Enrico Bandello, nicknamed Rico, in *Little Caesar*. They allege that LeRoy sought Robinson for the part of one of the film's minor mobsters—the character of Otero, played by George E. Stone (who had a substantial supporting role in the film version of *The Racket* as Scarsi's kid brother). In his autobiography,[4] LeRoy firmly refutes this urban legend. But even if he didn't, it seems unlikely that the actor who had risen to fame on Broadway as the Capone-like Nick Scarsi, who had played several leads in previous gangster movies, and who even looked a bit like Capone, would have been asked to take a supporting role in what was to be the most realistic depiction of the life and legend of Al Capone filmed up to that time.

Little Caesar offered moviegoers of 1930 a more brutal gangster anti-hero than they'd ever seen before on the screen. Robinson's Rico Bandello is no gentleman thief or ordinary street tough gone bad until regenerated by the love and support of an honest woman. In fact, Bandello seems to have no interest in women at all, except, possibly, as ornaments. He's an ungentlemanly, avaricious punk who kills because his victims stand in the way of his gaining power and prestige—or simply because he covets a nice piece of jewelry they happen to be wearing. And like Lon Chaney's Blackbird, he goes to his death unrepentant of his ways.

POET LAUREATE OF THE AMERICAN GANGSTER FILM

If the prolific and versatile Ben Hecht is the "Shakespeare of the movies," then the equally prolific but more focused William Riley Burnett is surely the "poet laureate of the American gangster film." The author of almost forty novels, the bulk of them on a gangland theme, and approximately sixty screenplays[5], many of them adapted from his own best-selling crime novels or the hardboiled crime fiction of others, Burnett's influence on the genre is as enduring as that of contemporaries Dashiell Hammett, Raymond Chandler, and James M. Cain, as well as Ben Hecht, put together. Yet today he is the least known, and the least read, among this elite group.

Film director John Huston, who collaborated with Burnett in adapting two of the author's novels, *High Sierra* (1940) and *The Asphalt Jungle* (1949), to the screen, and was a keen admirer of the man's work, felt Burnett was one of the most neglected of all American writers. "There are moments of reality in [his] books that are quite overpowering," Huston said.[6] And yet, of Burnett's many books about the inner lives of gangsters and thieves and the violent milieu in which they battle to survive, only *Little Caesar* and *The Asphalt Jungle* are today readily available in print.

A devotee of French realists like Gustave Flaubert and Émile Zola and their gritty novels about big-city life, Burnett left his hometown of

Springfield, Ohio, where he was working as a statistician for the state during the day while cranking out unpublished novels and short stories in the vein of his literary mentors at night, and headed for Chicago to experience gritty big-city life firsthand. The year was 1928, and the most famous name in the local papers at the time was Al Capone. Burnett took a night job as a desk clerk at a rundown hotel in a seedy part of town to pay the bills so that he could work during the day on the book he hoped would make him a published author. He immersed himself in the lowlife atmosphere and vernacular of the has-been pugs, prostitutes, and Capone wannabes that surrounded him, absorbing everything like a sponge. The result, *Little Caesar*, brought an end to his flow of rejection slips forever and took him to Hollywood, where he spent the next fifty years producing gangster novels as different from *Little Caesar* as they are from one another, and writing movies for every A-list screen tough guy from George Raft, Humphrey Bogart, and John Garfield to Alan Ladd, Frank Sinatra and Steve McQueen.

With *Little Caesar*, Burnett stripped down his style, making it terse and more Hemingway-esque than that of the descriptive European realists he'd started out emulating. More important, he departed from the traditional pulp-fiction formula of making gangster characters one-dimensional—as straw men set up to be blown away in the end by the hero or the law—and made his ambitious, conniving, greedy, violent gangster Rico Bandello the protagonist, giving him hopes and dreams and qualities of good and bad like all of us. He bestowed upon his gangsters—the doomed Roy Earle in *High Sierra,* the self-deluded Dix Handley in *The Asphalt Jungle,* and others—as well as the gangster in fiction at large, a recognizably human face (a pattern Mario Puzo would continue decades later in his best-seller *The Godfather*). On the page this human face is typically hailed as a "realistic," "honest," and "truthful" portrait. Translated to the screen, however, it is more often than not seen as glorifying the criminal, a criticism leveled at the screen version of *Little Caesar*, most other gangster movies Burnett was connected with (notably the 1932 *Scarface*), and the film version of *The Godfather*, too.

GUTTER MACBETH

The film of *Little Caesar* opens in a luncheonette where the down-and-out Rico and his pal Joe Massara (Douglas Fairbanks Jr.) spot an article in a newspaper about wealthy Chicago racketeer Diamond Pete Montana (the film's Big Jim Colosimo, played by Ralph Ince). They head for the Windy City to change their luck. Rico falls in with Montana's right-hand man, Sam Vettori (Stanley Field), the film's Johnny Torrio figure, and soon makes his mark as one of the South Side mob's most brutal enforcers. Meanwhile, Rico's pal Massara becomes a successful dancer at a nightclub run by North Side mob boss Arnie Lorch (Maurice Black), the film's O'Banion, and turns his back on his criminal past when he falls for his glamorous dance partner, Olga (Glenda Farrell).

Although Rico is ordered by his boss to stay out of the North Side, he coerces Massara into fronting a robbery of Lorch's club, during which Rico cold-bloodedly shoots one of the customers (played by Landers Stevens, the father of legendary film director George Stevens), who happens to be the head of the crime commission. Massara keeps silent about the shooting to all but Olga, who urges her lover to turn state's evidence against Rico, but Massara backs off when Rico threatens them with death if they dare to talk.

Determined to get Rico out of their lives, however, Olga ignores the threat and spills the beans to the cops, fingering Rico as the killer of the commissioner. Rico attempts to go through with his threat, but softens for the first time in his life and finds himself unable to kill his former pal.

The cops round up Rico's gang, and Rico goes on the run, a hunted man. Forced to hide out in a flophouse where fellow down-and-outers, unaware of Rico's real identity, snicker as they read in the newspaper about the gangster's fall from power, his pride gets the better of him, and he goes berserk with the egocentric rage of a child; emerges from hiding at last; and, with considerable irony, is fatally shot down by police beneath a billboard advertising Olga and Massara's top-billed dance routine at the Tipsy, Topsy, Turvy Theatre.

Contemporary reviewers lauded *Little Caesar* as a realistic portrait of the world of gangsterism, but they generally failed to comment upon the many parallels between the exploits of the fictional Rico and the actual Capone, whose name was even then a household word. What they did point out were the similarities in character between Robinson's Rico and *The Racket*'s Nick Scarsi, the role that brought Robinson his first taste of fame three years earlier and with which he was still strongly identified despite his absence from the controversial film version.

For example, writing in *The New Yorker*, critic John Mosher said: "Since his appearance on the stage in *The Racket*, Edward G. Robinson has grown to be the leading authority on the behavior and mannerisms of those gunmen and gangsters whose doings often occupy the attention of the press. Evidently all his experiences and research work in such a field are now employed in the study of Rico Bandello, the central figure of this movie." And in the *New York Herald Tribune*, Richard Watts Jr. noted: "Not even in *The Racket* was he [Robinson] more effective. Taking one of the most familiar roles in the universe, he makes it seem fresh and real. Never does he cease being a savage and terrifying killer, a man who is all the more sinister because of his reality."

This is the way W. R. Burnett saw the character, and how Edward G. Robinson brings him to life—as a sort of "gutter Macbeth." Indeed, *Little Caesar* is Robinson's film all the way. Its power and status as a classic gangster film of the pre-Code, early talkie era stem primarily from his performance, as the reticence of Mervyn LeRoy's direction—in stark contrast to the wallop LeRoy would deliver two years later in his direction of *I Am a Fugitive from a Chain* Gang—offers him little support. Although it was criticized as excessively brutal, *Little Caesar* is considerably more subdued in its mayhem than many of the silent-era gangster melodramas that preceded it. This is probably why *Little Caesar*, unlike the more violent and anarchic *The Public Enemy* (1931) and *Scarface* (1932) that quickly followed, seems so antiquated today. LeRoy averts the camera's eye from Rico's brutality at virtually every turn. For example, he shows us Rico's robbery of Lorch's nightclub and the murder of the commissioner in a series of arty, fast-paced dissolves designed, it seems, to obscure the thuggish nature of the mobster. And he keeps the key murder of Lorch (Rico's North Side rival) completely off-screen. We see Rico coveting Lorch's expensive stickpin, then proudly wearing it—the implication being that he murdered Lorch for the pin during an intervening dissolve. As a result, the task of putting across the violence of the man and the primitive instincts that drive him falls almost entirely upon Robinson's fortunately capable shoulders.

SCARFACE

As the title suggests, *Scarface* (1932) is more direct in modeling its story on the real Capone than even *Little Caesar* had been. It is based on the 1930 novel *Scarface* by a popular writer of detective fiction of the time named Maurice Coons, who wrote under the pseudonym Armitage Trail. A high school dropout with aspirations, like W. R. Burnett, of becoming a world-famous author, Coons, who was born in 1903, achieved writing success in his late teens turning out stories for pulp magazines. He researched *Scarface* as a visitor to Chicago in the late 1920s when Capone's power was at its zenith. He never lived to see the film version of his most famous crime novel, however. A literal heavyweight at 300-plus pounds, he dropped dead suddenly of a heart attack in 1931, shortly after moving to Hollywood to pursue a career as a screenwriter.

In the wake of the success of the Capone-influenced gangster movie *Little Caesar*, Howard Hughes bought the rights to the Coons/Trail book and commissioned *Little Caesar* author W. R. Burnett to adapt it into a screenplay for director Howard Hawks. Unhappy with the Burnett script, Hughes turned to several other writers, among them Seton I. Miller, John Lee Mahin, and Ben Hecht, who had written *Underworld*. Although all four writers received screen credit, it would appear that Hecht's contribution was the most substantial, as the film offers more than a few echoes of *Underworld*. For example, boasting about what he has planned for his opportunist moll if she sticks with him, Scarface shows her a billboard for Cook's Tours bearing the headline THE WORLD IS YOURS. In *Underworld*, George Bancroft's Bull Weed impresses moll Evelyn Brent about what the future has in store for her by pointing out a billboard for the AMC Investment Company bearing the same headline.

The Capone figure in *Scarface* is Tony Camonte (Paul Muni), an ex-member of New York City's Five Points Gang who has come to Chicago to work for Johnny Lovo (Osgood Perkins), a lieutenant of South Side mob boss Big Louis Costillo (Harry J. Vejar). Scarface becomes Costillo's bodyguard and kills him so that he and Lovo can take over the South Side themselves. Pulled in for questioning by the police, the arrogant Scarface lights a match for his cigarette on an officer's badge (a bit of business the Coen Brothers would reuse in their 1990 homage to the gangster movie genre and 1940s films noir, *Miller's Crossing*) and smugly denies everything. When asked where he received the ugly scar on his face, he gives Capone's own apocryphal explanation: "Got in the war."

Over his partner's objections, the ambitious Scarface decides to take over the North Side operation and orders the murder of its Irish boss, an execution that takes place in a flower shop. Another mobster, Gaffney (played by Boris Karloff) replaces the dead kingpin and orders the North Siders to assassinate Scarface. But the attempt fails and all-out war ensues between the North and South Side gangs. Feeling the pinch, Scarface's partner tries to cut a truce with the other side by having his partner rubbed out. But Scarface survives the attack, and his loyal bodyguard Gino (George Raft) kills the partner, Lovo, in reprisal.

With Lovo now out of the way, Scarface assumes control of the South Side mob as well as the affections of his dead partner's avaricious mistress Poppy (Karen Morely). Feeling his oats, Scarface then launches a vicious strike on St. Valentine's Day against the North Siders by luring several key members, including boss Gaffney, to a garage, where his men line them up against a wall and strafe them with tommy gun bullets. By a twist of fate, Gaffney escapes the massacre, but he's subsequently gunned down in a bowling alley, leaving the way clear for Scarface to take control of North Side operations.

In its only significant departure from the Capone story, the film concludes with Scarface's discovery that his beloved sister Cesca (Ann Dvorak), for whom his love is distinctly more than brotherly, is living in sin with his bodyguard Gino, and he kills the man in a jealous rage—only to learn afterward that the deceased and Cesca were legally man and wife. This sends Scarface further around the bend. With Cesca now turned against him, and the police hunting him for Gino's murder, Scarface loses his grip and (like Bull Weed in *Underworld*) seeks refuge in his steel-shuttered hideout. Cesca sneaks in with a gun, determined to revenge herself, but is unable to shoot him down when she comes to the realization that she harbors repressed longings for an incestuous relationship of her own. Instead, she takes up arms with him against the police as the street is cordoned off and the hideout pelted with gunfire and tear gas. She takes the first bullet and dies in his arms. With nothing to live for, the now totally flipped out Scarface, realizing he is nothing without her, commits "suicide by cop." He makes a run for it, knowing he'll be shot down, and dies in the street beneath the Cook's Tours sign advertising THE WORLD IS YOURS.

Scarface would be so overt and tough in its depiction of gangland morals and murder and so relentless in its mayhem that it would inspire controversy before the first frame of film was shot. Hollywood's self-censoring body, the Hays Office, viewed the script with horror and demanded a slew of changes in exchange for its seal of approval. Outraged, producer Hughes told the Hays Office to go stuff it and gave director Hawks carte blanche to make the film as realistic and bloodthirsty as he wished. When the film was finished, the Hays Office, as promised, denied its seal, leaving the film an easy target for state and local censor boards. Hughes knew from his experience with the silent version of *The Racket*

aised by critics, many of whom declared *Scar,*
 potent gangster pictures ever made. Citizen wa
 d it for much the same reason, calling it the most
 zing gangster picture ever made. As a result, the film
 cost plus a profit, but it was not the sensational commerci
 wanted; petulantly, he eventually withdrew it from circulatic
 er as he had done with the silent version of *The Racket.* Unlike
 , however, which is still unavailable to the public, *Scarface* was
 ereleased to television and home video after Hughes's death. It is
 versally admired as one of the genre's finest efforts—a tough, nose portrayal of a brutal Capone-style mobster and modern day
 Borgia that is almost as wall-to-wall with gunfire and brutality as
 ne and action films today.
 ctor Brian De Palma remade the Hawks classic in 1983 under the
 itle. Dedicated to Ben Hecht, the script by Oliver Stone and an
 ited De Palma updated the Capone story to the 1980s, when Castro's
 xiled boatloads of political prisoners, criminals, and other "undesir-
 o U.S. shores to get rid of them here and stir up trouble. In the film,
 these exiles is Al Pacino's Tony Montana, a scar-faced punk with an
 lthy (and unsavory) attachment to his sister (Mary Elizabeth
 ntonio). Montana rises to become a kingpin in Florida's flourishing
 rade, only to be brought down by his own brutal excesses.
 e the original *Scarface,* the remake ran into trouble with censors:
 er-the-top violence—torture by chain saw, nonstop shoot-outs, and
 cluding bloodbath aimed at topping (as well as parodying) Sam
 npah's ferocious finale to *The Wild Bunch* (1969)—almost earned
 lm an X rating. However, the film's distributor, Universal, resubmit-
 with minor cuts, and the Motion Picture Association of America
 A) granted it an R rating instead.
 he *Scarface* remake starts out as if it's going to amount to some-
 g, but then reverses gears as it roars to its flamboyant conclusion and
 ls up being a send-up of itself instead. Sporting a Cuban accent that
 nds more like the Frito Bandito, Pacino chews up the scenery and
 it out so broadly that his scar-faced Tony Montana comes across less
 primitive man dressed in street clothes like Paul Muni's Tony
 nonte in the original, than an ultra-violent cartoon character or tough
 action figure in a video game. And despite all the spectacular fire-
 er and gruesome bloodletting, the finale, wherein this Scarface
 wns his sorrows—*and his face*—in a plate of cocaine as his mansion is

hat he was in for; relenting, he had Hawks
to incorporate the Hays Office suggestions, a
the original ending so that Scarface goes to
ranting pile of mush.

Released with the seal, the film neverthele
across the land, whose censorship boards accu
the world of gangsters by portraying it too ob
more polemical anticrime and -corruption, ant
would appear from the censors' criticism of th
while W. R. Burnett's draft of a script for *Scarfac*
by Hughes, some of it must have rubbed off, bec
served and talked to real-life gangsters during l
hoods such as *Scarface*'s Tony Camonte as viewi
in the streets no differently than a soldier views k
tle. It is what one must do to survive. Unlike the r
Camonte isn't a sadist and cutthroat by nature; h
ing on all fours, a primitive man who sees everyth
of his own primitive understanding. Thus, when
fired upon by and then firing a tommy gun for the t
childlike excitement not simply a thirst for bloods
rather a gee-whiz kind of wonder at the awesome po
of such a tool.

Nevertheless, state censors demanded that *Sca*
take a more polemical stand, and it was held back fi
changes were made. Hughes went along, adding sev
by Richard Rosson because Hawks had by now moved
ect) to make the film more blatantly denunciating o
nomenon. In one of the added scenes, a newspaper
Pratt) accused of giving too many headlines to the ci
straight into the camera, decries the problem of gar
monishes the government and the public for their ow
bility in countering mob violence ("*You* can end it. Figl
In another, the city's chief of detectives (Edwin Maxw
glorification of gangsters, echoing the very accusations
foreword demanding a solution to the problem of gangste
well. And the film was finally released nationwide beari
signed specifically to appease censors everywhere: *The Shc*

Hughes's efforts to salvage his investment worked t
changes aimed at softening its content notwithstandin

highly pr
the most
denounc
demoral
back its
Hughes
altogeth
that film
finally r
now un
nonsen
Cesare
our cri
Dire
same t
uncred
Cuba e
ables"
one of
unhea
Mastra
drug t
Lil
its ov
a cor
Pecki
the f
ted i
(MP
T
thin
win
sou
spit
as
Cai
guy
po
dri

reduced to ruins and his flank of bodyguards decimated, isn't anywhere near as powerful as the less graphic but equally violent (for its time) and disturbingly incest laden conclusion to Howard Hawks's still-terrific 1932 original—even if it *is* much funnier.

THE UNTOUCHABLES

Today, Eliot Ness is an American folk hero. But in 1928, when he got the job of putting together a task force of incorruptible crime busters charged with prying some seams in the Capone organization, he was just another faceless Prohibition agent working for the Justice Department. Ness was keenly aware of the value of publicity, however, and he used it not only to advance his own career but to win public support for going after the Capone mob as well.

Ness pored through hundreds of personnel files to find nine men within the department whose law enforcement skills were unmatched and whose reputations were unassailable, then invited the press along to observe his elite squad in action as it began knocking over Capone's stills throughout the Chicago area. Losing income from the raids, the Capone mob repeatedly tried bribing Ness and his men to lay off. When these attempts failed, the mob dubbed Ness's squad the "Untouchables." Before long the nickname was picked up by the press, which ran with it.

Buoyed by the notoriety, Ness and his Untouchables got bolder and more aggressive. They infiltrated Capone's headquarters and put a tap on his phone, enabling them to learn the whereabouts of all of Capone's breweries throughout the city and the Midwest. They then constructed a heavy-duty ramming truck with which they could smash through the breweries' steel-enforced doors, catching Capone's men by surprise. Only two years into the job, Ness' Untouchables had succeeded in putting scores of Capone stills and breweries out of business and had confiscated hundreds of the Capone organization's delivery trucks—which they paraded by the mobster's headquarters on the way to a government warehouse just to rub things in.

Capone flew into one of his familiar rages at having his nose tweaked like this, and he ordered his hit men to step up their efforts to take out Ness. Their efforts failed. Capone never did get Eliot Ness. But then again, neither did Eliot Ness get Al Capone, who was nailed by the Treasury Department for the relatively unexceptional crime of holding out on his taxes. Ness and his Untouchables had cost the gangster's bootlegging rackets dearly, however. But Capone's other rackets—gambling, prostitution, and so on—continued to flourish, and more than made up for the shortfall.

With Capone jailed, the Untouchables disbanded and the redoubtable team went its separate ways, not to be heard from again until 1957. During the intervening years, Ness continued in law enforcement for a time, then he took a stab at politics. When that career move proved unsuccessful, he went into private business, floundering there as well. By 1956, he was a forgotten man and heavily in debt—until a chance encounter that same year with a sports reporter for United Press International named Oscar Fraley changed his fortunes. Although Ness couldn't understand why anyone would be interested in hearing about his almost thirty-year-old experiences going up against the Capone mob with the Untouchables, Fraley persuaded Ness to talk about them, and these conversations turned into a book. Published with little fanfare in 1957 by Julian Messner, a house specializing in children's books, *The Untouchables* unexpectedly shot to the top of *The New York Times* best-seller list and transformed the obscure former Prohibition agent into one of America's most famous—and storied—lawmen: a gen-u-ine modern day hero; a Wyatt Earp for the twentieth century. Unfortunately, Ness didn't live to enjoy his rediscovery and newfound fame. He died of a massive heart attack at age fifty-six, just a few months shy of the book's publication.

Desi Arnaz, TV star/producer and partner with wife Lucille Ball in Desilu Productions, bought the rights to the book and turned it into a two-parter for his company's dramatic anthology series on the ABC television network, *Desilu Playhouse*. Titled *The Scarface Mob*, the show, directed in hard-hitting semidocumentary by Phil Karlson—who had filmed the gritty cult classic about small town mob rule, *The Phenix City Story*, in a similar style a few years earlier—aired in the spring of 1959. It was such a ratings winner that Arnaz and his producer, Quinn Martin, stitched the two episodes together and released them in Europe as a feature film under the same title.

The Scarface Mob is a fairly straight and faithful adaptation of Ness' autobiographical account of his years battling the Capone mob—although for some reason the credits for the telefilm list it as being based on Eliot Ness and Oscar Fraley's "novel," whereas the book is allegedly nonfiction. The book doesn't suggest that Ness and his Untouchables were responsible for bringing down Capone, although it is possible to come away with that opinion because it focuses only on their brewery-busting activities. *The Scarface Mob* doesn't suggest that conclusion, either, but it does play looser with the historical record by giving another nemesis of the Ness team, mobster Frank Nitti (indelibly portrayed by Bruce Gordon), a more dominant role in the Capone organization than Nitti in fact had. It also provides Capone (Neville Brand) with a native Italian accent (albeit of the comic/theatrical "Hey, what's-a-u-a-name?" variety) even though the real Capone was Brooklyn-born. However, compared to the subsequent TV series *The Untouchables*—which had Ness and his men nailing every mobster and desperado of the Roaring Twenties and beyond—*The Scarface Mob*, narrated in tabloid-headline style by the powerful gossip columnist Walter Winchell, is practically a model of factual realism.

Although *The Scarface Mob* was not intended as a pilot for a television series, it drew such a huge audience that ABC persuaded Arnaz and Martin to develop it into a series for the network's 1959/60 schedule. Under the original book's title of *The Untouchables*, the series premiered in October and ran for 118 episodes over four years.

The TV series was controversial from the start—primarily for its violence, which in terms of explicitness was on a par with that of the original 1932 *Scarface* but fairly heavy-duty for television back then, but also for its ethnicity. In his autobiography *Straight Shooting*, star Robert Stack (who landed the role of Eliot Ness in *The Scarface Mob* and the TV series after Desilu's first choices of Van Johnson and Van Heflin turned it down), wrote:

> *The Untouchables* managed to get in more trouble in a shorter time than any show on TV. One of our biggest problems was the charge of ethnic bias in our scripts. Many of the villains, from Capone and Nitti to the least important, small-time thugs, had Italian names. No one ever suggested even remotely that Italian people as a whole had a leaning toward violent crime. But the controversy began. Together with Senator John Pastore, the powerful chairman of the Senate Communications Subcommittee, Frank Sinatra and Cardinal Spellman objected to the large number of Italian gangsters on the program. . . . Eventually we did stop using Italian names.[7]

This same controversy has dogged every movie and TV show about organized crime and the Mafia, from *The Godfather* films to *The Sopranos*, ever since. With regard to *The Untouchables*, it was apparently ignored by its politically correct detractors that one of Ness's closest lieutenants in the series, Enrico Rossi (Nicholas Georgiade), was a character of Italian descent, too. (Ironically, Georgiade played the uncredited role of a Capone hood in the two-parter that spawned the series. Paul Picerni, another of the series' Untouchables, played a Capone henchman in *The Scarface Mob* as well.) By the final season of *The Untouchables*, equal opportunity had been fully employed, and all ethnic groups were well represented as villains, including the Russians, in the form of a Slavic hood with the improbable name of Joe Vodka.

The Untouchables didn't just draw fire from Italian-Americans. The U.S. Bureau of Prisons objected to those episodes of the series, which, true to life, showed Capone living a rather more luxurious lifestyle behind bars than cons are expected to enjoy. FBI chief J. Edgar Hoover objected to the show because of its "inaccurate depiction" of his beloved T-men. Another senate subcommittee, echoing a time-honored criticism of gangster movies as far back as the 1928 version of *The Racket*, assailed the show for inciting crime and promoting juvenile delinquency. Meanwhile, the FCC skewered it for being too violent. And in the realm of the absurd, Al Capone's son threatened to sue the producers for defamation of his late father's character! (The suit never materialized, though not for lack of a willing mouthpiece, I'll bet.)

A popular but seldom top-rated series, despite all the notoriety surrounding it, *The Untouchables* finally shut down on September 10, 1963. Ness and his men had killed or put away most of the mob by then—from Jake "Greasy Thumb" Guzik, Capone's chief accountant, to Machine Gun Jack McGurn to hitman Mad Dog Coll—and the show was running out of steam, as well as villains. It went into syndication, but because of the furor it had caused during its original airing, as well as increased sensitivity about even make-believe gunplay that followed in the wake of the November 22, 1963, assassination of President John F. Kennedy, the series soon disappeared from U.S. airwaves almost entirely, finding continued visibility and success only in Europe.

The blockbuster performance of Francis Ford Coppola's *The Godfather* in 1972, and the cultural phenomenon it became, revived public interest in all things gangster, however, and a few local stations began running the old series again, usually at night.

There was even some discussion of resurrecting *The Untouchables* as a network prime-time series featuring a younger star as Ness. But these plans failed to materialize, at least right away, and so it fell to the movies to rescue the property from limbo.[8]

Appropriately, the director called in for the rescue was Brian De Palma, an old hand at the Capone saga with the updated *Scarface* four years earlier. However, he and writer David Mamet faced the same problem in adapting *The Untouchables* to the big screen in 1987 that director Phil Karlson and writer Paul Monash found themselves up against when they adapted Ness and Fraley's book into *The Scarface Mob*—namely, that the story of the Ness/Capone duel lacked a satisfying third act.

Although in real life Ness struggled mightily to put Capone out of business and behind bars, it was the Treasury boys who got the job done. In *The Scarface Mob,* Monash dealt with this dramatically unsatisfying resolution by having the usually taciturn Ness fly into an atypical rage when he hears that the mobster is going to prison for a crime (tax evasion) that paled in comparison to his others. De Palma and Mamet took a very different approach to solving the structural problem with which the facts had saddled them. They ignored the facts altogether and dreamed up a completely fictional finale wherein Ness (Kevin Costner) and his Untouchables come up with the idea of nailing Capone (Robert De Niro, who expressed interest in playing the part at the last minute, snatching it away from the already cast Bob Hoskins) on tax evasion and providing the Treasury boys with the evidence they need to do so.

This sets the stage for an elaborate, De Palma–style showpiece toward the end of the film where Ness and the sole surviving member of his team (Andy Garcia) stake out a Chicago train station to nab Capone's bookkeeper for the tax boys and are faced with the dilemma of saving a woman and her baby from the crossfire with Capone's hit men. De Palma modeled the highly touted scene (which was not in Mamet's script) after the classic Odessa Steps sequence in Sergei Eisenstein's *The Battleship Potemkin* (1925). I like some of De Palma's grandly cinematic set pieces—such as the finale of *Carlito's Way* where Al Pacino dodges his various assassins in Grand Central Station—but not this one. Shot in languorous slow motion (unlike Eisenstein's rapid-fire prototype), the scene seems to go on forever and is, like the finale of De Palma's *Scarface,* more funny than either shocking or suspenseful. This may have been intentional on De Palma's part as his version of *The Untouchables* operates on a similar level as his version of *Scarface.* It is like a blood-drenched video game or a violent historical cartoon. Not only does the unsmiling, morally upstanding Ness—who is even given a wholly fabricated family in the film—get Capone, he also gets Frank Nitti (Billy Drago), who falls from a skyscraper and crashes to his death through the roof of a car. (The real Nitti committed suicide in 1943.) There are a few isolated moments of fact in the film—such as the brewery raids, which are authentically portrayed, and the incident where Capone bashes one of his men to death with a baseball bat in a moment of pique—but the filmmakers don't let them interfere with the fiction.

BIG FELLAS

The revival of interest in Al Capone (a.k.a., Scarface, Snorkey, and the Big Fella) sparked by *The Scarface Mob* may have been what prompted Allied Artists to make the first big-screen biopic of the legendary gangster. Beefy Rod Steiger, who was even more of a Capone look-alike than Edward G. Robinson, was cast in the title role.

Narrated in Winchell style by James Gregory's Sergeant Schaeffer, a fictional Chicago cop suggestive of *The Racket*'s Captain McQuigg and *The Scarface Mob*'s Eliot Ness, *Al Capone* takes up the gangster's story with his arrival in Chicago in 1919 to help out his mentor, Johnny Torrio (Nehemiah Persoff). Its account of Capone's rise to the top of Chicago's South Side mob is, on the whole, fairly accurately portrayed, and gripping.

The ambitious Capone rubs out Big Jim Colosimo (Joe De Santis), then he and Torrio move against the North Side's O'Banion (Robert Gist). Things get too hot and Torrio retires, handing control to Capone, who immediately locks horns with George "Bugs" Moran (Mervyn Vye). Capone orders the St. Valentine's Day Massacre to eliminate Moran, gets massive amounts of negative publicity over the bloody affair and a police crackdown instead, and is convicted on tax evasion.

From here, the film goes factually off the rails, however, by having Capone sent to prison and beaten to death by his fellow inmates—presumably on the orders of Moran out of revenge and not because of his conspicuously lavish lifestyle behind bars. There are also a number of fictionalized scenes dealing with the gangster's womanizing. They don't add up to much. But they do provide a much-needed respite from Steiger's monotonous ravings and signature scenery-chewing as Capone.

"The most accurate and authentic gangster movie ever,"[9] is how producer-director Roger Corman describes his considerably more informed and effective, blow-by-blow account of the Capone/O'Banion/Moran power struggle, which culminated in the infamous St. Valentine's Day

Massacre of 1929. Although filmed on a relatively tight budget for a major studio theatrical feature—but a huge one ($1 million) by Corman standards—*The St. Valentine's Day Massacre* (1967) looks as good in terms of production values as some of the more epic and expensive gangster movies as *The Godfather* soon to come from the major studios. This is because Corman was able to make use of many sets left standing on the Twentieth Century Fox lot from other, more expensive Fox films: an ornate ballroom from *The Sound of Music* (1965) is used for Capone's mansion; a grimy bar/brothel from *The Sand Pebbles* (1966) is used for a speakeasy; and a turn-of-the-century New York City avenue on Fox's backlot is redressed to suggest Roaring Twenties Chicago. All give the film a very rich, period look.

The kaleidoscopic script does an excellent job of dramatizing the sometimes Byzantine events leading up to and following the massacre without playing too much havoc with the truth. Howard Browne, who, like Ben Hecht and Bartlett Cormack, had worked as a newspaper reporter in Chicago when the events portrayed in the film occurred, wrote the screenplay; thus he knew firsthand what he was writing about. As in *The Scarface Mob* and *Al Capone,* a Walter Winchell-esque narrator (Paul Frees, uncredited) is used to heighten the drama and to foretell the dire fates of the various dramatis personae while keeping the motivations of these characters and the flow of events clear for the viewer. This was no easy task as there are more plots, counterplots, and court intrigues going on than in an average installment of *I, Claudius*. Browne even provides some interesting bits of gangland lore along the way—such as the reason why the powerful Capone was unable to assume leadership of Chicago's Mafia. He wasn't Sicilian.

Corman's statement that *The St. Valentine's Day Massacre* is the most accurate and authentic gangster movie ever made may be stretching things a bit far, however, as there are a few factual slip-ups (that Capone was born in Italy, for example), as well as departures on grounds of dramatic license from the film's otherwise scrupulous, documentary-like approach. For example, the roughhouse scene between George Segal's Cagney-like Peter Gusenberg (a Moran gang member) and his blonde bombshell moll (Jean Hale) where he lets her have it in the face with a sandwich is clearly not part of the historical record but included as a tongue-in-cheek reference to a similar scene in *The Public Enemy* (1931) where Cagney lets his moll (May Clarke) have it in the face with a grapefruit. But Corman goes his homage one feminist step better by having Hale reciprocate by kneeing Segal in the groin.

Also, although the Chicago mobs certainly didn't stint in their efforts to try and rub each other out, the spectacular gunplay and widespread carnage in the film by the gangsters' preferred weapon of mass destruction, the tommy gun, suggests a war zone like Bosnia or Kosovo where going about one's daily business would have been impossible, rather than a functioning city, which is what Chicago was. In this regard, the film is much like the Howard Hughes/Howard Hawks *Scarface*.

On the whole, though, *The St. Valentine's Day Massacre* is probably the most factual Capone film yet made—even in spite of the physical miscasting of the tall, slim, and Irish Jason Robards as the beefy Italian mobster. Corman had wanted Orson Welles for Capone and Robards for Moran, but Fox nixed Welles, and Robards stepped in to fill Capone's shoes. Ralph Meeker was then given the part of Moran. The rest of the impressive cast consists of leading character actors and Fox contract players of the day, as well as alumni of previous Corman films, including Jack Nicholson, Dick Miller, Jonathan Haze, Betsy Jones-Moreland, and Barboura Morris, all of whom appear in bit parts without screen credit.

Known mostly for his output of drive-in horror and science fiction pictures during the heyday of that genre, the 1950s and '60s, the prolific Corman had made several lower-budget gangster films before *The St. Valentine's Day Massacre*, such as *Machine Gun Kelly* and *I, Mobster* (both 1958). *Machine Gun Kelly*, the better of the duo, is a highly fictionalized biopic of the low-rent, Depression-era bank robber who gave the feds their enduring nickname of "G-Men." It remains noteworthy as the film that gave stalwart movie tough guy Charles Bronson his first starring role.

I, Mobster, on the other hand, began as a paperback original published by Gold Medal books in 1951 to capitalize on the sensational Kefauver hearings into organized crime that were being televised. In the manner of Owen Kildare's *My Mamie Rose* and Charles Francis Coe's *Me, Gangster*, published earlier in the century, it purported to be the personal revelations of a Lower East Side slum kid who grew up to be a gangster—in this case, a top NYC crime boss. Hyped as a precaution to protect the author's identity, and thus his safety, the book is ascribed to "Anonymous." In fact, *I, Mobster*'s so-called "true confessions of a Mr. Big in America's crime cartel" were the work of pulp fiction writer Joseph Hilton Smyth (1901–1972), whose other novels in a similar, exploitative vein include *Angels in the Gutter* (1955, published under his pseudonym, Joseph Hilton) and *The Sex Probers* (1967). The film version of *I, Mobster*, which took seven years to reach the screen and was ultimately produced, one suspects, to capitalize on the sensational new set of televised hearings into labor racketeering by the McClellan Committee, deals with a mobster (vaguely reminiscent of Capone, as well as every other gangster ever portrayed on the screen) who rises from street punk to the top of the NYC underworld by murdering a syndicate chieftain named Moran (Grant Withers), then falls precipitously when he's called to testify before a senate committee, and gets rubbed out because he knows too much.

The doomed mobster, who realizes in the end that he's nothing more than a cheap hoodlum with a taste for fancy clothes, is played well by Steve Cochran, a specialist at the time in cad roles demanding looks and charm. Today, Corman considers *I, Mobster* to be little more than a conventional gangster picture. It does, however, offer an unusual twist on the age-old gangster movie cliché of the bad guy who is redeemed by the love of a good woman. Here, the bad guy drags the good woman (Lita Milan) down to his scummy level.

In 1975, Corman essentially remade *The St. Valentine's Day Massacre* as *Capone*. Directed by Steve Carver, with Ben Gazzara playing a cross between Rod Steiger and Marlon Brando's jowly Godfather in the title role, the remake relies heavily for many of its scenes—action and period shots in particular—on stock footage from the earlier film. As with *I, Mobster*, one again suspects that the film was made to capitalize on something else—in this case the success of Francis Ford Coppola's two *Godfather* films of 1972 and 1974. It is striking, however, to watch the original *St. Valentine's Day Massacre*, which was made six years before the Coppola films, in tandem with those films. In doing so, one notes a small but definite influence on Coppola's sprawling big-budget gangster sagas of Corman's small-budget gangster epic in terms of atmosphere and attention to period detail. This influence, perhaps, isn't so surprising because Coppola did get his start as a filmmaker in the early 1960s working with Roger Corman, and he subsequently cast his mentor in a cameo role as a congressional investigator in *The Godfather Part II*.

Roger Corman resurrected the Big Fella for the last time (as of this writing!) in *Dillinger and Capone* (1995), directed by Jon Purdy from a fanciful screenplay by Michael B. Druxman, for which Corman acted as executive producer. The film trades on the urban legend that it wasn't Dillinger who was killed outside Chicago's Biograph theatre on July 22, 1934, but someone else—a wringer for the notorious bank robber (Martin Sheen) who is mistakenly gunned down by the feds instead of the real McCoy. Meanwhile, the real Dillinger uses the lucky (for him) case of mistaken identity to his benefit by giving up his criminal career so that he can retire to a quiet life of anonymity. Capone (F. Murray Abraham) knows the truth, however, and coerces the bank robber out of retirement to pull one last, spectacular heist for the mob.

Clearly, Corman had neither accuracy nor authenticity in mind with this entry in his canon of Capone movies, as the real Dillinger was indeed shot and killed outside the Biograph that night, and Scarface was in prison serving his sentence for tax evasion when the shootout occurred.

Ironically, it was not the prolific, constantly repackaging, and ever-recycling Corman but Larry Cohen, another maestro of exploitation cinema, who seized upon the idea of offering moviegoers an African-American version of the enduring Al Capone saga. *Black Caesar* (1973), as the film is called, followed on the heels of such other popular black-themed, black-oriented crime movies of the period as *Shaft* (1971) and *Superfly* (1972)—and, perhaps, was inspired to be made also by the runaway success of *The Godfather*. It chronicles the bloody rise and fall of a shoeshine boy turned mobster named Tony Gibbs who becomes the "Godfather of Harlem" (an apt title for the film, as well).

"Nobody had ever made a black gangster movie with an Edward G. Robinson type character. Suit and tie, hat, a real Edward G. Robinson guy,"[10] said football-star-turned-actor Fred "The Hammer" Williamson, who plays Gibbs and claims to have provided director Cohen with the idea for the film, which became one of the year's top money-makers, earning $2 million in North America alone, a tidy sum back then. Its success spawned a slew of black-themed gangster films such as *Hell up in Harlem* (1973), *Truck Turner* (1974), *Foxy Brown* (1974), and *Bucktown* (1975) during the golden age of what has since come to be known as the black exploitation (a.k.a., "blaxploitation") film. This 1970s phenomenon spawned such descendants as *I'm Gonna Get You Sucka!* (1988), a hilarious spoof of the "blaxploitation" film formula by Keenan Ivory Wayans, and *Original Gangstas* (1996), writer-director Larry Cohen's very entertaining, tongue-in-cheek, but sincere homage to the subgenre he helped create. In the Cohen film many stars of the classic "blaxploitation" cycle were reunited, including Richard Roundtree, Jim Brown, Ron O'Neal, Pam Grier, and "the Hammer" himself, Fred Williamson.

Elmer Booth's "Snapper Kid" puts the moves on virginal Lillian Gish in order to drug her, then sell her into a life of prostitution. From D. W. Griffith's 1912 two-reeler *Musketeers of Pig Alley*, the film that established most of the basic ground rules of the American gangster picture.

Illiterate hoodlum until age thirty, reformed citizen, and an acclaimed author five years later: Owen Frawley Kildare, whose autobiography *My Mamie Rose* became the subject of Raoul Walsh's *Regeneration* (1915), the first feature-length gangster movie made in America.

The plot of the young criminal reformed by the love of a good woman became a staple of many gangster movies in the twenties. Here the plot is trotted out again for *Fools' Highway* (1924), a loose remake of *Regeneration*, starring Mary Philbin (on settee) as the good woman and Pat O' Malley (in dark jacket, "collared" by police) as her gangland lover who wants to go straight.

Director Raoul Walsh reworked the *Regeneration* formula in his last underworld drama of the silent era—*Me, Gangster* (1928), drawn from another fact-based story of a young hoodlum who'd turned his life around to become a noted writer and reformer, Charles Francis Coe.

A stoolie witness (Howland Chamberlain) gets the nothing-personal-just-business end of a gun in blacklisted writer-director Abraham Polonsky's hard-hitting yet poetic "mouthpiece movie" *Force of Evil* (1948), based on the sprawling novel *Tucker's People* by socialist writer Ira Wolfert. (Copyright© 1948, Loew's Inc.)

Lon Chaney's psychotic "lord and master of the underworld" in *The Penalty* (1920) is a *Little Caesar* and *Phantom of the Opera* rolled into one violent package.

Lon Chaney had one of his best gangster movie roles in Jack Conway's *While the City Sleeps* (1928) playing against type. He appears not as a mobster, but as a veteran Irish cop in New York City's plainclothes division who suffers from chronically sore feet and, despite his gruff exterior, a sentimental and lonely heart.

Escaped from death row for only an hour, gangster "Bull" Weed (George Bancroft) gives himself up to police in Josef von Sternberg's Academy Award–winning *Underworld* (1927). "There was something I had to find out," the gangster tells his captors. "And that hour was worth more to me than my whole life."

Underworld was such a hit for Paramount that the studio teamed stars George Bancroft (here with Leslie Fenton) and Evelyn Brent with writer-director Josef von Sternberg for a follow-up, *The Drag Net* (1928), a gangster picture full of "weird ideas," noted *Variety*. The film is presumed lost.

Another lost film, William A. Wellman's *Ladies of the Mob* (1928) starred "It" girl Clara Bow as the daughter of a gangster executed for murder, who is raised by her embittered mother to become a criminal in order to "get even" with the law.

Phyllis Haver as the publicity mad Roxie Hart, Victor Varconi (to her left) as Roxie's sap of a husband Amos, and Robert Edeson as flamboyant mouthpiece Billy Flynn in the rare first film version of Maurine Dallas Watkins' fact-based satire *Chicago* (1927). It would be a source of the hit Broadway musical and 2002 film of the same title which breathtakingly evokes the spirit of corruption, spin, and sin of Al Capone's Chicago during gangland's golden age better than any gangster movie without gangsters ever made.

"We rob banks." Faye Dunaway makes a sexy fashion statement in between bank jobs as the real-life Bonnie Parker in Arthur Penn's still-controversial *Bonnie and Clyde* (1967), a project that was kicking around a disinterested Hollywood for years until producer-star Warren Beatty got his hands on it. (Copyright © 1967 Warner Bros.)

Sexy and smart with no trace of vulnerability: Marie Windsor, the quintessential noir babe. Here, in Richard Fleischer's *The Narrow Margin* (1952), she's a moll witness to a mob killing under the protection (not that she needs it) of cop Charles McGraw. (Copyright © 1952 RKO Radio Pictures, Inc.)

From her trace of some sexy but indefinable foreign accent, her dreamy way of talking (a hint the character may be on drugs), mixture of strength and vulnerability and "come hither" eyes to her scarlet, perfectly shaped mouth, Gaby Rodgers radiates "bombshell"—literally—in Robert Aldrich's *Kiss Me Deadly* (1955), opposite Ralph Meeker. (Copyright © 1955 United Artists)

Thomas Meighan's incorruptible cop Captain McQuigg and Louis Wolheim's dapper bootlegger Nick Scarsi (a character patterned on Al Capone) square off in Lewis Milestone's censor-plagued film of Bartlett Cormack's incendiary gangland melodrama *The Racket* (1928), which was banned from release in Chicago for almost 20 years.

Paul Muni (right) as the Capone figure Tony Camonte with Osgood (father of Anthony) Perkins as the Torrio figure in the Howard Hughes production of *Scarface* (1932), another look at the violent Chicago underworld that caused as much trouble with the censors as Hughes's 1928 silent exploration of gangland, *The Racket*. (Copyright © 1932 United Artists)

Eliot Ness (Kevin Costner) stakes out the Chicago train station to nab Capone's book-keeper for the feds in *The Untouchables* (1987), and is faced with saving a woman and her baby from getting hit in the crossfire, a set piece inspired by the classic Odessa Steps sequence from Sergei Eisenstein's *The Battleship Potemkin* (1925), transposed to gang-land. (Copyright © 1987 Paramount Pictures Corp.)

Edward G. Robinson as W. R. Burnett's Caesar Enrico Bandello, nicknamed Rico, threat-ens pal Douglas Fairbanks, Jr. and Glenda Farrell in *Little Caesar* (1931). "The most naïve vanity seems to be the moving spirit of *Little Caesar*," noted *The New Yorker* of Robinson's gangster film persona. (Copyright © 1931 Warner Bros.)

Edward G. Robinson as *The Last Gangster* (1937), a rare excursion by the actor away from his Warner Bros. home to play a green-eyed mobster for another studio, MGM. (Copyright © 1937 Metro-Goldwyn-Mayer)

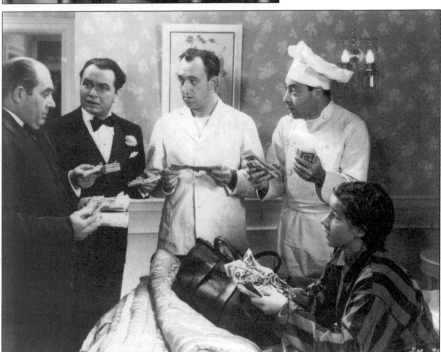

Many of Edward G. Robinson's best gangster films were comedies wherein he not only poked fun at the style of movie gangster he personified, but was able to expand upon that persona in ways his more dramatic parts didn't seem to allow. From *A Slight Case of Murder* (1938), arguably the funniest of his gangster comedies. (Copyright © 1938 Warner Bros.)

George Raft, Edward G. Robinson's contemporary and chief imitator in the dressed to kill department, plays the vain "Spats" Colombo, mastermind of the St. Valentine's Day Massacre, in Billy Wilder's farcical nod to the gangster movies of the thirties, *Some Like It Hot* (1958). The part was originally offered to Robinson. (Copyright © 1958 United Artists)

Peter Falk leads a cadre of greedy mob misfits, all of whom wind up in the clink, in *The Brink's Job* (1978), William Friedkin's under-appreciated docudrama with comedy about the notorious 1950 break-in of the Brink's payroll and securities-company in Boston. (Copyright © 1987 Dino De Laurentiis Productions)

Sadistic and delighting in violence, anarchic, ruthless and unsentimental: all are words conveyed by this 1939 studio portrait photo of the actor to describe the type of gangster defined on screen by James Cagney. (Photo by Scotty Welbourne)

Billed by the studio as "Hollywood's Most Famous Bad Man," James Cagney (center with white scarf) went straight (well, sort of) as a member of the Department of Justice in *G-Men* (1935) to pacify the country's moral crusaders upset by his series of roles as violent, remorseless gangster "heroes." (Copyright © 1935 Warner Bros.)

"Made it, Ma! Top of the world!" James Cagney goes out big time as the "mug to end all mugs," Cody Jarrett, in Raoul Walsh's apocalyptic gangster film, *White Heat* (1949). (Copyright © 1949 Warner Bros.)

Richard Widmark (center) made his film debut playing a psychopathic gangster in the Cagney mold in *Kiss of Death* (1947). (Copyright © 1947 Twentieth Century Fox Film Corporation)

In the 1931 The Public Enemy, gangster James Cagney let moll Mae Clarke have it the kisser with a grapefruit, but a lot had changed when the 1950s rolled around. Here, moll Gloria Grahame shows sadistic hood Lee Marvin the fruits of his handiwork on her face from a boiling pot of coffee in Fritz Lang's *The Big Heat* (1953). (Copyright © 1953 Columbia Pictures Industries)

Ronald Reagan with Angie Dickinson in his last movie role, and only one as a villain, in Don Siegel's remake of *The Killers* (1964). It's not every day that audiences get to see a future President of the United States roughing up his moll. (Copyright © 1964 Universal Pictures Corp.)

Escaped convict Duke Mantee (Humphrey Bogart) and his gang hold Leslie Howard, Bette Davis (seated at Bogart's right), and others hostage until he can make his getaway in *The Petrified Forest*. Warner Bros. wanted Edward G. Robinson for the gangster role, but star Howard refused to make the picture without Bogart. (Copyright © 1936 Warner Bros.)

Rushing toward death: Humphrey Bogart as an older, more world-weary version of Duke Mantee—the doomed "Mad Dog" Roy Earle in *High Sierra* (1941). The character is loosely based on bank robber John Dillinger. (Copyright © 1941 Warner Bros.)

Granite-jawed newcomer Lawrence Tierney starred as the notorious bank robber in Hollywood's first outright biopic (albeit a fanciful one) *Dillinger* (1945).

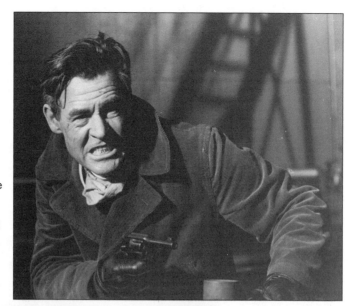

Taller, more muscular, more sinister than Bogart and more combustible than Alan Ladd, Robert Ryan, shown here as the racist gangster in *Odds Against Tomorrow* (1959), played more downright rotten bastards on the screen than either of them. (Copyright © 1959 United Artists)

Gangsters Sterling Hayden, Brad Dexter, Louis Calhern, and Sam Jaffe congratulate each other on the results of a job well done in the successful-heist-soon-to-go-wrong classic *The Asphalt Jungle* (1951) directed by John Huston from the book by W. R. Burnett.

The only syndicate kingpin ever to get the juice, Murder Incorporated's Louis Lepke Buchalter (Tony Curtis) goes to his well-deserved reward in *Lepke* (1975). (Copyright © 1975 Warner Bros, Inc.)

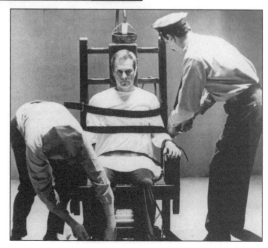

One mobster's family: organized crime kingpin Vito Corleone marries off his only daughter in between taking care of family business in *The Godfather* (1972). From left to right: Robert Duvall (Tom Hagen), Tere Livrano (Theresa Hagen), John Cazale (Fredo Corleone), Gianni Russo (Carlo Rizzi), Talia Shire (Connie Corleone), Morgana King (Mama Corleone), Marlon Brando (Vito Corleone), James Caan (Sonny Corleone), and Julie Gregg (Sandra Corleone). (Copyright 1972 Paramount Pictures, Inc.)

Robert De Niro as the young Vito Corleone in *The Godfather Part II* (1974). He grows his criminal empire by operating on animal cunning like the Cagney gangster in a world where *la vendetta* is the natural order of things and where only the strong can survive. (Copyright © 1974 Paramount Pictures Corporation)

Al Pacino as Michael Corleone in *The Godfather Part II* (1974). Echoes of the Bogart gangster, fated as if from birth to walk alone, he loses everything in the end, including his soul. (Copyright © 1974 Paramount Pictures Corporation)

Godfather-to-be Michael Corleone delivers some payback to two of the men involved in the attempted murder of his father in *The Godfather* (1972). (Copyright © 1972 Paramount Pictures Corporation)

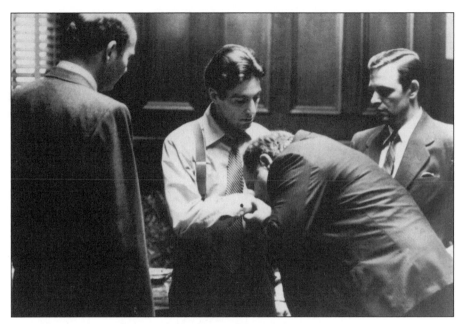

Michael (Al Pacino) shuts the door on his wife Kay and his youthful dreams of not being part of the family business when he assumes leadership of the Corleone criminal empire in *The Godfather* (1972). It was Paramount production chief Robert Evans who insisted upon this powerful close. (Copyright © 1972 Paramount Pictures Corporation)

"Noodles" Aaronson (Robert De Niro) returns to his Lower East Side roots after a stretch in prison in *Once Upon a Time in America* (1984), Sergio Leone's epic poem to the American cinema in general and the American gangster picture in particular, based on the novel *The Hoods* by onetime mobster Harry Grey. (Copyright © 1984 The Ladd Company)

7

The Green-Eyed Mobster

"Rico was standing in front of the mirror, combing his hair
with a little ivory pocket comb. Rico was vain of his hair.
It was black and lustrous, combed straight back from
his low forehead and arranged in three symmetrical waves.
Rico was a simple man. He loved but three things:
himself, his hair and his gun."

—W. R. Burnett,
Little Caesar (the novel), 1929

DRESSED TO KILL

A LTHOUGH IT REFERS TO A GENTLEMAN THIEF and not the sort of
fashion-plate, streetwise criminal represented by Rico Bandello
that we generally think of when we hear the word "gangster," the
title of a popular silent-era gangster film called *Dressed to Kill* (1928)
succinctly tells us what drives the Bandello-style of gangster, one of the
movies' Big Three types: the thug with a yen, indeed a hunger, for dressing to the nines because to him fancy clothes and all that go with them
make the man.

Variety's typically incisive review of March 14, 1928, its slangy prose
perhaps inspired by the picture itself, offers a good depiction of the fantasy view of this type of screen gangster: "[The] whole story is told against
a background of elegance. [The] master crook lives in a mansion. The
crook's crimes are always graceful and unhurried, symphonies of social

grace, which lend them a disarming attractiveness. Even at the end when the hero gives himself up to the machine gun fire of the gangsters to save the girl, he does it in the same debonair fashion, and drops dead before a billboard reading 'You Can't Win,' an impeccable figure in faultless evening dress."

The reality is harsher and more sordid, however, as this type of screen gangster is ruled by envy, grandiosity, greed, and the need to satisfy these feelings by whatever means necessary. They are the key to his survival, the sum and substance of his life, the mirror in which he sees himself whole.

The personification of this type of gangster on the screen is Edward G. Robinson. Beginning with his characterization of Rico Bandello in *Little Caesar*, every green-eyed mobster ruled by envy, grandiosity, and greed in the movies ever since is but a variation.

"MOTHER OF MERCY, IS THIS THE END OF RICO?"

Edward G. Robinson was born Emanuel Goldenberg in Bucharest, Romania, in 1893. His family came to the United States in 1902 and settled in New York City. After attending City College of New York and the American Academy of Dramatic Arts, "Manny," as his friends called him all his life, legally changed his name to the more Anglo-Saxon–sounding Edward G. Robinson in order to pursue a career in the mainstream theater where, in those days, ethnicity tended to close doors more often than open them.

He made his stage debut in 1915 in a play called *Under Fire*, where he had a small role as a French soldier. A year later, he made his film debut with a walk-on as a Hungarian émigré in the silent five-reeler *Arms and the Woman* (1916), a film that appears not to have survived. Scores of stage appearances as a variety of ethnic types and another small part opposite Richard Barthelmess and Dorothy Gish in the 1923 silent *The Bright Shawl* followed before Robinson finally hit pay dirt playing gangster Nick Scarsi in Bartlett Cormack's controversial *The Racket*. The 1927 play was a Broadway smash, and so was Robinson, whose performance as the dapper Italian-American mobster modeled on Chicago's Al Capone (albeit a more sophisticated version of Capone) was singled out by New York critics as being a marvelously realized creation of character. Ironically, it was the only gangster role Robinson ever played on stage.

Although Robinson lost out in getting the part of Nick Scarsi in the film version of the play (see Chapter 6), movie producers were soon knocking on his door to play other gangster roles for them. In *The Hole in the Wall* (1929), his first talkie, Robinson plays the Fox, a dapper, Scarsi-like ringleader of a gang of thieves and con artists posing as spiritualists. In *Night Ride* (1930), he plays another racketeer, again in the Scarsi mold, nailed by a crusading reporter (Joseph Schildkraut). Then director Tod Browning cast him as the Chinese-American Cobra Collins in the remake of the popular Browning-Chaney silent gangster film *Outside the Law* (1930). Asian or not, Robinson's characterization in the film is still more Nick Scarsi than Rico Bandello.

Robinson shifted to a new studio, Warner Brothers, his home for many years to come, for his next gangster picture, *The Widow from Chicago* (1930). In it he plays a dapper night club impresario and cutthroat beer baron named Dominic whose dour looks the heroine (Alice White), who is out to revenge her husband's murder by the mobster, likens to "the heavy in *Way Down East,*" the title of a popular nineteenth-century stage melodrama successfully filmed by D. W. Griffith in 1923. A heavy he may be, but he's still a heavy in the tradition of Nick Scarsi. Determined to keep doing things the way he's always done them—*his way*—he snarls lines like, "You nor nobody else in town can tell me where to get off!"

Movie reviewers were taking notice of this repetition in Robinson's gangster pictures of his most famous stage characterization and started describing them as being "in the best Nick Scarsi manner." It was time for a change.

Although Robinson was dismissive of *The Widow of Chicago* and of himself in it, his strong supporting performance as Dominic, which reviewers summed up as "a vivid and striking portrait of a coldly malignant killer," is very likely what prompted Warner Brothers and director Mervyn LeRoy to give him the starring role as another cold-blooded killer in the studio's *Little Caesar* (1930), wherein Robinson finally cast off the shadow of Nick Scarsi.

The scene in *Little Caesar* where Rico meets mob boss Diamond Pete and scrutinizes the well-heeled big shot from head to toe the way some men eye a woman neatly spells out the difference between Rico and Scarsi in a nutshell. The hungry look on Rico's face shows us his admiration for what Diamond Pete represents yet displays his contempt for the man at the same time. It is a look of unbridled envy coupled with mistrust and loathing ("He ain't so much!"); deep down, Rico *knows* that Diamond

Pete is a false idol. When Rico overthrows Pete and dons his trappings, believing they will turn him into a *true idol*, he finds they are only as illusory on him as on Pete, and just as easily snatched away. The film's classic finale, where he's gunned down dressed like a bum to escape the police, finds him wondering incredulously what the hell happened, and what it all meant: "Mother of mercy, is this the end of Rico?"

In his review of the film, *The New Yorker* critic John Mosher noted of Robinson's defining performance as Rico, the characterization that would firmly establish his gangster persona on the screen: "The most naïve vanity seems to be the moving spirit of Little Caesar. His eyes glitter at the sight of a scarf pin in the tie of a superior, and nothing will stop him until he has then disposed of that gentleman and assumed his leadership and his jewels. When he reaches high pinnacles where he must don a dinner coat, with spats, he is fearful that he looks a fool yet is fascinated by the elegance of his own appearance."

This is the key element that distinguishes Robinson's gangster persona from those of the other two members of the genre's pantheon elite: James Cagney and Humphrey Bogart. He's a killer, yes, but he's not a clever, homicidal crazy like Cagney or a desperate loner looking to break free of his self-made cage like Bogart. In many ways, he is, as *The New Yorker* critic suggests, a *fool* (even to himself), and thus less of a tragic figure than a *comic* one. This may be why many of Robinson's best gangster films following his star-making turn in *Little Caesar* are, in fact, outright comedies wherein he not only pokes fun at the Rico style of movie gangster he personified, but which also further explore and define that persona in ways his more serious portrayals of gangsters oddly prevented him from doing.

In his autobiography, *All My Yesterdays*, Robinson speculated upon his Rico characterization by suggesting that if Rico had expended his energies in other ways, and had not always followed the criminal tendency of pursuing short cuts, he might actually have achieved his dreams of being a great, great fellow. As if to prove this point, Bugs Ahearn, the gangster character Robinson plays in *The Little Giant* (1933), the first of his mob comedies, does just that.

Beer baron Bugs is a kinder, gentler version of Rico, but with just as many rough edges. When Prohibition is repealed, he decides to close up shop and retire as a millionaire gentleman. He's already begun preparing himself to go straight and mingle with the upper classes by reading Plato (whom he calls Pluto) and steeping himself in music and art. "I'm just crawlin' with culture," he says, pointing out the lack of perspective in an abstract painting he's just bought.

After liquidating his assets, he pays off his gang and heads for the West Coast, where he rents a Santa Barbara mansion complete with servants and hires the attractive young woman (Mary Astor) who leased him the place to be his personal secretary, unaware that she'd been forced to put the house on the market to get out from under a mountain of debt piled up by her late father, the victim of a phony stock deal.

Meanwhile, a svelte high-society dame (Helen Vinson) catches the eye of the former gangster, and he sets his sights on marrying her. However, Vinson and her family scorn the posturing ruffian as a joke—worse still, a joke with no money. Until they discover he's a millionaire. Unaware that Vinson and her family are frauds—in fact, it was Vinson's papa (Berton Churchill) who was behind the phony stock deal that ruined Astor's father, Robinson proposes marriage, and Vinson accepts—intending to divorce him after the ceremony and collect a hefty settlement.

The truth comes crashing in on Robinson when his prospective father-in-law unloads a fraudulent investment company on him, and the retired gangster finds himself in trouble with the law again, this time for selling bad bonds. Realizing he's been had by Vinson and her family, he strikes a deal with the DA (John Marston) to set everything straight, rings up his old gang, and orders them to fly to California to help him. (In an amusing shot, we see them priming themselves for action by polishing their machine guns on the plane.) "I got in over my head," Robinson tells them in a moment of self-reflection that might have profited Rico Bandello; then he turns them loose as enforcers to sell the phony bonds back to Vinson's old man, the fraudulent investment company's chiseling board of directors, and everyone else involved in the swindle.

In a surprising departure from the film's otherwise-comic tone, during these scenes one of the gang gruesomely tortures a recalcitrant board member into buying the bonds by holding a lighted cigar to the man's foot! The film then returns to being a comedy-fantasy as the money that flows in puts Robinson's company in the black, and he pays back everyone who was bilked by Vinson and her family, including his personal secretary, whom he subsequently marries when he realizes he was in love with her all along.

An amusing satire of the evolving Warner Brothers–style of gangster film in general and elements of *Little Caesar* in particular, *The Little Giant* is at its funniest in its opening scenes, where Robinson's crude,

Rico-like mob boss with pretensions to culture and respectability lays out his plans for storming high society. It tends to go a bit flat, however, when the locale shifts to the West Coast and the former gangster finds himself being taken for a ride—literally in one scene where he attempts to play polo and keeps falling off his horse.

Even while playing his gangster character for laughs, however, Robinson sharply retains his grasp on that character; particularly in the scenes with Astor (who sees him for what he is, and loves him for it), he adds greater resonance to the kind of green-eyed mobster *Little Caesar*'s Rico and *The Little Giant*'s Bugs Ahearn represent. The Robinson gangster may be a fool guided by envy, grandiosity, and greed—but he's also human and vulnerable, and not wholly incapable of doing the right thing. Some of Robinson's later gangster pictures of a more serious nature make the same point, notably *The Last Gangster* (1937), a rare excursion away from Warner Brothers to MGM, in which he plays a mob kingpin who, like Capone, is sent up the river on an income-tax charge and loses his criminal empire, as well as his wife and son. When he's released ten years later, he finds that his wife has remarried, and he vows revenge. A former crony (Lionel Stander) persuades him to reunite the old gang, but this is merely a ruse to get Robinson to reveal the whereabouts of some long-hidden loot. When the gang gets the money, Robinson is left holding the bag, and he swears revenge. In the somewhat syrupy end, though, Robinson's character does the right thing. He leaves his happily resettled wife and child alone, forswears vengeance against his former gang, and goes to his death a hero in the best tradition of Robinson's second-tier competitor in the green-eyed mobster division of Hollywood gangster movies, George Raft, when he's killed in a shoot-out with a former rival out to settle an old score.

More consistently funny than *The Little Giant*, even though screenwriters Jo Swerling and Robert Riskin (adapting the material from the story *Jail Breaker* by the ubiquitous W. R. Burnett) tend to telegraph too many of their jokes (as well as plot twists) ahead of time, is director John Ford's *The Whole Town's Talking*, a Robinson gangster comedy of 1935. In it, the actor plays dual roles: a meek office clerk with dreams of making it big as a writer and marrying his attractive coworker (Jean Arthur), and Killer Mannion, a look-alike gangster recently escaped from prison. Mistaken for the on-the-lam mobster, Robinson's meek clerk is arrested along with Arthur, whom the cops believe to be his moll. The mistake is cleared up, and the DA (Arthur Baron) gives Robinson a letter of passport substantiating his identity in case he's ever mistakenly picked up again.

Seeing a good human-interest story in all of this, an ambitious newspaper reporter (Wallace Ford) cooks up a scheme to have Robinson byline a series of derogatory articles about his villainous look-alike. Celebrating his lucky break into professional writing, Robinson pokes fun at his hard-drinking, cigar-chomping image as Rico by having his meek clerk with delusions of Rico choke on the booze and the smoke, which he's experiencing for the first time. Significantly, as the character gets progressively drunker and more used to the alcohol and cigar smoke, the more he starts to look and even behave like his alter-ego in the film, Killer Mannion (as well as Mannion's cinematic antecedent, Rico Bandello), further suggesting that there's a bit of the green-eyed mobster in the clerk and, perhaps, in all of us.

When the drunken Robinson stumbles home, he actually finds Mannion in the room waiting for him. The mobster coerces his look-alike into handing over the letter of passport so that Mannion can move freely about town, robbing banks to finance his get-away plans, while never being suspected. The seamless split-screen photography allowing the two Robinsons to interact with each other in the same shot, and even have one Robinson (as Mannion) intimidate the other by blowing cigar smoke into his face, is utterly convincing, and quite amazing for its time.

In the end, Robinson's meek clerk realizes that in order to bring down Mannion, he must summon the nerve of a mobster and take matters into his own hands. Consistent with the film's comic tone, as well as its dual identity theme, he tricks Mannion's gang into believing *he's* the real Mannion and orders them to shoot the actual Mannion, whom he insists is the look-alike clerk, on sight. He thus brings the charade to a close; collects the reward posted for Mannion's capture "dead or alive"; has the gang rounded up, adding to his celebrity; and wins the love of Jean Arthur. The British title of *The Whole Town's Talking* is perhaps even more effective in communicating the film's theme, as well as summing up the central thread that runs throughout the Robinson-style gangster picture: *Passport to Fame.* (The film was loosely remade in 1940 as *So You Won't Talk* as a vehicle for comic Joe E. Brown—he of the large tonsils—directed by Edward Sedgwick.)

Robinson, an *auteur* among actors, carried his theme that there's a bit of Rico in all of us into some of his serious gangster films as well, including two of his best—*Bullets or Ballots* (1936) and *The Amazing Dr.*

Clitterhouse (1938), the latter coscripted by John Huston. In *Bullets or Ballots*, his character is neither a good guy nor a bad guy, but a good guy with enough of the bad guy in him to convincingly pose as one in order to get the goods on the city's top mobster (Barton MacLane). And in *The Amazing Dr. Clitterhouse*, he plays a good guy, a respected doctor studying the criminal mind, who gets so wrapped up in his research that he *becomes* the bad guy when the latent criminal inside him comes out of the closet.

As I surveyed Robinson's gangster and crime films made in the 1930s and '40s, I began to notice what struck me as a subtle and amusing visual cue to whether his character is a good guy, a bad guy, or both, that appears throughout them—a cue Robinson seems to have inserted himself, in the form of his style of dress and how he wears his hats!

In *The Whole Town's Talking*, for example, Killer Mannion, like Rico, Bugs Ahearn, and the like, is immediately identifiable as a Robinson-style gangster due to his flashy, immaculately pressed suits and stylish headgear, which he wears with the brim pulled sharply down as if to conceal his shifty eyes. As the good-guy clerk, however, Robinson's clothing is ill fitting and rumpled, his headgear looking like it came off the cheap rack at Goodwill. In his gangster, crime, and films noir (such as *Double Indemnity*, 1944) of the '30s and '40s, Robinson mostly sustained this subtle clue to the nature of his character. In *Bullets or Ballots*, for example, he's the complete fashion plate, with the brim of his pricey-looking hat pulled down when he poses as a mobster to infiltrate the city's rackets; on the other hand, his clothes are bedraggled and the brim of his dumpy five-and-dime store fedora is worn up when he's his real self, good guy cop Johnny Blake. In the comedy *A Slight Case of Murder* (1938), based on a Broadway farce by Damon Runyon and Howard Lindsay, he pushes this amusing visual ID even further.

The film opens similarly to *The Little Giant*. Prohibition has been repealed, and Robinson's beer baron gangster, here named Remy Marko, is faced with the perplexing decision of what to do next. Unlike Bugs in *The Little Giant*, Marko sees the end of Prohibition as an opportunity to expand his business because the legal availability of beer will probably generate a whole new bunch of thirsty customers. So, he orders his mob to quit the strong-arm methods and just to sell the beer to customers honestly and aboveboard. He thus becomes, in his eyes, a legitimate businessman (albeit one who can't entirely shrug off his old habits). As a result,

Robinson's character, while dressing to the nines in the manner of Rico Bandello, wears his hat with the brim pulled *straight*.

Robinson followed up the very funny *A Slight Case of Murder* (remade in 1952 as *Stop You're Killing Me* with Broderick Crawford in the Robinson role) with several more gangster comedies, among them *Brother Orchid* (1940) and *Larceny, Inc.* (1942, costarring Crawford). Even though equally amusing, *Brother Orchid* is the quirkier of the pair—and arguably the darkest of all Robinson's gangster comedies.

Again, Robinson is the fashion plate hoodlum with a taste for expensive cigars, seeking refinement and *Kultur* or, as he puts it, to: "Get what I've been born to have—*class*!" He hands his protection racket over to a subordinate (Humphrey Bogart), and dubbing himself a retired socialite-sportsman, he sets off on a world tour, during which he's chiseled out of millions by the racketeers of high society—the antique dealers and stock brokers who prey on the gullible rich. He returns home five years later, itching to take up where he left off, but finds himself on the outs with his former cronies, who blame him for abandoning them and are now under Bogart's control.

The villainous Bogart deceives Robinson's devoted girlfriend (Ann Sothern) into arranging a meeting with Robinson, ostensibly to mend fences, but actually to rub him out. Robinson is wounded but escapes death, waking up in a monastery run by the order of the brothers of the flowers outside which his body was found. This leads to the film's funniest moment as Robinson regains consciousness in bed, finds himself surrounded by the brothers in robes, and, thinking he's dead, remarks with dumbfounded amazement: "I made it! I'm in heaven!"

It is in the monastery that Robinson, who is given the name Brother Orchid on account of the flowers he's assigned to garden, ultimately finds the class that has eluded him—albeit class of a very different kind than he'd always envisioned possessing.

What makes the film so quirky as a comedy is the surprising resistance Robinson's character gives to becoming a changed man. He struggles mightily to hold on to his old habits and old ways of thinking, and for most of the film his stubborn adherence makes him almost unlikable—especially when he treats the adoring, loyal, and long-suffering Sothern so shabbily, even contemptuously, which he does virtually up to the film's final moments. Although the film is a comedy-fantasy, Robinson's transformation from self-absorbed Rico-like bad guy to altruistic Brother

Orchid occurs the way it probably would in a serious drama on the same theme. It sneaks up on him in the end.

VARIATIONS ON A RICO THEME

All sharp-dressing, tough-talking movie gangsters with a yen for the good life at any cost are offshoots of Robinson's green-eyed mobster persona. One of the first to follow in his footsteps on the screen, but adding the missing element of sex appeal to that persona, is George Raft.

Although Raft always insisted that he based his portrayals of gangsters on actual mobsters he'd known (and even become lifelong friends with, such as Bugsy Siegel) while growing up in the crime-ridden neighborhood of Manhattan known as Hell's Kitchen—and that real-life mobsters, in turn, modeled their tough-talking manner on his screen image—it's undeniable that Edward G. Robinson's codifying Rico Bandello was there first.

The son of immigrants—his father was German, his mother, whose Latin looks he inherited, was Italian—George Raft was born "Ranft" in 1895. He later dropped the "n" to make the name easier for people to say and for the press to spell. He was barely into his teens when he dropped out of school and took off on his own to make it rich. Trading on his looks, he started out as a taxi dancer, the male equivalent of a dime-a-dance girl, in dives run by the mob. Future silent-screen legend Rudolph Valentino started out in the same line of work at the same clubs; in fact, they knew each other, and even bore an uncanny resemblance. Later, as screen stars, they would have to dodge the same rumors about their early starts as taxi dancers, a synonym, said the rumors, for "gigolo," or male prostitute.

Honing his skills as a dancer and dressing to the nines to fill out the image, Raft transitioned to ballroom dancing in the white tie and tails style of Fred Astaire at New York's plusher nightspots, then toured nightclubs across the country and in Europe with his ballroom act for several years before landing his first roles on stage and in the movies, typically playing a hoofer. His supporting role as Paul Muni's bodyguard and ill-fated brother-in-law in the 1932 *Scarface* is often cited as his first screen appearance. In fact, it was his twelfth. But it was *Scarface* that led to his becoming a star of gangster and crime films, albeit a second tier one, for although Raft may have been "sexier" on the screen than Robinson, he lacked Robinson's ebullience, charm, and commanding presence and always tended to give stiff, rather one-note performances. In all probability, if director Howard Hawks hadn't suggested that Raft habitually flip a coin in *Scarface* to give his character some color and personality, the actor may have gone unnoticed in the film and never had a career as a movie gangster in the Robinson or any other mold.

Unlike Robinson, Raft was loath to play wholly unregenerate gangster types on the screen—perhaps because so many real-life gangsters were his pals. Also, he may have intuited that his Valentino-ish looks and sharp clothes were not sufficient to make audiences warm to *his* gangster characters as they did to Robinson's, no matter how ruthless and low-down they were, because of Robinson's innate likability as a performer. So, as he gained more box office clout, Raft insisted that the bad guys he played be good/bad buys with codes of honor, loyalty, and decency—and to let the bad/bad guy parts go to Humphrey Bogart, who often supported him, as well as Robinson and Cagney, in Warner Brothers gangster pictures before becoming a star in the 1940s.

For example, in *Invisible Stripes* (1939), a work of fiction drawn from a book about the problem of recidivism in prisons by Lewis E. Lawes, the real-life warden of Sing Sing from 1920 to 1941, Raft plays a man paroled from prison the same day his gangster pal Bogart finishes a five-year stretch. Determined to go straight, unlike Bogart, who is determined to get even with society for his years in stir, Raft is unable to keep a job because of being branded an ex-con. Raft's girlfriend dumps him for the same reason. Worst of all, he sees his hothead younger brother (William Holden) going down the same path that landed him in prison.

Needing to "get from rags to riches quick" so he can set Holden up in business as a garage mechanic and keep him on the straight and narrow, Raft joins up with Bogart's gang for a series of bank jobs. One of the heists goes bad, however, and Holden is mistakenly incriminated, forcing Raft between a rock and hard place: love for his sibling and loyalty to Bogart.

In *Each Dawn I Die*, released the same year, Raft plays a similarly decent sort, this time behind bars opposite James Cagney as an investigative reporter sent up the river on a frame whom Raft takes under a protective wing. Raft's gangland heavy goes out in a blaze of honor at the end, this time during a prison break triggered by the film's real bad/bad guys—the crooked bureaucrats and conniving politicians who are in the pocket of the mob.

With the aptly titled *Each Dawn I Die*, Raft, who was tired of playing gangsters, even good ones, and getting killed in the last reel, announced to the studio, "No more!" From now on, he wanted to be the tough-guy hero who was left standing at the end and who got the girl. So, he hung up his fashionable black hat, exchanged it for a fashionable white one, and insisted on playing only nice guys. At which point, his career steadily began to decline until he found himself appearing more and more often in supporting roles, often in gangster pictures, playing the same kind of heavy with a heart of gold that made him a second tier star.

A good example is the 1955 *A Bullet for Joey*, where he supports the top-billed Edward G. Robinson, a cop who enlists Raft's help in bringing to justice a bunch of low-down dirty rats worse than any racketeer—communists! In exchange for the gangster's help, Robinson promises him a fair trial, eliciting one of the funniest, thoroughly Raftian ripostes in the actor's career as a screen tough guy: "If I get a fair trial, I'm dead. What *I* need is an unfair trial."

One of Raft's most memorable gangster roles in the shadow of Robinson was also one of his last. Ironically, the part was originally offered to Robinson, who turned it down. The picture, Billy Wilder's *Some Like It Hot* (1959), remains one of the best-loved gangster come-dies of all time, and the definitive comic treatment of the familiar tale of rubes on the run from the mob—a gangster film subgenre that extends as far back as *Lights of New York* (1928) and the 1942 *Broadway,* in which Raft had starred.

Arguably the funniest gangland comedy ever made, *Some Like It Hot* is loosely based on a 1932 German comedy called *Fanfaren das Liebe* (*Fanfares of Love*) about two Depression-era musicians who don the appropriate disguises to get work in, respectively, an all-gypsy band, all-female band, and an all-black jazz band. Wilder and his co-screenwriter, I. A. L. Diamond, transposed the setting to gangland Chicago during the last years of the Roaring Twenties and the heyday of Al Capone.

In their version, down-and-out musicians Tony Curtis and Jack Lemmon have to go on the run after they witness the St. Valentine's Day Massacre, ordered here by Raft's Capone-like "Spats" Columbo and his coterie of comic thugs. They lam it to Florida disguised, respectively, as Josephine and Daphne, members of an all-girl jazz band hired to play at a resort for millionaires. Curtis falls for the band's lead singer (Marilyn Monroe) and assumes a second identity as a yachtsman and Cary Grant wannabe in order to land her. Meanwhile, "Daphne" is pursued by real millionaire Joe E. Brown, an oft-married eccentric, who is not only blind to Lemmon's charade but doesn't much care ("Nobody's perfect!") when he finds out that "she" is a he.

Some Like It Hot includes many satiric winks at the classic gangster films of the genre's golden age—as when Raft stops a young mobster from irritatingly flipping a coin in his face, growling, "Where did you learn that stupid trick?"—an amusing reference to Raft's own coin-flipping turn in the 1932 *Scarface*. Later, the irascible Raft threatens to shove a grapefruit in the puss of a mobster who's annoying him à la the classic scene in *The Public Enemy* where James Cagney lets girlfriend Mae Clarke have it in the kisser with the same fruit. There is also a typically acerbic Wilder wink in the scene where Raft's character is mowed down by a machine-gun toting assassin—played by Edward G. Robinson Jr.

Raft, who died in 1980, lived to see his own colorful life story brought to the screen in *The George Raft Story* (1961), a dubious account of the actor's rise from the dance halls of New York to near-the-top star status at Warner Brothers in the 1930s to the slow burnout of his star in the '40s and '50s. Fresh off playing a real-life gangster of the Roaring Twenties (whom Raft had probably known) in *The Rise and Fall of Legs Diamond* (1960), Ray Danton, an actor with Valentino-looks too, filled Raft's shoes in the biopic.

In *The Brink's Job* (1978), Peter Falk and his gang of green-eyed mobster misfits form a whole cadre of Robinson-style comic hoods—as did their real-life counterparts behind the notorious break-in of the Brink's payroll and securities-company in Boston on January 17, 1950, that the film authentically chronicles.

Touted as "the crime of the century," the Brink's job was pulled off by a minor Boston underworld figure named Tony Pino and eleven of his closest confederates, among them the colorful Adolphe "Jazz" Maffie and Specs O'Keefe. Although no fashion plate himself, the rumpled Pino masterminded the robbery with his associates during a two-year period, breaking into the Brink's building several times in advance to have duplicate keys made for the counting-room doors and security cages, studying the company's elaborate alarm system at the manufacturing firm where it was made, and even making copies of the uniforms worn by Brink's guards so they could slip in and out of the place unnoticed. Pino and his gang even conducted a dress rehearsal a month before the robbery right inside Brink's itself. The robbery netted the mob a cool $2.7 million—big bucks anytime, but especially in 1950.

The gang members had each agreed to keep the loot on ice for six years until the statute of limitations on the crime ran out in Massachusetts. The extraordinary discipline they had mustered in planning and executing the heist fell apart at this stage of the game, however. Disputes arose over splitting the take; several gang members believed they had been stiffed by other members, and they all began turning on one another. O'Keefe and fellow gang member Albert "Gus" Guscoria were subsequently arrested in Pennsylvania for armed robbery and sent up the river for three years. Fearing they might talk, Maffie and others began spending the loot. Neither O'Keefe nor Guscoria (who died in jail) did talk. But when O'Keefe was released and learned that Maffie had spent most of his share (he had placed it in Maffie's safekeeping while imprisoned), he demanded an extra share. Believing O'Keefe would squeal on them if not taken care of, the gang hired a hitman to kill him. After two attempts on his life, the second one almost successful, O'Keefe finally spilled his guts to the cops. Pino, Maffie, and most of the others in the gang were rounded up, tried, and sentenced to life in prison. Most of the $2.7 million was never recovered.

Although the film is drawn from Noel Behn's nonfiction account of the case, *Big Stick-Up At Brink's*, Walon Green's screenplay and William Friedkin's direction of *The Brink's Job* seem to have been inspired in equal measure by the gangster comedies of Edward G. Robinson, and by Mario Monicelli's classic Italian spoof of caper films, *Big Deal on Madonna Street* (1958), because much of the film is played for laughs.

Pino (Peter Falk) and his cadre of small-time hoods with big-time dreams of wealth and style are portrayed as a most unlikely group to pull off such a grandiose scheme, which is not far from the truth. In fact, the authorities were fully aware that Pino and his pals were casing the Brink's facility, but they ignored them in the belief that they were a bunch of fools who were too stupid to pull off such an enterprise. They had every reason for this opinion, too, because Pino's biggest job up to that time had been the knock-over of a single safe in a gumball factory, which had netted him a whopping thirteen bucks. And most of his colleagues had failed to score even that much success in their criminal endeavors.

The Brink's job would be different, though, for, as Pino spots early on, the joint's reputation for state-of-the-art security is greatly exaggerated. He confirms this by stealing a couple of bags full of cash and securities from the back of an unwatched Brink's truck. Later, he sneaks into the

Brink's garage at night to case the place, and he finds security measures there to be equally lax.

"This joint is mine. I own this place!" he remarks in cockeyed wonderment and with Robinson's flare for expressing ownership rights. "That building is asleep. [That money] is screamin' at me through the walls. It's yelling, 'Hey, Tony, come in here and grab me. Get me out o' here!'"

Together with henchmen Vinnie Costa (Pino's brother-in-law, played by Allen Goorwitz), "Gus" Guscoria (Kevin O'Connor), Sandy Richardson (Gerard Murphy), Joe McGinnis (Peter Boyle), "Jazz" Maffie (Paul Sorvino), and safecracker Specs O'Keefe (Warren Oates), Pino pulls off "the crime of the century," which director Friedkin stages in suspenseful but humorous fashion, climaxing with a fictional scene where the boys whoop and holler and roll around on a mountain of cash inside the vault.

In addition to being a good gangland comedy in the Robinson tradition, *The Brink's Job* works well also as a docudrama of the famous robbery and its aftermath because it is shot in quasi-documentary style at the actual Boston locations, including the still-standing Brink's garage on Prince Street, where the crime took place. Many of these sites had to undergo an expensive face-lift, however, to make them appear as they did back in the 1950s. The real Vinnie Costa, "Jazz" Maffie, and Sandy Richardson, the sole surviving participants in the Brink's robbery at the time of filming, served as consultants on the film.

Director William Friedkin was no stranger to the documentary or to the gangster genre. He had cut his directorial teeth shooting documentaries for the news division of WBKB-TV in Chicago, and later for David L. Wolper Productions and ABC News. His gangster film debut, *The French Connection* (1971), about a Marseilles drug cartel setting up shop in New York City, won Academy Awards for Friedkin as best director, for star Gene Hackman as best actor, and for the film as best picture. Shot in the style of a documentary too, the most memorable element of this otherwise meandering and overrated film is its classic car chase through the crowded streets of the Big Apple. It seems that this scene's sole reason for being, however, was to top Steve McQueen's equally hair-raising joyride up and down the streets of San Francisco in the much superior mob movie *Bullitt* (1968), a film on the familiar theme of tracking down the conspirators behind the mob hit of an underworld informant. *Bullitt* too is directed in documentary style (by Peter Yates) and shares the same producer as *The French Connection*, Philip D'Antoni.

If *The French Connection* is Friedkin's most overappreciated picture, *The Brink's Job* is, in my opinion, his most underappreciated. It is an extremely entertaining look back at a classic American caper, one that occasionally bordered on farce, pulled off by a bunch of foolish Rico Bandello/Bugs Ahearn/Killer Mannion wannabes. Ironically, the making of the film mirrored its subject matter and tone when, during production, some aspiring Tony Pinos in the Boston underworld absconded with several cans of the film's rushes at gunpoint, later demanding a hefty ransom for their safe return. Because the rushes were only work prints and the original negatives were in safekeeping, Friedkin refused. Unlike Pino and his gang, the thieves got nothing, but they were never caught either, nor were the stolen reels ever recovered.

On a more serious note, the embattled production became the focus of an investigation into charges of extortion involving payoffs to local mob figures connected with the Teamsters' union. Several Beantown racketeers were charged, found guilty, and sent to the slammer like their forebears in the Brink's mob—the greedy and grandiose Tony Pino and his gang.

The actor who comes closest to sharing the Robinson persona on the screen, and who shares Robinson's ability to switch effortlessly back and forth between dramatic and comic roles as gangsters, is Chazz Palminteri. His Oscar-nominated supporting performance in Woody Allen's Roaring Twenties mob comedy *Bullets Over Broadway* (1994), in fact, has Robinson's shadow all over it. As Cheech, a thug with a taste for fine clothes assigned by his mobster boss to chaperone moll Jennifer Tilly to and from rehearsals for a play the boss is bankrolling, Palminteri's performance draws a straight line to Robinson's Bugs Ahearn in *The Little Giant,* Remy Marko in *A Slight Case of Murder*, and Little John Sarto in *Brother Orchid.* Crawling with *Kultur* and talent ("They told me I had to read and write in school, before I burnt it down") he didn't know he had, Cheech picks up playwright John Cusack's highfalutin work of "art" and injects it with the in-the-street naturalism ("You don't know how people talk") it needs to come alive on stage. Come opening night, Cheech experiences all the jitters of the playwright himself as the curtain goes up, for that is what he has become.

Although *Bullets Over Broadway* is not as consistently funny as the best of Robinson's mob comedies, the performance of Chazz Palminteri as Cheech is spot-on hilarious, as well as human and touching in its exploration of character—precisely in the manner of Robinson's humorous hoods.

8
"Made it, Ma!
Top o' the World!"

"No one expresses more clearly the delights of
violence, the overtones of a semiconscious sadism,
the tendency toward destruction, toward anarchy
[than James Cagney]."
—Poet and critic Lincoln Kirstein, 1932

THE BIG SWITCH

WHEN *THE PUBLIC ENEMY* (1931) went into production on the
Warner Brothers lot, it starred Edward Woods as the vicious
title character and a virtual unknown named James Cagney
in the supporting role of Woods's underworld pal.

When the early rushes were screened, however, director William A.
Wellman discovered that the kinetic Cagney was blowing Woods off the
screen. So, he scrapped the early footage and resumed shooting with
Cagney in Woods's role, and vice versa.

Wellman's decision paid off at the box office and made gangster movie
history. It is Cagney's star-making performance as the amoral, violence-
prone, almost psychopathic public enemy incarnated in the character of
Tom Powers, that—much like Edward G. Robinson's character (and performance) in *Little Caesar*—sustains this classic early talkie gangster
film and gives it a timeless punch.

KILLER INSTINCT

James Francis Cagney was born in 1899 in the same West Side neighborhood of New York as George Raft: Hell's Kitchen. After graduating from high school, he enrolled at Columbia University to study art but had to drop out of school to help support his family. He got his introduction to show business when he joined a drama club sponsored by a local settlement house, and he went into vaudeville shortly thereafter to pursue a career as a dancer, also like Raft.

Cagney made his Broadway debut in the chorus of the 1920 musical *Pitter Patter*. He then toured the vaudeville circuit for several years before returning to Broadway in 1925 to play a hobo in the Maxwell Anderson play *Outside Looking In*, an adaptation of the novel *Beggars of Life*[1] by author Jim Tully, whose acclaimed writings of life on the American road led to the nickname "poet laureate of the hobos."

Larger roles in a variety of stage comedies, revues, and musicals followed until Cagney got noticed in the 1930 slice-of-life drama *Penny Arcade*, playing the kind of ruthless tough guy he would make indelibly his own on the screen, here a rumrunner who frames his sister's boyfriend for murder. Warner Brothers bought the screen rights to the play with the stipulation that Cagney come along to recreate his role in the film version, retitled *Sinner's Holiday* (1930); Cagney's costar in the play, Joan Blondell, came as part of the package too, largely because of Cagney's insistence.

Cagney went from *Sinner's Holiday* into his first full-fledged gangster picture for Warner Brothers, *Doorway to Hell* (1930), based on a Rowland Brown story called "A Handful of Clouds," referring to "The kind that come out of the end of a .38 automatic," explains Cagney's character in the film, whose plot is loosely based on the career of Al Capone's organizational mentor, Johnny Torrio.

Cagney plays Steve Mileaway, the top lieutenant of mobster Louis Ricarno (Lew Ayres). When Ayres decides to go straight, he turns his empire over to Cagney (as did Torrio to Capone, although there is nothing in Cagney's performance suggestive of Capone). Ayres's plans to go straight are thwarted, however, when his wife and Cagney betray him, and gang rivals murder his brother. Ayres returns to the rackets to exact revenge and ultimately seals his doom pursuing that goal.

Critics of the time were unanimous in their praise of *Doorway to Hell* and singled out Ayres and Cagney for their credible performances. In light of Cagney's subsequent superstardom playing gangster roles and Ayres's becoming the screen's kindly, caring Dr. Kildare, revisionist critics now tend to unfairly dismiss this gripping little gangster film on the basis that it would have been more compelling if Cagney and Ayres had switched roles—as occurred in Cagney's next brush with the law on film: *The Public Enemy*.

The script for *The Public Enemy* by Kubec Glasmon, John Bright, and Harvey Thew is based on ex-newspaperman Bright's unpublished "Beer and Blood," a veiled account of the quick rise and quicker fall of Chicago hoodlum Hymie Weiss, a successor to the North Side mob's assassinated leader Dion O'Banion. The same assassins belonging to the South Side Torrio/Capone mob subsequently gunned down Weiss, too. A novelization of Glasmon and Bright's script for *The Public Enemy* based on Bright's unpublished work was published by Grosset and Dunlap under both their by-lines as a Photoplay edition tie-in to promote the film's release in 1931.

The film picks up the saga of its Hymie Weiss character, Tom Powers, in 1909, when he and his pal Matt (Frank Coghlan Jr. and Frankie Darro, respectively) are kids living in the slums of an unnamed city (presumably Chicago), delivering growlers of beer to neighborhood saloons. Under the tutelage of a Shylock named Putty Nose (Murray Kinnell), they become petty thieves, then graduate summa cum laude to armed robbery. As grown ups (now played by Cagney and Edward Woods, respectively), they fall in with mobsters Paddy Ryan (Robert Emmett O'Connor), the film's Dion O'Banion figure, and Nails Nathan (Leslie Fenton), a character based on real-life O'Banion lieutenant Nails Morton, and become successful rumrunners.

A rival gang at the height of the bootleg wars kills Woods. Cagney goes vengefully amuck, killing Woods's murderers in a saloon shoot-out that we hear but don't see—a trademark of director Wellman, who liked putting the audience's imagination to work in such scenes—during which he, too, is wounded.

While Cagney is recuperating in a hospital, his upstanding older brother (Donald Cook), a World War I vet and night-school student, encourages him to get out of the rackets. Cagney agrees to return home when released from the hospital and think about it. Several days later, Cook gets a phone call letting him know that his brother is on the way. But when Cagney fails to show up, Cook begins to suspect the worst. To the accompaniment of "I'm Forever Blowing Bubbles" on the Victrola, the boys' doting mother (Beryl Mercer) euphorically prepares a room for her "baby's" return home. Suddenly there is a knock at the door. When Cook opens it, Cagney's corpse, swathed in a white hospital sheet and looking like a mummy, pitches headlong into the room in the film's disturbing last image.

Although *The Public Enemy* follows the early gangster tradition of realistically detailing the environmental conditions that give rise to criminality, it makes the case that a Tom Powers, the specific criminal at the center of this story, may be born, not made. Cagney's Powers is a fundamentally bad lot who treats everyone (with the exception of pal Woods) cruelly and opportunistically. Almost as soon as the film begins, he is shown tripping a female playmate for the hell of it as she tries out a pair of roller skates he's just given her (probably for that purpose)—skates that he'd stolen from someone else. When his policeman father (Purnell Pratt) takes a strap to him for his thievery, the young tough refuses to utter a cry, his face filling instead with hatred and contempt for his old man and for the authority he represents—an authority that seeks to curb the hoodlum's killer instincts. Freed to unleash these instincts under the lawless conditions of Prohibition, the adult Powers does just that, and becomes an even more vicious and brutal character—a killer of men and, in the film's most famous scene where he lets Mae Clarke have it in the face with a grapefruit[2], an abuser of women. Unlike the green-eyed mobster etched by Edward G. Robinson, who is motivated to kill for reasons of envy and ego, the Cagney gangster, as typified by Tom Powers, fights, robs, and kills mostly because *he likes to*.

Cagney's performance inspired raves from film critics of the day and turned *The Public Enemy*, an otherwise somewhat uneven film that wavers in tone from uncompromising toughness to almost syrupy sentimentality, into a major box office hit. Influential *New York Herald Tribune* movie reviewer Richard Wattis Jr. called it "the most ruthless appraisal of the meanness of a petty killer that the cinema has yet devised. Its central character is a homicidal little rat, and there is never any effort to show him as anything else. James Cagney plays [the character] with a simple, relentless honesty that should immediately place him among the top personages of the screen. From the time you see him engaged in his first robbery to the moment when he walks out on the girl he is about to win in order to shoot down the horse that had thrown the head of his gang, he is utterly merciless, utterly homicidal, and utterly real." The *National Board of Review* put it even more succinctly: "The real power of *The Public Enemy* ... lies in the stunning—stunning in the literal sense—acting of James Cagney."

"It Didn't Fit"

Even before *The Public Enemy* was released, Warner Brothers knew it had a new gangster star on its hands. What was more natural then than to team him with the studio's number-one gangster star, Edward G. Robinson? So, the studio did just that with *Smart Money* (1931), a gem of a gangland comedy-drama, also penned by John Bright and his writing partner Kubec Glasmon, along with Lucien Hubbard and Joseph Jackson, the authors of the original story, who earned an Oscar nomination for their work.

The terrific script full of surprising twists and turns and some of the sharpest banter in movies has Cagney playing sidekick to Robinson's Nick the Barber, the unlucky at love but lucky at cards, high-rolling operator of a string of gambling houses the city's ambitious and politically incorrect DA (he refers to Nick as a "greaseball") is determined to shut down.

Cagney's character here is as cocksure of himself as Tom Powers, and just as unsentimental in his treatment of everyone but Robinson, to whom he is consistently loyal and always gives the straight dope. But he lacks Powers's anarchic spirit and killer instinct as the tone of *Smart Money* is more Robinson-style gangster than Cagney-style. His killer instincts curbed, Cagney's character therefore gets little to do except be second fiddle to Robinson's Nick,[3] a just as grandiose and foolish but nice-guy version of Rico, whose performance steals the show.

Warner's pairing of Robinson and Cagney in what is essentially a Robinson vehicle proved how different Cagney's command of the screen (and screen persona) was from Robinson's, and that making them compete with each other in the same film only served to diminish the full power of one or the other (in this case Cagney) from coming through. The film itself acknowledges that Cagney isn't Robinson (and vice versa) in an amusing repartee that takes place at the beginning when Robinson spots Cagney sporting one of his flashy bow ties. "Say, is that my tie?" he barks, then adds sarcastically, "Why didn't you put on that new, checkered suit while you were about it?" Cagney comes back at him with the double-meaning barb, "It didn't fit."

As good as *Smart Money* is, and as good as Cagney is in it, even playing second fiddle, a Lew Ayres or an Edward Woods could have played Cagney's part in the film just as well. The studio realized it had two equally commanding but very distinct screen personalities to build films around, and neither of them needed a partner to draw big at the box office. Neither Warner Brothers nor any other Hollywood studio ever teamed Robinson and Cagney on screen ever again.

GOING STRAIGHT

> *"You dirty rat, I'm going to get rid of you just like you gave it to my brother!"*
> **—Matt Nolan (James Cagney),**
> **Taxi! (1932)**

Coupled with Robinson's *Little Caesar* and Paul Muni's *Scarface* (which was released a year after *The Public Enemy* but made at the same time), Cagney's charismatic, thoroughly vicious gangster antihero proved too much for many of the country's most influential religious and civic groups. Protesting the "glorification" of crime and violence in gangster films—Cagney's particularly—they raised the specter of state-by-state censorship with renewed vigor.

Will H. Hays, the former U.S. Postmaster General turned movie morals czar who headed up the industry's self-monitoring Motion Picture Producers and Distributors of America (MPPDA), joined the chorus of disapproval when he got wind of a proposed film to be based on the life and crimes of real-life public enemy John Dillinger, whose nefarious career had only recently come to an end when he'd been shot outside a Chicago movie theater. Hays fired off a telegram to the heads of the various studios, stating firmly, "No picture on the life or exploits of John Dillinger will be produced, distributed or exhibited by any member [of the MPPDA]. This decision is based on the belief that the production, distribution or exhibition of such a picture would be detrimental to the public interest."[4] And, of course, to the best interest of the movie industry as well, Hays hinted not so subtly.

The studios reacted by agreeing to the creation of a strict set of moral guidelines governing its films, called the Motion Picture Production Code, and they allowed that they would give a green-light to no project that had not been granted a Code Seal of Approval.

Insofar as depicting crime and violence was concerned, the Code's guidelines strictly forbade the production of any film that, in its words, might "make criminals seem heroic or justified," because this would, the

Code maintained, "inspire potential criminals with a desire for imitation." There were many other stipulations, all aimed mostly at the gangster films that, reflecting the infiltration of gangland into American life,
had begun to proliferate on America's movie screens.

Whether Robinson's high-living kingpins or Cagney's pugnacious cutthroats were guilty of inspiring potential criminals, or just other actors,
is still open to question as the debate on the impact of reel violence on
human behavior rages on. What was not open to question, however, was
that the gangster characters Robinson and Cagney played were undeni-
ably the heroes of these films (albeit antiheroes) if only because they are
the films' protagonists. It satisfied neither the Hays Office, the Code, nor
the nation's moral crusaders that Rico Bandello and Tom Powers and
their like got what they deserved come the fade out. The spotlight, the
crusaders insisted, must be shifted.

Gangster movies—especially those featuring Robinson and Cagney—
were moneymakers, however, and the movies are a business as well as an
art. So, the studios began searching for a loophole. And they found one.
"A wave of kidnappings had focused national attention on the Federal
Bureau of Investigation," noted screen censorship maven Murray Schumach. "They [the studios] now made the FBI agents the heroes, but gave
the same fat parts to the gangsters."[5]

Another way of outwitting the Code was to tone down the mayhem or
give it a slapstick twist by making gangster comedies in which mobsters
were treated as figures of fun, as in some of the post–*Little Caesar* Robinson vehicles and such pictures as *Little Miss Marker* (1934), a wholesome
comedy with a gangland milieu based on a Damon (*Guys and Dolls*) Runyon story. The film made a star out of little Shirley Temple in the title
role.

And so, in the wake of the Code's creation, Robinson and Cagney put
their gats and roscoes to work for the law instead—at least temporarily.
As you will recall from Chapter 7, Robinson took the part of an honest
New York City cop in *Bullets or Ballots*—although the studio had it both
ways by having his character pose as a gangster in the mold of Rico
Bandello, too. Meanwhile, the studio's press department announced that
Cagney, "Hollywood's Most Famous Bad Man," was going straight as a
member of the Department of Justice in *G-Men* (1935).

Cagney's Brick Davis in *G-Men* is a former slum kid and an associate of
racketeers seeking revenge for the murder of his best friend. He's offered
a job on the right side of the law as a G-Man only because the Justice

Department sees he has the right kind of connections—and tempera-
ment—to infiltrate the mob and bring it to its knees. And by taking the
job and bringing down the mob, he gets his pal's killer in the bargain.

One needn't scratch much below the surface to see that Cagney's G-
Man is temperamentally and in many other ways barely indistinguishable
from *The Public Enemy*'s Tom Powers, or from other characters Cagney
had already played who were ostensibly on the right side of the law—like
the quick with his fists hack driver Matt Nolan in *Taxi!* (1932), for example, who goes up against a syndicate with a powerful hold on the city's
taxi business to revenge his brother's death by these racketeers. Later, in
Great Guy (1936), Cagney walks a similar tightrope as a prizefighter
turned racketbuster for the government's Bureau of Weights and
Measures who uses tactics not unlike those of the racketeers he's up
against to bring them down. Cagney's tough guys simply don't feel right
going straight. They're like a picture spilling out of the frame. So, it
wasn't long before that character was back on the wrong side of the law,
where he truly belonged.

BAD TO THE BONE

> "Let's go and say a prayer for a boy
> who couldn't run as fast as I could."
> **—Jerry Connelly (Pat O'Brien),**
> **Angels with Dirty Faces (1938)**

As Rocky Sullivan in *Angels with Dirty Faces* (1938), Cagney was back
being bad—and badder than ever. Well, almost. *Angels* satisfied the Code
in a number of ways. First, it gave Cagney's vicious Rocky an upstanding
counterpart in the form of Pat O'Brien's Jerry Connelly, a childhood pal
who has chosen God over gangland. Second, it has Rocky, sentenced to
death for a life of crime, go to his death seemingly a changed man when
O' Brien persuades him to do a good deed as his last act on earth. He asks
Cagney to erase the heroic image a gang of slum kids have of Rocky as an
idealized tough guy by going to the chair a frightened, sniveling coward.
The genius of Cagney's performance—the best thing in this fast-moving
but at times somewhat mawkish melodrama—is that when his character
does break down hysterically on the way to the chair, we're not sure
whether the character's hysteria is faked or not.

Cagney's next gangster film, Raoul Walsh's expansively titled *The Roaring Twenties* (1939), was much more ambitious. It not only sought to recapture the look, sound, and feel of the bygone era it chronicles but also to chart the rise and fall of its characters from Prohibition through to the 1929 Crash. In fact, the film begins even earlier, during World War I, when star Cagney and supporting players Humphrey Bogart and Jeffrey Lynn meet in the trenches, become pals, and share with each other their postwar dreams and aspirations.

Cagney, a garage mechanic prior to becoming a doughboy, intends to get his old job back and marry Priscilla Lane as the girl who has been writing to him throughout the war, although they have never met. Lynn plans to study law. Only the surly, chip-on-his-shoulder Bogart seems destined for a life of crime, as is suggested by his shooting of an enemy soldier seconds after the armistice has been announced.

Stateside, unemployment for returning vets is running high, and Cagney is unable to get his old job back. Anticipating the real-life gangster he would play more than a decade later in the biopic *Love Me or Leave Me* (1955), he's dumped by his pen pal gal too, even though he has helped her to realize her ambition to become a singer. With the financial backing of speakeasy owner Gladys George, Cagney establishes a successful taxi business that serves as a front for an even more profitable bootleg operation, and he hires wartime pal Lynn to be his mouthpiece. Meanwhile, Bogart becomes a big-time crook and bootlegger also, and as the lawless decade rolls on, he and Cagney become business associates, then rivals.

The upright Lynn decides to go straight and joins the district attorney's staff. But he really earns Cagney's enmity when he marries Priscilla Lane, the gangster's old flame. The Crash bankrupts the high-rolling Cagney, and he finds himself a down-and-outer, driving a hack. Coincidentally, he picks up Lane as a passenger, and she begs for his help as Bogart, worried that her husband (Bogart's former mouthpiece) will use his knowledge of Bogart's illegal activities to bring the mobster down, is threatening murder.

Out of a renewed sense of loyalty and purpose—or, perhaps, like the noble hero of the Dickens classic *A Tale of Two Cities*, who yearns for a better place—the brawling and tough but inherently decent Cagney goes to bat for his wartime buddy and kills Bogart. Gunned down for his sins shortly thereafter, he expires on the snowy steps of a church as the bells symbolically ring an end to the era and to the tough-guy-in-life but redeemed-in-death Roaring Twenties character he personified.

The Roaring Twenties works so well and so seamlessly that it is hard to believe its production was such a troubled one. Three credited writers (and probably an equal number of uncredited ones, given the way the studio system operated) were required to turn the kaleidoscopic original story by Mark Hellinger[6] into a concise, workable screenplay; Walsh stepped in late as director when producer Hal B. Wallis dropped Anatole Litvak; and there were several last-minute casting changes as well. Nevertheless, none of these difficulties show on screen. The film is energetically and believably acted (especially by Cagney, and by Gladys George as the B girl who loves him) and convincingly directed by Walsh. It remains the last great gangster picture of the 1930s—the genre's golden age—and a noteworthy re-creation of the violent era it summed up, as America and the gangster and crime film moved into the even more tumultuous eras of World War II, the Cold War, and beyond.

MUG TO END ALL MUGS

> "A copper, a copper, how do you like that boys? A copper and his name is Fallon. And we went for it, I went for it. Treated him like a kid brother. And I was gonna split fifty-fifty with a copper!"
> —*Cody Jarrett (James Cagney),*
> **White Heat (1949)**

As popular as Cagney's gangster and crime films were, and as persuasive as he is in them, he often acknowledged that the genre was not really a favorite with him. He won his only Oscar playing legendary song-and-dance man George M. Cohan in *Yankee Doodle Dandy* (1942), the type of vehicle—along with *Footlight Parade* (1933) in which he also starred—the actor said he much preferred. In fact, after *Yankee Doodle Dandy,* he stored his gangster persona in mothballs for a time in order to pursue a variety of parts in a succession of comedies, dramas, and war thrillers, such as *13 Rue Madeleine* (1946), some of them made by his own company, Cagney Productions (headed by his brother William), into which the actor sunk substantial amounts of his own money. Alas, few of these Cagney-produced films scored well with the public, or the critics, and by the late 1940s, the actor wanted a hit. So, he went back to the studio and to the type of film that had made him a star in Raoul Walsh's *White Heat*

(1949), one of the hallmarks of the genre in which Cagney gives a searing performance as "the mug to end all mugs," Cody Jarrett.

Jarrett is not your average screen tough guy; he's a total psychopath whose dream of making it "to the top o' the world" in the annals of crime take on an apocalyptic significance by the end of the film as Jarrett realizes his old-style desperado methods don't stand a chance in the post-war, high-tech world of sophisticated detection devices able to track his every move and slick undercover cops who act with the cunning duplicity of the most ruthless spies.

During a train robbery at the beginning of the film, Jarrett murders the engineers in cold blood because they overhear his name and are able to identify him. To further throw off the cops, he confesses to another robbery committed at the same time in another state, but where no one was killed, and gets a minor stretch. Knowing he's guilty of the murders, the police plant undercover cop Hank Fallon (Edmond O'Brien) in Jarrett's cell to befriend the gangster and get the goods on him by helping him escape. Fallon carries out the assignment with such cold-blooded efficiency that ultimately it is the dangerous but sick Jarrett who wins our sympathy. When Jarrett discovers that Fallon, the only person beside his mother the paranoid gangster has ever allowed to get close to him, is a cop stringing him along, he loses what sanity he has left and goes violently berserk. For Fallon, however, it is not enough to have succeeded in exposing the gangster; he volunteers to be the one to shoot Jarrett down.

Wounded, Jarrett triumphantly shouts, "Made it, Ma! Top o' the world!" as he goes to his spectacular death pumping bullets into the petroleum tanks atop which he's been trapped, and he is blown to eternity in a mushroom-shaped cloud of smoke and fire—a classic moment in cinema that also stands as a frightening metaphor of the dangers of our nuclear age where there are so many Cody Jarretts out there, driven by all sorts of dark dreams.

Surprisingly, Cagney didn't think *White Heat* was that special, calling it "just another cheapjack job" and the character of Jarrett, except for his craziness, only "a cheapie one-two-three-four kind of thing."[7] But Jarrett is one of the all-time great screen antiheroes, and Cagney's incarnation of that character one of the towering performances in cinema, gangster or otherwise.

Cagney commands the screen throughout, blistering it in many individual scenes, such as the remarkable one in prison when he learns of his mother's death and goes wild with such unbridled anger and grief, screaming like a wounded animal, and starts slugging guards right and left as they try to restrain him and carry him away. But he's just as powerful in quieter moments, such as the scene where he realizes his "pal" Fallon is really an undercover cop out to get him. The look of astonishment, pain, despair, then vengeful rage that fleets across Cagney's face in a virtual instant is an example of screen acting at its best.

O'Brien's performance as Fallon is no less sturdy, and subversive, for he, the cop, is the real villain of the piece—a definite shift in tone from the gangster films of the '30s. There are times when he even fools us into believing his friendship with and concern for Jarrett are genuine, which is no mean acting trick, and when he drops the masquerade, we feel almost as disappointed, angry, and betrayed as Jarrett. Fallon's ability to pierce so coldly and efficiently the sick man's armor and to destroy him may make Fallon one helluva great undercover cop, but as a human being, he's repugnant.

Many years later, undercover work in gangland would take a very different twist. In the true story *Donnie Brasco* (1997), FBI agent Joe Pistone (Johnny Depp) goes undercover to get the goods on the Bonanno crime family during the government's 1978 crackdown on organized crime. To burrow his way inside the mob, he wins the trust and even the friendship of a low-level hitman (Al Pacino) just as Edmond O'Brien's Fallon worms his way into Cagney's confidence in *White Heat*. The difference is that Depp, whose undercover nom de crime is Donnie Brasco, actually comes to like Pacino's character. Pacino considers Depp a protégé and takes an almost brotherly interest in the lad. As Depp submerges deeper into the activities of the Bonanno mob, he starts to lose his moral bearings. The dividing line between what he is and what he pretends to be grows fainter and fainter as his loyalties become divided and as he gets hooked on the danger and anarchic freedom of the criminal lifestyle. His conscience suffers too from the knowledge that by having gained Pacino's trust and gotten the mobster to vouch for him with the Bonanno family, he has set the man up to surely get whacked when the feds close in and Depp's cover is exposed.

In this contemporary passion play set in gangland, the blood of Depp's conflicted FBI mole doesn't run as cold as O'Brien's ruthless undercover assassin in *White Heat* even though the men they must get close to in order to get their jobs done are not dissimilar. Both Pacino and Cagney are remorseless killers vulnerable to the dream of making it to the top of the world. The difference is that Cody Jarrett's dream is born out of psychosis whereas the dream of Pacino's character, who has always been a bottom feeder, is born of a need to be looked up to by at least some member of the Bonanno Family.

Donnie Brasco shows why the FBI—for much of its longevity, especially under the longtime tenure of totalitarian chief J. Edgar Hoover—went after headline-grabbing desperadoes like John Dillinger or seditious elements posing a threat to capitalist society like the communists rather than pitting its vast law enforcement resources against America's most insidious criminal network, the mob.[8] The mob was "dirty." And danger lurked in getting too close to that dirt; some of it might rub off, as it had on so many state and local police organizations since the Roaring Twenties.

Having pushed his gangster persona in *White Heat* seemingly as far as it could go and yet sustain audience loyalty, Cagney pushed it further still in his next underworld melodrama *Kiss Tomorrow Goodbye* (1950), produced by his own company for release through Warner Brothers. Here his gangster protagonist is even more vicious, scheming, paranoid, and misogynistic than Cody Jarrett, but without Jarrett's compensating mental illness. In other words, he's *completely* rotten, a thief and killer with a heart of stone, who is more "anti" and less "hero" than any antihero Cagney ever played, including Cody Jarrett. But every antihero requires an even nastier type, like Edmond O'Brien's Fallon in *White Heat*, to go up against, and unfortunately *Kiss Tomorrow Goodbye* doesn't provide one. It offers only a bunch of ruthless, morally corrupt characters that are collectively as unsavory as Cagney but lacking in his charisma.

Superior to *Kiss Tomorrow Goodbye* as a drama and even as a gangster film is MGM's *Love Me or Leave Me* (1955), the musical biography of Nebraska-born show business legend Ruth Etting (Doris Day), who rose from the ranks of Chicago chorus girls to become one of the highest-paid torch singers of the Roaring Twenties with the help of her crippled mobster husband and agent, Marty "the Gimp" Snyder. The role of Snyder offered Cagney an opportunity to shine in his last great (but not final) role as a thug with an uncontrollable temper and a thin skin prior to his retirement from the screen in the 1960s.

In the film, as in Etting's life, Cagney's obsessively domineering control over the singer drives her to drink and ultimately drives him to ruin. When she finally hits the big leagues, she swears off the booze and off Cagney, dumping him for her accompanist, John ("Myrl" in real life) Alderman, played by Cameron Mitchell, with whom she has fallen in love. In a jealous rage, Cagney shoots Mitchell, but the musician survives his wounds, keeping Cagney from facing a murder charge, but the mobster's life with Day is over. He has nothing left but a splashy new Los Angeles nightclub he's sunk all his money into, and which looks to be a white elephant even before it opens on account of all the negative publicity he's gotten over the shooting incident.

The grateful songstress publicly acknowledges her debt to Cagney, however, in the moving finale by going on, without Cagney's foreknowledge, as the headliner on opening night, turning the club's debut into a smashing success.

Ruth Etting and Myrl Alderman, who had married, and Marty Snyder were all living when *Love Me or Leave Me* was produced, and not only gave the filmmakers permission to tell their story on the screen warts and all, but even acted as technical consultants. Despite all the traditional MGM gloss layered upon it, this may be why the film has such a strong sense of authenticity both in the Jazz Age era it evokes and in the emotions it conveys. Daniel Fuchs and Isobel Lennart's incisive, often biting, and Oscar-winning script doesn't skirt around the unattractive nature of the stormy Etting/Snyder relationship—namely, that it is he, the uncultured, control-freak gangster, who, for all those faults, genuinely adores Etting, and puts himself out in every way to help her realize her career ambitions. And if Etting is a victim of Snyder's domineering ways, which clearly she is, it is also clear that her acceptance of that status quo for so long in order to get what she wanted makes her at the very least a somewhat willing one.

As Ruth Etting, Doris Day is a bit whiny during the emotional scenes, but she knows how to belt out a song, and the film lets her shine with twelve of them, many of them Roaring Twenties standards made famous by Etting herself. But the film really belongs to James Cagney, whose lacerating yet touching performance as the monstrous but somehow endearing Snyder is up there with the best of his career. A climactic scene where Day comes to the aid of the jailed mobster and offers bail money that he figuratively throws back at her with blistering pride is stingingly powerful in its ring of truth.

DIRTY RATS

"To get paid to do what you love . . . ain't that the dream?"
**—Maquire (Jude Law), hitman and photographer,
Road to Perdition (2002)**

James Cagney's distinctive tough-guy gangster with psychotic overtones has shaped the performances of many actors who have played gangsters in the modern cinema. For example, Broadway actor Richard Widmark made his screen debut in Twentieth Century Fox's noir gangster film *Kiss of Death*[9] (1947), playing a hood in the mold of Cagney's Tom Powers in *The Public Enemy*. If anything, Widmark's over-the-top performance in *Kiss of Death* even outdoes in psychotic violence the actions of Cagney's "mug to end all mugs" two years later in *White Heat*.

Widmark's wiry mob hitman, Tommy Udo, whose skeletal features suggest a grinning death's head, especially when he gets worked up, lacks the Cagney gangster's streetwise cleverness. But in the film's most famous scene, he outdoes Cagney in unfeeling brutality when, purely for fun, he shoves the elderly, wheelchair-bound mother (Mildred Dunnock) of a suspected stoolie down a flight of stairs.

Like Cagney's gangsters, Widmark's maniacal Udo has an insatiable appetite for killing and is motivated primarily by the need to have that appetite fed (it can never be satisfied). Even when relaxing at a boxing match, the blows and blood whet his appetite for more, prompting him to jump from his seat and order the fighters to "stop dancing" and tear each other up. Courtesy of the screenplay by gangster movie pioneer Ben Hecht (with Charles Lederer), Widmark even gets to spew a variation on the line of dialogue most associated with the Cagney gangster when, much in the Cagney manner, he accuses a pal who has fallen out of favor of being "a dirty little rat!"

Richard Widmark followed up his Oscar-nominated debut turn in *Kiss of Death* playing another twisted, violent gang leader in Twentieth Century Fox's *The Street with No Name* (1948) and then a pathological, racist hoodlum in the same studio's *No Way Out* (1950). After that, he transitioned full-time to playing heroic leads and antiheroes—albeit ones who quite often had a veneer of sleaze common to the villains he played in the past. A quarter of a century later, though, Widmark was back to his bad old ways as an American crime lord, now retired and on vacation traveling by train across 1930s Europe, in *Murder On the Orient Express* (1974), the screen adaptation of one of the British Queen of Crime's rare literary excursions[10] into the uncozy world of the mob.

Widmark's appropriately named character in the film is Ratchett, and his past crimes include kidnapping and murder. Unlike the Cagney-esque gangsters Widmark had played early in his career, however, the character's violent nature is more muted here—but only because the character is older and has already made all the bones he needs or wants. He was lethal enough in his day, however, to warrant becoming the victim of the titular murder, a revenge killing that Christie's redoubtable Belgian sleuth Hercule Poirot (Albert Finney), also on board, is charged with solving when the Orient Express becomes snowbound. He does so brilliantly, as always, in this ingenious mixture of traditional Christie-style whodunit combined with elements of the real-life Lindbergh baby kidnapping case of 1932 and American gangland lore.

In the 1950s, the diminutive Mickey Rooney, a fixture of many MGM musicals and comedies of the 1930s and '40s, turned to playing pint-sized wise guys with big chips on their shoulder in the Cagney mold in a number of genres, most notably in war films—such as the underrated *The Bold and the Brave* (1956), where he earned a best supporting actor Oscar nomination as a motor-mouthed, card-playing grunt—and in crime films, such as Don Siegel's B-movie classic *Baby Face Nelson* (1957).

An absorbing, typically well-crafted Siegel action film made on a shoe-string, the film picks up the story of the notorious '30s gunman and bank robber of the title (a diminutive psychotic killer whose real name was Lester Gillis) shortly after Nelson is released from prison. After carrying out a murder contract, he finds himself on the run from the law. He joins up with the even more notorious bank robber John Dillinger (Leo Gordon), who gives the pint-sized pistolero his enduring nickname of "Baby Face." When Dillinger is killed, Nelson assumes leadership of the Dillinger gang.

Hunted by the FBI, the dangerously unstable Baby Face refuses to lie low, committing a series of daring bank jobs that result in the gang's being squeezed by the law even harder. When the feds begin to close in, the self-serving Nelson engineers his escape by feeding his associates to the law. But the authorities track him and his moll (Carolyn Jones) to their hideout, where the killer takes on all comers in a furious gun battle from which he escapes. Wounded in the process, he manages to flee if not to the top of the world, to a nearby cemetery—and goes out a legend in independent style, blood spewing from his mouth, when Jones grants his final request to fire a fatal bullet into his brain pan before the law arrives.

"What gave the picture its vitality [was that] we made no apologies for Nelson," Don Siegel told his biographer, Stuart Kaminsky. "If you felt anything for him, it was because of his size and his rebellious attitude towards society."[11] He could be speaking as well of the Cagney gangster in everything from *The Public Enemy* and *Angels with Dirty Faces* to *White Heat* and *Love Me or Leave Me*.

Mickey Rooney grabbed no Oscar nominations for his dynamic performance in this all-but-forgotten B-picture, which mainstream critics dismissed at the time as just another low-rent gangster movie, and may now be a lost film because its negative is said to have deteriorated like so many unwanted and uncared for silent films. But Rooney did win the Cesar, the French film industry equivalent of the Oscar, for his charismatic performance in the film, which, like many Siegel films of the period, was a bigger hit throughout Europe than here.

Also dripping with pathology in the Cagney mold is Jude Law's ferret-like Irish hitman/picture snatcher (he likes to shoot what he kills) in *Road to Perdition* (2002), based on the graphic novel (i.e., long form comic book) of the same title. Tom Hanks stars as a top hitman for Irish mobster Paul Newman, who treats Hanks like a son. However, when Hanks's own boy witnesses a mob killing committed by Newman's actual son (Daniel Craig), the boy must be silenced. So, Hanks takes him on the run, with Jude Law's twisted top assassin #2 in hot pursuit, camera gear in tow.

The crux of the picture is the relationship between fathers and sons. Hanks develops a closer bond with his boy as their getaway progresses, whereas at the same time his relationship with his surrogate father Newman completely deteriorates. This aspect of the story is clearly what captures the interest of director Sam Mendes because he focuses so much of the film's running time on it—which is all well and good, except that Hanks's character of a 5:00 to 9:00 hitman cum 9:00 to 5:00 Ward Cleaver isn't altogether credible. So, despite Hanks's valiant effort to involve us with the character by giving him an aura of *weldschmerz* similar to the type of gangster played by Humphrey Bogart that is trapped in a cul-de-sac of his own making, we care, but not really, and only until the film is over.

Courtesy of its extraordinary Oscar-winning cinematography by the late great Conrad L. Hall, *Road to Perdition* pulls us in by thickly enveloping us in the atmosphere of the time (the Great Depression) and place (the Midwest of Frank Nitti and Al Capone) in which the story is set. But the story itself pulls us in very little—except when Jude Law's Maguire (a character not in the original graphic novel, I'm told) comes on the scene to juice things up with his unpredictability and his air of impending violence, characteristics that Cagney's goons always bring with them, too.

LAST OF THE INDEPENDENTS

In Don Siegel's crime-busting follow-up to *Baby Face Nelson*, *The Lineup* (1958), based on the popular 1950s TV series of the same name (and later syndicated as *San Francisco Beat*), for which Siegel directed the pilot episode, the character of the hitman played by Eli Wallach is described by his mob boss (Robert Keith) as a "wonderfully pure pathological study. A psychopath with no inhibitions." These words serve equally well as a portrait of Cagney's Tom Powers, Cody Jarrett, and other gangster types. That Wallach's character in the film is named Dancer makes the link to Cagney even stronger, as Cagney began his show business career as a dancer, and moves like one on screen, even when playing tough guys—perhaps *especially* when playing them.

In the vein of Rooney's Baby Face Nelson, Dancer is not so much the traditional outsider (Robinson's Rico Bandello, for example, who aspires to be what he covets from afar) as he is a misfit, someone who simply *doesn't fit anywhere*, not comfortably anyhow, in the role of insider or outsider. A virtual law unto himself, he is, in that sense, the personification of the word "outlaw" in contemporary life.

Although James Cagney and Don Siegel never made a movie together, Cagney's gangsters and the antihero figures in Siegel's films, gangster or otherwise, have this in common. They are "outlaws," too—not so much in the rugged individualist sense as in the sense of what might be described as being a breed apart, truly the "last of the independents."

"Last of the independents" also is an apt term for Don Siegel (1912–1991), who carved a career as one of the most subtly (and often not subtly) subversive directors (Martin Scorsese calls them "smugglers") working inside the Hollywood studio system during its heyday—a filmmaker who got away with as much as he did in films like the classic *Invasion of the Body Snatchers* (1956) and the aforementioned *Baby Face Nelson* and *The Lineup* because the low budgets Siegel was often saddled with kept him and his films well under the studio's radar screen.

Graduating to A budgets in the 1960s and '70s, Siegel remained the "last of the independents" by continuing to make the same kind of films he'd always made, but with bigger stars playing his iconoclastic and misfit antiheroes, such as Clint Eastwood, whose best, most interesting films immediately after achieving international stardom in the Sergio Leone "spaghetti-western" *A Fistful of Dollars* (1967), were all made by Don

Siegel[12]: the crime films *Coogan's Bluff* (1968), *Dirty Harry* (1972), and *Escape from Alcatraz* (1979); the western *Two Mules for Sister Sara* (1970); and the gothic Civil War drama *The Beguiled* (1971), a film that virtually defines the Siegel oeuvre.

The Chicago-born, Cambridge University–educated Siegel began his four-decade movie career first as an editor of montages, then as second-unit director in the 1940s at Warner Brothers, where he also made his directorial debut with two short films, *Star in the Night* (1945) and *Hitler Lives* (1946), that won Oscars in the best short subject category. The studio then decided to give him a shot at directing a full-length feature, *The Verdict* (1946), a noirish period murder mystery starring the screen's Laurel and Hardy of menace, Peter Lorre and Sydney Greenstreet. Producer Mark Hellinger, who had recently moved from Warners to Universal to prepare the Hemingway story *The Killers* for filming, offered that plum assignment to Siegel around the same time. But Siegel, having already committed to making *The Verdict*, was forced to turn down the offer, and the opportunity to direct what would become one of the key films noir of the postwar period went to the German-born filmmaker Robert Siodmak. Disproving the axiom that there are no second chances in life, when the same studio, Universal, opted to remake *The Killers* seventeen years later, it offered the job to Siegel again; this time, he was available to accept.

Another reason why Siegel was able to tweak the formulaic nose of the studios while not alienating the system that readily employed him was that his attitude toward both the movie business *and* to the material he filmed, as well as his outlook on life, was generally more sardonic than nihilistic or threatening. The opening scene of his remake of *The Killers* offers a good demonstration of this when the title hit men, played by Lee Marvin and Clu Gulager, invade a school for the blind to whack their target and are wearing dark glasses—presumably to avoid identification (by whom? the blind?), not just because of the strong southern California sun—which they never remove.

Siegel's version of *The Killers* was to have been the first movie made expressly for television. It was scheduled to air in the fall of 1963, but in the wake of the nation's trauma over the assassination of President Kennedy, Universal decided to shelve the completed film,[13] at least temporarily, fearing that its subject matter of cold-blooded murder—including a sequence in which a man is killed by a sniper firing a high-powered rifle from the window of a building—might offend American viewers. In 1964, Universal took the film off the shelf, however, and released it as a theatrical feature in Europe, where, to the studio's surprise, it was a big hit both with audiences and overseas critics, who had long embraced Siegel's work.

Siegel's *The Killers* retains many of the ingredients that made the 1946 version a noir classic—a duplicitous dame, the use of flashbacks— but it abandons the high-contrast, black-and-white photography of the original for a bright, almost garish look that is partly because of the requirements of color television at the time but also because much of the remake takes place outdoors in broad daylight.

The man (John Cassavetes) the killers have been contracted to rub out is no longer an ex-prizefighter as in Hemingway's story and the Siodmak film but rather a former race car driver who is now working at the school as a therapist. Marvin mercilessly beats up a blind receptionist (Virginia Christine) for information as to Cassavetes's whereabouts in the school. A janitor discovers the battered woman, she tells him what happened, and the janitor alerts Cassavetes over the intercom that two men with guns are coming for him.

Expecting them and long resigned to his fate, Cassavetes makes no attempt to run and is brutally executed where he stands. Marvin becomes obsessed with knowing why Cassavetes didn't run—"why he'd rather die"—and it is through him, rather than Hemingway's third-party narrator or Edmond O'Brien's insurance investigator in the Siodmak film, that the story is told and the truth revealed.

From a former racing partner (Claude Akins) of Cassavetes's, the killers learn the murdered man had fallen for an expensive, scheming dame (Angie Dickinson) and that his infatuation had destroyed the partnership and his career. Following a racing incident in which he'd almost been blinded, Cassavetes had fallen on hard times. From a thug (Norman Fell); Dickinson; and a high-toned, ruthless gangster played by Ronald Reagan (in his last movie role—and only movie role as a bad guy), Marvin unravels the rest of the story.

At Dickinson's urging, Cassavetes had signed on to drive the getaway car in a $1 million payroll heist planned by Reagan. But Cassavetes allegedly double-crossed the gang, dumped Dickinson, and absconded with the stolen loot on his own, at which point Reagan had put the contract out on him. Marvin rightly deduces that this explanation doesn't gel with Cassavetes's character and beats the truth out of Dickinson that it was she and Reagan who'd double-crossed the gang, taken the money, and pinned the blame on Cassavetes, then had him killed to keep him from talking. In the best noir tradition, the Cassavetes character, blindsided by the woman he'd loved, had disappeared to lick his wounds and fatalistically await life's next, hopefully last, kick in the groin.

His partner having been murdered by Reagan, Marvin demands the stolen $1 million from this bunch of crooks for himself. He kills Reagan to get it and is wounded in the process. Dickinson exploits her sex appeal to con the wounded hitman, but he's no chump like Cassavetes, easily sees through the charade, and pumps a bullet into her. Then, he stumbles outside with the suitcase of money and tries to make it to his car. But it's no use, and he knows it. He is resigned to his fate, just as Cassavetes had been. In a finish that sums up the sardonic tone of the entire film, Marvin takes aim with his finger at an approaching police car as if to plug it like a kid playing cops and robbers, then falls dead on the grass.

After his career soared in the late 1960s and '70s when American critics finally "discovered" him too, Siegel became disheartened with moviemaking after his last two pictures (*Rough Cut*, 1980, and the aptly titled *Jinxed*, 1984) turned into troubled productions, largely because of excessive meddling by their respective stars and producers, and went toes-up at the box office. So, like Cassavetes and Marvin in *The Killers*, he resigned himself to the inevitable and retired.

Appropriately, his final gangster film (one of his best), *Charley Varrick*, came fairly late in his career (1973). It bears the subtitle "Last of the Independents," the logo of its title character (played by Walter Matthau), a former stunt pilot turned bank robber, and Siegel's view of himself.

Ironically, Siegel almost didn't get to make the film. The story of a guy who robs a bank located off the beaten path, unaware that the bank is a drop for laundered Mafia money, and becomes the target of a manhunt by the mob and the cops, the project, based on a book called *The Looters*[14] by John Reese, had been kicking around Hollywood for years. At one point, Howard Hawks, the director of the original *Scarface*, was going to make it with Peter Bogdanovich serving as producer. But then Hawks went on to make the 1970 Western *Rio Lobo* (his last picture show) with John Wayne, and *The Looters* fell once more into limbo. Fortuitously, it eventually crossed Siegel's path, and he saw in the material and its acerbic antihero, who beats out the mob and the police, the perfect foundation for a Siegel film.

Working closely with the screenwriter (Dean Reisner, who shared screen credit with Howard Rodman, the author of an earlier version of the script), Siegel shaped the material, as he had done on most of his earlier films, even more to his liking, but this time with more clout as he was serving as his own producer. *Charley Varrick* thus became the first film to bear Siegel's own handwritten "A Siegel Film" above the title in the opening credits.

Only once does this intricately woven gangland thriller suffer a lapse—when Matthau beds down the secretary (Felicia Farr) of the bank's mob-controlled national manager (John Vernon) to set him up for a double-cross, and she all-too-readily goes along. Otherwise, the film is a prime example of Siegel's taut, tough (though never repellently violent) approach to the genre, with a wonderfully wry performance by Matthau as the sly, duplicitous, pragmatic, engaging, and one-of-a-kind mug Charley, the "last of the independents."

"LADY, I DON'T HAVE THE TIME"

In the 1964 version of *The Killers*, the inquisitive hitman played by Lee Marvin (1924–1987) wrings the truth out of Angie Dickinson by calmly promising to dangle her from the hotel room window and drop her to the street far below if she doesn't talk. When he calmly goes through with his promise, and she begs him to stop, finally agreeing to talk, the astonished look on her face as he pulls her back inside seems to say: "My God, you really would have done it, wouldn't you?" Indeed he would have, for in the sadism department, the Lee Marvin gangster goes the Cagney gangster many times better.

Marvin's thugs in crime movies (and outlaws in many of the Westerns he also made during his career) are second cousins to Cagney's Tom Powers and Cody Jarrett, minus the hang-ups. Marvin's sadistic criminals enjoy what they do because, like Cagney, they feel they have a right to do it, and they are thus *in the right*. And they are even more matter-of-fact about it than Cagney. For example, when Angie Dickinson makes one last try at conning the wounded Marvin in *The Killers*, he says straightforwardly, "Lady, I don't have the time," and matter-of-factly plugs her.

There is no softness at all in the Marvin gangster. When Cagney shoves the grapefruit in Mae Clarke's face in *The Public Enemy* after she suggests he has eyes for someone else, he's making the point, in his own skewed way, that he loves her and nobody but her. But when Marvin lets moll Gloria Grahame have it in the kisser with a boiling pot of coffee to make a point in the classic *The Big Heat* (1953), the point he's making is not an expression of love, not even a skewed one.

Coming at the tail end of film noir's heyday, Fritz Lang's *The Big Heat* derives from a *Saturday Evening Post* serial (later published in book form) by William P. McGivern. Sydney Boehm, a newspaper reporter turned screenwriter in the Ben Hecht, W. R. Burnett, and John Bright tradition, wrote the script. Glenn Ford's honest cop and loving family man is the archetypal Lang hero whose belief system is put to the test when he gets embroiled in the case of a fellow officer's suicide. His superiors and the cop's widow (Jeanette Nolan) pressure Ford to ease up on the case, but he stubbornly refuses and digs deeper and deeper, learning that the deceased cop was on the take from an urbane mob kingpin played by Alexander Scourby, who has a host of police officials and politicians in his pocket as well.

When Ford still won't back off, Scourby orders him killed by Marvin, who plants a bomb in Ford's car wired to explode on ignition. But Ford's wife (Jocelyn Brando[15]) is the one who is killed. Embittered, and now more determined than ever to nail Scourby out of hatred and vengeance, Ford descends into the perilous noir underworld that threatens to turn him into the alter ego of Lee Marvin's character, albeit one on the right side of the law.

Aided by some war buddies, a few loyal associates in the department, and Marvin's scarred moll, Ford finally prevails over the mobsters by bringing them to justice—and prevails over himself by recovering his humanity and belief in others.

Alternately hailed as a realistic study of postwar urban corruption and vilified for its brutality, *The Big Heat* was a very potent film in its time. It may seem less strong to viewers today who have become inured to such brutality on the screen, but Brando's accidental death still comes as a shocker, and the scene where Marvin disfigures Grahame with the hot coffee ranks right up there with Cagney's apocalyptic "Made it, Ma, top o' the world" as one of the all-time most powerful moments in movies. In fact, *The Big Heat* boasts two such moments involving hot coffee, one where Marvin hurls it in Grahame's face, and another at the end of the film when she hurls it in his to get even—after which he shoots her in the back. As I said before, the Marvin gangster is neither soft nor sentimental.

Director Robert Altman later echoed Marvin's sadistic gangster and this classic scene in his offbeat and amusing *The Long Goodbye* (1973), freely adapted by Leigh Brackett from the novel by Raymond Chandler. In it, mobster Mark Rydell smashes a bottle of Coca-Cola in the face of his gorgeous girlfriend as a warning to meddling private eye Phillip Marlowe (Elliot Gould) that this is how he treats people he likes, so just imagine how he treats those he dislikes.

After winning his only best actor Oscar, for the Western spoof *Cat Ballou* (1965), and becoming a major star, Marvin more frequently chose roles in films that cast him as iconoclastic heroes with a bone to pick with any kind of authority, such as *The Dirty Dozen* (1967). But he returned brilliantly to his familiar role of no-nonsense gangster with a heart of stone in John Boorman's *Point Blank*[16] (1967), wherein he plays the ultimate killing machine.

Point Blank is based on a novel by Richard Stark[17] called *The Hunter* about a career crook named Parker who is double-crossed by his mob partners after a successful heist and left for dead. But he recovers from his wounds and sets out to collect his fair share—and only that—no matter what the cost. The film is a seminal crime thriller of the 1960s because of the elliptical, nonlinear style of its narrative, and Lee Marvin's "anti-est" of antihero protagonists. Renamed Walker in the film, he is even more violent, more sadistic, and more duplicitous than the guys and gals who wronged him because he firmly believes he's in the right; all he wants is to get the cut of the stolen loot he was denied, and not one penny more. He thus sees his cause as a righteous, almost noble, one that fully justifies his every action, no matter how brutal (in this film Marvin actually goes through with tossing a miscreant from a high-story window). And in terms of the world Walker inhabits, he probably sees correctly. Reminiscent of the films of Italian director Michelangelo Antonioni, *Point Blank* doesn't draw to a conclusion so much as come to a stop, suggesting, perhaps, that in such a world nobody wins because nothing is ever resolved.

Its qualities, particularly Marvin's steely performance as the savagely single-minded Walker, who, like Cagney, never second-guesses himself, strongly influenced the ultraviolent, morally ambiguous crime thrillers to come in the 1970s and beyond, many of them modeled—like *Point Blank*—on the classic films noir of the '40s and '50s. Labeled "neo-noirs," this string of films continues unbroken to this day. It consists of such potent additions to the form populated by cold-blooded killers who see themselves in the right as the gangland thrillers of Quentin Tarantino (*Reservoir Dogs*, 1992; *Pulp Fiction*, 1994; *Jackie Brown*, 1997), *L.A.*

Confidential (1997), and *Get Carter* (2000), Stephen T. Kay's surprisingly effective America-located remake starring Sylvester Stallone of Mike Hodges's stellar British gangster film of 1971 of the same title starring Michael Caine.[18]

"YOU THINK I'M *FUNNY?*"

Another study in contrast between the Robinson gangster and the Cagney gangster is their unpredictability. With Robinson's green-eyed mobster—as well as Bogart's imprisoned loner yet to be discussed—what you see is fundamentally what you get. They lack the unpredictability of the Cagney gangster; with him, friend or foe, you always have to be on your toes.

The Cagney gangster is a human scorpion—passive one second, stinging you to death the next. One sees the character's dangerous unpredictability as early as *The Public Enemy*, where it even underpins the famous grapefruit scene, all the way through to such later films as *White Heat*. The latter provides an especially vicious example of the capricious nature of the character's unpredictable sadism. Instead of shooting the quivering man, Cagney's Cody Jarrett lets a prison stoolie (Paul Guilfoyle) off the hook by locking him in the trunk of a car. When the stoolie complains about a lack of air, however, Jarrett whips out a gun and ventilates the trunk with bullet holes, killing the stoolie just seconds after having spared his life.

Cocksure, tough, and diminutive like Cagney—as well as hailing from New York, too—actor Joe Pesci followed in the footsteps of the Cagney gangster throughout the 1990s in such films as Martin Scorsese's *Good-Fellas* (for which he won a best supporting actor Oscar in 1990) and *Casino* (1995) and *8 Heads in a Duffel Bag* (1997) by assuming this aspect of the actor's mantel.

In *GoodFellas*, for example, Pesci is a strutting psychopathic thug in the Cagney manner whose deadly ambition to become mob royalty leads to his getting whacked instead. In a nightclub scene (largely improvised, it appears) surrounded by mob hangers-on and close pal Henry Hill (Ray Liotta), whom he's regaling with funny stories, Pesci's character exhibits an abrupt change in mood when Liotta compliments him as a funny guy, and Pesci takes offense: "You think I'm *funny?*"

At first we (like Liotta's character) think Pesci is joking; then we're not so sure; then we're convinced he isn't joking at all and that he's going to kill Liotta any second over the perceived insult. Then, just as quickly, the atmosphere of impending violence evaporates as he laughs at how convincingly he'd strung Liotta along.

We almost feel the air sucked from the room, our lips going as dry as Liotta's, during this scene as the tension mounts then falls from Pesci's quixotic shift from clown to potentially explosive lethal weapon back to clown again. It is an act of sadism that would make the Cagney gangster proud. But the true brilliance of Pesci's performance in the scene, however, is the subtle persuasiveness with which he conveys the terrifying idea that at any time the wind might have blown the other way, and the character might very well have crossed the line from kidder to killer.

9
Bustin' Out

"Remember what Johnny Dillinger said about guys
like you and him. He said you were just rushing towards
death. Yeah, that's it. Just rushing towards death."

—Doc Banton (Henry Hull),
High Sierra (1941)

FOLK HERO

ALTHOUGH HE RAN WITH SUCH GUN-HAPPY crazies as Baby Face
Nelson, America's most notorious bank robber, John Dillinger,
was not an especially violent criminal himself. He was once
charged with killing a patrolman during an Indiana bank raid, but he
staunchly denied the charge, and it was never proven. Why, then, did the
FBI consider him to be the most dangerous "mad dog" criminal in America? The answer has to do with image.

Born in the Midwest in 1902, Dillinger grew up in a strict, religious
environment, against which he rebelled early on. A wild kid, he had his
first brush with the law at age seventeen when he got a ticket for speeding. He later joined the navy to escape his repressive home life, but he
found the rigorous discipline and routine of military life equally confin-
ing and deserted. He committed his first serious crime, the robbery of an
Indiana grocery store, the same year, 1923. He was twenty-one.

Arrested quickly, he had the book thrown at him, even though the
store robbery was his first offense, and got a ten-year stretch. The state's

governor later described the sentence as an injustice that had much to do with the bitterness toward society that Dillinger developed. Paroled in 1933, Dillinger was reported to have said, "They stole nine years of my life. Now, I'm going to do some stealing of my own." And this he did—by himself at first, then with a gang.

A fancy dresser and ladies' man, he allegedly was courteous to one and all during his crimes. He had a particular MO. He would carefully case the targeted banks, assessing security measures and escape routes ahead of time so as to ensure a minimum of gunplay and violence. Reportedly, he never stole from any depositors or bystanders who happened to be in the bank, just from the cash drawers and the vault. This led to the public's mythologizing him as an American Robin Hood, who robbed from the rich (the banks)—although never went so far as to give any of his ill-gotten gains to the poor.

Captured again, he escaped from jail before his trial, using a toy gun whittled from wood and painted with black shoe polish. This stunt made him an object of public celebration. He then sped in a stolen car across state lines—his only federal crime, but enough to set the FBI on his trail. The Bureau got a black eye, however, when its agents failed to catch the "gentleman bandit" despite a number of opportunities. Its image plummeted when, during another failed attempt at capturing the notorious gangster, FBI agents shot and killed several innocent bystanders. The angry public vilified J. Edgar Hoover's Bureau and the special agent assigned to the job of catching Dillinger, Melvin Purvis. The humiliated Hoover declared Dillinger a "yellow rat" and directed Purvis and his men to shoot the "mad dog" on sight.

This opportunity came when Anna Sage, an illegal alien facing deportation to her native Romania, notified the Bureau that Dillinger was staying at her Chicago brothel and made a deal to set a trap for the gangster in exchange for her freedom. She told Purvis she would be accompanying Dillinger and his girlfriend to a movie, Dillinger's second favorite pastime after bank robbing. Because Dillinger had recently undergone plastic surgery on his face, Sage said, she would wear an orange dress to help the agents pick out the trio. Purvis and his men waited for them to come out of the theater. As soon as Purvis spotted Sage in her orange dress (which looked reddish under the marquee lights, giving rise to her subsequent nickname of the "Lady in Red"), he lighted a cigar, the signal to his fellow agents to draw their guns. Then Purvis shouted, "Stick 'em up, Johnny!" Dillinger allegedly drew his own gun and fled into an alley beside the theater, where Purvis and his agents followed, and, per Hoover's instructions, shot the "mad dog" dead.

Several Hollywood studios announced plans for a movie about Dillinger before the gangster's body was even cold. But movie morals czar Will H. Hays quickly put the kibosh on such plans with his famous industry directive (see Chapter 8), and it wasn't until 1941 that a film loosely based on the gangster's life and legend—his folk-hero status, his alleged appeal to women, his skill as a master bank robber, his unwarranted reputation as a "mad dog" killer—was finally made: *High Sierra*. And the job of incarnating the thinly veiled Dillinger character, here named "Mad Dog" Roy Earle, fell to a heretofore second banana in gangster movies at the Warner Brothers factory named Humphrey Bogart.

SON OF PRIVILEGE

"It looks like I'll spend the rest of my life dead."
—Duke Mantee (Humphrey Bogart),
The Petrified Forest (1936)

The son of an eminent surgeon, Dr. Belmont DeForest Bogart, and a successful commercial artist, Maud Humphrey Bogart (legend has it that she used her toddler son as the model for the first series of Gerber baby-food ads), Humphrey Bogart was born in 1899. He grew up in New York City like fellow Warner Brothers gangsters Edward G. Robinson, James Cagney, and George Raft. Unlike them, however, he grew up surrounded by the rich and sometimes famous rather than the thugs all four would later play on the screen.

Bogart attended the prestigious Trinity School in New York and prep school at Phillips Academy in Andover, Massachusetts. His parents wanted him to go to Yale, but he was expelled from prep school before graduation and joined the navy instead. While serving in World War I, he received the scar on his lip that caused the distinctive lisp that became his screen trademark later on.

After the war, Bogart returned to New York and went to work for stage and film impresario William A. Brady, a close family friend. It was Brady who suggested that Bogart go into acting, and he made his Broadway debut playing two parts in the 1922 melodrama *Drifting* (where he was credited in the playbill as both H. D. Bogart and as Humphrey Bogart).

The play was produced by Brady and directed by John Cromwell, who would direct Bogart (playing a good guy) a quarter of a century later in the excellent film noir *Dead Reckoning* (1947).

A larger stage role followed the same year in *Swifty*, for which the aspiring actor received the worst notices of his fledgling career. The show closed after twenty-four performances. Bogart nonetheless persevered and won parts in a succession of Broadway melodramas and comedies over the next few years. The image he created in them, however, couldn't have been more removed from the one he established on the screen. "He usually was cast as romantic juveniles, his stage equipment a tennis racquet and a pair of flannels,"[1] wrote Clifford McCarty (no relation to the author).

Bogart journeyed to Hollywood in the early 1930s to pursue a film career. Even though he got work, his film roles were fairly minor, and he returned to New York and Broadway, where he landed the part in the play that would dramatically change his image and would launch him on the road to movie stardom. In Robert Emmett Sherwood's drama *The Petrified Forest*, which opened on January 7, 1935, and ran for almost 200 performances, Bogart was cast as Duke Mantee, a gangster who has escaped from prison. On the run, he takes several hostages at a roadside café in the Arizona desert while preparing his getaway to Mexico. Although the role of Mantee is a supporting one, Bogart used it to maximum advantage, all but stealing the show out from under its lead star, Leslie Howard. Warner Brothers bought the screen rights and signed Howard to re-create his starring role in the film version, but decided to pass on Bogart in favor of one of its already established gangster stars, Edward G. Robinson, despite the fact that the type of gangster Robinson incarnated on the screen was altogether different from that of Duke Mantee. Fortunately, Leslie Howard used his clout to insist that Bogart come along too—in fact, Howard said he wouldn't do the film unless Bogart played Mantee. The studio gave in and Bogart returned to Hollywood—and to the studio that would be his home for a good many years—on a permanent basis.

Sherwood wrote *The Petrified Forest* to express his changing views on pacifism and isolationism. In view of the rise of Hitler in Europe, he now saw the need for sacrifice—even violent sacrifice—in the face of great evil, if that evil is to be thwarted so that future generations will have a chance. The protagonist, a failed poet and pacifist played by Howard, is wandering—literally as well as spiritually—through the arid Arizona landscape and stops at the roadside café as the drama opens.

Howard befriends the waitress (Bette Davis), a kindred spirit who longs to better her life someday by realizing her dream of becoming an artist. Escaped convict Bogart arrives, and he and his gang hold Howard, Davis, and everyone else in the café captive until his moll shows up with the getaway money. During their forced confinement, Davis and Howard grow closer; as the police close in on the desperate Bogart, Howard sees a way to both help Davis achieve her dream *and* stop the criminal. He signs his life insurance policy over to her, then manipulates Bogart into shooting him as the police arrive, giving them the opportunity to bring the gangster down.

A stage-bound, talky, and somewhat improbable drama and film—unless you swallow its heavy-handed symbolism whole—*The Petrified Forest*[2] works on the nerves as well as it does largely because of Bogart's performance as the stoop-shouldered, trapped-like-a-rat Mantee, who all but shuffles when he walks as if his feet are still bound by chains. Mantee is the prototype of the loner gangster who seems fated almost from birth to be imprisoned inside himself, and desperate to "bust out," a figure that Bogart would enshrine on the screen.

Unlike the Robinson and Cagney gangster, the Bogart gangster isn't so much motivated by envy or the thrill of violence as the need to get by in a world he perceives as completely hostile to him. Whether he's an underling or the mob's top man, is in jail or walking the streets, the Bogart gangster always seems to be looking over his shoulder (Bogart's good guys characters, among them Rick in *Casablanca* [1942], possess this quality to a degree as well). Somewhat out of step with the dynamic, hell-bent gangster characters of the '30s personified by Robinson and Cagney, Bogart's brooding, desperate thugs are much closer in spirit to the anti-heroes of '40s films noir—the milieu, not coincidentally, in which the actor would finally come into his own and become a star.

FILM NOIR

By the 1940s, the quasi-romantic and "straight from the headlines" style of gangster film prevalent in the 1930s had given way to a new style of gangster film inspired in part by the hard-boiled crime novels of Dashiell Hammett, Raymond Chandler, James M. Cain, and, of course, our prolific old friend W. R. Burnett. The silent-era gangster regenerated by the love of a good and honest woman and the brutal misfits and outsiders of the

'30s who always got what they deserved in the end were being replaced by a new type of antihero—the disillusioned "nonhero," who finds himself walking a tightrope through a dark world of greed, cynicism, and corruption, a world of wealthy and powerful criminals, double-dealing dames, shadowy corners, and ominous rain-slicked streets that threaten him at every crooked turn. Sometimes, that crooked turn gets him. At other times, in fact most of the time, he manages to crawl out of the moral pit he has fallen into and defeat the dark forces—often at the sacrifice of his own life.

In most of these films, the protagonist nonhero is not a gangster himself (another departure from the '30s formula). He is, say, a private eye, a cop, an insurance investigator, or sometimes just an innocent bystander, who gets mixed up either by accident or by profession with the world of gangsters and must face up to his own corruptibility. At the time, this new style of gangster and crime film didn't have a name. In fact, the makers of these films didn't even recognize they were collectively bringing a new style to the genre—a style that would soon creep into other types of films as well (the Western, the war film) and would be accepted by critics a decade later not just as a new style but as a distinct subgenre of the crime film with its own iconography and conventions. It was the French critics, deprived of American movies during the war, who, upon seeing this backlog of films one right after the other during peacetime, gave this new filmmaking style its enduring name: *film noir*, or "black film," a term that reflects both the moral universe of these films and their stark low-key lighting. With tongue not entirely in cheek, Robert Mitchum, the quintessential nonhero of many classic films noir such as *Out of the Past* (1947), attributed this stark look to lack of money and having to scrimp on lights.

Having been a major influence on the evolution of film noir, Hammett, Chandler, Cain, Burnett, and a host of lesser pulp-fiction writers found themselves in the enviable position of being more in demand than ever, and seeing more and more of their books and stories turned into movies as the production of films noir reached a full head of steam. Sometimes, the results were mixed; on other occasions, the film versions of their work proved to be as influential and enduring as the original itself. For example, Howard Hawks's convoluted classic *The Big Sleep* (1946), with Humphrey Bogart as Raymond Chandler's good-guy private eye Philip Marlowe, continues to cast a spell on audiences and moviemakers to this day because of its amusing script full of quintessential noir

perils and colorful characters, and, of course, the sparks generated between Bogie and costar Lauren Bacall. Michael Winner's 1978 remake,
which updated Chandler's book to that year and featured an aging and
sleepier than usual Robert Mitchum in the Bogart role, has its admirers
as well, although it seems more like a send-up of film noir than a serious,
modern-day take on the real thing.

James M. Cain, W. R. Burnett, and Raymond Chandler (reluctantly)
even became screenwriters, turning out a slew of original noir scripts as
well as adaptations. Sometimes, they even adapted each other's work,
as in Billy Wilder's classic noir about insurance fraud and murder, *Double
Indemnity* (1944), which Chandler scripted (with Wilder) from Cain's
book.

The eldest of the quartet, Dashiell Hammett, was, like W. R. Burnett,
already an old hand at seeing his work translated to the big screen, but
film noir gave that work a new lease on life. For example, two versions of
Hammett's quasi-gangster novel *The Maltese Falcon* had already been
made in the 1930s—*The Maltese Falcon* (a.k.a., *Dangerous Female*,
1931) and *Satan Met a Lady* (1936)—before screenwriter John Huston
tackled the job again for his directorial debut in 1941 and turned it into a
film classic. Likewise, Hammett's *The Thin Man* had evolved into a successful series with William Powell and Myrna Loy that MGM started in the
'30s and continued into the '40s. And his 1932 novel *The Glass Key* was
made twice, first in 1935 with George Raft, then again in 1942 with Alan
Ladd. More recently, the double-threat team of Joel and Ethan Coen paid
homage to *The Glass Key,* to the '30s gangster film, *and* to film noir in
Miller's Crossing (1990), featuring Gabriel Byrne in a variation on the
Raft/Ladd role of a loyal (or is he?) aide to his embattled boss.

"Your Head Always Loses"

"Bogart had yet to hit it big and was playing supporting roles. [*High
Sierra*] made him a star,"[3] exaggerates *Sierra* director Raoul Walsh, but
only slightly. *High Sierra* was a film noir. And it was film noir that made
Bogart a star.

Bogart's scene-stealing performance as Duke Mantee notwithstanding,
The Petrified Forest didn't catapult him immediately into the big leagues
at Warner Brothers as one of its top-tier gangster stars alongside Robinson and Cagney (or Raft). As noted in previous chapters, Robinson's and

Cagney's gangster films were starting to get fired upon by civics groups and other do-gooders for their "excessive" violence. Not oblivious to Bogart's value as a charismatic movie villain, the studio signed the actor to a long-term contract and took some of the heat off its two top screen bad guys by casting Bogart opposite them as the even *worse* guy. Even before *The Petrified Forest* was released, the studio cast Bogart as the nemesis of Edward G. Robinson's good-guy undercover cop in *Bullets or Ballots*. A year later, Bogart, as gangster and crooked boxing promoter "Turkey" Morgan, was slugging it out once more against Robinson, an honest manager, and Robinson's champion fighter *Kid Galahad* (1937). Later, in *Angels with Dirty Faces,* Cagney's good-kid-gone-wrong was pitted against unscrupulous lawyer and racketeer Bogart—and they continued their on-screen duel the following year in *The Roaring Twenties*. Occasionally, though, the Bogart gangster would take center stage all by himself, as in William Wyler's "nature or nurture" social drama *Dead End* (1937), based on the hit play by Sidney Kingsley that premiered on Broadway in 1935 at the peak of the Great Depression and ran for 687 performances. In the film, Bogart plays Baby Face Morgan, who, like Cagney in *Angels with Dirty Faces*, becomes the idol of a bunch of impressionable slum kids when he comes home to his Lower East Side roots to visit his mother and a former girlfriend.

In between these supporting roles as gangsters, Bogart sometimes got a supporting role as a good guy—as in *Marked Woman* (1937), where he's a crusading district attorney who brings down mob kingpin Eduardo Cianelli by persuading Bette Davis, a "hostess" (polite word for prostitute) in one of the gangster's "nightclubs" (polite word for brothel), to turn state's evidence against her double-dealing, murderous boss. Bogart's character, David Graham, is loosely based on Thomas E. Dewey—the Rudy Guliani of his day—a special prosecutor, future governor of New York, and failed presidential candidate (against Harry Truman in 1948), who got his reputation as a zealous crime fighter when he busted mob chieftain Lucky Luciano on prostitution charges with the help of several disgruntled "hostesses" in Luciano's employ, just as in the film.

In several of Warner Brothers's B pictures, such as *Crime School* and *Racket Busters* (both 1938), Bogart has the starring role, playing the good guy in the former and the bad guy in the latter. But it was *High Sierra*, an A picture in which Bogart got his meatiest gangster role (and the lead role this time) since Duke Mantee in *The Petrified Forest*, that led to his being cast as private eye Sam Spade in John Huston's *The Mal-*

tese Falcon, the film that turned Bogart into a star, and, ultimately, a screen icon.

Ironically, Bogart was almost shut out of both films. The studio wanted George Raft for the part of "Mad Dog" Roy Earle in *High Sierra* and Sam Spade in *Falcon*. But Raft had grown tired of playing gangsters and dying at the end of movies, balked at playing Earle, and the studio gave in. Although *Falcon* would have given Raft the opportunity to play a good (if shady) guy who wins the girl (although he has to turn her over to the cops at the end) and survives at the fade out, the insecure actor balked at putting his fortunes in the hands of first-time director Huston, and the studio gave in to him. Bogart, who was the studio's back-up choice, got both parts by default—much to the delight of *Sierra* director Raoul Walsh and *The Maltese Falcon*'s Huston, both of whom had itched for Bogart over Raft in the first place. In a double dose of irony, Bogart triumphed in both films and went on to become a much bigger star than Raft had ever been.

"Mad Dog" Roy Earle in *High Sierra* is an older, even world-wearier version of Duke Mantee. He is a man who carries his fate with him like a backpack. He is also a chronic self-deceiver in the mold of *Falcon*'s Sam Spade and the protagonists of many other films written and/or directed by John Huston. A notorious bank robber with an inflated reputation for viciousness like Dillinger, Bogart's Earle is sprung from prison by a mob crony (Donald MacBride) to mastermind the stickup of a luxurious hotel in a desert resort town. On his way to rendezvous with the hold-up men MacBride has lined up to work with him, Bogart helps out an old man (Henry Travers) experiencing car trouble and falls for Travers's daughter (Joan Leslie), who is crippled with a clubfoot. Having no idea of Bogart's actual identity and grateful to him for his help, Travers and Leslie warmly accept Bogart and welcome him into their family. Thus begins the self-deception that ultimately leads to his doom as Bogart convinces himself that he can erase his past and settle down to a normal life with Leslie after he pulls off this last job.

To further his aims, he finances the operation to repair Leslie's foot in the belief that the grateful girl will come to love him in return—even though the worlds they are from, not to mention their ages, separate them like a gulf. Although the hotel robbery goes off without a hitch, two of Bogart's confederates (Arthur Kennedy and Alan Curtis) are killed when their car crashes during the getaway. The cops force a confession from the caper's inside man (Cornel Wilde) at the hotel, and Bogart becomes a hunted man.

The operation on Leslie a success, Bogart pursues his quickly vanishing dream and shows up to propose to her, but finds that she's already engaged to her childhood sweetheart. Thereafter, he goes to hell fast. Blowing a last chance for real happiness, however short-lived it may be, with the girl (Ida Lupino) who truly loves him, he winds up trapped in the Sierra mountains where the police use her to lure him out into the open so they can shoot him down like the "mad dog" they and the media claim him to be.

High Sierra is a terrific movie. And Bogart is terrific in it. He makes us empathize with Roy Earle without lapsing into sentimentality toward him. He makes us want to shout at the character to open his eyes to reality (and his heart to Lupino's love) and not to go down the self-destructive road he seems bent on taking, even though we know, as does he, that at the end of whatever road he takes the same fate is waiting for him.

For the Bogart gangster, there is no bustin' out of the trap life has set for him—because of the way he's chosen to live that life. With Duke Mantee, this is particularized in the character's shuffling walk, symbolic of a shackled nature that inherently prevents him from outrunning his fate—a fate that is never far away. With Roy Earle, it is the character's furtive glances and over the shoulder looks, as if constantly on guard for the figure that is dogging his trail—himself.

Oddly enough, in spite of his strong performance as Roy Earle and the unique gangster persona now associated with him, Bogart was not assigned by the studio to appear in another outright gangster film until *The Big Shot* in 1942. John Huston's intervening classic *The Maltese Falcon* was only marginally a gangster film, and as noted, Bogart was on the right side of the law in that one, although his character flew awfully close to the edge from time to time. And the 1942 *All Through the Night*, made prior to *The Big Shot*, cast Bogart as a big-time gambler but loyal U.S. citizen who brings down a bunch of Nazi spies.

The Big Shot seems to have been made only to trade on the success of *High Sierra* as it is little more than a weak imitation. Bogart plays ex-con Duke Berne, another doomed loner in the mold of Roy Earle and the earlier Duke Mantee. When an armored-car robbery he was pushed into goes wrong due to the duplicity of an accomplice (Stanley Ridges), Bogart lands back in prison, but he manages to escape, and together with his moll (Irene Manning), he heads for the mountains to elude police. Manning gets killed, however, and Bogart surrenders to his fate, but only after getting even with Ridges.

Cowritten and directed by his pal John Huston, the 1949 film noir *Key Largo* cast Bogart not as a gangster, gambler, crooked lawyer, nor even a criminal, but as a returning World War II veteran. In a twist on *The Petrified Forest*, it is Bogart who, along with several others, is taken hostage this time—in another role reversal on Bogart's earlier film career, the hostage taker is played by none other than Edward G. Robinson, now back on the wrong side of the law as Johnny Rocco, a deported Mafioso on the lam patterned on real-life mobster Lucky Luciano.

Nevertheless, there is still much of the desperate loner running from himself in Bogart's noirish nonhero Frank McCloud, who at one point expresses a belief that could be the mantra of the Bogart gangster: "When your head says one thing and your whole life says another, your head always loses."

Key Largo is based on Maxwell Anderson's stage play of the same title, which debuted at the Ethel Barrymore Theater in 1940 and ran for 105 performances. It starred Paul Muni as an American veteran of the Spanish Civil War who had cut and run, leaving his comrades to die. A disillusioned Lord Jim hounded by guilt over his cowardice, he seeks absolution from the father and sister, who are living in the Florida Keys, of one of the men he deserted. In the Keys he finds his courage at last, protecting the father and sister from a group of thugs, including a former Spanish adversary from the battlefields of Spain who is fleeing to points south.

Seeing gangster-ism as a perfect metaphor for fascism, the film version updates the story to the film noir post–World War II years and changes the protagonist's adversaries from fascists on the lam to American goombas on the run led by Robinson's Johnny Rocco.

In the Muni role, Bogart's ex–Army major Frank McCloud is no coward but equally disillusioned, having returned stateside to find that the values he fought for are outmoded and that the lot of vets such as himself is not an easy one. Similar to the play, he arrives in the Florida Keys to look up the father (Lionel Barrymore) and, in this case, widow (Lauren Bacall) of an army pal. Here, he runs up against Robinson's flashy Johnny Rocco and his quartet of thugs. In a complete reversal of fortune from their Warner Brothers years of the 1930s, Robinson is the bad guy who threatens and beats up Bogart, now the good guy. Bogart's character allows himself to be intimidated by the gun-wielding hood in silk shirts because he's no longer willing to take up another cause, he says. "I had hopes once, but gave 'em up," Bogart's character admits.

"What were they?" Robinson demands to know with a sneer.

"A world with no place for Johnny Rocco," Bogart replies, submitting wearily later, however, that, "One Rocco more or less ain't worth dyin' for."

Robinson's Johnny Rocco is a classic John Huston character, a self-deceiver who dreams of regaining his status as a mob kingpin—the "stuff that dreams are made of" in the parlance of Huston's *The Maltese Falcon*. But Bogart's character in *Key Largo* is no less of a self-deceiver, at least initially, in his belief that he no longer cares whether gangsters such as Johnny Rocco—the fascists of the post–World War II era—take over or not. But in the final analysis, he does care, does fight back, and defeats Rocco in the spirit of his dead war buddy.

CURTAINS

Movingly, Humphrey Bogart, who died of lung cancer in 1957, ended his film career where it had taken off—in gangland. His penultimate film, *The Desperate Hours* (1955), drew the actor's career almost full circle; its plot, like *Key Largo*, again recalls Bogart's first big success on the screen, *The Petrified Forest*. And his role, that of an escaped convict, Glenn Griffin, who takes a suburban family hostage while planning his getaway, is not dissimilar to *Forest*'s Duke Mantee in a number of ways.

Set in Indianapolis rather than the Arizona desert, *The Desperate Hours* begins with Bogart, his brother (Dewey Martin), and a thug named Kobish (Robert Middleton) looking for a place to hide after breaking out of jail. They pick a house at random and hold the family hostage while Bogart phones his moll with the gang's whereabouts so she'll know where to bring getaway money. The police and the FBI mount roadblocks and put a tail on her. Realizing she's being followed, she ditches her car and calls Bogart for a change in plans. He tells her to mail the getaway money to the office of the man (Fredric March) whose house they're holed up in, and he orders March to go to work as if everything's OK and bring the envelope home at the end of the day, or the gang will kill March's wife (Martha Scott) and daughter (Mary Murphy).

As the cops tighten their net around the Indianapolis suburb where they believe Bogart is hiding, the gang's nerves start to fray. Martin, Bogart's younger brother, decides to make a break for it while he still can but is killed when he runs into the police, who find March's address in his pocket. They waylay March as he returns with the envelope full of cash and inform him of their plans to storm the house. Realizing what might happen to his family if they do, March asks for time to get Bogart out of the house on his own. The cops give him ten minutes. His nerves stretched to the breaking point, March cleverly gets the upper hand on Bogart with an unloaded gun and orders the gangster out of the house into a hail of police bullets.

Like *The Petrified Forest*, *The Desperate Hours* is based on a successful Broadway melodrama (by Joseph Hayes, who adapted it from his own best-selling novel of the same title). Directed by actor Robert Montgomery, the taut play premiered at the Ethel Barrymore Theatre on February 10, 1955, and ran for more than 200 performances. An up-and-coming New York actor named Paul Newman starred as a much younger, less world-weary version of the character played by Bogart in the film version (Karl Malden played the Fredric March role).

As Newman's name as yet meant little to moviegoers, the film's director, William Wyler, asked Joseph Hayes—for whom *The Desperate Hours* was turning into a cottage industry as he'd been signed to write the screen adaptation[4] of his play—to age the Newman character twenty years for veteran screen gangster and superstar Bogart. Wyler had wanted Spencer Tracy for the role of the nerve-frayed family man who finally gets the better of the gangster, but top stars Bogart and Tracy disagreed over who was to get top billing. "Each one said, 'My name goes first.' As if the public cared," Wyler reportedly said in disgust: "It was really stupid."[5] So, Tracy bowed out, and the part went to Fredric March instead. It is the less flashy and, therefore, more difficult role, but March brings it off with stinging conviction. The tense by-play between the rough, school-of-hard-knocks Bogart and the dignified and likable average suburban family man March echoes many similar sequences between Bogart's Duke Mantee and Leslie Howard's failed poet and existential wanderer Alan Squier in *The Petrified Forest*. Like Mantee, Bogart's Glenn Griffin in *The Desperate Hours* exhibits a grudging respect for his hostage and a bitter contempt for him at the same time. He envies and hates March's Dan Hilliard for the same reasons, for everything about Hilliard—his strength in the face of adversity, his reciprocated love for his family, his comfortable middle-class lifestyle—points up just how much of a loner—and loser—in life the trapped gangster, bound by his own fate, truly is.

The Harder They Fall (1956), Bogart's last film, returned the actor once more to the role of honorable good guy in a world of crooks, albeit a flawed one like Sam Spade, who flirts with the dark side for most of the film's running time, but finds his moral center in the final reel. Bogart plays a down-on-his-luck sportswriter hired by gangster/fight promoter Rod Steiger as a press agent to steer a strapping young boxer with a glass jaw (Mike Lane) to the heavyweight championship—as Steiger fixes fight after fight to ensure that outcome. The film was written by Budd Schulberg to expose the influence of gangland on the fighting game as he had previously revealed its influence on the longshoreman's union in *On the Waterfront.* Schulberg loosely based the Mike Lane character on Primo Carnera, a real-life heavyweight champion with a glass jaw.

Through Bogart, the gentle Lane discovers his successful bouts have all been rigged. Out of pride (and the need for money to support his parents in Argentina), he decides to go through with the big heavyweight title fight, which has not been rigged, on his own. Knowing the glass-jawed Lane doesn't a stand a chance in an unfixed match, Steiger, on behalf of himself and his associates, including Bogart, bets everything on Lane's odds-against opponent in anticipation of collecting a fortune.

In one of the most grueling boxing scenes staged for a film (by director Mark Robson, who had earlier made another impressive boxing picture, the 1949 *Champion* with Kirk Douglas), Lane gives his all in the ring, but is beaten to a bloody pulp. The reprehensible Steiger makes a fortune but pays off the savagely beaten Lane in peanuts. This kicks Bogart's troubled conscience into gear; he gives Lane his substantial share of the winnings and puts the Argentine giant on the next plane home to South America. Then, in the best tradition of Sam Spade, Bogart outlines for his old boss what's going to happen next—for the benefit of "every bum who ever got his brains knocked loose in the ring," he's going to expose the fight game's infiltration by crooks like Steiger to the press, a dirty secret Bogart's own work as a flack for Steiger had ironically served to keep hidden. Bogart then announces his intention to get the sport outlawed "even if it takes an act of Congress." Typical of the Bogart persona, it is the character's past, and hope of outrunning it, that drives him—a trip he must make alone.

"YOU MOVE FAST, BUT THINK SLOW"

The Bogart gangster had an enormous influence on the underworld melodramas of '40s and '50s film noir. Shades of him can be seen in most of the heroes, antiheroes, and nonheroes populating the films of this period. Alan Ladd's cold-blooded hitman in *This Gun for Hire*[6] (1945), based on a novel by Graham Greene and adapted to the screen by W. R. Burnett, is just one example of a now-iconographic antihero of the post–*The Petrified Forest,* post–*High Sierra* gangster movie for whom Bogart's Duke Mantee and "Mad Dog" Roy Earle clearly paved the way.

Diminutive, tight-lipped and unsmiling, motivated to violence to survive, and looking perpetually trapped, Philip Raven, the role that launched Alan Ladd to stardom, is spiritually akin to the existential loner suggestive of John Dillinger whom Bogart personified on-screen.

Four years after the release of *High Sierra*, Hollywood finally got around to making an outright biography of the notorious Dillinger. Titled *Dillinger* (1945), it featured a granite-jawed newcomer named Lawrence Tierney as the bank robber; he gives a taciturn performance possessing little of the Bogart gangster's complexity or charisma.

The film consists of a series of overworked gangster movie clichés strung together into superficial narrative whose resemblance to the historical record is remote to say the least. It suggests that Dillinger's criminal career derived from his womanizing ways, that he committed acts of lawlessness to keep his women in style. The film gets right to the point in its opening scene when he robs a grocery store for some cash to buy another round of drinks for an admiring bimbo he's got his eye on.

The act lands him in the clink, however, where he strikes up a relationship with a career criminal named Specs Green (Edmund Lowe) and several other lifers, whom he agrees to spring from the jail as soon as he's released. Once paroled, he makes good on his word and robs a movie theater to finance the breakout, taking up with a pretty cashier (Anne Jeffreys) who urges him to commit bolder and bolder crimes to keep her well heeled.

With Specs as mastermind, Dillinger and his gang pull off a series of daring bank jobs and are soon riding high. But Dillinger and Specs soon clash over Dillinger's propensity for violence ("You're a little too free with the gun, John," Specs says, dressing him down). With cunning duplicity, the pragmatic Specs sets Dillinger up to get him out of the way, but the wary gangster evades capture, kills Specs in reprisal, and assumes leadership of the gang. The hot-tempered, gun-happy Dillinger proves to be no criminal mastermind, however, and the gang is soon out of money and on the run, so it splits up. Dillinger finds himself going it alone, with his expensive babe in tow. As the law closes in, he and his moll go into hiding. Suffering soon from cabin fever, she decides she's had enough and demands a night out at the movies. To disguise his face, he dons a pair of glasses with Coke-bottle lenses that make him look like Albert Dekker's bug-eyed mad scientist in *Dr. Cyclops* (1940), and she puts on a red dress so that the coppers will have no trouble spotting them. In one of the film's rare concessions to the true story of Dillinger, the gangster is summarily shot down while fleeing into an alley next to the theater after the show.

It is incredible to believe that the Academy of Motion Picture Arts and Sciences considered screenwriter Philip Yordan's "original story" worthy of an Oscar nomination when W. R. Burnett and John Huston's superb script for *High Sierra* had gone un-nominated, but it did. There is some justice, however, in the fact that at least *Dillinger* didn't win.

The Tierney *Dillinger* manufactures an image of the notorious gangster that is almost wholly fabricated. It portrays him as a dull-brained, dead-eyed, somnolent cutthroat given to greedily snatching cash from frightened depositors even after he's emptied the bank till, and who delights in committing acts of sadism more in the style of the Cagney gangster than the Bogart gangster, albeit without a trace of the Cagney gangster's charm and wit. Apparently, the weight of movie morals czar Will H. Hays's 1934 dictum against making a movie about Dillinger, even if in name only, was still being felt by Tinseltown in 1945. And, it seemed, it would continue to be felt for some years, as many films inspired by Dillinger's life and legend have cast the folk-hero outlaw in a similar light as a womanizing, "mad dog" killer.

For example, in 1965's redundantly titled *Young Dillinger* (dead at thirty-one, Dillinger scarcely lived long enough to be anything but), the future public enemy number one (played here by Cagney-ish Nick Adams) is again driven to a life of crime because of a girl. His teenage sweetheart (Mary Ann Mobley) wants him to marry her, but the dirt-poor Dillinger says he can't afford a marriage license, much less support her. So, she pushes him into robbing a safe in her wealthy father's warehouse. He's caught and gets a twenty-year sentence in jail that embitters him against the world.

While in the slammer, he makes friends with a veritable "Who's Who" of future public enemies: Pretty Boy Floyd (Robert Conrad), Baby Face Nelson (John Ashley), and Homer Van Meter (Dan Terranova). He promises to spring them when he's out. With Mobley's help, he escapes from prison and makes good on his promise. With Mobley in tow, Dillinger and his gang pull off several small-time robberies, then fall in with a criminal mastermind straight out of *The Maltese Falcon* played by beefy Victor

Buono to commit a series of big-time bank jobs. Hunted by the law, the gang retreats to a Midwest mountain cabin (located in what looks like California's scenic Lake Tahoe area), and is surrounded. Mobley takes a bullet, but her gangster lover gets away at the end of the film to receive his just desserts some other day as Adult Dillinger.

Macho director John Milius's 1973 debut feature, also called *Dillinger*, comes considerably closer to painting an accurate picture of the legendary bank robber's life and times than any other Hollywood film, including *High Sierra*, which had only been suggestive of the Dillinger story. The film has an authentic period feel, bolstered by a great score of period and rural Americana songs arranged by Barry De Vorzon; unlike Lawrence Tierney and Nick Adams, the actor who plays Dillinger (Warren Oates) even looks like Dillinger—as does Bogart's Roy Earle, although Oates's resemblance to the real-life criminal is more striking, and he is closer to the right age.

In the "bust the Code" tradition of many gangster films made since the 1970s in the wake of *Bonnie and Clyde*, especially those made on low budgets by tightwad companies such as American International Pictures, director (and ardent gun enthusiast) Milius's *Dillinger* is primarily an action movie where the emphasis is on firepower and graphic violence. Nevertheless, it does probe somewhat deeper into the truth of the Dillinger legend—and the gangster's preoccupation with sustaining that legend, a path that entraps him, and from which, like *High Sierra*'s Roy Earle, he cannot escape.

"Milius shows the effort, the narcissism, that goes into the making of a legend," write film historians Michael Pye and Lynda Myles. "Dillinger and his girl, the half-Indian Billie Frechette [Michelle Phillips], debate crossing the border to safety; but they stay in America, knowing that flight would break the legend."[7]

It is the symbiotic relationship between that legend, however, and the house on which it has become a plague—the FBI—that forms the greatest link to the Bogart gangster, most especially Duke Mantee and "Mad Dog" Roy Earle. The FBI *must* destroy the legend of Dillinger to avoid the further diminution of its own reputation, which is being cut down more and more each day because of the Bureau's failure to capture or kill the desperado. Thus, the conflict between Dillinger and the feds is no longer one of anarchy versus law and order but of image, and both sides— like Bogart's Duke of Earle and the cops in pursuit—are equally trapped into living up to their respective reputations right to the bitter end.

"Hunter and hunted are interdependent," Pye and Myles write. Melvin Purvis (Ben Johnson), the FBI agent assigned by Hoover to get the bank robber dead or alive, "is as much a mythomaniac as Dillinger himself: the two define each other and give each other stature."[8] We are told via an end title that Purvis, who left the Bureau and went into private business after the Dillinger case, took his own life in 1961 with the same gun he had used to shoot dead Dillinger outside the Biograph Theatre, thus bringing their dance of death full circle.

Closer in essence to the loner antihero, personified by Bogart, who is infernally trapped inside his own troubled soul and looking to bust out are many of the heavies played in gangster and other genre films by Robert Ryan (1909–1973). Taller, more muscular, more sinister than Bogart, and more combustible than Alan Ladd, Ryan played more outright rotten bastards on the screen than any of them—certainly more than Ryan, a devotee of Shakespeare who thirsted after the kind of light comedy and dignified hero roles that always went to Cary Grant and Gregory Peck, would have preferred.

Robert Ryan made his most notable gangster movies during the '40s and '50s, the period when he was also at his busiest. In most cases, these films remain notable largely because of the powerful work Ryan delivered in them. He made his screen debut in a minor role in *Queen of the Mob* (1940). Later, as the no longer Italian Nick Scarsi but now WASP-ish Nick Scanlon in the remake of *The Racket*, he clarified the distinction between the two types of gangsters, the former a green-eyed mobster type like Robinson, the latter a doomed, out-of-step loner like Bogart.

Maverick writer/producer/director Samuel Fuller gave Ryan another strong role in the colorful, widescreen gangster film *House of Bamboo* (1955) about the corruptive influence of the American underworld on postwar Japan. Ryan heads up a powerful syndicate that runs a numbers racket in Tokyo during the American occupation. His cronies are all ex-GIs who stayed on to make a killing, like him. His rules are rigid. Anyone who gets out of line gets a new pair of shoes made of cement. Robert Stack plays an American detective sent to Tokyo to work with Japanese officials in toppling Ryan's criminal organization.

The script by Harry Kleiner (with additional dialogue by Fuller) is a re-working of the 1948 *The Street with No Name* (also written by Kleiner, with Mark Stevens and Richard Widmark in the Stack and Ryan roles, respectively) and *White Heat*, relocated to an exotic setting. Stack infiltrates the organization to get close to Ryan, a paranoid type always looking over his shoulder for the hangman like Roy Earle (but with a sadistic streak like Cagney's Cody Jarrett). Ryan comes to like Stack and trust him. He bends the organization's rules to accommodate him and comes to rely on Stack more and more as both confidante and friend. Stack builds on the relationship to manipulate the gangster into a corner so that he can destroy him. When Stack's duplicity is revealed, Ryan reacts like a wounded animal. The conclusion substitutes *White Heat*'s apocalyptic petroleum-tank showdown between the undercover cop and the doomed gangster with a lengthy shoot-out in a Tokyo amusement park.

Robert Wise's *Odds Against Tomorrow* actually does put Ryan's paranoid thug in the Bogart vein atop some petroleum tanks for the climactic shoot-out. Part of a trio of bank robbers made up of a down-on-his-luck ex-con (Ryan), a disgraced ex-cop (Ed Begley), and a nightclub singer (Harry Belafonte) in debt to the mob, who come together to pull off a heist in a small upstate New York town (exteriors were filmed in the waterfront hamlet of Hudson), Ryan's desperate loner character here is like Bogart's Duke Mantee and Roy Earle carried to the tenth power. His fear of a world and everyone in it that is hostile to him is out of all control and is explosively manifested in his virulent racism. He virtually sweats antipathy toward the black Belafonte, and it is this racism, driven by the character's ignorance and paranoia, that ultimately leads to the failure of the bank job, and Ryan's self-immolation atop the petroleum tanks.

It is this fiery finale, however, that is the film's least convincing moment because it strikes one as being so openly derivative of *White Heat,* whereas the rest of the film—written by John O. Killens (a "front" for the blacklisted Abraham Polonsky) and Nelson Gidding from a novel by William P. McGivern—stands so solidly on its own. The film is at its most persuasively incendiary in the scenes where the race-baiting Ryan and the object of his fear and scorn Belafonte square off against each other verbally. And the film's real sparks fly in the scenes between Ryan and film noir icon Gloria Grahame as the "hotcha" femme fatale he really should be afraid of who gets turned on by talk of murder.

In real life, Ryan couldn't have been more dissimilar to the vicious, paranoid thugs he played on the screen, which may be why he understood and played them so well: He knew what he despised. Interestingly, this was also true of Edward G. Robinson (an art collector), James Cagney (a painter), and even Humphrey Bogart in his later years when he married Lauren Bacall and became a laid-back sailor on his yacht, the *Santana.*

Only George Raft seemed to have enjoyed associating with the types he played on the screen, while not actually being one of those types himself, except in his relish of the high life.

Dissimilar too in real life from the not-so-smart, psychically wounded tough-guy characters trying to get by in a noir world that he often played on screen is John Garfield (1913–1952). Born Julius Garfinkle, the stage-trained Garfield more often played shady but decent nonheroes (as in *Force of Evil*; see Chapter 1) or vulnerable young rebels without (but occasionally with) a cause. His naturalistic acting style—part Cagney, part Bogart, part New York Group Theatre—and charisma set the pace for such actors as Montgomery Clift, Marlon Brando, and James Dean who were to follow.

Garfield's few screen performances as outright thugs were clearly of the Bogart school. This is nowhere more evident than in *He Ran All the Way* (1951), his last film before his untimely death of coronary thrombosis in 1952. It is a gangster movie strikingly similar, in fact, to *The Desperate Hours*, Bogart's swansong as a movie thug. Garfield plays a hood involved in an armed robbery gone bad who takes refuge in an apartment in a lower-class neighborhood, holding the family that lives there hostage until the heat blows over.

Like Bogart's Glenn Griffin in *Hours*, Garfield's Nick Robey is drawn to the homey, close-knit lifestyle of the family he has taken hostage. Unlike the family Griffin takes hostage, however, this one is of the same background and economic class as the hostage taker. Even Garfield's philosophy of "trust no one" (but especially cops) is shared by these people because of their similar position on the social and economic ladder. Thus, Garfield's character is even more drawn to their lifestyle than Bogart's character is to the lifestyle of his victims. The gulf isn't as wide; thus, the lifestyle of his victims is more realistically attainable to Garfield's character.

At the same time, his character is both ambivalent toward—and sometimes dangerously resentful of—the family's close-knittedness because it is so at odds with his own upbringing (his parents tossed him out at a young age). It is this lifelong internal tug of war and the paranoia it has engendered that leads him to tipping the scales against himself. He forces the family's grown daughter (played by Shelley Winters), who has fallen in love and wants to run away with him, into making a fateful choice between his life and that of her father (Wallace Ford) during the climactic getaway when things really get sticky between the old man and the young thug. And Garfield's Nick Robey finds out—as Bogart's Griffin does—that forcing choices in others out of your own paranoia can be a fatal mistake. "You think slow, Nick—you move fast, but think slow," one of Garfield's criminal associates points out to him early in the film. It is a line that could serve as the epitaph not only for Garfield's Nick Robey in *He Ran All the Way*, but also for all manner of screen bad guys in the mold of the Bogart gangster right up through Tom Hanks's Prohibition-era hitman on the run from his employers (and from himself) in *Road to Perdition* (2002), where Hanks's Michael O'Sullivan finds himself boxed into a corner by the life he has chosen to lead.

Maverick director Sam Peckinpah, whose films are profuse with desperate loners, took a crack at reworking the story with a Dillinger-style desperado in *The Getaway* (1972)[9], based on a noir novel published in 1959 by maverick pulp-cum-socialist writer Jim Thompson. Steve McQueen stars as Doc McCoy, a convicted bank robber in the Bogart mold serving a ten-year stretch in Huntsville prison. After the parole board denies McQueen's request for an early release, he accepts an offer from crooked board member Ben Johnson to rob an oil-company payroll at a small-town Texas bank in exchange for his freedom. He sends his moll (Ali McGraw) to finalize the deal. To accomplish this, she sleeps with Johnson.

As soon as McQueen is released, he and McGraw (his getaway driver) begin planning the heist with Johnson's henchmen (Al Lettieri and Bo Hopkins), unaware that they are planning a double-cross. During the getaway, Hopkins is killed. McQueen smells a rat, and he plugs Lettieri before Lettieri can plug him. Then the outlaw couple flees with the loot—with Lettieri, who survives his wounds, more of Johnson's thugs, and the cops in hot pursuit. Several wild car chases, a tense sequence involving a garbage truck, and much gunplay ensue as McQueen and McGraw struggle to keep alive as they head for El Paso and to freedom across the Mexican border.

The film ends quite differently from Thompson's bleak portrait of an ill-fated loner and his equally ill-starred moll. Like Bogart, McQueen successfully communicates the character's aloneness, his bottled-up sense of being trapped in a prison without walls that is of his own making. But McQueen was a big enough star by 1972 to be able to call the shots—especially when his own production company (First Artists) was making the picture—and vetoed any suggestion of coming up a loser at the end of his films. As a result, *The Getaway* feels compromised, even though it is an exciting combination of gangster movie, heist picture, and modern-day Western, filled with many suspenseful and powerfully put together action sequences, Peckinpah-style. Aside from the compromised finish, its major flaw is the casting, or *miscasting*, of McGraw as a gun totin' babe good with cars and a talent for trouble. Peckinpah defended her performance, but compared to the gals in Chapter 5, McGraw's polished porcelain moll in *The Getaway* is clearly more Bryn Mawr College than school of hard knocks.

A GOOD THING FOR A BAD MAN

Having turned in a spot-on performance as the Robinson-style gangster Cheech in Woody Allen's *Bullets Over Broadway* (1991), Chazz Palminteri topped himself by turning in a triple-threat performance as a Robinson, Cagney, *and* Bogart-style gangster in *A Bronx Tale* (1993), wherein he synthesizes each archetypal gangster persona into one New York City hood.

The film marked actor Robert De Niro's directorial debut and is based on an award-winning one-man play by Palminteri himself about growing up among all sorts of gangsters on 187th Street in the Bronx during the 1960s. Cannily, Palminteri the writer gives Palminteri the actor the best part, that of Sonny, the so-called "number one man in the neighborhood" whom everyone treats like a god, mostly out of fear. When one of the kids on the street who looks up to him witnesses Sonny commit a murder but refuses to rat him out to the cops, Sonny takes a special shine to the boy, whose name is Calogero (writer Palminteri's actual first name and his alter-ego in the film). Calogero's bus driver father (Robert De Niro) discourages the friendship. "You did a good thing for a bad man," he counsels the boy whom he wants to grow up to be an honest working man like himself, not a gangster like Sonny. Ironically, even though Sonny scorns all working men as suckers, he wants the same for the boy: "This is my life, not yours," he says, "I do what I have to do."

The bulk of the film, a coming-of-age story set in gangland, deals with the emotional tug of war Calogero experiences learning about life from his real father and his surrogate one, both of whom want the boy to grow up to be the best man he can possibly be and are admirable teachers in their own very different ways.

A Bronx Tale perfectly captures the innocent glow of growing up and of the era in which Calogero's coming of age takes place. Like Martin

Scorsese, his frequent collaborator and directorial mentor, De Niro layers the film's soundtrack with a playlist of contemporary pop hits—in this case a cavalcade of classic '50s and '60s "doo wop"—to whisk us back in time and to comment on the action. Occasionally the match up of song and story gets a bit strained, wavering between the delightfully unexpected and subtly right to the too-heavy-handed and on-the-nose. Likewise, the tone of the film itself wavers, alternating between caricature and character, toughness and schmaltz.

What really holds *A Bronx Tale* together, though, and it does so like glue, is Palminteri. His performance as Sonny encompasses the full range of gangland archetypes in the cinema, from the green-eyed mobsters dressed to the nines personified by Robinson, to the homicidal thugs personified by Cagney, to the desperate, brooding loners personified by Bogart who've been sentenced to life in a prison of their own making, and from which there will never be any bustin' out.

PART THREE
THE FAMILY

"I'm a businessman, Tom.
I don't like violence. Blood is a big expense."
—*Sollozzo (Al Lettieri),*
The Godfather *(1972)*

10
Once Upon a Time in New York

"This is a night for Americans!"
—*Bill the Butcher (Daniel Day-Lewis)*,
Gangs of New York (2002)

AMERICAN EAGLE

IN A POWERFUL APPRECIATION OF SAM PECKINPAH'S classic Western *The Wild Bunch* (1969), actor Robert Culp asserts that one of the film's important subthemes is "the only good American is a dead American." This is a riff on the genocidal frontier sentiment that "the only good Indian is a dead Indian." Peckinpah's riff has an altogether different meaning, however, says Culp, one that is neither genocidal nor unpatriotic, but that "the Americans who are now all lost and gone were much better than we are, and what we have lost in them we can never get back."[1]

This subtheme of *The Wild Bunch* is the dominant one in Martin Scorsese's *Gangs of New York*. It runs straight through to the end when Scorsese's camera collapses time to show the modern skyline of his beloved New York City growing and taking shape on a foundation of graves, marked and unmarked, belonging to the dead, good and bad, who *made* the city—just as the stalwart likes of Peckinpah's good, bad, and ugly roughnecks made this country.

The influence of *The Wild Bunch* on *Gangs of New York* is not surprising in that director Scorsese and especially co-screenwriter Jay Cocks are aficionados of Peckinpah's work, *The Wild Bunch* especially, and had long desired to make a film of similar conviction and visceral power. *Gangs of New York,* a project Scorsese and Cocks had nurtured for twenty years, presented them with the opportunity, and they decided to use it to go Peckinpah's film one better. *The Wild Bunch* ends on a note of both triumph and tragedy as the bunch go to their bloody grave in a blaze of— not glory, perhaps, but honor—taking on an entire army of Mexican federales in a suicidal attempt to get back one of their own who has been captured and tortured.

"'Let's put the end of *The Wild Bunch* at the beginning of [*Gangs of New York*],' Cocks said," reports film critic Michael Sragow. "[Of course] Doing a similar scene at the start of *Gangs of New York* meant Cocks and Scorsese would risk comparisons to the greatest action scene in modern movies and face the obstacle of equaling or topping it at the end of their own film, 'But,' [said Cocks] 'at least we'd set ourselves a good challenge!'"[2]

Alas, it is a challenge that *Gangs of New York* fails to meet.

As the curtain rises on the gangland drama, we have not yet come to know, let alone become emotionally invested in, any of the characters we see in the opening melee, and so we feel nothing for those who lose their lives (as we do for the Wild Bunch)—except, perhaps, to turn away grimacing at all the bloodshed. Thus, the opening scene of *Gangs of New York* delivers on the carnage but not on the visceral punch.

More successful is the filmmakers' goal to emulate *The Wild Bunch*'s elegiac qualities. Their admiration for the good and bad dead on whose bones today's Big Apple spires upward is both forceful and sustained, and largely reflected in the larger than life character of Bill the Butcher (Daniel Day-Lewis), a charismatic rogue, cutthroat, and first generation mob boss based on the real life William "Bill the Butcher" Poole (1821–1855), whom Scorsese and Cocks learned about when they read Herbert Asbury's nonfiction *The Gangs of New York: An Informal History of the Underworld* (originally published by Alfred A. Knopf in 1928), which became the primary source material for their film.

Asbury (1889–1963) is another of that breed we've encountered many times throughout these pages: the newspaper reporter-turned-scribe. Born in Missouri, Asbury attended Carleton College in Minnesota, graduating from there to reporting on issues of sin, religious intolerance, and hypocrisy in the Midwest for H. L. Mencken's controversial *American Mercury* magazine, as well as covering the crime beat for a host of

New York City newspapers, ranging from the *Sun* and the *Tribune* to the *Herald*.

It was the latter experience that led him to write *The Gangs of New York*, which grew out of a piece he'd first published in a 1927 issue of *American Mercury* called "The Old Gangs of New York." Mixing history and folklore, the book canvassed the lawless legacy of the notorious Bowery and Five Points areas of lower Manhattan—the setting of the first gangster films such as *Regeneration*—from the beginning of the nineteenth century through the Civil War draft riots of the 1860s to the influx of Italian immigrants as the century turned. The book was a top-seller, prompting Asbury to give up newspaper reporting to pursue an even more successful career as a writer of nonfiction, as well as a less successful one as a novelist, playwright, and screenwriter. His subsequent top-selling chronicles of gangland America include *The Barbary Coast: An Informal History of the San Francisco Underworld* (Alfred A. Knopf, 1933) and *Gem of the Prairie: An Informal History of the Chicago Underworld* (Alfred A. Knopf, 1940).

The first of his "informal histories" to get the film treatment was his tale of the San Francisco underworld, which served as the inspiration for the 1935 Howard Hawks picture *Barbary Coast,* although the film version is more fiction than non, taking little from the book other than some tidbits of Barbary pirate lore and the real-life setting. Republic Pictures went the same route when it brought Asbury's *The Gangs of New York* to the screen under the title *Gangs of New York* in 1938, directed by James Cruze. The screenplay (cowritten by crime reporter-turned-screenwriter Samuel Fuller) about a cop (Charles Bickford) who uses his resemblance to a notorious gangster (Bickford also) to seize control of the New York mob and take it down is fiction; also, the period is updated to modern day. The film was a hit critically and commercially for the small studio, so Republic followed it in 1940 with *Gangs of Chicago*, which appears unrelated in any way to Asbury's informal survey of Chicago's underworld history published the same year.

Martin Scorsese's approach to bringing Asbury's work to the screen is not altogether different from that of Hawks and Cruze in that he too mixes fact (but more of it) with fiction in *Gangs of New York*—largely out of a *need* to take dramatic license given the sheer volume of characters, events, and years covered. The main period focused on, however, is the 1860s, and the main locale is Five Points, where the seeds of organized crime in America took root.

Although Asbury's book bulges with unforgettable characters, Bill the Butcher and Boss Tweed (Jim Broadbent)—that sly, manipulative, corrupt vote stealer of Tammany Hall infamy—are the most fascinating to have found their way from Asbury's book into the film, and they also are the most watchable. Indeed, they are clearly the filmmakers' favorite characters, particularly Bill the Butcher. Unfortunately (but perhaps out of commercial necessity) the scriptwriters felt they needed a top-billed foil for Bill that could be played by a rising, hot young star. And so they pit Bill against a fictional protagonist, Amsterdam Vallon (played by Leonardo DiCaprio), the son of a rival gang leader (Liam Neeson) slain by Bill in the opening battle. Now grown up and bent on revenge, DiCaprio insinuates himself into Bill's good graces in order to get close enough to the mobster (a virtual cat with nine lives) to be able to slit his throat.

DiCaprio is fine as Vallon, and so is Cameron Diaz as his love interest (another fictional character). But the almost three-hour film unquestionably slows to a crawl whenever the action shifts away from the activities of those scurrilous but wonderfully engaging rats Bill the Butcher and Boss Tweed. It is *their* picture—especially Bill's; he is the picture's hero (or antihero), certainly in *Wild Bunch* terms, and Daniel Day-Lewis brings him powerfully to life.

As the vengeful DiCaprio gets close to the man who killed his father, even *he* comes to develop a grudging admiration for Bill's survival instincts, political shrewdness, personal pride, and patriotic fervor for the city and country the mob boss lays claim to as a native son. Bill is so patriotic, in fact, that he wears an American eagle not on his sleeve but on his glass eye.

DiCaprio is also taken aback when the man he's determined to destroy, and who has the blood of scores of men on his hands (unlike the real Bill the Butcher, whose nickname derived solely from his occupation as a meat cutter), honors the memory of DiCaprio's father by remembering him as the only worthy adversary among his many victims. This revelation is not enough to stay DiCaprio's hand when he and Bill finally go mano a mano, but it does drive home a contradictory and surprising truth about Bill the Butcher and his like—that they could be xenophobic, intolerant, crafty killers who also valued such qualities as respect and honor, particularly in their enemies.

"Honor" and "respect" would later become hard, sometimes lethal, currency to the American Mafia, which, as *Gangs of New York* comes to a close, is still a quarter of a century away from blossoming in the Lower

East Side as immigrants from Sicily flooded into the city. In fact, an 1890s gang calling itself the Five Pointers run by an Italian émigré named Paolo Vaccarelli (calling himself "Paul Kelly") would grow in power as the century turned, eventually boasting such influential alumni as Johnny Torrio and Al "Scarface" Capone.

The scope of *Gangs of New York* doesn't stretch that far, nor does the film suggest that the gangs portrayed on screen are the antecedents of the Mafia in America; it only acknowledges that the Five Points area was a breeding ground for criminal organizations of all stripes to take root and grow. What the film does do, with gusto, is echo the observation of the dying James Cagney at the conclusion of *The Public Enemy* when he says, "I ain't so tough." Compared to the old gangs of New York, Scorsese's picture says, today's goodfellas really "ain't so tough" either.

PAY OR DIE

Often considered synonymous with "criminal organization," the term "La Mano Nera" (the "Black Hand") actually refers to a method of intimidation used by immigrant criminals to extort protection money from among the population of their fellow Italian immigrants, who had begun to move beyond the borders of Five Points into what was to become New York's Little Italy. Those who refused to fork cash over to the Black Handers were murdered and mutilated, a slip of paper bearing a black palm print and the words *pay or die* left with the body to warn others. This method of intimidation was such a moneymaking enterprise that many Mafiosi adopted it as well.

Pay or Die (1960), director Richard Wilson's less fanciful follow-up to his uneven biopic about Al Capone, chronicles this all-but-forgotten episode in New York's gangland history by focusing on the cop who exposed the Black Handers at the expense of his own life. He is Lt. Joseph Petrosino, an immigrant policeman in Little Italy whose crusade against the Black Hand extortionists during the years 1906 and 1909 exposed the existence of the Sicilian-controlled New York Mafia—that criminal organization, you'll recall, that J. Edgar Hoover never heard of for much of his law enforcement career.

As the film begins, Petrosino (Ernest Borgnine) is himself skeptical that there is a criminal conspiracy behind the Black Hand phenomenon. While studying to make captain, a promotion he's repeatedly denied because of interdepartmental prejudice and his lack of proficiency in reading English, Petrosino comes up with the idea of putting together a team of fellow immigrants on the force to win hearts and minds within the Italian community, enabling him to go after the Black Handers. The commissioner (Robert F. Simon) goes along with the idea, and Petrosino's so-called "Italian Squad"—a forerunner of Eliot Ness's Untouchables— gets its first assignment, which is to protect the visiting Italian singer Enrico Caruso (Howard Caine) from becoming a target of the Black Handers over his refusal to pay protection money. The Black Handers plant a bomb in Caruso's car, but Petrosino and his squad foil the assassination attempt, and the bomber is killed.

In the wake of the Italian Squad's debut success, the Black Handers get bolder, and influential members of the Italian community, believing the squad needs a leader of greater stature than Petrosino, urge the commissioner to replace him. But Petrosino is kept on, and through his courage and persistence, he and his squad get the frightened citizens to come to them when threatened by the Black Handers. As a result, the squad scores an impressive record of arrests and convictions.

When an important criminal witness (Robert Ellenstein) commits suicide rather than go against the Mafia code of silence, however, Petrosino comes to the realization that the Black Handers are not just a bunch of loose-knit extortionists but the single arm of a larger criminal enterprise being run from afar by Mafia elders in Sicily. He sails there to unearth as much as he can about the Mafia's tentacled reach into the new country and to smoke out the identity of the *capo*[3] running things in New York.

Overseas in Italy, Petrosino learns that one of Little Italy's most respected citizens (Frank Corsaro) is the *capo*, and he gets ahold of the names and photos of numerous other *capos* the Sicilian puppetmasters have sent to the United States to develop similar organizations. In a surprising but factual twist, Petrosino is killed by Mafia goons before he can return to New York with the evidence. And although his protégé (Alan Austin) does manage to nail the top villain in Little Italy, the film ends with the implication that the Mafia's infiltration of New York and the rest of the country will go on, and ultimately expand far beyond the small-time criminal of extorting mom and pop shopowners.

A decade earlier than Wilson's film, MGM's *Black Hand* (1950) chronicled essentially the same episode, but in more fictionalized terms. The screenplay by Luther Davis centers on Johnny Columbo, the son of an immigrant lawyer who is murdered by the Black Handers for trying to expose them. When Columbo grows to adulthood, he thirsts for revenge against the men responsible for his father's death. Taken under the wing of a tough Italian cop (J. Carrol Naish), a character modeled on the real-life Joseph Petrosino, he turns away from his dreams of *la vendetta*, however, and joins Naish in organizing the Italian community to fight back against the Black Handers and their Mafiosi leaders.

Pay or Die and *Black Hand* are beautifully photographed by Lucien Ballard and Paul C. Vogel, respectively. Tough and violent, the two films capture in noirish black and white the ethnic atmosphere of New York's teeming Little Italy in the early years of the twentieth century as vividly as *The Godfather Part II* and Sergio Leone's *Once Upon a Time in America* do in color. Most interestingly, both films openly made use at the time of the terms *Mafioso*, *Mafiosi*, and *Mafia* with little protest from Italian-American groups of the kind that would later swirl around so many movies and TV shows about organized crime in America, from Francis Ford Coppola's *Godfather* films to *The Sopranos*. In *Black Hand*, Naish's Italian cop even alludes instructively to the purported derivation of the word Mafia, an acronym of *Morte alla Francia Italia anela* ("Death to the French cries Italy"), when he educates his protégé about the Bourbon kings' domination of Italy in the late eighteenth and early nineteenth centuries. Perhaps J. Edgar Hoover should have spent more time at the movies.

Of these two worthy films dealing with the history of la Mano Nera, *Black Hand* is the least dramatically persuasive overall. The very Irish Gene Kelly is a mighty odd choice for the role of the revenge-seeking young Italian Johnny Columbo, although he acquits himself in the part fairly well. Also, the film is oddly structured; Kelly is supposed to be the hero, but he disappears for large chunks of the picture as the story focuses on Naish's character, ostensibly a supporting one but the most interesting character in the film. And the film's revelation of the *capo*'s identity comes as no real surprise because we see him engineer the murder of Kelly's father at the beginning of the movie.

MURDER, INCORPORATED

For the enterprising mob, it was just one small but profitable step from extorting money from people for *not* killing them to the just as venal, but often more profitable, business of hiring out killings—just as the land barons of the Old West used to put gunslingers on the payroll to get their dirty work done.

Although the shadowy figure of the contract killer had lurked about the edges of the gangster film almost from the beginning, the details of his occupation, including his motives and methods, had gone largely unexplored by filmmakers, even during the genre's heyday of the 1930s because of the restrictions imposed by the Motion Picture Production Code. Even the two contract killers played by William Conrad and Charles McGraw who take center stage in Robert Siodmak's *The Killers* remain shadowy characters. The real focus and subject of the film is their quarry, who seems a resigned target, and how he got into the fix that set them on his trail.

As the power of the Code started waning, however, motion picture makers began to delve more deeply into such previously taboo subject matter as the mob's long-standing tradition of murder for hire, a subject that broke into the news in the early 1950s during the televised Kefauver hearings into organized crime. It was during these hearings that Murder, Inc. (as the press dubbed it with gallows humor)—the corporate signature of the syndicate's professional hit squad, an organization that had first hit the headlines in the early '40s—hit the headlines again.

Murder, Inc., was the enforcement arm of the burgeoning crime syndicate created by legendary mobsters Charles "Lucky" Luciano and Meyer Lansky in the 1930s. Louis Lepke Buchalter, the mob's top union racketeer, ran the operation aided by Albert Anastasia, his "lord high executioner." Notorious mobsters Joe Adonis, Bugsy Siegel, Frank Costello, Vito Genovese, and Abner "Longy" Zwillman were other "members of the board."

Allegedly, Murder, Inc., targeted only those mob miscreants thought to be double-crossing the organization, those in peril of being squeezed by the feds into spilling their guts on mob activities, or those who failed to follow the orders of the national syndicate. Cops, politicians, and journalists were off limits due to the heat their murders might generate, as witness the furor that had followed the gangland rubout of reporter Jake Lingle (see Chapter 2)—and Lingle had been on the mob's payroll!

Similar to a board of directors meeting at a Fortune 500 company, a unanimous vote of approval was required of all board members before a contract could be issued. Murder Inc. chief operating officer Buchalter and his manager of operations Albert Anastasia would then give the contract to one of their staff—Louis Capone (no relation to Al), Mendy Weiss, or Abe "Kid Twist" Reles—to execute, and they would assign the hit to one of a number of contract killers who freelanced for them. In this way, the theory went, the killers, if ever caught, would be unable to identify the top men who had ordered the hit, thus a legal system of plausible denial was established for those top men in the event of questioning by police.

Exposure came as a result of a tip given to a New York assistant district attorney named Burton Turkus that led to the arrest of Abe "Kid Twist" Reles and two of his freelancers, Buggsy Goldstein and Dukey Maffetore. When Goldstein and Maffetore began spilling their guts to authorities, Reles knew his days were numbered. So he made a deal to sing too. Reles fingered other contract killers on the Murder, Inc., payroll and implicated Buchalter as well. At the time, Buchalter was serving a life sentence in Leavenworth on narcotics and other charges. Murder was not among these charges, however, and so a possible parole for Buchalter seemed in the cards—until Reles named him as the head of Murder, Inc.

Buchalter was charged with ordering the murder of a union leader and his successful prosecution resulted in a non–life sentence with no possibility of parole—death in the electric chair. Buchalter and subcontractors Mendy Weiss and Louis Capone went to the chair in 1944. Reles, the once-loyal staffer who had exposed Murder, Inc., never lived to testify against them (or anyone else), though. He died in 1941 after a fall from the top floor of a Coney Island hotel where he was being held under police protection on assistant DA Turkus's orders.

Reles's death was ruled accidental; bed sheets were found hanging from Reles's window, and it was assumed that the hoodlum, perhaps because of claustrophobia or fear for his life, had fallen while trying to escape. Most chroniclers of organized crime, however, believe Reles was killed on Lucky Luciano's orders to keep him from doing more squealing than he already had, and that the contract killer (whoever he was) had simply paid one of Reles's guards to look the other way at the opportune moment.

"In all the history of crime, there has never been an example of organized lawlessness equal to the Syndicate," Turkus writes (with Sid Feder) in his best-selling account of the case, *Murder Inc: The Story of the Syndicate*, published by Farrar, Straus and Young in 1951. He goes on: "Details are not for the squeamish. In a ten-year period, upward of one thousand murders were committed from New England to California, Minnesota to New Orleans and Miami, by the combination,[4] either directly or through the technique it developed. They were done for the

Syndicate. The technique became, and, in fact, remains to this day, the blueprint for organized gang throat-cutting. However, murder, I must emphasize, was not the big business. The rackets were. The assassinations were ordered, contracted and performed solely to sustain those rackets." The bodies of the victims were dumped in swamps and farmlands all along the East Coast.

Capitalizing on the revelations of the Kefauver hearings about organized crime and Murder, Inc., Warner Brothers went back to its "straight from the headlines" formula of the 1930s and concocted a semi-fictional account of the exposure of Murder, Incorporated, titled *The Enforcer* (1951) in the United States; abroad it was titled *Murder, Inc.* It stars Humphrey Bogart (in his last role for the studio[5]) not as the head or even a member of the organization of killers, which one might have expected, but as a crusading prosecutor in the mold of Burton Turkus out to bring the ringleaders to justice. In a character modeled on Louis Lepke Buchalter, Everett Sloane plays the CEO of the murder-for-hire organization.

Studio contract director Bretaigne Windust began the film but was summarily replaced by an uncredited Raoul Walsh, who stepped in for a number of weeks of extra shooting. This may account for some of unevenness of the film, long stretches of which are talky and dull, whereas others are full of violent, even shocking, action. The collaborative nature of filmmaking makes it uncertain which scenes belong to Windust and which to Walsh, an old hand at the hard-hitting style of gangster film pioneered by Warner Brothers, who had most recently directed the powerful *White Heat* for the studio, but the likelihood is that the "zestier" footage is Walsh's.

One of the film's strongest scenes is the opener, which details the death of the Abe "Kid Twist" Reles character (played by Ted Corsia) for having informed on the mob. Stashed in a high-rise hotel under guard until he can testify, the terrified witness knows that a contract has been put out on him and that it's only a matter of time before it's carried out. He overcomes one of his guards by brutally slamming the man's head into the bathroom sink, then climbs out the window to flee. Too high up, however, he dangles precariously from the ledge. Bogart arrives and climbs out after him, extending a hand, but the witness loses his grip and falls to his death on the street below in the manner of the actual Reles.

The film's most gruesome scene (also based on fact) has Bogart and his men discovering one of the assassination squad's mass graves in a New Jersey swamp and unearthing bundles of pairs of shoes, the only traces remaining of the victims, whose bodies were buried separately in lime. Another of Murder, Inc.'s methods of execution—death by ice pick in the back of the victim's neck—is also accurately portrayed.

Published the same year *The Enforcer* was released, Burton Turkus's memoir of bringing the murderers of Murder, Inc., to justice reached the screen itself in 1960. Produced by Twentieth Century Fox and titled *Murder, Inc.,* after Turkus's book, the film unfolds in the noirish style of *The Untouchables*, the hit ABC series whose popularity at the time probably had a lot to do with inspiring the studio to make the picture.

Murder, Inc. offers a more factual account of the killer organization's rise and tumble after being exposed than *The Enforcer* and also uses real names. Henry Morgan plays Turkus, the narrator of the story; David J. Stewart (a prolific TV character actor at the time who was just then beginning to shine in film roles but died suddenly at age fifty-two) is utterly reptilian as the villainous Louis Lepke Buchalter; and Peter Falk appears (in only his third film role) as the cagey but ultimately doomed Abe "Kid Twist" Reles, a performance that earned him an Academy Award nomination as best supporting actor.

Like *The Enforcer, Murder, Inc.* also had two directors (Burt Balaban and Stuart Rosenberg), but in this case, each received screen credit. Again, the presence of two helmsmen behind the camera may explain the uneven qualities of the film, in which scenes of powerful impact are similarly offset by long expanses of unexciting celluloid. The roles of an ill-fated couple (Stuart Whitman and May Britt), who get caught up in a deadly syndicate power play when they agree to hide the fugitive Stewart, are considerably expanded here, if only to give us someone for whom to root. But the film belongs to Stewart and Falk; as with Daniel Day-Lewis in *Gangs of New York*, it is mostly when they are on screen that this minor but engaging docudrama about the mob's ugly but profitable murder-for-hire business really cooks.

Most of the mob's infamous supporting characters eventually moved up the ladder in gangster movies to receive star billing of their own, and Murder, Inc.'s Louis Lepke Buchalter is no exception. In Menachem Golan's requisitely bloodthirsty *Lepke* (1975), a fair amount of biographical research obviously went into its subject; nevertheless, the filmmakers do manage to pull a few boners along the way. For example, the script at one point has mob kingpin Lucky Luciano (Vic Tayback) address syndicate colleague Ben Siegel as "Bugsy," a hated nickname that prompted the narcissistic psychopath to go ballistic if used in his presence. In another gaffe, Lepke (Tony Curtis) tells how he ordered the death of gangster Jack "Legs" Diamond and had the body dumped off a Coney Island pier, when in fact "Legs" Diamond was disposed of (allegedly at the order of mobster Dutch Schultz) in a hotel room in Albany, New York.

As with Roger Corman's *The St. Valentine's Day Massacre*, these are minor lapses, however, in a screenplay that otherwise strives to deliver the real dope. In fact, the picture plays like a filmed rap sheet.

Lepke opens in 1923 when the title character is one of many impoverished teens eking out an existence in New York's Lower East Side. Several arrests for petty thievery land him in reform school. When he gets out as an adult, he joins up with boyhood pal Gurrah Shapiro, a member of a protection racket run by small-time hood Little Augie Orgen. Lepke kills Orgen, takes over the protection operation, and quickly expands activities to the city's labor unions. His success and reputation earn him a spot in Luciano's syndicate, where Lepke heads up Murder, Inc., the syndicate's deadly squad of enforcers. Curiously, the term "Murder, Inc." is never used in the film. But its methods are graphically depicted—and embellished upon, sometimes amusingly, as in a scene where hitman Mendy Weiss fulfills one contract by whacking his victim with an exploding plate of spaghetti, and another with a detonated stack of newspapers.

By contrast, most of Lepke's own victims are offed by less colorful means, such as the traditional ice pick and tommy gun. These scenes of murder are interspersed with tedious peeks into Lepke's serene home life with vapid bride Bernice (Anjanette Comer), whose obliviousness to what her husband does for a living to keep them in such riches is astonishing. She makes the naïve wife of Michael Corleone ("Never ask me about my business, Kay") in *The Godfather* films seem like a hardened skeptic by comparison.

Eventually Lepke's ambitions overtake him when he tries to horn in on Luciano's narcotics operation. A gang war erupts, and he becomes a hunted man forced to go into hiding. He bargains with the feds to turn himself in so long as he's not tried for murder, but the feds double-cross him and turn him over to New York prosecutor Thomas E. Dewey, who charges Lepke with running Murder, Inc., and gets him sent to the chair—the only syndicate kingpin ever to get the juice in New York.

Director Golan's staging of Lepke's execution in the "dance hall" (death-row slang for the electric chair) is harrowing, and the grisliest such scene in movies until Frank Darabont's death row epic *The Green Mile* (1999).

Known more for its arty style than its bloodthirstiness, Irving Lerner's noirish and suspenseful *Murder by Contract* (1958) is another B gangster film that, like *The Phenix City Story*, exerted a strong influence on such up-and-coming young filmmakers as Martin Scorsese[6] for its boldness, its style, and its inventiveness on a no-budget. Lerner's film takes a more cerebral look at the mechanics of murder for hire than any of the other films discussed. Vince Edwards plays one of three killers contracted to rub out a wealthy socialite who is to testify against their gangster boss. Herschel Bernardi and Phillip Pine are Edwards's fellow contractees. Most of the action in this compelling sleeper is confined to the area in and around the target's heavily guarded apartment, a veritable fortress that the persistent Edwards manages to penetrate in a most unusual manner during the film's closing minutes—only to fall victim to the oldest law of all, Murphy's Law, as everything goes wrong for him, at the worst possible time.

"NEVER RAT ON YOUR FRIENDS"

The more things change, the more they stay the same—an adage that applies as much to reel life as to real life. The same social ills that gave rise to the gangs of New York in the early decades of the twentieth century have not been eradicated. Poverty, drugs, bigotry, class and ethnic warfare, homelessness, and greed are still with us. Inevitably, so are the gangs and gangsters such ills produce or nurture. Their violent exploits continue to fascinate filmmakers and audiences.

The enduring popularity of the gangster genre, together with some financial help from his friends in the rock music world, enabled aspiring director Martin Scorsese to bring the postwar saga of the New York underworld and its hold on Scorsese's own Lower East Side/Little Italy roots into the modern cinema via his breakthrough film *Mean Streets* (1973).

An American New Wave film in the style of the European New Wave cinema of the 1960s but with a rough, urban style all its own, *Mean Streets* is a gritty portrait of the legacy and influence of organized crime on three second-generation Italian-Americans. In many ways, the film is a warm-up for Scorsese's more polished, and even more highly acclaimed, exploration of the same world in *GoodFellas* (1990), as well as the final entry in the director's trilogy on modern gangland, the westbound

Casino (1995). For all three films, the previously discussed Scorsese period epic *Gangs of New York* can, and should, be viewed as a preamble.

Like the iconic character of the former juvenile delinquent who grew up to be a priest played by Pat O'Brien in *Angels with Dirty Faces,* Scorsese's alter ego in *Mean Streets*, played by Harvey Keitel, is torn between his religious convictions (his desire to become a priest) and his conflicting attraction to the anarchy and excitement of the New York underworld—much as Scorsese himself was conflicted in his early years between the idea of entering the priesthood and his addiction to the world of movies.

The underworld of *Mean Streets* is represented by Keitel's uncle (Cesare Danova), a successful restaurateur and Mafioso. As Keitel searches his soul, he and a pal (David Proval) get progressively more involved in low-level loan-sharking and numbers racketeering while the Cagney-esque third member of their group, the hot-tempered and violent Johnny Boy (Robert De Niro), gets in over his head with a vicious small-time hood (Richard Romanus) bent on moving up the syndicate ladder and becoming a *capo*.

Part coming-of-age tale on the order of Federico Fellini's *I Vitelloni* (1953), part crime-cum-morality tale on the order of François Truffaut's *Shoot the Piano Player* (1960), and part '70s gangster film, *Mean Streets* effectively shows how little the underworld-influenced landscape of Scorsese's Little Italy had changed since the early days of the Black Handers when gangland muscle posed similar threats and the allure of gangsterism forced similarly tough moral choices on the confused young savages of the streets who were trying to find themselves and their future. In a way, the film says, only the background music of this world has changed—having shifted from old country tarantellas and new country Big Band to the rock 'n' roll of Chuck Berry and Screamin' Jay Hawkins.

Today's post–*Mean Streets* gangster films are rougher, sexier, and more foul-mouthed than their antecedents, but the themes remain constant. For example, Phil Joanou's *State of Grace* (1990), a tale of contemporary Irish mobsters battling for a piece of the Mafia pie in New York's Hell's Kitchen (the setting of many of James Cagney's gangster movies), is *Mean Streets* by way of Raoul Walsh's *Regeneration*. Gary Oldman's hotheaded and none-too-bright Jack Flannery in *State of Grace* is the fraternal twin of Robert De Niro's Johnny Boy in the Scorsese film. And Sean Penn's Irish tough Tommy Noonan, like the hero of the Walsh film, turns his back on his past and tries to regenerate himself with the help of a good woman (Robin Wright Penn), his childhood sweetheart. She also happens to be the estranged sister of two gangsters (Ed Harris and Oldman).

Penn decides to become a cop. Knowing he will inevitably be pitted against Harris and Oldman if he stays in Hell's Kitchen, he heads for Boston and joins the force there. But a New York cop (the ubiquitous John Turturro, who pops up in contemporary gangster pictures more than any actor except Robert De Niro) draws Penn back to Hell's Kitchen for an undercover job: infiltrating the Harris/Oldman gang (based on the real-life Irish-American gang of the 1970s called the Westies).

Posing as an enforcer for hire, Penn rejoins the gang to inform on its activities and takes up his relationship with his childhood sweetheart where it left off. When she threatens to end the affair because he's seemingly gone back to his bad old ways, Penn reveals that he's an undercover man. But this only places more strain on the relationship because the men he's after are her brothers, and however much she disapproves of their lifestyle, she still feels a sense of loyalty toward them. Penn suffers a crisis of conscience as well because he feels a similar sense of loyalty toward Oldman, his friend since childhood.

State of Grace is the complete film buff's gangster movie. In addition to recalling the films already mentioned, its climactic set piece, a bloody shoot-out in an empty bar on St. Patrick's Day that film-school grad Joanou films in slow motion, is one-quarter Sam Peckinpah and three-quarters Brian De Palma. Joanou knows the medium and the genre all right, but *State of Grace* might have been a better film if he'd spent less time mimicking other, better films and filmmakers, and more time paring down Dennis McIntyre's script, which is much too convoluted for the threadbare story it has to tell.

The same year *State of Grace* appeared, Scorsese continued his reflections on the post-1950s history of the mob in New York in the classic *GoodFellas*, a film that combines brutal realism, caustic satire—and a great soundtrack of '50s and '60s rock music hits—in the manner of *Mean Streets*, which its story of a young man drawn to the get-rich-quick world of the mob expands upon. *GoodFellas*, however, is not based on an original script drawn from Scorsese's own experiences but rather on reporter Nicholas Pileggi's gritty nonfiction account *Wiseguy* (Mafia slang for "made man") of the rise and fall of Irish/Italian-American and ex-Mafia goon Henry Hill. The film was retitled *GoodFellas* (a Mafia synonym for "wiseguy") prior to its release so as to avoid confusion in the moviegoing public's mind with a popular network TV series of the time called *Wiseguy*, which also dealt with organized crime on the mean streets of New York.

Ray Liotta stars as Hill, a kid from Brooklyn who, like Harvey Keitel's character in *Mean Streets*—and a long line of others going all the way back to Elmer Booth in *Musketeers of Pig Alley*, Rockliffe Fellowes in *Regeneration*, the Robinsons and the Cagneys—is captivated early on by the expensive clothes the goodfellas in the neighborhood wear and by the power they can wield. He decides to be a goodfella himself and starts doing odd jobs running numbers for syndicate boss Paul Cicero (Paul Sorvino), who makes his *real* money not by running numbers but, in Hill's admiring words, by "offering protection for people who can't go to the cops."

Hill later falls in with two other local hoods, Jimmy Conway (Robert De Niro) and Tommy DeVito (Joe Pesci), the latter reminiscent of De Niro's Johnny Boy in *Mean Streets* and also very much in the Cagney mold, who kills people for not treating him with respect (or, as Pesci's character calls it, "for busting my balls").

In contrast to Pesci's Cagney-like gangster, De Niro's Jimmy Conway, although by no means above whacking a guy—and even enjoying it a little—is more coolheaded and restrained. Ironically, the actual hood De Niro's character in *GoodFellas* is based on—James "Jimmy the Gent" Burke—was in fact more like the Irish-American tough guys Cagney played on the screen in terms of addiction to violence. Burke's adopted nickname of "Jimmy the Gent" may even have been inspired by the 1934 Cagney gangster movie of that title.

De Niro's personal code—and the mob's credo—is "Never rat on your friends and always keep your mouth shut." Liotta's Hill eventually breaks that code to survive and ironically turns on De Niro largely because of De Niro himself.

When De Niro and Pesci whack a guy, Liotta gets in deep by helping them dispose of the body. The three goodfellas—only one of whom (Pesci's character) is full-blooded Italian—rise in the Sicilian-run mob, but then everything falls apart for them. Liotta gets involved in a drug-trafficking sideline, a venture prohibited by mob boss Sorvino, and finds himself on the outs with his former patron. A contract is put out on Pesci for having murdered a fellow wiseguy without syndicate approval, and his fate is sealed at the very moment he thinks he's being initiated into the upper echelons of the family. Meanwhile, De Niro's character engineers the notorious 1978 Lufthanasa robbery at Kennedy Airport, netting the gang a fortune in cash and jewels, most of which De Niro—following in the greedy, self-destructive, no-honor-among-thieves footsteps of the characters in *The Asphalt Jungle, The Killing,* and *The Brink's Job*—opts to keep for himself.

When the feds start closing in, and De Niro starts knocking off his co-conspirators in the Lufthansa heist, Liotta (who is one of them) realizes the jig is up and makes a deal with the feds to rat on his former pals in exchange for freedom. As a result of Liotta's evidence, De Niro, Sorvino, and many of the film's other characters based on real-life mobsters are sent to jail in what was at the time one of the biggest gangland crack-downs in American history.

GoodFellas ends with Liotta's Henry Hill entering the Federal Witness Protection Program and mourning his lost glory days as a high-rolling goodfella with the observation, "I miss the action. Now, I'm just a schnook like everybody else."

Well, not quite.

As a result of the U.S. Supreme Court's overturning of New York's so-called "Son of Sam law," which had prohibited criminals from sharing in the profits of books or movies about their crimes, the actual Henry Hill pocketed almost $200,000 for his story. Later he made even more money appearing (in disguise) on various TV talk shows, discussing his vanished career in organized crime. Who says crime doesn't pay?

Scorsese's vivid kitchen-sink look at the workings of organized crime in the post-Eisenhower years of *Mean Streets* and *GoodFellas* reveals a society that is totally upside down—a society ruled by blood and ritual, where greedy guys and killers are named after saints and their wives and daughters after the Virgin Mary; a society where notions of right and wrong have become so skewed that ratting on your friends, even if they're killers, is wrong, and everything from petty larceny to murder is okay, just part of the daily routine—like a regular 9:00 to 5:00 job. "It got to be normal," observes Liotta's Jewish outsider wife (Lorraine Bracco). "It didn't seem like crime at all."

At first glance, Scorsese's *Casino* (1995), cowritten by Scorsese with Nicolas Pileggi based on Pileggi's book, seems like it's *GoodFellas* all over again, as if the director is supping at the *GoodFellas* trough one more time—and one time too often. But *Casino* is not *GoodFellas* redux. It's the final act in what can now be seen—like John Ford's "Cavalry Trilogy"—as Scorsese's "Mob Quartet," a series of films that traces the rise and fall of organized crime (as we've come to know it, mainly through movies themselves) in America, from its rough, streetwise, pre–Civil War roots (*Gangs of New York)* to its corporatization in the 1980s (*Casino*). Although at 180 minutes (the lengthiest of all Scorsese gangster films) *Casino* takes mighty long to explore this final chapter, it's a compelling tale nonetheless.

As with *GoodFellas*, the names of many of the real-life characters are changed—perhaps to protect the guilty. A veteran of all but *Gangs of New York*, Robert De Niro stars as Sam "Ace" Rothstein, a hot-shot odds maker the mob puts in charge of making its profitable Vegas casinos even *more* profitable. "Ace" is based on the still-living (he even has his own website) Frank "Lefty" Rosenthal, who operated the mob's desert casinos during the high-flying 1970s and 1980s.

Similar to Edward G. Robinson in the classic *Smart Money*, a film whose fictional plot the factual *Casino* mirrors in many striking ways, De Niro's "Ace" is a smart cookie when it comes to operating gambling houses, but blind as a bat when it comes to love. His rocky and much too loud (the modern mob prefers its employees to keep a low profile) relationship with expensive (and ultimately tell-all) junkie call girl Ginger McKenna (Sharon Stone, giving the performance of her life) proves his undoing, just as Robinson's character in *Smart Money* and other films is undone by his own chronic mistakes of the heart.

Adding to the overall unraveling of the mob's Vegas hold is its uncontrollable enforcer Nicky Santoro (Joe Pesci), an old-style urban tough guy and killer in the Cagney mold whose in-your-face attitude and extreme violence De Niro is unable to rein in. "No matter how big a guy might be, Nicky would take him on," De Niro narrates. "You beat Nicky with fists, he comes back with a bat. You beat him with a knife, he comes back with a gun. And you beat him with a gun, you better kill him, because he'll keep comin' back and back until one of you is dead."

Pesci's character also is based on an actual guy—Tony "the Ant" Spilotro, the mob's sometimes ultra heavy-handed muscle in Vegas during the final boom to bust years.

Even for a town built on and for excess, the activities of "Ace," Ginger, and Nicky prove excessive and finally get wildly out of hand, drawing heat from the feds, who use the trio to drive the Mafia snake out of the playground/paradise in the Nevada desert once and for all, bringing an end to an era that began in the 1930s with the entrepreneurial Bugsy Siegel's vision of a gambling oasis in the sand.

Describing how the big corporations then took over the mob's casino holdings and turned Vegas from a mecca for gamblers only into an entertainment conglomerate for the entire family, "Ace" regretfully concludes that the place now operates "like Disneyland."

The epoch of Bill the Butcher, the Black Handers, the Capones, the Nicky Santoros, and their like is over, says *Casino*, having come to end, like much else, on America's western frontier.

Taking its place—in the way that the gangster picture has supplanted the Western—is a new epoch, one characterized by a less individualistic and robust but no less devastating breed of criminal, the "corporate crook," who makes the words of John Garfield's mouthpiece in *Force of Evil* seem no longer like self-justification but instead downright prophetic: "What gangsters? It's just business."

11
An Offer Hollywood Couldn't Refuse

"Leave the gun. Take the cannoli."
—*Clemenza (Richard Castellano),*
The Godfather (1972)

NOTHING PERSONAL—JUST BUSINESS

THE LATE NOVELIST MARIO PUZO (1920–1999) said that his main reason for writing *The Godfather* was to get out of debt. His earlier novels, *The Dark Arena* (published in 1955) and *The Fortunate Pilgrim* (published in 1965), had earned him many excellent reviews but not much in royalties. With *The Godfather*, he was aiming for a popular success. And he achieved his goal—in spades.

Published in 1969, the novel sold more than 500,000 copies in hardcover and more than 10 million copies in paperback by the time the film version was released three years later. It has sold many more millions since.

To put the frosting on the cake (or the sauce on the pasta, as it were), Puzo's novel also earned a great deal of critical acclaim for a commercial best-seller. *The Saturday Review* called it "A staggering triumph . . . the most revealing novel ever written about the criminal underworld of the Mafia." Sounds like a review of W. R. Burnett's *Little Caesar* forty years earlier. Similar to *Little Caesar*, Puzo's novel set the standard for a whole new generation of novels about gangsters and the criminal underworld. And like Mervyn LeRoy's film version of *Little Caesar*, Francis Ford Coppola's movie of *The Godfather* became the yardstick by which all subsequent gangster pictures are measured.

Puzo's epic novel (which the author admitted to researching almost entirely at the library) is a richly detailed roman à clef about the history and structure of organized crime in the United States, from the early twentieth century to the bloody Mafia wars between New York's powerful Five Families in the late 1940s. The story and characters are modeled on a wide spectrum of events and underworld figures, politicians, entertainers, and other historical personages of that era. The novel's aging Godfather, Don Vito Corleone, for instance, is a composite of many real Mafia crime bosses but is primarily a portrait of Frank Costello, one of the original pioneers of the syndicate, along with Meyer Lansky, Lucky Luciano, and Bugsy Siegel.

Like the fictional Vito Corleone, Costello's power derived from the number of corrupt politicians, judges, and police officials he had in his pocket and whose strings he could pull at any time for the benefit of his criminal organization. And like the real life Frank Costello, the fictional Vito Corleone is opposed to getting involved in selling narcotics, deeming them "bad business" and "bad for business," and his reluctance to use his political strings to assist his fellow mobsters involved in the drug trade is what, in part, triggers the gang war for power among the Five Families that constitutes the book's plot.

Michael Corleone, the youngest son in the novel, who ultimately claims his father's throne, is also a composite, but the character's most striking resemblance is to mobster Vito Genovese. Michael murders a crooked cop and an ambitious drug dealer for their participation in an assassination attempt on his father's life and is then forced to hide out in Sicily until things blow over. When he returns to the United States, his superior cunning makes him the natural candidate to take over the family's beleaguered operation after the deaths of his father and older brother Sonny. The equally cunning Vito Genovese had likewise escaped to Italy to avoid a mob-related murder charge, and he too eventually returned to assume leadership—in his case, of the powerful Luciano crime family.

In addition to exploiting the lore of the Mafia in skillful dramatic terms, the book also provides a richly authentic look at Italian-American life, which the Italian-American Puzo did not have to research at the library. The film version would be even more suffused with Italian-American flavor, and this would create a furor because the particular Italian-

Americans being portrayed were gangsters. Neither the book nor the movie suggests that all Italian-Americans are Mafiosi. Nevertheless, Italian-American pressure groups forced the makers of the film to excise all reference to the words *Mafia* and *La Cosa Nostra* from the script.[1] Less familiar Italian words relating to the mob, such as *capo*, *caporegime*, and *consigliere* would remain, however, and would enter the gangster film vocabulary.

Paramount Pictures was not the likeliest of studios to make Puzo's book into a movie. Unlike Warner Brothers, which had pioneered the sound-era gangster film with *Little Caesar* and *The Public Enemy* and breathed new life into the gangster picture in the 1960s with *Bonnie and Clyde*, Paramount had no long-standing association with the genre. Furthermore, Paramount was still smarting over the box office failure of its last gangster picture, which had also been about the Mafia, had also boasted a strong Italian-American flavor, and had even included a reference to a Mafia family named Corleone.

Titled *The Brotherhood* (1968), it stars Kirk Douglas as an old-style Mafia don like Vito Corleone whose reluctance to go along with the organization's more "progressive" crime ventures lands him on the hit list. His younger brother (Alex Cord), a college grad like Michael Corleone but who is destined to head the organization, is assigned the hit as a way of proving himself. Douglas learns that a fellow member of the syndicate's board of directors (Luther Adler) was responsible for the murder of his and Cord's Mafioso father years earlier. When Douglas kills Adler in revenge, he has to go into hiding in Sicily. Cord tracks him down and tries to persuade him to patch things up with the mob, but Douglas knows the Mafia code makes that impossible and that he's a doomed man. Douglas also knows that Cord is doomed, too, if he doesn't carry out the hit, so Douglas coerces him into it by exchanging the Sicilian kiss of death. Although the film ends upon Douglas's death, the look of devastation coupled with grim determination on Cord's face after pulling the trigger suggests that the drama is not yet over, and that as the vicious circle of the brotherhood comes around, he will turn into Douglas and exact his own *la vendetta* against the mob someday. Douglas even hints at this future moments before his death when he tells Cord, "Me like papa, you like me. It's like we're all the same guy."

Although strongly acted, especially by Douglas, who also produced and gave himself the showiest part, and quite powerful in spots—the scene where Douglas takes the man who murdered his father "for a ride" is particularly taut—*The Brotherhood* was avoided by audiences in droves, as the legendary producer Samuel Goldwyn was wont to say. Nevertheless, the publishing buzz on *The Godfather* was so strong that Paramount picked up the film rights to the book anyway; perhaps because the book was in manuscript form, the studio got away with paying a bargain price of only $8000. It proposed to make the movie on a modest (even at the time) budget of $2.5 million, a price tag that would virtually guarantee the studio a profit, especially if the book became a best-seller. To keep within that $2.5 million, however, the studio decided to update Puzo's story to the present, thereby eliminating the need for costly period sets, costumes, and vintage cars.

Many directors turned the project down—perhaps because it seemed to them that the studio was aiming for a low-budget (in Hollywood terms) cheapie—before Coppola finally came on board. According to Robert Evans, Paramount's production chief at the time, Coppola was chosen for the assignment because he was Italian-American and would thus be able to invest the film with a strong ethnic flavor. Coppola was also a young director in need of a breakout hit. He had won an Oscar for writing the screenplay for *Patton* (1970), but his films as a director had ranged from the fast-vanishing *You're a Big Boy Now* (1966) and *The Rain People* (1969) to such highly visible box office flops as *Finian's Rainbow* (1968). Undoubtedly the studio felt that because Coppola was both young *and* hungry, he would be easier to control than some veteran. So, he got the job.

The likes of Laurence Olivier, Edward G. Robinson, and Richard Conte (who would ultimately get the role of the godfather's chief rival, the Machiavellian Don Barzini) were considered for the title role. Orson Welles, whom Twentieth Century Fox vetoed as Al Capone in Roger Corman's *The St. Valentine's Day Massacre*, actively campaigned for the part as well. But Coppola wanted Marlon Brando.

Brando had not had a box office hit in years. Furthermore, his name was anathema to the studio, which had lost a sizable amount of money producing Brando's profligate directorial debut (and swansong) *One-Eyed Jacks* (1961). To Coppola and other filmmakers of his generation, however, Brando was an icon whose performance as Terry Malloy, the working-class stiff who risks his life to expose mob corruption of the longshoreman's union at the risk of his life in *On the Waterfront*, had transformed film acting. The role of the aging patriarch of the kind of criminal organization Brando's Terry Malloy had exposed would bring the actor full circle.

To convince Paramount executives such as Robert Evans that Brando was the right man for the job, Coppola persuaded the legendary actor to do a screen test in full godfather makeup. This did the trick. The executives didn't even recognize Brando at first, and the actor got the part—for which he took a percentage of the film's profits rather than a salary, a decision that would eventually earn him millions when the film became a blockbuster. Ironically, Brando captured his only two Academy Awards as best actor for these two gangster movies—made almost twenty years apart.

For the pivotal role of Michael Corleone, the reluctant war-hero son who ultimately becomes an even more brutal don than his old man, the studio sought someone with the right mix of star power and bankability. Coppola wanted the relatively unknown Al Pacino, whom Paramount's Evans was vehemently against also. But Coppola won that battle as well. He handpicked the rest of the cast and even wrote the script in collaboration with Puzo.

One of the few things Evans did get his way on is the film's conclusion. Coppola had shot the book's ending, in which Michael's long-suffering wife, Kay, who is much more aware of Michael's dark activities in the book than in the film, takes communion and prays for her husband's lost soul. Reportedly, Evans suggested that the film conclude with Michael's final betrayal of Kay when she asks for the truth about his alleged complicity in the murder of his sister's husband, and he lies to her again big time, then shuts the door on her (and us, the audience) as he takes his place as dynastic head of the secrecy-bound criminal empire. This ending is tremendously effective.

With *The Godfather*, Francis Coppola took a cinematic genre in which every story had seemingly been told and pushed it in an epic new direction with gripping narrative force. Brutal, bloody, shocking, scary, funny, socially and politically observant, and meticulously performed by everyone from the leads to the bit players, the film offers a panoramic glimpse into the closed society of organized crime in the United States—a society ruled by *la vendetta*, where the second most sought-after currency, respect, is acquired through fear and intimidation. It's a society where even murder is "nothing personal—just business." Coppola had made a movie that, to borrow the words of one of his influences, the legendary Japanese director Akira Kurosawa, was rich and "entertaining enough to eat." Not for nothing was the film quickly ballyhooed in ads as the *"Gone with the Wind* of Gangster Movies."

Coppola had also made a financial blockbuster, the first blockbuster (followed by *Jaws* in 1975 and *Star Wars* in 1978) of the 1970s—the decade that changed the American film industry by giving rise to the "blockbuster mentality," which continues to dominate the focus and direction of the Hollywood studios today. Paramount demanded a sequel as quickly as possible. Success has many fathers, and it nettled Coppola that Evans claimed so much parental responsibility when, in fact, he and the writer/director had fought on casting and many other matters virtually every step of the way, from preproduction to final cut. So that there would be no mistaking whose film the sequel was right from the start, Coppola demanded and received creative autonomy. He would not only cowrite the script (in collaboration once more with Puzo) and direct the film but would produce *The Godfather Part II* (1974) as well.

Although the first film had been almost unanimously well received by the nation's movie critics and other opinion makers, one negative criticism leveled at it was that Coppola had created too sympathetic a portrait of his Mafia characters by putting too human a face on them. They *are* killers, after all, so the criticism went, even if they do have wives and families.

Coppola's point about the banality of evil, that not all gangsters are eye-rolling, saliva-oozing goons brandishing guns, was apparently lost on these critics. (Interestingly, many book reviewers acclaimed Puzo for having made his frightening cast of Mafioso characters seem human and possible.) Coppola took this criticism to heart, however, and was determined in the sequel to clearly make the point that Michael Corleone, an antihero who holds his family together through the turmoil of the Mafia wars in the first film, is a Machiavellian schemer whose soul is unmistakably damned by the final reel of the second. The first film ends with the christening of Michael's godson and Michael's concurrent baptism of fire as his father's rightful heir. The sequel begins with Michael's son Tony's first communion and Michael's own symbolic first communion as head of the Family, dispensing favors, orders, and "justice" as his father had done at the beginning of the first film. The point that what drives Michael is not what drove his father, that Michael is a bitter and more ruthless character who is finally capable of murdering his own brother Fredo (John Cazale), is potently made by flashing back in time throughout the sequel in order to contrast the two godfathers' characters at similar points in their lives.

The flashbacks—in which the young Vito flees Italy following the murders of his family by local Mafiosi and builds his power base in the United States as an adult (Robert De Niro[2]) by taking a leaf from the book of the Black Handers—are taken substantially from portions of Puzo's novel unused in the first film. When *The Godfather* and *The Godfather Part II* were sold to network television, Coppola re-edited the two films and combined them so that they unfolded chronologically. He also added numerous sequences that had been cut for length and other reasons, such as pacing, from the theatrical versions. The epic result, which premiered on NBC in 1976 as *The Godfather Saga*, enabled viewers to marvel at how convincingly De Niro turns into Brando in terms of voice and mannerism. But the loss of the flashback structure in *The Godfather Saga*, which continues to be shown on television, mutes our understanding of the differences between Michael and his father, Vito.

Vito is a product of his old-country roots. He sees the world as a hostile landscape where only the strong can survive. Accepting this as the way of things, he functions on the instinctive level of pure animal cunning to stay king of the jungle. Even *la vendetta* is to him no more than the natural order of things in such a world. He is more like the Robinson gangster—with, perhaps, a dash of the Cagney gangster thrown in.

By contrast, Michael has more of the Bogart gangster in him. A college graduate and war hero who wanted no part of his father's world yet is pulled back into it anyway by circumstances and by choice, he is a bitter man, a wounded idealist who comes to view the world he presides over as a sewer where everyone is corrupt, corrupting, or corruptible. This outlook eventually destroys him, turning him by the close of *The Godfather Part II* into a paranoid despot who has completely sacrificed his soul.

Coppola saw the sequel not as a way of simply cashing in on the success of the first film but as a chance to expand his canvas into a broader and much richer tapestry. *The Godfather Part II* chronicles the business of organized crime in the United States from 1900 to the 1960s, weaving fact with fiction in the manner of its predecessor. The opening sequence in Sicily depicts the funeral of Vito's slain father, the murder of his mother, and his escape to New York's Little Italy, which production designer Dean Tavoularis reconstructs in spectacular fashion. Coppola's use of the Neopolitan opera *Senze Mamma*, a popular musical of the period written by the director's paternal grandfather, serves as a coda to the Little Italy flashbacks where the adult Vito murders the Black Hander Fanucci (Gaston Moschin) and begins his rise to power in the underworld. When he becomes a successful figure in organized crime, Vito returns to his native hill village in Sicily to revenge his parents by slaying the Mafiosi who ordered their execution. In the modern sequences, Coppola introduces a Meyer Lansky character named Hyman Roth (Lee Strasberg), the syndicate boss and financial wizard who plays up to Michael but secretly plots to overthrow him. These scenes take the film to Cuba (the Dominican Republic served as stand-in), where organized crime's holdings in nightclubs and casinos are confiscated in the wake of guerrilla fighter Fidel Castro's takeover of the corrupt, mob-influenced Batista government.

The film also includes a reenactment of the Kefauver/McClellan hearings into organized crime and labor union racketeering of the 1950s in which actor Joe Spinell plays a character modeled on Joe Valachi, a real-life mob hitman and informer, who amuses the senators on the committee with his slangy description of mob killers like himself as "button men," just as Valachi had done. As an in-joke, Coppola assigned the roles of the senators on the committee to various nonactors who had been instrumental in advancing his career, among them Phil Feldman (the producer of Coppola's *You're a Big Boy Now*) and producer-director Roger Corman. Character actor Peter Donat plays the gimlet-eyed committee chair based on McClellan, here named Senator Questadt. At the conclusion, Michael's Mafia "soldiers" brutally take care of "all family business," including the execution of Hyman Roth and Michael's brother Fredo, as the ruthless criminal chieftain gazes upon the chilly waters of Lake Tahoe from the windows of his heavily fortified estate.

Coppola said of *The Godfather Part II* in the film's pressbook: "The only way [it] can be an excellent film is, if when it's done and seen, the audience, including myself, looks at it and says that it was essential that it was made." He succeeded. *The Godfather Part II* is that rarity indeed, a sequel that not only deepens our understanding of the original film but also betters it artistically. It also remains the only sequel to date to repeat the success of its predecessor in capturing a best picture Oscar. As of this writing, it also remains Coppola's masterpiece, his arguably more ambitious and certainly more controversial *Apocalypse Now* (1979) notwithstanding.

The Godfather Part II was big box office for the studio, but at twice the budget of its predecessor, not quite the cash cow the original had been. Nevertheless, the two films together opened the floodgates for the greatest outpouring of gangster movies from Hollywood (and abroad) since the first great wave in the 1930s following the advent of talking pictures and the second in the 1950s when the Kefauver and McClellan committee hearings were televised. *The Valachi Papers* (1972), a European production set in the United States, was part of that wave.

Based on the best-selling book of the same title by reporter Peter Maas, *The Valachi Papers* examines the growth of organized crime in the United States from the days of the Black Handers and "Mustache Petes"[3] to the 1970s as seen through the eyes of the aforementioned mob hitman and informer, Joe Valachi. A few location scenes were filmed in New York City where most of the events of the story occurred, but the picture was shot mainly on the gigantic sound stages of Cinecitta studios in Italy— the same studio where Martin Scorsese and his production designer Dante Ferretti would recreate the Five Points area of Civil War–era New York in *Gangs of New York*.

The cast is predominantly Italian as well, with a few American and British performers included to enhance the international flavor. Charles Bronson, who had achieved fame mostly in supporting roles up to that time, would shoot to international stardom as Valachi. Perhaps to offset some of the ethnic controversy that had plagued *The Godfather* during production, the film is introduced with a quote by former U.S. Attorney General Robert F. Kennedy: "Crime is a question of criminal. It is not a matter of race, color or religion."

We first meet Valachi in the Atlanta Penitentiary, where he's serving a sentence for murder. Big-time mob boss Vito Genovese (Lino Ventura) is incarcerated in the same pen on a narcotics rap and suspects Valachi of being the one who ratted on him, a charge Valachi, a loyal Mafia "soldier" all his life, vehemently denies. When Genovese gives him the Sicilian kiss of death nonetheless, Valachi comes to the realization that his loyalty to the mob all these years has been for nothing, and so he makes a deal with the feds to protect him and his family in exchange for giving the lowdown on the activities of the Mafia (which Valachi calls La Cosa Nostra), testimony he will later repeat on live television before the McClellan committee.

As Valachi spills his guts, the film flashes back to the late 1920s when Valachi, a small-time hood just released from prison, lands the job of bodyguard to big-time "Mustache Pete" boss Salvatore Maranzano (Joseph Wiseman in an entertainingly ripe performance). Maranzano and rival Joey "the Boss" Masseria (Alessandro Sperli) are done away with by Lucky Luciano (Angelo Infanti, a virtual double for the real Lucky) and other ambitious mobsters, leading to the formation of New York's notorious Five Families criminal network. Valachi gets carried along and eventually becomes a hitman for the brutal Vito Genovese and his sidekick of Murder, Inc. fame, Albert Anastasia. Valachi is an eyewitness to the mob's deadly intrigues and corruptive influence on America over the next several decades, culminating with the historic 1957 underworld conference in Apalachin, New York, which is raided by the feds and ultimately leads to Genovese's downfall as the *Capo di tutti capi* ("boss of bosses"). For giving them the goods on the mob (even though much of his testimony is disbelieved at the time), Valachi is placed in tight security at a federal correctional facility in Texas, where he dies in 1971, having outlived his former boss, the vengeful Genovese, by six months.

Coming on the heels of Coppola's admittedly bigger-budgeted but also more fastidiously made *The Godfather* (*The Valachi Papers* was released later the same year), Terence Young's film of Maas's book seems a bit slipshod, as if it had been rushed into release before the printed celluloid was dry in order to grab onto *The Godfather*'s coattails. The English lip-synching of the mostly Italian cast seems always just a bit off (although of course this could just be the fault of the print I screened for this book). Given that Young directed three of the best action pictures ever made—the James Bond films *Dr. No* (1962), *From Russia, with Love* (1963), and *Thunderball* (1965)—the action sequences are not altogether convincing and seem clumsily staged, the explosions of "blood squibs" as mobster bodies are racked by gunfire occasionally as off-synch as the actors' lips. That said, the film is gripping nonetheless. The scene where one of Valachi's close pals is castrated for dallying with Genovese's slutty showgirl mistress is as harrowingly effective as the scenes of violence in Coppola's film. And Stephen Geller's script, which often veers wildly from broad comedy to stark drama, does a good job of laying out the complex cast of real-life characters, explaining their sometimes Byzantine relationships, and providing some solid inside dope on the history of the mob in the manner of *The Godfather* but without the label of "fiction." Charles Bronson is somewhat impassive (a characteristic of his performances in his later years) as Valachi, a dumbfella who basically just goes along until he can no longer risk doing so, but his performance, like the film itself, fully engages our interest.

More substantial than *The Valachi Papers* and arguably even more fastidiously produced than *The Godfather* and its sequel is Sergio Leone's *Once Upon a Time in America* (1984), which achieves the near impossible by being as epic in scope as Coppola's first two *Godfather* films, and almost as good. It also provides viewers a refreshing change, offering a look at the Jewish gangsters of Lower East Side Manhattan during the same years spanned by Coppola's films.

Based on the hefty 1953 novel *The Hoods* by Harry Grey, nom de plume of former gangster and ex-con Harry Goldberg, who had turned to writing about the world of Jewish and Italian gangsters he grew up in after getting out of prison, *Once Upon a Time in America* is "spaghetti Western" auteur Leone's most complex film, as well as his most expansive. It chronicles the lives of its gangster characters from before the Roaring Twenties to the late 1950s, shifting back and forth in time in the manner of *The Godfather Part II*—although here the shift is prompted by the memories of its lead character David "Noodles" Aaronson (Robert De Niro). Like Leone's spaghetti Westerns, it is primarily a tale of betrayal, vengeance, and loss.

Noodles is the only surviving member of a quartet of Jewish gangsters whose power in the New York underworld and labor rackets once equaled that of their Mafia counterparts. Noodles returns to his Lower East Side roots after many years of self-imposed exile, haunted by the memory that it was he who was responsible for the deaths of his boyhood pals and former cronies in crime. At the peak of the gang's success, Noodles's ambitious and unbalanced partner, Max (James Woods), the leader of their clique, had set in motion a daring plan to knock over a federal bank, a crime that would have resulted in the fullest wrath of the law coming down on them—and likely death for them all. To save Max from himself and to salvage the gang's future (a prison sentence being preferable to being killed), Noodles had exposed the robbery plan to the cops, hoping it could be nipped in the bud with no casualties. But the betrayal went wrong, and Noodles's cronies were killed after all. Years later, having received a mysterious invitation that brings him back to New York, the guilt-ridden Noodles discovers that he, too, had been betrayed, and that his betrayer now awaits—indeed invites—Noodles's revenge. The film concludes with a curious yet haunting ambiguity, leaving us to wonder over the fate of Noodles's betrayer and the future of Noodles himself.

Unlike *The Godfather* and *The Godfather Part II*, *Once Upon a Time in America* is not quite the sum of its parts. But many of those parts—from the breathtaking re-creation of New York in the teens, twenties, and thirties; the equally breathtaking color photography by Tonino Delli Colli; and the stylized reverence for the genre to the performances of De Niro and Woods—are magnificent indeed. The film, however, was not a box-office hit in America, where Warner Brothers—the ideal studio, one would have thought, to get behind such a film—timidly released a severely truncated (and thus extremely confusing) 139-minute cut-down of Leone's 229-minute original in order to get in a few more showings each day. Fortunately, the latter is now available on DVD. It remains Sergio Leone's best film (one that casts the style of his spaghetti Westerns in welcome relief) and a passionate nod to the genre's roots in America and his love of movies at large. Unfortunately, it was also his last film. He died in 1989.

Coppola's *Godfather* films and Sergio Leone's *Once Upon a Time in America* had turned the subject of organized crime in America into grand opera and epic myth, respectively. By contrast, John Huston's *Prizzi's Honor* (1985), based on the 1982 novel by Richard Condon, treats it as grand farce. A satiric look at the Mafia's skewed morality and equally skewed sense of honor, the film has as its protagonist Charley Partanna (Jack Nicholson), a dumbfella and hitman for Brooklyn's powerful Prizzi crime family (a comic version of the Corleones). Charley is being groomed by the mob for big things, but his future hinges on marrying one of the Prizzi daughters, Maerose (Anjelica Huston, the director's daughter). But she unexpectedly stands him up. Out of honor to Nicholson, the Prizzis disown her until he agrees to take her back or marries someone else. As she schemes to win Nicholson back, he falls for the mysterious Irene (Kathleen Turner), a professional killer like him, and marries her—not realizing she's the brains behind a recent scam of the Prizzi's Las Vegas operation. The heated situation comes to a head when the cops crack down on the Prizzis after Turner shoots a police offer's wife while in the process of committing another crime she and Nicholson had hoped would put her in the mob's good graces. So, the Prizzis order Nicholson to whack Turner, while at the same time another Family member for whom Nicholson's continued existence is an obstacle to becoming the mob's top man contracts Turner to whack Nicholson. In the end, all concerned, particularly Nicholson, learn a less-than-honorable lesson about the perils of working and marrying outside the Family.

The greatest irony in this ironic black comedy is that whereas all the characters (cops and mobsters alike) obsess over the meaning of the word "honor," what they are really talking about is power and territoriality—vested interests. But they have deceived themselves into thinking otherwise, and their, as well as our, world, John Huston and Condon observe, is not the better for their self-deception. Despite this serious subtext, and its overt resonances of *The Godfather* ("It's only business" is how the death warrant on Turner is described), *Prizzi's Honor* is primarily a comedy (and a delightful one) in the tradition of the gangster comedies made by Edward G. Robinson, to whose upwardly mobile gangster character without a lot of brain power Nicholson's Charley Partanna is definitely kin. The film is also a shaggy dog story in the mold of the director's earlier crime comedy *Beat the Devil* (1954), although not as free-wheeling as that film, whose script was virtually made up as the shooting progressed.

In Richard Condon, who fashioned a career writing dark contemporary thrillers (*The Manchurian Candidate, Winter Kills*) with a satiric edge, Huston finds an ideal collaborator, and Condon's script (written with Janet Roach) follows Condon's novel fairly closely. Both book and film are essentially a romance about two mismatched lovers swallowed up in a game of mob power and politics that each of them comes to understand too late. The film's irony and humor emerge mostly through its script and the performances of its stars (Anjelica Huston won a best supporting actress Oscar for her deliciously ripe turn as the Machiavellian Maerose), but Alex North's underrated score, with its repeated refrains of Rossini's *The Thieving Magpie*, contributes strongly to the irony and humor as well.

THE GODFATHER RIDES AGAIN

As the "blockbuster mentality" spread throughout Hollywood and the major studios went full tilt into the franchise business, Paramount concluded that because *The Godfather Part II* had ended in the 1960s with Michael Corleone still very much alive, the mine had yet to be played out. It wanted another sequel. Coppola wasn't interested, however, and shelved the offer to make *The Godfather Part III* for almost twenty years.

In the interim, Mario Puzo turned out another Mafia-themed novel in 1984 called *The Sicilian*, a fictionalized account of the life and death of the legendary Sicilian bandit and revolutionary Salvatore Guiliano, who was assassinated in 1950 for warring against the Italian government, the country's rich landowners, and powerful Mafiosi. The character of Michael Corleone makes a brief appearance in the novel, but not the film version, which came out in 1987, starring Christopher Lambert as Guiliano.

In the manner of Puzo's *The Godfather*, *The Sicilian* was a pageturner. Under the direction of Michael Camino, the filmmaker who sunk

United Artists with his spectacularly expensive flop *Heaven's Gate* (1980), however, the film of the novel is a large-scale but plodding affair that lacks both the operatic drama of Coppola's two *Godfather* films as well as a charismatic leading man. Prior to its release, more than thirty excruciatingly tedious minutes (I know they're tedious because the full version is available on videocassette) were cut from the film to improve its chances at U.S. box offices by getting a few more showings each day like the shortened *Once Upon a Time in America*. But the cut version flopped nonetheless because the public, perhaps expecting—indeed, hoping for—another *Godfather*, got a dead fish instead.

Meanwhile, like Puzo and Michael ("They keep pulling me back in") Corleone, Francis Coppola too found himself returning in the interim to gangland with *The Cotton Club* (1984), an extravagant musical period piece about the famous Harlem night club (*Thunderbolt*'s Dreamland Café was suggestive of the same establishment) of the Roaring Twenties and thirties whose clientele included not just movie gangsters such as James Cagney (played in a cameo by look-alike Vincent Jerosa) but some of the era's most notorious mobsters, such as Dutch Schultz and Lucky Luciano. Even the club's owner, Irishman Owney Madden, was a mobster who had made his bones as a member of the Five Points gang.

Spectacularly staged by Coppola in a style reminiscent of his *Godfather* films, *The Cotton Club* recreates the look, the music, and the gunplay of the era, but suffers from an inadequate script (by novelist William Kennedy and Coppola) that focuses attention in the wrong direction—the banal lives of its two fictional heroes (Richard Gere and Gregory Hines), whereas the background story of the real-life gangsters surrounding them is implicitly more colorful and interesting. In the end, it is not the travails of Gere or Hines that stick in the mind but rather the machinations of supporting players James Remar (as Dutch Schultz) and Bob Hoskins (as Owney Madden).

Ironically, Coppola finally resumed his place at the helm of the *Godfather* franchise for the same reason he'd taken it initially: he needed a hit and an infusion of capital.

Paramount had been talking about doing *The Godfather Part III* for years, without Coppola; stars such as John Travolta and Sylvester Stallone had been courted for the project, which was to have focused on Michael's son, Tony, now grown and heading up the family business. Following the poor box-office showing of Coppola's long-cherished biopic *Tucker: The Man and His Dream* (1988), Paramount chairman Frank Mancuso approached Coppola about taking the reins on *The Godfather Part III*, and this time the director was interested. To sweeten the offer, Mancuso agreed to give the director the same degree of creative control he had had on *The Godfather Part II*, plus a $5 million salary and 15 percent of the film's gross. This proved the proverbial offer that couldn't be refused. Coppola, collaborating again with Puzo, agreed to come up in six months with an original script focusing on the further adventures of Michael Corleone. Paramount wanted the picture for a Christmas 1990 release, however, and so the collaborators were forced to pare down their schedule and turn out their script in a brisk six weeks instead. Coppola was revising the script even as shooting began in November 1989, and he would continue to do so throughout the film's production, tallying approximately thirty drafts before the film was finally completed.

Pressure mounted on Coppola during the editing stage of the nearly three-hour film, and rumors spread throughout the industry that the movie was in trouble and would not be ready in time for the lucrative holiday season—a deadline also for Academy Award consideration that year. The film opened on time, however, and proved to be the hit everyone expected it to be. But it was not the blockbuster *The Godfather* had been, nor did it receive the critical accolades heaped upon *The Godfather Part II*. Like its predecessors, it earned numerous Academy Award nominations, including best picture, but unlike them it failed to capture any awards.

The film picks up the saga of Michael Corleone in 1979, as the now sixty-year-old don (Pacino again) is receiving the Order of San Sebastian, the highest honor the Catholic Church bestows upon a layman. He is haunted by the murder of his brother Fredo and failed marriage to his ex-wife Kay. Through the Vito Corleone Foundation, a charitable organization fronted (innocently) by his daughter, Mary (Sofia Coppola), Michael makes a multimillion-dollar donation to assist the Vatican with some real estate and loan troubles in exchange for controlling interest in International Immobiliare, an outwardly respectable but secretly shady European conglomerate whose largest shareholder is the Vatican Bank. Pope Paul VI himself must ratify the deal, but the pontiff's untimely passing and the delay in electing a new Pope stalls Michael's takeover plans long enough for his former syndicate associates to thwart his dream of washing away his sins and becoming respectable, as he'd promised Kay long ago.

Unhappy that Michael has severed himself from them and is going it alone in the lucrative Immobiliare deal, the heads of the other crime families back in New York conspire to pull Michael back into the Mafia world of violence and treachery—a conspiracy that, among other things, involves assassinating the honest new Pope (Raf Vallone), and, ultimately, Michael himself.

In between coping with Mafia plotters, crooked Vatican officials, and cutthroat European businessmen, Michael faces trouble on the home-front as well. His grown son, Tony (Franc D'Ambrosio), has rejected the family business (just as Michael himself had sought to do at Tony's age) to become an opera singer. Meanwhile, his daughter, Mary, is carrying on a tempestuous affair with her first cousin Vincent (Andy Garcia), the hot-headed illegitimate son of Michael's late brother, the hotheaded Sonny Corleone, who was killed in the first film. Michael has taken Vincent under his wing and enthrones him as the family's next godfather (thereby perhaps paving the way for a *Godfather Part IV*). Michael is also attempting to reunite with his ex-wife, Kay. All these intrigues come to a climax in the vigorous last half hour, during Tony's operatic debut, when, with Vincent's help, Michael bloodily settles "all family business" once more—this time for good, he hopes.

The Godfather Part III is not without its virtues. Its rich, warm photography by Gordon Willis (who shot *Parts I* and *II* as well); its sump-tuous production design by Dean Tavoularis (and others); and its operatic sweep are each consistent with the first two films in the series. But its flaws are not insignificant. Considering the whopping (for its time) $55 million budget (more than four times that of *The Godfather Part II*), its failure to provide a wrap-up to the multigenerational Corleone saga in keeping with the epic vision of the first two installments is a disappoint-ment. Coppola intended the film to be contemplative (like Leone's *Once Upon a Time in America*), but the effect it produces is ennui. Compared to the first two films, it lacks narrative force and is quite dull in stretches. Its mostly new cast of Mafiosi characters and scheming outsiders is simply no match for the colorful Don Barzinis, Clemenzas, Tessios, Sollozzos, Hyman Roths, and other underworld figures who populate the earlier films, riveting our interest even as they repel us.

Coppola's casting of his daughter Sofia (who is herself a film director now) in the pivotal role of Michael's beloved daughter also fails to serve the film very well. She is awkward and inexperienced like the character she plays, but in this case living the part doesn't work, and she fails to bring Mary alive. To the role of Vincent, Michael's surrogate son and heir as godfather, Andy Garcia brings a considerable amount of fire and grit, but the character is fairly one-dimensional and hardly the stuff of which gangland sagas are made.

The film's most serious flaw, however, is the change Coppola and Puzo have wrought in the main characters. They are simply not the same people they were at the close of *The Godfather Part II*—a detail that becomes strikingly apparent when *Parts II* and *III* are watched back-to-back.

Connie (Talia Shire), Michael's long-suffering and vulnerable sister, has transformed into a scheming Lady Macbeth. In *The Godfather Part II*, Diane Keaton's Kay revenges herself on Michael by aborting their third child to keep it from being born into the amoral life her husband leads that she calls "this Sicilian thing"—an act that loses her custody of their other children when they divorce and condemns her, in Michael's unforgiving heart, to total banishment. Yet in *Part III* the two attempt reconciliation, which is more than a bit hard to swallow given the past they share. But the most extreme, and most damaging, change is to Michael's character.

Soulless monsters may grow old and tired—like Richard Widmark's Mafioso kidnapper and murderer in *Murder on the Orient Express*—but the core of their being that made them monsters does not vanish with age. Guilt, the need for redemption, and heartfelt regret over paradise lost are simply not feelings that we can associate with the cold and righteous patriarch Michael had fully become when *The Godfather Part II* faded to black. Nor would Michael, who cynically observed to the naïve Kay way back in the first film that even governments are corrupt and order people killed, comment with such surprise and chagrin (as he does in *The Godfather Part III*) that "the higher I go, the crookeder it gets." We do feel a sense of loss at the end of *Part III*, but this has more to do, I think, with nostalgia for the overall series than emotional investment in this particular installment. The film offers a nicely ironic touch, though, by having the character of Joey Zasa (Joe Mantegna), a character modeled on Joe Colombo, the boss of the Profaci Family whose Italian-American Civil Rights League forced the removal of all reference to the words *Mafia* and *Cosa Nostra* from the first film, mowed down (as Colombo was) by mob bullets after proclaiming that the Mafia and La Cosa Nostra don't exist.

Have we seen the last of the Corleones on the big screen? Possibly not. In conjunction with the estate of the late Mario Puzo and Paramount Pictures, Random House publishers held a contest early in the new millennium that challenged published authors around the country to submit story outlines for a continuation of the Corleone saga, picking up where the 1969 novel left off, not Coppola's *The Godfather Part III*. The contest winner announced in February 2003 by Random House was Mark Winegardner, a former director of the creative writing program at Florida State University. His past novels include *The Veracruz Blues* (1997) and *Crooked River Burning* (2001), neither of which focuses on crime and criminals. The author has his work cut out for him as it is difficult to imagine a story line about the next generation of Mafiosi such as the Corleones that has not already been explored in HBO's brilliant portrait of the modern day mob, *The Sopranos*.

Epilogue:
Through the Looking Glass

Christopher: "Louis Brazzi sleeps with the fishes."
Big Pussy: "Luca Brazzi. Luca . . . "
—The Sopranos, Season 1

MY LIFE AS A MOVIE

ONCE ASKED WHY REAL GANGSTERS sounded so much like their movie counterparts, George Raft replied that it was because gangster movies (his in particular, he noted) taught gangsters how to talk.

Raft's explanation is more than just an offhand quip or self-aggrandizing patter; it is an astute observation. America's gangsters have always been fascinated with movies about them and their exploits, and they have always been interested in the movie business because of the huge amount of money that can be made. For example, Mafia kingfish Charles "Lucky" Luciano felt his story was destined for the movies, and perhaps in an effort to make sure he had creative control, spearheaded the mob's failed efforts in the 1930s to take over the industry's labor unions and seize control of Hollywood itself. Luciano's point man in this operation was Benjamin "Bugsy" Siegel, the nattily attired mobster who put Las Vegas on the map and, in the process, became something of a media star himself.

The story of Bugsy Siegel has special significance to this chronicle of bullets over Hollywood because Bugsy's rise and fall is not just a rattling good gangster story with all the genre's trimmings—money, power, vio-

them the Countess diFrasso (Bebe Neuwirth), a woman with close ties to Italian dictator Benito Mussolini. Consumed by romantic and patriotic fervor, Siegel carries on a brief affair with her in the hope that she'll arrange a meeting between him and Mussolini so he can assassinate the fascist leader. He gives up on the idea, though, when Mussolini's vengeful countrymen do the job instead.[2]

Siegel's relationships with West Coast mobster Mickey Cohen (Harvey Keitel) and the ambitious Hill are the core of the film. His increasingly flamboyant business schemes with Cohen and all-consuming infatuation with Hill separate him more and more from his East Coast partners. The huge cost overruns of the syndicate-financed Flamingo Hotel finally put him on the outs with the mob, which also suspects Hill of stashing some of the construction money in a Swiss bank account (without Siegel's knowledge, the script maintains). When bad weather dampens the expensive gambling casino's opening night and Siegel is forced to close the place down, the syndicate decides it's had enough of the loose cannon. Even Meyer Lansky, Siegel's oldest friend and chief protector, can no longer defend Siegel's impetuous actions. In a scene reminiscent of the conclusion of *Casablanca* (1942), not to mention *Bonnie and Clyde*, Siegel and Hill say their good-byes at the airport, their parting glances filled with longing and a sense of fatalism, and Siegel flies to Los Angeles to meet his doom. As the film ends, a title card informs us that Siegel's Las Vegas dream, which netted the gangster only a gruesome death, went on to make its syndicate heirs billions of dollars.

Warren Beatty gives an appropriately larger-than-life, movie-star performance as Bugsy Siegel. He is by turns comic, frightening, endearing, and in Hill's words, a "psychotic asshole." Beatty's Bugsy is perfectly in tune with the film's glitzy style and its theme—the tragedy (if indeed it can be called that) of a hood who forgets he is a hood and enters the realm of Hollywood fantasy where sees himself as the romantic lead, destined to get both the girl and the gold—but who takes a bullet through the eye instead.

BADA BING

"What do you think this is the Army, where you shoot 'em a mile away? You've gotta get up close like this and—

bada bing—you blow their brains all over
your nice Ivy League suit."
—*Sonny Corleone (James Caan),*
The Godfather (1972)

Today, almost sixty years since the untimely passing of Bugsy Siegel, the mob itself seems to have gone through the looking glass. Real-life wiseguys and goodfellas more and more have come to define themselves—and the image of the mob—by *The Godfather*, *GoodFellas*, and other American gangster pictures they've seen over the years. More and more also, they have come to identify with and, like children, even come to behave in the same manner as their screen icons Robinson, Cagney, Bogart, Muni, Garfield, De Niro, and Pacino. This indelible, often comic, influence of the American gangster picture—especially those of Coppola and Scorsese—on today's friendly neighborhood mobsters is nowhere more vividly portrayed than in the HBO television series *The Sopranos*.

An Italian-American born in New Jersey (*The Sopranos'* locale), the show's creator, David Chase, was hooked early on by such gangster movies as *The Public Enemy* and such TV shows as *The Untouchables*. He began his television career as a writer on the James Garner TV detective show *The Rockford Files* (NBC, 1974–1980). *The Sopranos* grew out of an idea he'd conceived originally as a feature film, a mob comedy about a wiseguy who has difficulty handling his aging mother and winds up in therapy. Later, he was approached to develop a family drama about the mob in the manner of *The Godfather*, but for television. He put the two ideas together and out came *The Sopranos*, a dysfunctional take on traditional "family values" TV fare like *The Waltons,* with characters named "Big Pussy" replacing those named "John-Boy" and people getting whacked instead of bidding each other "good night." Call it the Corleones meet Ozzie and Harriet.

The first TV show, network or cable, set against the backdrop of the Mafia with mobsters and their families as both the protagonists and the villains, *The Sopranos* premiered on HBO in 1999. Picking up where its major big screen antecedents, *The Godfather* and *GoodFellas*, left off, it has become the first great gangster saga of the new millennium. As this book goes to press, *The Sopranos* has entered its fifth season on television and seems destined to sit among the stars of gangland on the theatrical screen someday as well.

The show's blue-collar mobsters, their wives, and their children are inspired by the real-life wiseguys and their families who moved out of such cities as New York and Newark when Chase was growing up and into suburban neighborhoods like his own. Although mobsters, their reasons for moving to the more family-friendly (no pun intended) suburbs were the same as those of most other big-city transplants, Chase has said, and *The Sopranos* plays on that idea.

Tony Soprano, his wife Carmela, daughter Meadow, and son Tony Jr. are an otherwise average suburban family, coping with the same mundane pressures all families have about school, teenage dating, gaining too much weight, caring for older parents, and so on. It's just that Tony Sr. has the added pressure of being the don of New Jersey (whose front is "Waste Management Consultant"), and his wife and kids must deal with the ramifications of that.

In this environment, it's not oversized photos of the latest pop stars one sees hanging on walls everywhere, but blow-ups of more personal and enduring icons like Edward G. Robinson and Humphrey Bogart. Conversations are dotted not just with slang and the F–word, but with lines of dialogue from gangster movies like *The Godfather* series, their specific source identified not by title but by the roman numeral *I*, *II*, or *III*. And when someone gets a bullet through the eye, it's not called a "Bugsy Siegel Special" but rather a "Moe Green Special." It is an environment governed as much by fantasy and wish fulfillment as by tradition, the show is saying—perhaps even moreso.

"For me," Chase explained in a 2000 interview with the online fan site Sopranosforum.com, "[*The Sopranos*] is a mob story about what's happening in the mob right now—as opposed to the *Godfather* movies, which were about the past. They were the '40s and '50s. *GoodFellas* was about the '60s through the '80s. So, they were period pieces. And *The Sopranos* isn't a period piece. It's about the mob today."

And what of the mob today? Laments *The Sopranos*' galvanizing antihero on Prozac played by James Gandolfini: "You know how many mobsters are selling screenplays and screwing things up? The Golden Age of the mob is gone, it's never coming back—and the mob has only itself to blame."

But it lives on—in the movies, on television, and through the looking glass.

Acknowledgments

M Y LATE FATHER, EUGENE MCCARTY, for introducing me to the movies and taking me to hundreds of them when I was young—and for making me stick it out to the end of *Citizen Kane* on the late show when I was twelve to find out what "Rosebud" was. I haven't been the same since.

My late mother, Sally McCarty, for encouraging my passion for movies by ignoring the teachers and guidance counselors in school who cautioned that I was in danger of developing no other interests. I developed many—and it was often the movies that led me to them.

My wife, Cheryl; behind every successful writer, there's a working spouse. You can retire soon, hon, I promise.

Laureen Rowland, my former agent at the David Black Agency—and now founder and publisher of her own imprint (Hudson Street Press)—for getting the ball rolling. Good luck in your new life; let's not lose touch. Joy Tutela, my new agent at the David Black Agency, for picking up that ball and for making the transition on my part enjoyable and effortless. To paraphrase Humphrey Bogart at the end of *Casablanca:* I think this is the beginning of a great relationship.

Marnie Cochran, my editor at Da Capo, for having the courage and the understanding to allow me a chance to give my thoughts on the American gangster picture a new lease on life. I hope I haven't let you down. Erin Sprague, my project editor on the book, for your keen eye in catching my gaffes, and for ensuring an exceptionally smooth production process.

Entertainment attorney Scott Schwimer, my right hand shark in Hollywood—for your faith in me, your professional courtesy in and out of the water, and, above all, your good humor.

Director Richard Fleischer, for graciously taking the time to share anecdotes and your experiences with me—an interview that was, alas, never published—about the making of some of your early gangster and crime films at RKO and other studios; happily some of your fascinating tidbits have found their way herein.

Kevin Brownlow, for your courtesy and your hospitality on the occasions I visited London some years ago, and for being a continuing source of inspiration to people like myself who try to write about the history and their love of the movies.

Rob Edelman, my fellow writer and fellow adjunct in the trenches of academe, for encouraging me to do this book so he'd have something to assign his students to read in a class on crime films. Thanks, Rob, for the jumpstart.

Documentary filmmaker Elaina B. Archer, for your enthusiasm for this project in general and for your belief in my take on the American gangster picture in particular—as well as for convincing me I wasn't crazy in seeing more than a little of Marlon Brando's Terry Malloy from *On the Waterfront* in Rockliffe Fellowes's Owen Conway from *Regeneration.*

My son Christopher McCarty, for helping me to mine the rich resources of Albany's labyrinthine State Education Library; Ken Hanke, for sharing some of his research on Hollywood's early talkies with me; Danny Burk, Ray Cabana, John Foster, and Doug Palmer (of Tory's Mystery Movies) for helping me find and screen some important rare films; Eric Caidin (Hollywood Book & Poster), Mary Corliss (Museum of Modern Art) for helping me locate some of the hard-to-find photos included in the book; and Lorraine Lubudziewski, for her ace graphics help.

APPENDIX I:

The Oscars

MAJOR AWARD NOMINATIONS AND WINNERS*
1927–PRESENT

ALL GANGSTER MOVIES ARE CRIME MOVIES. But not all crime movies (films noir or prison pictures, for example) are necessarily gangster movies. In keeping with this theorem, the following list is confined to nominees and winners for gangster pictures only, from before the Oscars were called Oscars to the present. As a result, multiple nominated and award-winning films dealing with crime (but not gangsters or the milieu of gangland), such as *I Am a Fugitive from a Chain Gang*, 1932, are excluded.

1927/1928
Best Picture
   The Racket (Paramount)
Best Writing (Original Story)
   Ben Hecht,* *Underworld* (Paramount)

1928/1929
Best Picture
   Alibi (Feature Productions)

---

* Denotes winner.

Best Actor
  Chester Morris, *Alibi*
  George Bancroft, *Thunderbolt* (Paramount)

1930/1931

Best Director
  Clarence Brown, *A Free Soul*
Best Actor
  Lionel Barrymore,* *A Free Soul* (MGM)
Best Actress
  Norma Shearer, *A Free Soul*
Best Writing (Adaptation)
  Seton Miller and Fred Niblo Jr., *The Criminal Code* (Columbia)
  Francis Faragoh and Robert N. Lee, *Little Caesar* (First National)
Best Writing (Original Story)
  Rowland Brown, *Doorway to Hell* (First National)
  John Bright and Kubec Glasmon, *The Public Enemy* (First National)
  Lucian Hubbard and Joseph Jackson, *Smart Money* (First National)

1931/1932

Best Writing (Original Story)
  Lucien Hubbard, *Star Witness* (Warner Brothers)

1932/1933

Best Director
  Frank Capra, *Lady for a Day* (Columbia)
Best Actress
  May Robson, *Lady for a Day*
Best Writing (Adaptation)
  Robert Riskin, *Lady for a Day*

1934

Best Picture
  The Thin Man (MGM)
Best Director
  W. S. Van Dyke, *The Thin Man*
Best Actor
  William Powell, *The Thin Man*

Best Writing (Adaptation)
   Frances Goodrich and Albert Hackett, *The Thin Man*
Best Writing (Original Story)
   Arthur Caesar,* *Manhattan Melodrama* (MGM)

1936

Best Writing (Original Story)
   Frances Goodrich and Albert Hackett,
   After the Thin Man (MGM)

1937

Best Picture
   Dead End (Samuel Goldwyn–United Artists)
Best Supporting Actress
   Claire Trevor, *Dead End*
Best Cinematography
   Gregg Toland, *Dead End*

1938

Best Director
   Michael Curtiz, *Angels with Dirty Faces*
   (Warner Brothers)
Best Actor
   James Cagney, *Angels with Dirty Faces*
Best Writing (Original Story)
   Rowland Brown, *Angels with Dirty Faces*

1940

Best Writing (Original Screenplay)
   Preston Sturges,* *The Great McGinty* (Paramount)

1941

Best Picture
   The Maltese Falcon (Warner Brothers)
Best Supporting Actor
   Sydney Greenstreet, *The Maltese Falcon*
Best Writing (Screenplay Adaptation)
   John Huston, *The Maltese Falcon*

1942
Best Supporting Actor
  Van Heflin,* *Johnny Eager* (MGM)

1945
Best Writing (Original Screenplay)
  Philip Yordan, *Dillinger* (Monogram)

1946
Best Director
  Robert Siodmak, *The Killers* (Universal)
Best Writing (Original Screenplay)
  Raymond Chandler, *The Blue Dahlia* (Paramount)
Best Writing (Screenplay Adaptation)
  Anthony Veiller, *The Killers*

1947
Best Supporting Actor
  Richard Widmark, *Kiss of Death* (Twentieth Century Fox)
  Thomas Gomez, *Ride the Pink Horse* (Universal)
Best Writing (Original Screenplay)
  Eleazar Limpsky, *Kiss of Death*

1948
Best Actress
  Barbara Stanwyck, *Sorry, Wrong Number*
    (Paramount)
Best Supporting Actress
  Claire Trevor,* *Key Largo* (Warner Brothers)

1949
Best Writing (Original Screenplay)
  Virginia Kellogg, *White Heat* (Warner Brothers)

1950
Best Director
  John Huston, *The Asphalt Jungle* (MGM)
Best Supporting Actor
  Sam Jaffe, *The Asphalt Jungle*

Best Writing (Original Screenplay)
>   Edna Anhalt and Edward Anhalt,* *Panic in the Streets*
>   (Twentieth Century Fox)

Best Writing (Screenplay Adaptation)
>   Ben Maddow and John Huston, *The Asphalt Jungle*

Best Writing (Original Story and Screenplay)
>   Joseph L. Mankiewicz and Lesser Samuels,
>   *No Way Out* (Twentieth Century Fox)

Best Cinematography
>   Harold Rosson, *The Asphalt Jungle*

1951

Best Director
>   William Wyler, *Detective Story* (Paramount)

Best Actress
>   Eleanor Parker, *Detective Story*

Best Supporting Actress
>   Lee Grant, *Detective Story*

Best Writing (Screenplay Adaptation)
>   Philip Yordan and Robert Wyler, *Detective Story*

1952

Best Writing (Motion Picture Story)
>   Martin Goldsmith and Jack Leonard, *The Narrow Margin* (RKO)

1953

Best Supporting Actress
>   Thelma Ritter, *Pickup on South Street*
>   (Twentieth Century Fox)

1954

Best Picture
>   *On the Waterfront** (Columbia)

Best Director
>   Elia Kazan,* *On the Waterfront*

Best Actor
>   Marlon Brando,* *On the Waterfront*

Best Supporting Actor
>   Lee J. Cobb, *On the Waterfront*

Karl Malden, *On the Waterfront*
Rod Steiger, *On the Waterfront*
Best Supporting Actress
Eva Marie Saint,* *On the Waterfront*
Best Writing (Original Story and Screenplay)
Budd Schulberg, *On the Waterfront*
Best Cinematography (Black & White)
Boris Kaufman,* *On the Waterfront*

1955
Best Actor
James Cagney, *Love Me or Leave Me* (MGM)
Frank Sinatra, *The Man with the Golden Arm*
(United Artists)
Best Supporting Actress
Peggy Lee, *Pete Kelly's Blues* (Warner Brothers)
Best Writing (Motion Picture Story)
Daniel Fuchs,* *Love Me or Leave Me*
Best Writing (Original Screenplay)
Daniel Fuchs and Isobel Lennart,* *Love Me or Leave Me*
Best Writing (Original Story and Screenplay)
Betty Comden and Adolph Green, *It's Always Fair Weather* (MGM)
Best Cinematography (Color)
Harry Stradling, *Guys and Dolls* (MGM)

1956
Best Writing (Original Screenplay)
William Rose, *The Ladykillers* (Continental)
Best Cinematography (Black & White)
Burnett Guffey, *The Harder They Fall* (Columbia)

1957
Best Actor
Anthony Franciosa, *A Hatful of Rain* (Twentieth Century Fox)

1958
Best Director
Robert Wise, *I Want to Live!* (United Artists)

Best Actress
    Susan Hayward,* *I Want to Live!*
Best Screenplay (Screenplay Adaptation)
    Nelson Gidding and Don Mankiewicz, *I Want to Live!*
Best Cinematography (Black & White)
    Lionel Lindon, *I Want to Live!*

1959

Best Director
    Billy Wilder, *Some Like It Hot*
        (United Artists)
Best Actor
    Jack Lemmon, *Some Like It Hot*
Best Screenplay (Screenplay Adaptation)
    Billy Wilder and I. A. L. Diamond,
        Some Like It Hot
Best Cinematography (Black & White)
    Charles Lang Jr., *Some Like It Hot*

1960

Best Supporting Actor
    Peter Falk, *Murder, Inc.*
        (Twentieth Century Fox)

1961

Best Supporting Actor
    Peter Falk, *Pocketful of Miracles*
        (United Artists)

1967

Best Picture
    Bonnie and Clyde (Warner Brothers–Seven Arts)
Best Director
    Arthur Penn, *Bonnie and Clyde*
Best Actor
    Warren Beatty, *Bonnie and Clyde*
Best Actress
    Faye Dunaway, *Bonnie and Clyde*

Best Supporting Actor
    Gene Hackman, *Bonnie and Clyde*
    Michael J. Pollard, *Bonnie and Clyde*
Best Supporting Actress
    Estelle Parsons,* *Bonnie and Clyde*
Best Original Story and Screenplay
    David Newman and Robert Benton, *Bonnie and Clyde*
Best Cinematography
    Burnett Guffey,* *Bonnie and Clyde*

1971
Best Picture
    *The French Connection** (Twentieth Century Fox)
Best Director
    William Friedkin,* *The French Connection*
Best Actor
    Gene Hackman,* *The French Connection*
Best Supporting Actor
    Roy Scheider, *The French Connection*
Best Screenplay (Adaptation)
    Ernest Tidyman,* *The French Connection*
Best Cinematography
    Owen Roizman, *The French Connection*

1972
Best Picture
    *The Godfather** (Paramount)
Best Director
    Francis Ford Coppola, *The Godfather*
Best Actor
    Marlon Brando,* *The Godfather*
Best Supporting Actor
    James Caan, *The Godfather*
    Robert Duvall, *The Godfather*
    Al Pacino, *The Godfather*
Best Screenplay (Adaptation)
    Mario Puzo and Francis Ford Coppola,* *The Godfather*

1973

Best Picture
  *The Sting** (Universal)
Best Director
  George Roy Hill,* *The Sting*
Best Actor
  Robert Redford, *The Sting*
Best Screenplay (Original)
  David S. Ward,* *The Sting*
Best Cinematography
  Robert Surtees, *The Sting*

1974

Best Picture
  *The Godfather Part II** (Paramount)
Best Director
  Francis Ford Coppola,* *The Godfather Part II*
Best Actor
  Al Pacino, *The Godfather Part II*
  Albert Finney, *Murder on the Orient Express* (Paramount)
Best Supporting Actor
  Robert De Niro,* *The Godfather Part II*
  Michael V. Gasso, *The Godfather Part II*
  Lee Satrasberg, *The Godfather Part II*
  Jeff Bridges, *Thunderbolt and Lightfoot* (United Artists)
Best Supporting Actress
  Talia Shire, *The Godfather Part II*
  Ingrid Bergman,* *Murder on the Orient Express*
Best Screenplay (Adaptation)
  Francis Ford Coppola and Mario Puzo,* *The Godfather Part II*
  Paul Dehn, *Murder on the Orient Express*
Best Cinematography
  Geoffrey Unsworth, *Murder on the Orient Express*

1975

Best Supporting Actress
  Sylvia Miles, *Farewell, My Lovely* (Avco Embassy)

1977
Best Screenplay (Original)
  Robert Benton, *The Late Show* (Warner Brothers)

1981
Best Picture
  Atlantic City (Paramount)
Best Director
  Louis Malle, *Atlantic City*
Best Actor
  Burt Lancaster, *Atlantic City*
Best Actress
  Susan Sarandon, *Atlantic City*
Best Screenplay (Original)
  John Guare, *Atlantic City*

1984
Best Screenplay (Original)
  Daniel Petrie Jr., and Danilo Bach,
    Beverly Hills Cop (Paramount)

1985
Best Picture
  Prizzi's Honor (Twentieth Century Fox)
Best Director
  John Huston, *Prizzi's Honor*
Best Actor
  Jack Nicholson, *Prizzi's Honor*
Best Supporting Actor
  William Hickey, *Prizzi's Honor*
  Robert Loggia, *Prizzi's Honor*
Best Supporting Actress
  Anjelica Huston,* *Prizzi's Honor*
Best Screenplay (Adaptation)
  Richard Condon and Janet Roach, *Prizzi's Honor*

1986
Best Director
  David Lynch, *Blue Velvet* (De Laurentiis)

1987
Best Supporting Actor
  Sean Connery,* *The Untouchables* (Paramount)

1988
Best Supporting Actor
  Dean Stockwell, *Married to the Mob* (Orion)

1990
Best Picture
  The Godfather Part III (Paramount)
  GoodFellas (Warner Brothers)
Best Director
  Francis Ford Coppola, *The Godfather Part III*
  Martin Scorsese, *GoodFellas*
  Stephen Frears, *The Grifters* (Miramax)
Best Actress
  Anjelica Huston, *The Grifters*
Best Supporting Actor
  Al Pacino, *Dick Tracy* (Touchstone)
  Andy Garcia, *The Godfather Part III*
  Joe Pesci,* *GoodFellas*
Best Supporting Actress
  Lorraine Bracco, *GoodFellas*
  Annette Bening, *The Grifters*
Best Screenplay (Adaptation)
  Nicholas Pileggi and Martin Scorsese, *GoodFellas*
  Donald E. Westlake, *The Grifters*
Best Cinematography
  Vittorio Storaro, *Dick Tracy*
  Gordon Willis, *The Godfather Part III*

1991
Best Picture
  Bugsy (TriStar)
Best Director
  Barry Levinson, *Bugsy*
Best Actor
  Warren Beatty, *Bugsy*

Best Supporting Actor
   Harvey Keitel, *Bugsy*
   Ben Kinglsey, *Bugsy*
Best Screenplay (Original)
   James Toback, *Bugsy*
Best Cinematography
   Allen Daviau, *Bugsy*

1992
Best Cinematography
   Stephen Byrum, *Hoffa* (Twentieth Century Fox)

1993
Best Supporting Actress
   Holly Hunter, *The Firm* (Paramount)

1994
Best Picture
   Pulp Fiction (Miramax)
Best Director
   Woody Allen, *Bullets Over Broadway* (Miramax)
   Quentin Tarantino, *Pulp Fiction*
Best Actor
   John Travolta, *Pulp Fiction*
Best Actress
   Susan Sarandon, *The Client* (Warner Brothers)
Best Supporting Actor
   Chazz Palminteri, *Bullets Over Broadway*
   Samuel L. Jackson, *Pulp Fiction*
Best Supporting Actress
   Jennifer Tilly, *Bullets Over Broadway*
   Dianne Wiest,* *Bullets Over Broadway*
   Uma Thurman, *Pulp Fiction*
Best Screenplay (Original)
   Woody Allen and Douglas McGrath,
      Bullets Over Broadway
   Quentin Tarantino and Roger Avery,*
      Pulp Fiction

1995
Best Supporting Actor
  Kevin Spacey,* *The Usual Suspects* (Polygram)
Best Supporting Actress
  Sharon Stone, *Casino* (Universal)
Best Screenplay (Original)
  Christopher McQuarrie,* *The Usual Suspects*
Best Cinematography
  Lu Yue, *Shanghai Triad* (Sony Pictures Classics)

1997
Best Picture
  L.A. Confidential (Warner Bros.)
Best Director
  Curtis Hanson, *L.A. Confidential*
Best Supporting Actor
  Robert Forster, *Jackie Brown* (Miramax)
Best Supporting Actress
  Kim Basinger,* *L.A. Confidential*
Best Screenplay (Adaptation)
  Paul Attanasio, *Donnie Brasco* (TriStar)
  Brian Helgeland and Curtis Hanson,* *L.A. Confidential*
Best Cinematography
  Dante Spinotti, *L.A. Confidential*

1998
Best Supporting Actor
  Billy Bob Thornton, *A Simple Plan* (Paramount)
Best Screenplay (Adaptation)
  Scott Frank, *Out of Sight* (Universal)
  Scott B. Smith, *A Simple Plan*

2000
Best Picture
  Traffic (USA Films)
Best Director
  Steven Soderbergh,* *Traffic*
Best Supporting Actor
  Benicio Del Toro,* *Traffic*

Best Screenplay (Adaptation)
   Stephen Gaghan,* *Traffic*

2001
Best Director
   David Lynch, *Mulholland Dr.* (Universal Focus)
Best Actor
   Ben Kingsley, *Sexy Beast* (Fox Searchlight)
   Denzel Washington,* *Training Day* (Warner Bros.)
Best Supporting Actor
   Ethan Hawke, *Training Day*
Best Cinematography
   Roger Deakins, *The Man Who Wasn't There* (USA Films)

2002
Best Picture
   Chicago* (Miramax)
   Gangs of New York (Miramax)
Best Director
   Rob Marshall, *Chicago*
   Martin Scorsese, *Gangs of New York*
Best Actor
   Daniel Day-Lewis, *Gangs of New York*
Best Actress
   Renee Zellweger, *Chicago*
Best Supporting Actor
   John C. Reilly, *Chicago*
   Paul Newman, *Road to Perdition* (Twentieth Century Fox/Dreamworks)
Best Supporting Actress
   Catherine Zeta-Jones,* *Chicago*
Best Screenplay (Original)
   Jay Cocks, Steve Zaillian, and Kenneth Lonergan, *Gangs of New York*
Best Screenplay (Adaptation)
   Bill Condon, *Chicago*
Best Cinematography
   Dion Beebe, *Chicago*
   Michael Ballhaus, *Gangs of New York*
   Conrad L. Hall,* *Road to Perdition*

2003

Best Picture
  Mystic River (Warner Bros.)
Best Director
  Clint Eastwood, *Mystic River*
  Fernando Meirelles, *City of God* (Miramax)
Best Actor
  Sean Penn,* *Mystic River*
Best Supporting Actor
  Tim Robbins,* *Mystic River*
Best Supporting Actress
  Marcia Gay Harden, *Mystic River*
Best Screenplay (Adaptation)
  Brian Helgeland, *Mystic River*
  Braulio Mantovani, *City of God*
Best Cinematography
  Cesare Charlone, *City of God*

2004

Best Actress
  Catalina Sandino Moreno, *Maria Full of Grace* (Fine Line Features)
Best Supporting Actor
  Jamie Foxx, *Collateral* (Dreamworks Studios/Paramount Pictures)

Appendix II: The American Gangster Picture (Feature Length)

A SELECTED FILMOGRAPHY, 1915–PRESENT

THE FOLLOWING IS THE MOST COMPREHENSIVE CHRONOLOGY of feature-length (fifty minutes or longer) gangster pictures made in America from the silent era to the present ever published. That boast aside, I don't claim the list is definitive—just a very thorough start for future historians of the American gangster picture to build upon.

As in Appendix I, the represented films were selected on the basis of focusing primarily (although not necessarily wholly) on urban gangsters, their country cousins, and organized crime, or for projecting a strong sense of the gangland milieu (like the musical *Chicago*).

Gangster-oriented short subjects, documentaries, made-for-TV or cable movies, and direct-to-video features are excluded. The name in parenthesis following each title is the director of record.

1915
Frame-Up, The (Otis Turner)
Gentleman from Indiana, The (Frank Lloyd)
Regeneration (R. A. [Raoul] Walsh)

1916
Cycle of Fate, The (Marshall Neilan)
Her Father's Gold (W. Eugene Moore)
Intolerance (the "modern story," a.k.a., *The Mother and the Law*) (D. W. Griffith)

Redemption of Dave Darcey (Paul Scardon)
Reggie Mixes In (Christy Cabanne)
Sign of the Spade, The (Murdock MacQuarrie)
Temptation and the Man (Robert F. Hill)
Thrown to the Lions (Lucius Henderson)
Wrong Door, The (Carter De Haven)

1917

Hate (Walter Richard Stahl)
Kick In (George Fitzmaurice)

1918

Convict 993 (William Parke)
Finger of Justice, The (Louis William Chaudet)
Flash of Fate, The (Elmer Clifton)
Hell's End (J. W. MacLaughlin)
Midnight Patrol, The (Irvin Willat)
Pretty Smooth (Rollin S. Sturgeon)
Romance of the Underworld, A (James Kirkwood)
Whirlpool, The (Alan Crosland)
Wicked Darling, The (Tod Browning)
Wildcats of Paris, The (Joseph De Grasse)

1920

Cradle of Courage, The (William S. Hart and Lambert Hillyer)
Love Madness (Joseph Henabery)
Penalty, The (Wallace Worsley)
Scarlet Dragon, The (Frank Reicher)
Wanted at Headquarters (Stuart Paton)
White Moll, The (Harry Millarde)

1921

Below the Deadline (J. P. McGowan)
Big Brother (Allan Dwan)
Frontier of the Stars, The (Charles Maigne)
Night Rose, The (Wallace Worsley)
Outside the Law (Tod Browning)
Voices of the City (Wallace Worsley)

1922

Boomerang Bill (Tom Terriss)
Bootleggers, The (Roy Sheldon)
Bootlegger's Daughter, The (Victor Schertzinger)
Flesh and Blood (Irving Cummings)
Light in the Dark, The (Clarence Brown)

1923

Big Brother (Allan Dwan)
Shock, The (Lambert Hillyer)
Slippy McGee (Wesley Ruggles)

1924

Beautiful Sinner, The (W. S. Van Dyke)
Fools' Highway (Irving Cummings)
Jack o' Clubs (Robert F. Hill)

1925

Beautiful City, The (Kenneth Webb)
My Lady's Lips (James P. Hogan)
Soft Shows (Lloyd Ingraham)
That Royale Girl (D. W. Griffith)
Unholy Three, The (Tod Browning)

1926

Blackbird, The (Tod Browning)
Boob, The (William A. Wellman)
Exclusive Rights (Frank O'Connor)
Jade Cup, The (Frank Hall Crane)
Road to Mandalay, The (Tod Browning)

1927

Birds of Prey (William James Craft)
Broadway After Midnight (Fred Windemere)
Cabaret (Robert G. Vignola)
Chicago (Frank Urson)
City Gone Wild, The (James Cruze)
Girl from Chicago, The (Ray Enright)
New York (Luther Reed)

Undertaker's Wedding, The (John Bradshaw)
Underworld (Josef von Sternberg)

1928

Big City, The (Tod Browning)
Bitter Sweets (Charles Hutchison)
Blindfold (Charles Kelin)
Chicago After Midnight (Ralph Ince)
Drag Net, The (Josef von Sternberg)
Dressed to Kill (Irving Cummings)
Four Walls (William Nigh)
Gang War (Bert Glennon)
Ladies of the Mob (William A. Wellman)
Lights of New York (Brian Foy)
Me, Gangster (Raoul Walsh)
Midnight Rose (James Young)
Ned McCobb's Daughter (William J. Cowen)
Racket, The (Lewis Milestone)
Romance of the Underworld, A (Irving Cummings)
State Street Sadie (Archie Mayo)
Stool Pigeon (Renaud Hoffman)
Tenderloin (Michael Curtiz)
Tenth Avenue (William C. DeMille)
Way of the Strong, The (Frank Capra)
While the City Sleeps (Jack Conway)
Yellow Contraband (Leo Maloney)

1929

Alibi (Roland West)
Below the Deadline (J. P. McGowan)
Big News (Gregory La Cava)
Broadway (Paul Fejos)
Broadway Babes (Mervyn LeRoy)
Carnation Kid, The (E. Mason Hopper)
Come Across (Ray Taylor)
Dark Streets (Frank Lloyd)
Eyes of the Underworld (Leigh Jason)
Hole in the Wall, The (Robert Florey)
House of Secrets, The (Edmund Lawrence)

Man, Woman, and Wife (Edward Laemmle)
Mighty, The (John Cromwell)
New York Nights (Lewis Milestone)
Racketeer, The (Howard Higgin)
Skin Deep (Ray Enright)
Synthetic Sin (William A. Seiter)
Thunderbolt (Josef von Sternberg)
Voice of the City (Willard Mack)
Welcome Danger (Clyde Bruckman)

1930

Big Chase, The (Walter Lang)
Big Fight, The (Walter Lang)
Big House, The (George Hill)
Big Money (Russell Mack)
Born Reckless (John Ford)
Conspiracy (Christy Cabanne)
Costello Case, The (Walter Lang)
Czar of Broadway, The (William James Craft)
Doorway to Hell (Archie Mayo)
Easy Street (Oscar Micheaux)
Fall Guy, The (A. Leslie Pearce)
Framed (George Archainbaud)
Ladies Love Brutes (Rowland V. Lee)
Little Caesar (Mervyn LeRoy)
Murder on the Roof (George B. Seitz)
Night Ride (John S. Robertson)
Officer O'Brien (Tay Garnett)
One Night at Susie's (John Francis Dillon)
Outside the Law (Tod Browning)
Pay Off, The (Lowell Sherman)
Playing Around (Mervyn LeRoy)
Remote Control (Nick Grinde, Malcolm St. Clair, and [uncredited]
   Edward Sedgwick)
Roadhouse Nights (Hobart Henley)
See America Thirst (William James Craft)
Shooting Straight (George Archainbaud)
Sinner's Holiday (John G. Adolfi)
Squealer, The (Harry Joe Brown)

Street of Chance (John Cromwell)
Those Who Dance (William Beaudine)
Unholy Three, The (Jack Conway)
Up the River (John Ford)
Widow From Chicago, The (Edward F. Cline)

1931

Bad Company (Tay Garnett)
Big Gamble (Fred Niblo)
Blonde Crazy (Roy Del Ruth)
Caught Cheating (Frank R. Strayer)
City Streets (Rouben Mamoulian)
Criminal Code, The (Howard Hawks)
Dance, Fools, Dance (Harry Beaumont)
Enemies of the Law (Lawrence C. Windom)
Finger Points, The (John Francis Dillon)
Forgotten Woman, The (Harold Young)
Free Soul, A (Clarence Brown)
Gang Buster, The (A. Edward Sutherland)
Good Bad Girl, The (Roy William Neill)
Guilty Generation, The (Rowland V. Lee)
Hell Bound (Walter Lang)
Homicide Squad (Edward L. Cahn and George Melford)
Hush Money (Sidney Lanfield)
Lady from Nowhere, The (Richard Thorpe)
Last Parade, The (Erle C. Kenton)
Lawless Woman, The (Richard Thorpe)
Little Caesar (Mervyn LeRoy)
Maltese Falcon, The (a.k.a., *Dangerous Female*)
  (Roy Del Ruth)
Mr. Lemon of Orange (John G. Blystone)
Night Beat (George B. Seitz)
Public Enemy, The (William A. Wellman)
Quick Millions (Rowland Brown)
Ruling Voice, The (Rowland V. Lee)
Scareheads (Noel M. Smith)
Secret Six, The (George Hill)
Smart Money (Alfred E. Green)
Star Witness (William A. Wellman)

Tip-Off, The (Albert S. Rogell)

Young Donovan's Kid (Fred Niblo)

1932

Afraid to Talk (Edward L. Cahn)

Beast of the City (Charles Brabin)

Big City Blues (Mervyn LeRoy)

Diamond Trail, The (Harry L. Fraser)

Disorderly Conduct (John W. Considine Jr.)

Docks of San Francisco, The (George B. Seitz)

Exposed (Albert Herman)

From Broadway to Cheyenne (Harry L. Fraser)

Handle with Care (David Butler)

Hatchet Man, The (William A. Wellman)

Hell's House (Howard Higgin)

Hotel Continental (Christy Cabanne)

Girl from Chicago, The (Oscar Micheaux)

Last Ride (Duke Worne)

Madame Racketeer (Alexander Hall and Harry Wagstaff Gribble)

Man Against Woman (Irving Cummings)

Mouthpiece, The (James Flood and Elliott Nugent)

Night After Night (Archie Mayo)

Okay America (Tay Garnett)

Pride of the Legion (Ford Beebe)

Rackety Rax (Alfred L. Werker)

Radio Patrol (Edward L. Cahn)

Scarface (Howard Hawks)

State's Attorney (George Archainbaud)

Sin's Pay Day (George B. Seitz)

Taxi! (Roy Del Ruth)

Texas Tornado (Oliver Drake)

That's My Story! (Sidney Salkow)

Three on a Match (Mervyn LeRoy)

Under-Cover Man (James Flood)

Washington Merry-Go-Round (James Cruze)

Wet Parade, The (Victor Fleming)

1933

Blondie Johnson (Ray Enright)

Blood Money (Rowland Brown)
Broadway Through a Keyhole (Lowell Sherman)
Emergency Call (Edward L. Cahn)
Gambling Ship (Louis J. Gasnier)
Girl in 419, The (Alexander Hall)
He Couldn't Take It (William Nigh)
Hold Your Man (Sam Wood)
House on 56th Street, The (Robert Florey)
Important Witness, The (Sam Newfield)
Lady for a Day (Frank Capra)
Lady Killer (Roy Del Ruth)
Little Giant, The (Roy Del Ruth)
Mad Game, The (Irving Cummings)
Mayor of Hell, The (Archie Mayo)
Midnight Mary (William A. Wellman)
Parachute Jumper (Alfred E. Green)
Penthouse (W. S. Van Dyke)
Phantom Broadcast, The (Phil Rosen)
Picture Snatcher (Lloyd Bacon)
Riot Squad (Harry S. Webb)
Shadows of Sing Sing (Phil Rosen)
Silk Express, The (Ray Enright)
Story of Temple Drake, The (Stephen Roberts)
This Day and Age (Cecil B. DeMille)
What's Your Racket? (Fred Guiol)
Woman Who Dared, The (Millard Webb)

1934

Against the Law (Lambert Hillyer)
Big Shakedown, The (John Francis Dillon)
Fighting Rookie, The (Spencer Gordon Bennet)
Fugitive Lovers (Richard Boleslawski)
Gay Bride, The (Jack Conway)
Girl in Danger (D. Ross Lederman)
Harlem After Midnight (Oscar Micheaux)
He Was Her Man (Lloyd Bacon)
Heat Lightning (Mervyn LeRoy)
Hide-Out (W. S. Van Dyke)
Hollywood Hoodlum (B. Reeves Eason)

Inside Information (Robert F. Hill)
I've Got Your Number (Ray Enright)
Jimmy the Gent (Michael Curtiz)
Kansas City Princess (William Keighley)
Limehouse Blues (Alexander Hall)
Lineup, The (Howard Higgin)
Little Miss Marker (Alexander Hall)
Mandalay (Michael Curtiz)
Manhattan Melodrama (W. S. Van Dyke)
Men of the Night (Lambert Hillyer)
Midnight (Chester Erskine)
Midnight Alibi (Alan Crosland)
St. Louis Kid, The (Ray Enright)
Texas Tornado (Oliver Drake)
Three on a Match (Mervyn LeRoy)
Very Honorable Guy, A (Lloyd Bacon)
What's Your Racket? (Fred Guiol)
Woman Unafraid (William J. Cowan)
World Accuses, The (Charles Lamont)

1935

Another Face (Christy Cabanne)
Baby Face Harrington (Raoul Walsh)
Bad Boy (John G. Blystone)
Behind the Evidence (Lambert Hillyer)
Black Fury (Michael Curtiz)
Calling All Cars (Spencer Gordon Bennett)
Cocaine Fiends, The (William A. O'Connor)
Confidential (Edward L. Cahn)
Dr. Socrates (William Dieterle)
G-Men (William Keighley)
Girl Who Came Back, The (Charles Lamont)
Glass Key, The (Frank Tuttle)
Go into Your Dance (Archie Mayo)
Ladies They Talk About (Howard Bretherton)
Let 'Em Have It (Sam Wood)
Mary Burns, Fugitive (William K. Howard)
Men Without Names (Ralph Murphy)
On Probation (Charles Hutchison)

People's Enemy, The (Crane Wilbur)
Public Hero #1 (J. Walter Ruben)
Shadow of Silk Lennox, The (Ray Kirkwood and Jack Nelson)
She Couldn't Take It (Tay Garnett)
Show Them No Mercy (George Marshall)
Special Agent (William Keighley)
Stolen Harmony (Alfred Werker)
Temptation (Oscar Micheaux)
Whipsaw (Sam Wood)
Whole Town's Talking, The (John Ford)
Woman Wanted (George B. Seitz)

1936

Anything Goes (Lewis Milestone)
Big Show, The (Mack V. Wright)
Bridge of Sighs (Phil Rosen)
Bulldog Edition (Charles Lamont)
Bullets or Ballots (William Keighley)
Crime Patrol, The (Eugene Cummings)
Exclusive Story (George B. Seitz)
Florida Special (Ralph Murphy)
Grand Jury (Albert S. Rogell)
Great Guy (John G. Blystone)
Gun Grit (William A. Berke)
Human Cargo (Allan Dwan)
Lady from Nowhere (Gordon Wiles)
Law in Her Hands, The (William Clemens)
Man Hunt (William Clemens)
Missing Girls (Phil Rosen)
Muss 'Em Up (Charles Vidor)
Night Waitress (Lew Landers)
Nobody's Fool (Irving Cummings)
Old Corral, The (Joseph Kane)
Parole (Lew Landers)
Petrified Forest, The (Archie Mayo)
Public Enemy's Wife (Nick Grinde)
Return of Jimmy Valentine, The (Lewis D. Collins)
Satan Met a Lady (William Dieterle)
Special Investigator (Louis King)

Step on It (Henri G. Samuels)

Sworn Enemy (Edward L. Marin)

Trapped by Television (Del Lord)

Two Against the World (William McGann)

Wanted! Jane Turner (Edward Killy)

Woman Trap (Harold Young)

Women Are Trouble (Errol Taggart)

Yellow Cargo (Crane Wilbur)

Yellowstone (Arthur Lubin)

1937

Alcatraz Island (Edward Killy)

Bank Alarm (Louis J. Gasnier)

Big City, The (Frank Borzage)

Big Shot, The (Edward Killy)

Born Reckless (Malcolm St. Clair)

Carnival Queen (Nate Watt)

Charlie Chan on Broadway (Eugene Forde)

Clipped Wings (Stuart Paton)

Criminal Lawyer (Christy Cabanne)

Dark Manhattan (Harry L. Fraser)

Dead End (William Wyler)

Escape By Night (Hamilton MacFadden)

Frame-Up, The (D. Ross Lederman)

Game That Kills, The (D. Ross Lederman)

Gangsters on the Loose (a.k.a., *Bargain with Bullets*) (Harry L. Fraser)

Girls Can Play (Lambert Hillyer)

Great Hospital Mystery, The (James Tinling)

Her Husband Lies (Edward Ludwig)

Hideaway (Richard Rosson)

I Promise to Pay (D. Ross Lederman)

Idol of the Crowds (Arthur Lubin)

Interns Can't Take Money (Alfred Santell)

Kid Galahad (Michael Curtiz)

King of the Gamblers (Robert Florey)

Last Gangster, The (Edward Ludwig)

Manhattan Merry-Go-Round (Charles Reisner)

Marked Woman (Lloyd Bacon)

Midnight Taxi (Eugene Forde)

Missing Witnesses (William Clemens)
Night Club Scandal (Ralph Murphy)
On Such a Night (E. A. Dupont)
Outer Gate, The (Raymond Cannon)
Paid to Dance (Charles C. Coleman)
Partners in Crime (Ralph Murphy)
San Quentin (Lloyd Bacon)
She Had to Eat (Malcolm St. Clair)
That Certain Woman (Edmund Goulding)
They Gave Him a Gun (W. S. Van Dyke)
Underworld (Oscar Micheaux)
We Who Are About to Die (Christy Cabanne)
You Only Live Once (Fritz Lang)
Youth on Parole (Phil Rosen)

1938

Amazing Dr. Clitterhouse, The (Anatole Litvak)
Angels with Dirty Faces (Michael Curtiz)
Border G-Man (David Howard)
City Girl (Alfred L. Werker)
Convicts At Large (Scott E. Beal)
Crashing Hollywood (Lew Landers)
Crime School (Lewis Seiler)
Crime Takes a Holiday (Lewis D. Collins)
Dangerous to Know (Robert Florey)
Devil's Party, The (Ray McCarey)
Gang Smashers (Leo C. Popkin)
Gangs of New York (James Cruze)
Gangster's Boy (William Nigh)
Held for Ransom (Clarence Bricker)
Hunted Men (Louis King)
I Am a Criminal (William Nigh)
I Am the Law (Alexander Hall)
I Demand Payment (Clifford Sansforth)
I Stand Accused (John A. Auer)
Illegal Traffic (Louis King)
Juvenile Court (D. Ross Lederman)
King of Alcatraz (Robert Florey)
King of Chinatown (Nick Grinde)

Law of the Underworld (Lew Landers)
Mr. Moto's Gamble (James Tinling)
Paroled from the Big House (Elmer Clifton)
Prison Train (Gordon Wiles)
Racket Busters (Lloyd Bacon)
Saint in New York, The (Ben Holmes)
Slight Case of Murder, A (Lloyd Bacon)
State Police (John Rawlins)
Tenth Avenue Kid (Bernard Vorhaus)
This Marriage Business (Christy Cabanne)
Tip-Off Girls, The (Louis King)
Two Gun Man from Harlem (Richard C. Kahn)
Up the River (Alfred Werker)
Wanted by the Police (Howard Bretherton)
When G-Men Step In (Charles C. Coleman)
You and Me (Fritz Lang)

1939

Ambush (Kurt Neumann)
Angels Wash Their Faces (Ray Enright)
Arson Racket Squad (Joseph Kane)
Back Door to Heaven (William K. Howard)
Big Town Czar (Arthur Lubin)
Blackwell's Island (William McGann and [uncredited] Michael Curtiz)
Blind Alley (Charles Vidor)
Café Hostess (Sidney Salkow)
Call a Messenger (Arthur Lubin)
Disbarred (Robert Florey)
Each Dawn I Die (William Keighley)
Escape, The (Ricardo Cortez)
Fugitive at Large (Lewis D. Collins)
Golden Boy (Rouben Mamoulian)
Hell's Kitchen (E. A. Dupont and Lewis Seiler)
Heroes in Blue (William Watson)
Homicide Bureau (Charles C. Coleman)
Invisible Stripes (Lloyd Bacon)
Irish Luck (Howard Bretherton)
I Stole a Million (Frank Tuttle)
I Was a Convict (Aubrey Scotto)

King of the Underworld (Lewis Seiler)
Lady and the Mob, The (Benjamin Stoloff)
Main Street Lawyer (Dudley Murphy)
Man Who Dared, The (a.k.a., *City in Terror*) (Crane Wilbur)
Missing Daughters (Charles C. Coleman)
One Hour to Live (Harold D. Schuster)
Persons in Hiding (Louis King)
Religious Racketeers (Frank O'Connor)
Risky Business (Arthur Lubin)
Roaring Twenties, The (Raoul Walsh)
6,000 Enemies (George B. Seitz)
Society Lawyer (Edward L. Marin)
Star Reporter (Howard Bretherton)
Street of Missing Men (Sidney Salkow)
Torchy Plays with Dynamite (Noel M. Smith)
Twelve Crowded Hours (Lew Landers)
Undercover Doctor (Louis King)
You Can't Get Away with Murder (Lewis Seiler)

1940

Am I Guilty? (Sam Newfield)
Angels over Broadway (Ben Hecht and Lee Garmes)
Black Friday (Arthur Lubin)
Brother Orchid (Lloyd Bacon)
Earl of Chicago, The (Richard Thorpe)
East of the River (Alfred E. Green)
Fugitive from Justice, A (Terry O. Morse)
Gambling on the High Seas (George Amy)
Gang War (Leo C. Popkin)
Gangs of Chicago (Arthur Lubin)
Great Plane Robbery, The (Lewis D. Collins)
House Across the Bay, The (Archie Mayo)
I Can't Give You Anything but Love, Baby (Albert S. Rogell)
I Take This Oath (Sam Newfield)
It All Came True (Lewis Seiler)
Johnny Apollo (Henry Hathaway)
Man Who Talked Too Much, The (Vincent Sherman)
Marked Men (Sam Newfield)
My Son Is Guilty (Charles Barton)

Notorious Elinor Lee, The (Oscar Micheaux)
On the Spot (Howard Bretherton)
Outside the Three Mile Limit (Lewis D. Collins)
Parole Fixer (Robert Florey)
Queen of the Mob (James P. Hogan)
Saint Takes Over, The (Jack Hively)
So You Won't Talk (Edward Sedgwick)
While Thousands Cheer (Leo C. Popkin)

1941

Big Boss, The (Charles Barton)
Blues in the Night (Anatole Litvak)
Bride Wore Crutches, The (Shepard Traube)
Buy Me That Town (Eugene Forde)
Caught in the Act (Jean Yarbrough)
Citadel of Crime (George Sherman)
City of Missing Girls (Elmer Clifton)
Confessions of Boston Blackie (Edward Dmytryk)
Dangerous Game, A (John Rawlins)
Doctors Don't Tell (Jacques Tourneur)
Double Cross (Albert H. Kelley)
Gambling Daughters (Max Nosseck)
Gangs Inc. (a.k.a., *Paper Bullets*) (Phil Rosen)
Get-Away, The (Edward Buzzell)
Hard Guy (Elmer Clifton)
High Sierra (Raoul Walsh)
Hit the Road (Joe May)
Lady Scarface (Frank Woodruff)
Maltese Falcon, The (John Huston)
Mob Town (William Nigh)
Monster and the Girl, The (Stuart Heisler)
Murder on Lenox Avenue (Arthur Dreifuss)
Mystery Ship (Lew Landers)
Out of the Fog (Anatole Litvak)
Penalty, The (Harold S. Bucquet)
Public Enemies (Albert S. Rogell)
Riot Squad (Edward Finney)
Rise and Shine (Allan Dwan)
Shadow of the Thin Man (W. S. Van Dyke)

Stork Pays Off, The (Lew Landers)
Strange Alibi (D. Ross Lederman)
Tall, Dark and Handsome (H. Bruce Humberstone)
Tight Shoes (Albert S. Rogell)

1942

All Through the Night (Vincent Sherman)
Baby Face Morgan (Arthur Dreifuss)
Big Shot, The (Lewis Seiler)
Broadway (William A. Seiter)
Broadway Big Shot (William Beaudine)
Come Out Fighting (William Beaudine)
Four Jacks and a Jill (Jack Hively)
Gallant Lady (William Beaudine)
Glass Key, The (Stuart Heisler)
Highways by Night (Peter Godfrey)
I Live on Danger (Sam White)
Johnny Eager (Mervyn LeRoy)
Lady Gangster (Florian Roberts, a.k.a., Robert Florey)
Larceny, Inc. (Lloyd Bacon)
Lucky Jordan (Frank Tuttle)
Man from Headquarters (Jean Yarbrough)
Man with Two Lives, The (Phil Rosen)
Mayor of 44th Street, The (Alfred E. Green)
Meet the Mob (Jean Yarbrough)
Mississippi Gambler (John Rawlins)
Police Bullets (Jean Yarbrough)
Roxie Hart (William A. Wellman)
Sealed Lips (George Waggner)
Secrets of a Co-ed (Joseph H. Lewis)
This Gun for Hire (Frank Tuttle)
Two Yanks in Trinidad (Gregory Ratoff)

1943

Confessions of a Vice Baron (S. Roy Luby, William A. O'Connor, Melville
    Shyer, and Herman E. Weber)
Cosmo Jones, Crime Smasher (James Tinling)
Eyes of the Underworld (Roy William Neill)
Fog over Frisco (William Dieterle)

Gentle Gangster, A (Phil Rosen)

Hit the Ice (Charles Lamont and Erle C. Kenton)

Johnny Come Lately (William K. Howard)

Man of Courage (Alexis Thurn-Taxis)

Mr. Lucky (H. C. Potter)

Never a Dull Moment (Edward C. Lilly)

No Place for a Lady (James P. Hogan)

One Dangerous Night (Michael Gordon)

Petticoat Larceny (Ben Holmes)

Silent Witness (Jean Yarbrough)

Taxi, Mister (Kurt Neumann)

Truck Busters (B. Reeves Eason)

1944

Dark Mountain (William Berke)

Dixie Jamboree (Christy Cabanne)

Follow the Leader (William Beaudine)

My Buddy (Steve Sekely)

Murder, My Sweet (Edward Dmytryk)

Racket Man, The (D. Ross Lederman)

Roger Touhy, Gangster (Robert Florey)

What a Man! (William Beaudine)

1945

Blonde Ransom (William Beaudine)

Crime Inc. (Lew Landers)

Dillinger (Max Nosseck)

Gangs of the Waterfront (George Blair)

Johnny Angel (Edward L. Martin)

Sensation Hunters (Christy Cabanne)

Steppin' in Society (Alexander Esway)

This Gun for Hire (Frank Tuttle)

Wonder Man (H. Bruce Humberstone)

1946

Angel on My Shoulder (Archie Mayo)

Below the Deadline (William Beaudine)

Big Sleep, The (Howard Hawks)

Black Angel (Roy William Neill)

Black Market Babies (William Beaudine)
Bowery Bombshell (Phil Karlson)
Chase, The (Arthur Ripley)
Criminal Court (Robert Wise)
Decoy (Jack Bernhard)
Gentleman Joe Palooka (Cy Endfield)
Gilda (Charles Vidor)
Glass Alibi, The (W. Lee Wilder)
Her Kind of Man (Frederick De Cordova)
Hoodlum Saint, The (Norman Taurog)
Inside Job (Jean Yarbrough)
Joe Palooka, The Champ (Reginald Le Borg)
Killers, The (Robert Siodmak)
Last Crooked Mile, The (Philip Ford)
Mr. Ace (Edward L. Marin)
Nobody Lives Forever (Jean Negulesco)
Somewhere in the Night (Joseph L. Mankiewicz)
Strange Journey (James Tonling)

1947

Big Fix, The (James Flood)
Big Town After Dark (William C. Thomas)
Body and Soul (Robert Rossen)
Dead Reckoning (John Cromwell)
Desert Fury (Lewis Allen)
Desperate (Anthony Mann)
Devil Ship (Lew Landers)
Devil Thumbs a Ride, The (Felix E. Feist)
Gangster, The (Gordon Wiles)
Hard Boiled Mahoney (William Beaudine)
High Tide (John Reinhardt)
Intrigue (Edward L. Marin)
Joe Palooka in the Knockout (Reginald le Borg)
Johnny O'Clock (Robert Rossen)
Killer Dill (Lewis D. Collins)
Kiss of Death (Henry Hathaway)
Man I Love, The (Raoul Walsh)
Newshounds (William Beaudine)
Out of the Past (Jacques Tourneur)

Railroaded (Anthony Mann)
Ride the Pink Horse (Robert Montgomery)
Road to the Big House (Walter Colmes)
Shoot to Kill (William A. Berke)
Slippy McGee (Albert H. Kelley)
Too Many Winners (William Beaudine)

1948

Alias a Gentleman (Harry Beaumont)
Angels' Alley (William Beaudine)
Big Town Scandal (William C. Thomas)
Cry of the City (Robert Siodmak)
Enchanted Valley, The (Robert Emmett Tansey)
Force of Evil (Abraham Polonsky)
Hazard (George Marshall)
Hollow Triumph (a.k.a., *The Scar*) (Steve Sekely)
I Walk Alone (Byron Haskin)
Incident (William Beaudine)
Jinx Money (William Beaudine)
Key Largo (John Huston)
Parole, Inc. (Alfred Zeisler)
Race Street (Edwin L. Marin)
Raw Deal (Anthony Mann)
Song Is Born, A (Howard Hawks)
Sorry, Wrong Number (Anatole Litvak)
Stage Struck (William Nigh)
Street with No Name, The (William Keighley)

1949

Abandoned (Joseph M. Newman)
Angels in Disguise (Jean Yarbrough)
Arctic Manhunt (Ewing Scott)
Bribe, The (Robert Z. Leonard)
C-Man (Joseph Lerner)
Chicago Deadline (Lewis Allen)
Criss Cross (Robert Siodmak)
Crooked Way, The (Robert Florey)
Dangerous Profession, A (Ted Tetzlaff)
Fighting Fools (Reginald Le Borg)

Flaxy Martin (Richard L. Bare)
Gun Crazy (Joseph H. Lewis)
Hideout (Philip Ford)
Illegal Entry (Frederick De Cordova)
Incident (William Beaudine)
Joe Palooka in the Big Fight (Cy Endfield)
Johnny Allegro (Ted Tetzlaff)
Johnny Stool Pigeon (William Castle)
Manhandled (Lewis R. Foster)
Mr. Soft Touch (Gordon Douglas and Henry Levin)
Port of New York (Laszlo Benedek)
Red, Hot and Blue (John Farrow)
Scene of the Crime (Roy Rowland)
Set-Up, The (Robert Wise)
Sorrowful Jones (Sidney Lanfield)
Streets of San Francisco (George Blair)
They Live By Night (Nicholas Ray)
Thieves' Highway (Jules Dassin)
T-Men (Anthony Mann)
Too Late for Tears (Byron Haskin)
Tough Assignment (William Beaudine)
Trapped (Richard Fleischer)
Undercover Man, The (a.k.a., *Chicago Story*) (Joseph H. Lewis)
White Heat (Raoul Walsh)

1950

Armored Car Robbery (Richard Fleischer)
Asphalt Jungle, The (John Huston)
Between Midnight and Dawn (Gordon Douglas)
Black Hand, The (Richard Thorpe)
Blonde Bandit, The (Harry Keller)
Breaking Point, The (Michael Curtiz)
Customs Agent (Seymour Friedman)
Damned Don't Cry, The (Vincent Sherman)
Danger City (William Dieterle)
Deported (Robert Siodmak)
Destination Murder (Edward L. Cahn)
D.O.A. (Rudolph Mate)
Federal Agent at Large (George Blair)

Federal Man (Robert Tansey)

Guilty Bystander (Joseph Lerner)

Gun Crazy (Joseph H. Lewis)

Gunman in the Streets (a.k.a., *Time Running Out*) (Frank Tuttle)

Highway 301 (Andrew L. Stone)

Hi-Jacked (Sam Newfield)

Joe Palooka in Humphrey Takes a Chance (Jean Yarbrough)

Joe Palooka in the Squared Circle (Reginald Le Borg)

Johnny One-Eye (Robert Florey)

Kiss Tomorrow Goodbye (Gordon Douglas)

Love That Brute (Alexander Hall)

Ma and Pa Kettle Go to Town (Charles Lamont)

Motor Patrol (Sam Newfield)

Night and the City (Jules Dassin)

No Way Out (Joseph L. Mankiewicz)

Panic in the Streets (Elia Kazan)

Quicksand (Irving Pichel)

Rader Secret Service (Sam Newfield)

Red Light (Roy Del Ruth)

711 Ocean Drive (Joseph M. Newman)

Shakedown (Joseph Pevney)

Side Street (Anthony Mann)

Southside 1–1000 (Boris Inkster)

Sun Sets at Dawn, The (Paul H. Sloane)

Try and Get Me (a.k.a., *The Sound of Fury*) (Cyril [Cy] Endfield)

Under My Skin (Jean Negulesco)

Underworld Story, The (Cy Endfield)

Where the Sidewalk Ends (Otto Preminger)

1951

Appointment with Danger (Lewis Allen)

Cry Danger (Robert Parrish)

Detective Story (William Wyler)

Double Dynamite (Irving Cummings)

Enforcer, The (Bretaigne Windust and [uncredited] Raoul Walsh)

Fat Man, The (William Castle)

FBI Girl (William Berke)

He Ran All the Way (John Berry)

His Kind of Woman (John Farrow)

Hoodlum, The (Max Nosseck)
Lemon Drop Kid, The (Sidney Lanfield and Frank Tashlin)
M (Joseph Losey)
Mob, The (Robert Parrish)
People Against O'Hara, The (John Sturges)
Racket, The (John Cromwell)
Racket Girls (Robert C. Dertano)
St. Benny the Dip (Edgar Ulmer)
Strip, The (Leslie Kardos)
Unknown Man, The (Richard Thorpe)

1952

Because of You (Joseph Pevney)
Bloodhounds of Broadway (Harmon Jones)
Captive City, The (Robert Wise)
Deadline—U.S.A. (Richard Brooks)
Hoodlum Empire (Joseph Kane)
Kansas City Confidential (Phil Karlson)
Loan Shark (Seymour Friedman)
Macao (Josef von Sternberg and [uncredited] Nicholas Ray)
Meet Danny Wilson (Joseph Pevney)
Models, Inc. (Reginald Le Borg)
Narrow Margin, The (Richard Fleischer)
Stop, You're Killing Me (Roy Del Ruth)
This Woman Is Dangerous (Felix E. Feist)
Turning Point, The (William Dieterle)

1953

Big Heat, The (Fritz Lang)
Crime Wave (Andre de Toth)
Dance Hall Racket (Phil Tucker)
Forbidden (Rudolph Mate)
I, the Jury (Harry Essex)
99 River Street (Phil Karlson)
Pickup on South Street (Samuel Fuller)
Second Chance (Rudolph Mate)
Vice Squad (Arnold Laven)

1954

Big Chase, The (Arthur Hilton)
Black Tuesday (Hugo Fregonese)
Dangerous Mission (Louis King)
Down Three Dark Streets (Arnold Laven)
Dragnet (Jack Webb)
Drive a Crooked Road (Richard Quine)
Long Wait, The (Victor Saville)
Miami Story, The (Fred F. Sears)
On the Waterfront (Elia Kazan)
Private Hell 36 (Don Siegel)
Rogue Cop (Roy Rowland)
Shield for Murder (Edmond O'Brien and Howard W. Koch)

1955

Big Combo, The (Joseph H. Lewis)
Bullet for Joey, A (Lewis Allen)
Chicago Syndicate (Fred F. Sears)
City of Shadows (William Witney)
Crashout (Lewis E. Foster)
Desperate Hours, The (William Wyler)
Finger Man (Harold D. Schuster)
Gangbusters (Bill Karn)
Guys and Dolls (Joseph L. Mankiewicz)
Headline Hunters (William Witney)
Hell on Frisco Bay (Frank Tuttle)
Hell's Island (Phil Karlson)
House of Bamboo (Samuel Fuller)
I Cover the Underworld (R. G. Springsteen)
I Died a Thousand Times (Stuart Heisler)
Illegal (Lewis Allen)
Inside Detroit (Fred F. Sears)
It's Always Fair Weather (Gene Kelly and Stanley Donen)
Killer's Kiss (Stanley Kubrick)
Kiss Me Deadly (Robert Aldrich)
Las Vegas Shakedown (Sidney Salkow)
Love Me or Leave Me (Charles Vidor)
Naked Street, The (Maxwell Shane)
New Orleans Uncensored (William Castle)

New York Confidential (Russell Rouse)
Pete Kelly's Blues (Jack Webb)
Phenix City Story, The (Phil Karlson)
Six Bridges to Cross (Joseph Pevney)
Tight Spot (Phil Karlson)
Violent Saturday (Richard Fleischer)

1956

Accused of Murder (Joseph Kane)
Behind the High Wall (Abner Biberman)
Blonde Bait (Herbert Glazer and Elmo Williams)
Fighting Trouble (George Blair)
Girl Can't Help It, The (Frank Tashlin)
Harder They Fall, The (Mark Robson)
He Laughed Last (Blake Edwards)
Houston Story, The (William Castle)
Killing, The (Stanley Kubrick)
Man in the Vault (Andrew V. McLaglen)
Miami Expose (Fred F. Sears)
Outside the Law (Jack Arnold)
Price of Fear, The (Abner Biberman)
Slightly Scarlet (Allan Dwan)
Steel Jungle, The (Walter Doniger)
Storm Fear (Cornel Wilde)
When Gangland Strikes (R. G. Springsteen)

1957

Baby Face Nelson (Don Siegel)
Big Boodle, The (Richard Wilson)
Brothers Rico, The (Phil Karlson)
Burglar, The (Paul Wendkos)
Chicago Confidential (Sidney Salkow)
Designing Woman (Vincente Minnelli)
Escape from San Quentin (Fred F. Sears)
Garment Jungle, The (Vincent Sherman and
    [uncredited] Robert Aldrich)
Guns Don't Argue (Richard C. Kahn and Bill Karn)
Helen Morgan Story, The (Michael Curtiz)
Hell Bound (William J. Hole Jr.)

Joker Is Wild, The (Charles Vidor)
Nightfall (Jacques Tourneur)
Plunder Road (Hubert Cornfield)
Short Cut to Hell (James Cagney)
Slaughter on Tenth Avenue (Arnold Laven)

1958

Bonnie Parker Story, The (William Witney)
Damn Citizen (Robert Gordon)
Gang War (Gene Fowler Jr.)
I, Mobster (Roger Corman)
I Want to Live (Robert Wise)
Johnny Rocco (Paul Landres)
King Creole (Michael Curtiz)
Lineup, The (Don Siegel)
Machine Gun Kelly (Roger Corman)
Man Who Died Twice, The (Joseph Kane)
Murder by Contract (Irving Lerner)
Never Steal Anything Small (Charles Lederer)
Party Girl (Nicholas Ray)
Stakeout on Dope Street (Irvin Kershner)
Thunder Road (Arthur Ripley)
Touch of Evil (Orson Welles)

1959

Al Capone (Richard Wilson)
Arson for Hire (Thor Brooks)
Big Operator, The (Charles Haas)
Cry Tough (Paul Stanley)
FBI Story, The (Mervyn LeRoy)
Guns, Girls, and Gangsters
  (Edward L. Cahn)
Inside the Mafia (Edward L. Cahn)
New Orleans After Dark (John Sledge)
Odds Against Tomorrow (Robert Wise)
Scarface Mob, The (Phil Karlson)
Some Like It Hot (Billy Wilder)
Trap, The (Norman Panama)

1960

Gangster Story (Walter Matthau)
Ma Barker's Killer Brood (Bill Karn)
Murder Inc. (Burt Balaban and Stuart Rosenberg)
Music Box Kid, The (Edward L. Cahn)
Pay or Die (Richard Wilson)
Pretty Boy Floyd (Herbert J. Leder)
Purple Gang, The (Frank McDonald)
Rise and Fall of Legs Diamond, The (Budd Boetticher)
Squad Car (Ed Leftwich)
Walking Target, The (Edward L. Cahn)

1961

Blast of Silence (Allen Baron)
George Raft Story, The (Joseph M. Newman)
King of the Roaring Twenties, The
    (Joseph M. Newman)
Mad Dog Coll (Burt Balaban)
Most Dangerous Man Alive, The (Allan Dwan)
Pocketful of Miracles (Frank Capra)
Portrait of a Mobster (Joseph Pevney)
Run Across the River (Everett Chambers)
Secret of Deep Harbor (Edward L. Cahn)
20,000 Eyes (Jack Leewood)
Underworld U.S.A. (Samuel Fuller)
You Have to Run Fast (Edward L. Cahn)

1962

Fallguy (Donn Harling)
Kid Galahad (Phil Karlson)
Scarface Mob, The (Phil Karlson)

1963

Johnny Cool (William Asher)
Lonnie (William Hale)
Man from the Diner's Club, The (Frank Tashlin)
Right Hand of the Devil, The (Aram Katcher)

1964

Killers, The (Don Siegel)
Moonshine Mountain (Herschell Gordon Lewis)
Robin and the 7 Hoods (Gordon Douglas)

1965

Mickey One (Arthur Penn)
One Way Wahini (William O. Brown)
Young Dillinger (Terry O. Morse)

1966

Harper (Jack Smight)
Money Trap, The (Burt Kennedy)

1967

Big Mouth, The (Jerry Lewis)
Bonnie and Clyde (Arthur Penn)
Busy Body, The (William Castle)
Gunn (Blake Edwards)
Happening, The (Elliot Silverstein)
Point Blank (John Boorman)
St. Valentine's Day Massacre, The (Roger Corman)
Thoroughly Modern Millie (George Roy Hill)
Tony Rome (Gordon Douglas)
Warning Shot (Buzz Kulik)

1968

Brotherhood, The (Martin Ritt)
Bullitt (Peter Yates)
Coogan's Bluff (Don Siegel)
Fireball Jungle (Joseph G. Prieto)
Lady in Cement (Gordon Douglas)
Madigan (Don Siegel)
Never a Dull Moment (Jerry Paris)
Pick-Up, The (Lee Frost)
Skidoo (Otto Preminger)
Sol Madrid (Brian G. Hutton)
Split, The (Gordon Flemyng)

They Ran for Their Lives (John Payne and Oliver Drake)
Wild 90 (Norman Mailer)

1969

Fabulous Bastard from Chicago, The (Greg Corarito)
Girl Who Knew Too Much, The (Francis D. Lyon)
Mafia Girls (Ed Ross)
Marlowe (Paul Bogart)
Stiletto (Bernard L. Kowalski)

1970

Bloody Mama (Roger Corman)
Bullet for Pretty Boy, A (Larry Buchanan)
Cotton Comes to Harlem (Ossie Davis)
Moonshine War, The (Richard Quine)

1971

Chandler (Paul Magwood)
French Connection, The (William Friedkin)
Gang That Couldn't Shoot Straight, The (James Goldstone)
Grissom Gang, The (Robert Aldrich)
Shaft (Gordon Parks)

1972

Across 110th Street (Barry Shear)
Black Gunn (Robert Hartford-Davis)
Come Back Charleston Blue (Mark Warren)
Cool Breeze (Barry Pollack)
French Connection II (John Frankenheimer)
Getaway, The (Sam Peckinpah)
Godfather, The (Francis Ford Coppola)
Hammer (Bruce Clark)
Hickey & Boggs (Robert Culp)
Hit Man (George Armitage)
Little Cigars (Chris Christenberry)
Mechanic, The (Michael Winner)
Prime Cut (Michael Ritchie)
Slaughter (Jack Starrett)

Superfly (Gordon Parks Jr.)

Sweet Jesus, Preacher Man (Henning Schellerup)

Valachi Papers, The (Terence Young)

1973

Badge 373 (Howard W. Koch)

Black Caesar (Larry Cohen)

Charley Varrick (Don Siegel)

Coffy (Jack Hill)

Cops and Robbers (Aram Avakian)

Crazy Joe (Carlo Lizzano)

Dillinger (John Milius)

Don Is Dead, The (Richard Fleischer)

Friends of Eddie Coyle, The (Peter Yates)

Hell up in Harlem (Larry Cohen)

Hit! (Sidney J. Furie)

Long Goodbye, The (Robert Altman)

Mean Streets (Martin Scorsese)

Slaughter's Big Rip-Off (Gordon Douglas)

Sting, The (George Roy Hill)

Stone Killer, The (Michael Winner)

Superfly T.N.T. (Ron O'Neal)

That Man Bolt (Henry Levin and David Lowell Rich)

Walking Tall (Phil Karlson)

White Lightning (Joseph Sargent)

1974

Big Bad Mama (Steve Carver)

Black Belt Jones (Robert Clouse)

Black Godfather (John Evans)

Black Lolita (Stephen Gibson)

Bootleggers (Charles B. Pierce)

Family, The (Sergio Sollima)

Foxy Brown (Jack Hill)

Godfather Part II, The (Francis Ford Coppola)

McQ (John Sturges)

Mr. Majestyk (Richard Fleischer)

Murder on the Orient Express (Sidney Lumet)

Newman's Law (Richard Heffron)

Nickel Ride, The (Robert Mulligan)
99 and 44/100 Percent Dead (John Frankenheimer)
Outfit, The (John Flynn)
Thieves Like Us (Robert Altman)
Truck Turner (Jonathan Kaplan)

1975

Black Bird, The (David Giler)
Brannigan (Douglas Hickox)
Bucktown (Arthur Marks)
Capone (Steve Carver)
Crazy Mama (Jonathan Demme)
Farewell, My Lovely (Dick Richards)
Funny Lady (Herbert Ross)
Hustle, The (Robert Aldrich)
Lepke (Menachem Golan)
Man Who Would Not Die, The
   (Richard Arkless)
Report to the Commissioner (Milton Katselas)
Sheba Baby (William Girdler)
Walking Tall: Part II (Earl Bellamy)
White Line Fever (Jonathan Kaplan)
Yakuza, The (Sydney Pollack)

1976

Bugsy Malone (Alan Parker)
J. D.'s Revenge (Arthur Marks)
Killing of a Chinese Bookie, The (John Cassavetes)
Meet Johnny Barrows (Fred Williamson)
Scorchy (Hikmet Avdedis)
St. Ives (J. Lee Thompson)

1977

Final Chapter: Walking Tall (Jack Starrett)
Portrait of a Hitman (Allan A. Buckhantz)
Speedtrap (Earl Bellamy)

1978

Big Sleep, The (Michael Winner)

Brink's Job, The (William Friedkin)
Driver, The (Walter Hill)
Fingers (James Toback)

1979

Cuba (Richard Lester)
Hot Stuff (Dom DeLuise)
Love and Bullets (Stuart Rosenberg)
Saint Jack (Peter Bogdanovich)

1980

Gloria (John Cassavetes)
Little Miss Marker (Walter Bernstein)
Man with Bogart's Face, The (Andrew J. Fenaday)

1981

Absence of Malice (Sydney Pollack)
Atlantic City (Louis Malle)
Body and Soul (George Bowers)
Eye for an Eye, An (Steve Carver)
Sharkey's Machine (Burt Reynolds)
Thief (Michael Mann)

1982

I, the Jury (Richard T. Heffron)
One Down, Two to Go (Fred Williamson)
Sting II, The (Jeremy Paul Kagan)
Vigilante (William Lustig)

1983

Big Score, The (Fred Williamson)
City Heat (Richard Benjamin)
Detroit 9000 (Arthur Marks)
Hammett (Wim Wenders)
Scarface (Brian De Palma)

1984

Against All Odds (Taylor Hackford)
Beverly Hills Cop (Martin Brest)

Code of Silence (Andrew Davis)
Cotton Club, The (Francis Ford Coppola)
Evil That Men Do, The (J. Lee Thompson)
Johnny Dangerously (Amy Heckerling)
Once Upon a Time in America (Sergio Leone)
Perfect Strangers (Larry Cohen)

1985

Prizzi's Honor (John Huston)
Stick (Burt Reynolds)
To Live and Die in L.A. (William Friedkin)
Year of the Dragon (Michael Cimino)

1986

52 Pick Up (John Frankenheimer)
F/X (Robert Mandel)
Wise Guys (Brian De Palma)

1987

House of Games (David Mamet)
Positive I.D. (Andy Anderson)
Sicilian, The (Michael Cimino)
Tough Guys Don't Dance (Norman Mailer)
Untouchables, The (Brian De Palma)

1988

Keaton's Cop (Robert Burge)
Married to the Mob (Jonathan Demme)
Tequila Sunrise (Robert Towne)
Things Change (David Mamet)
Verne Miller (Rod Hewitt)

1989

Backtrack (Dennis Hopper as Alan Smithee)
Beverly Hills Bodysnatchers (Jonathan Mostow)
Big Bad Mama II (Jim Wynorski)
Bloodhounds of Broadway (Howard Brookner)
Disorganized Crime (Jim Kouf)
Family Business (Sidney Lumet)

Harlem Nights (Eddie Murphy)
Hit List (William Lustig)
Johnny Handsome (Walter Hill)
Mob War (J. Christian Ingvordsen)
Road House (Rowdy Herrington)

1990

Another 48 Hours (Walter Hill)
Chicago Joe and the Showgirl (Bernard Rose)
Dick Tracy (Warren Beatty)
Freshman, The (Andrew Bergman)
Godfather Part III, The (Francis Ford Coppola)
GoodFellas (Martin Scorsese)
Grifters, The (Stephen Frears)
Havana (Sydney Pollack)
Hot Spot, The (Dennis Hopper)
King of New York, The (Abel Ferrara)
Miami Blues (George Armitage)
Miller's Crossing (Joel Coen)
Mob Boss (Fred Olen Ray)
My Blue Heaven (Herbert Ross)
Narrow Margin (Peter Hyams)
Return of Superfly, The (Sig Shore)
Revenge (Tony Scott)
State of Grace (Phil Joanou)
Two Jakes, The (Jack Nicholson)

1991

Billy Bathgate (Robert Benton)
Bugsy (Barry Levinson)
F/X2 (Richard Franklin)
Hitman, The (Aaron Norris)
Marrying Man, The (Jerry Rees)
Mobsters (Michael Karbelnikoff)
New Jack City (Mario van Peebles)
One False Move (Carl Franklin)
Oscar (John Landis)
Point Break (Kathryn Bigelow)

Rage in Harlem, A (Bill Duke)
Thick as Thieves (Steve DiMarco)

1992

American Me (Edward James Olmos)
Amongst Friends (Rob Weiss)
Deep Cover (Bill Duke)
Diary of a Hitman (Roy London)
Diggstown (Michael Ritchie)
Equinox (Alan Rudolph)
Guncrazy (Tamra Davis)
Hoffa (Danny DeVito)
Leather Jackets (Lee Drysdale)
Mad Dog Coll (a.k.a., *Killer Instinct*) (Greydon Clark and Ken Stein)
Night and the City (Irwin Winkler)
Public Eye, The (Howard Franklin)
Reservoir Dogs (Quentin Tarantino)
Ruby (John Mackenzie)

1993

Amongst Friends (Rob Weiss)
Bronx Tale, A (Robert De Niro)
Carlito's Way (Brian De Palma)
Deadfall (Christopher Coppola)
Firm, The (Sydney Pollack)
Mad Dog and Glory (John McNaughton)
Menace II Society (Albert and Allen Hughes)
Outfit, The (T. Christian Ingvordsen)
True Romance (Tony Scott)

1994

Bullets Over Broadway (Woody Allen)
Client, The (Joel Schumacher)
Confessions of a Hitman (James Foley)
Federal Hill (Michael Corrente)
Getaway, The (Roger Donaldson)
Hits! (William R. Greenblatt)
Last Seduction, The (John Dahl)
Professional, The (a.k.a., *Leon: The Professional*) (Luc Besson)

Pulp Fiction (Quentin Tarantino)
Sugar Hill (Leon Ichaso)
Trial by Jury (Heywood Gould)

1995

Assassins (Richard Donner)
Bulletproof Heart (Mark Malone)
Casino (Martin Scorsese)
Coldblooded (Wallace Wolodarsky)
Dillinger and Capone (Jon Purdy)
Get Shorty (Barry Sonnenfeld)
Heat (Michael Mann)
Last Word, The (Tony Spiradakis)
Underneath, The (Steven Soderbergh)
Usual Suspects, The (Brian Singer)

1996

Albino Alligator (Kevin Spacey)
Bound (Andy and Larry Wachowski)
For a Few Lousy Dollars (Michael Bafaro)
Funeral, The (Abel Ferrara)
Kansas City (Robert Altman)
Last Days of Frankie the Fly, The (Peter Markle)
Last Man Standing (Walter Hill)
Mad Dog Time (Larry Bishop)
Mulholland Falls (Lee Tamahori)
Public Enemies (Mark L. Lester)
Pure Danger (C. Thomas Howell)
Red Line (John Sjogren)
Things to Do in Denver When You're Dead (Gary Fleder)

1997

Acts of Betrayal (Jack Ersgard)
Blood and Wine (Bob Rafelson)
City of Industry (John Irvin)
Cop Land (James Mangold)
Donnie Brasco (Mike Newell)
8 Heads in a Duffel Bag (Tom Schulman)
Hoodlum (Bill Duke)

Jackie Brown (Quentin Tarantino)
L.A. Confidential (Curtis Hanson)
Lost Highway (David Lynch)
Mean Guns (Albert Pyun)
Truth or Consequences N.M. (Kiefer Sutherland)

1998

Another Day in Paradise (Larry Clark)
Big Hit, The (Kirk Wong)
Black (Hector Barca)
Body Count (Robert Patton-Spruill)
Crazy Six (Albert Pyun)
Hoods (Mark Malone)
Mafia! (Jim Abrahams)
Montana (Jennifer Leitzes)
Newton Boys, The (Richard Linklater)
One Deadly Road (Frank Adonis)
Out of Sight (Steven Soderbergh)
Perpetrators of a Crime (John Hamilton)
Simple Plan, A (Sam Raimi)
Small Time (Jeffrey Reiner)
Suicide Kings, The (Peter O'Fallon)
When It's Over (Richard Mancuso)

1999

Analyze This (Harold Ramis)
Blood, Guts, Bullets and Octane (Joe Carnahan)
Gloria (Sidney Lumet)
Gunshy (Jeff Celentano)
Hitman's Run (Mark L. Lester)
In Too Deep (Michael Rymer)
Limey, The (Steven Soderbergh)
Mickey Blue Eyes (Kelly Makin)
Mob Queen (Jon Carnoy)
Ordinary Decent Criminal (Thaddeus O'Sullivan)
Payback (Brian Helgeland)
Runner, The (Ron Moler)
Thick as Thieves (Scott Sanders)

2000

Brother (Takeshi Kitano)
Crew, The (Michael Dinner)
Get Carter (Stephen T. Kay)
Traffic (Steven Soderbergh)
Very Mean Men (Tony Vitale)
Wannabes (Charles A. Addessi and William DeMeo)
Way of the Gun, The (Christopher McQuarrie)
Whole Nine Yards, The (Jonathan Lynn)

2001

Corky Romano (Rob Pitts)
Heist (David Mamet)
Knockaround Guys (Brian Koppelman and David Levien)
Lethal Force (Alvin Ecarma)
Made (Jon Favreau)
Mulholland Dr. (David Lynch)
Score, The (Frank Oz)
3,000 Miles to Graceland (Demien Lichtenstein)
Training Day (Antoine Fuqua)

2002

Analyze That (Harold Ramis)
Big Trouble (Barry Sonnenfeld)
Chicago (Rob Marshall)
Empire (Franc Reyes)
Gangs of New York (Martin Scorsese)
Good Thief, The (Neil Jordan)
Narc (Joe Carnahan)
One Eyed King (Robert Moresco)
Road to Perdition (Sam Mendes)

2003

Bad Boys II (Michael Bay)
Confidence (James Foley)
Cooler, The (Wayne Kramer)
Duplex (Danny DeVito)
El Padrino (Damian Chapa)
Hollywood Homicide (Ron Shelton)

Gigli (Martin Brest)
Italian Job, The (F. Gary Gray)
Kill Bill Vol. 1 (Quentin Tarantino)
Man Apart, A (F. Gary Gray)
Matchstick Men (Ridley Scott)
Medallion, The (Cordon Chan)
Mystic River (Clint Eastwood)
Once Upon a Time in Mexico (Robert Rodriguez)
Shade (Damian Nieman)
S.W.A.T. (Clark Johnson)
2 Fast 2 Furious (John Singleton)

2004

After the Sunset (Brett Ratner)
Catch That Kid (Bart Freundlich)
Cellular (David R. Ellis)
Criminal (Gregory Jacobs)
Kill Bill Vol. 2 (Quentin Tarantino)
Ladykillers, The (Joel Coen)
Last Shot, The (Jeff Nathanson)
Maria Full of Grace (Joshua Marston)
Never Die Alone (Errnest R. Dickerson)
Perfect Score, The (Brian Robbins)
Punisher, The (Jonathan Hensleigh)
Starsky and Hutch (Todd Phillips)
Torque (Joseph Kahn)
Walking Tall (Kevin Bray)
Whole Ten Yards, The (Howard Deutch)

Notes

PROLOGUE

1. Fittingly, the other two, *Rooster Cogburn* (1975) and *The Shootist* (1976), which marked Wayne's last screen appearance, were Westerns.

2. Herbert Asbury, *The Great Illusion: An Informal History of Prohibition* (New York: Doubleday, 1950), 136.

3. David Chase, "Made Man" (interview), in *Fade In* 6:3:40.

CHAPTER 1

1. In 1999, as the result of pressure from the NAACP, the Directors Guild of America dropped Griffith's name from its coveted D. W. Griffith Award for Lifetime Achievement, which had been in place since 1958 when the DGA inaugurated the award, and renamed it the DGA Award for Lifetime Achievement. "It was the right thing to do," NAACP President Kweisi Mfume told the Associated Press. "This award should have never been given under the name of D. W. Griffith. It was the NAACP that first protested in 1915 against *The Birth of a Nation*. We've lived with the horrors that took place." Many noted film critics, film historians, filmmakers, and film buffs countered that this decision, which was made without a DGA membership vote, was "political correctness" run amuck. Eulogized Pulitzer prize–winning novelist, film critic, and Oscar-nominated screenwriter James Agee upon Griffith's death in 1948: "There is not a man working in movies, or a man who cares for them, who does not owe Griffith more than he owes anybody else" (*The Nation*, September 4, 1948).

2. By some estimates, as many as half of the motion pictures made in this country before 1950, and as much as 80 percent of all silent era films, have been lost to us forever as the result of chemical decomposition, neglect, and wanton destruction over the years. Many studios regularly destroyed scores of their silent films because, in the studio's eyes, the advent of the talkies rendered these films commercially worthless, and they were just taking up storage space. Also, as the nitrate stock these films were printed on contained silver compound, the studios found they could profitably extract this valuable silver by setting the negatives a-boil.

3. Defined early on by the motion picture industry as a film lasting five reels (approximately one hour) or longer.

4. Charles Dickens, *American Notes*, 102.

5. D. W. Griffith supervised the making of a four-reeler titled *The Gangsters* (a.k.a., *The Gangsters of New York*), directed by James Kirkwood for the Reliance Film Company a year earlier than the film based on Kildare's memoir appeared. Likewise, a two-reeler titled *The Gangsters and the Girl*, a West Coast variation on Griffith's *The Musketeers of Pig Alley,* saw release in 1914 as well. Their less than 50-minute running times restrict them from being considered *feature length*, however.

6. Raoul Walsh, *Each Man in His Time* (New York: Farrar, Strauss and Giroux, 1974), 115.

7. Ibid., 119.

8. Ibid., 17.

9. Although he never became a star, Fellowes had a prolific career in silent-era films playing mostly bad-guy roles. His career seems to have hit a snag when the talkies arrived, however, and he was reduced to taking bit parts in major studio movies, such as Warner Brothers' quasi-gangster film *Lawyer Man* (1932), and playing conventional heavies in such B Westerns as *Rusty Rides Alone* (1933). He apparently retired from the screen by the mid-1930s as there are no screen credits listed for him after that, and he died in Los Angeles in 1950 at age 67.

10. A Swedish import and major star of silent era films in America whose career waned with the arrival of the talkies due to her heavy accent and health problems, Anna Q. Nilsson made one of her last screen appearances in a cameo role with fellow silent screen legends Buster Keaton and H. B. Warner as one of the "waxworks" in Billy Wilder's acerbic tale of the collision of old and new Hollywood, *Sunset Boulevard* (1950).

CHAPTER 2

1. From the collection *Big Brother and Other Stories* by Rex Beach (New York: Harper and Brothers, 1923).

2. *Big Brother* was remade by RKO as a talkie in 1931, directed by Fred Niblo. The title changed to *Young Donovan's Kid*, the remake starred Richard Dix as the gangster and Jackie Cooper as the boy and featured Boris Karloff, who was about to achieve screen immortality in *Frankenstein* that same year, in a supporting role as a lowlife "cokehead."

3. Peter Bogdanovich, *Allan Dwan: The Last Pioneer* (New York: Praeger Publishers, 1971), 67–68.

4. The father of Oscar-winning screenwriter Budd Schulberg, who would pen two of the most notable gangster films of the 1950s, *On the Waterfront* (1954) and gangster movie icon Humphrey Bogart's last picture, *The Harder They Fall* (1956).

5. In the real-life case, several killers assigned to carry out the hit did in fact disguise themselves as priests to track Lingle's movements unnoticed.

6. Phone conversation with the author, January 1996.

7. William "Stage" Boyd used the stage name "Stage" to differentiate himself from movie actor William Boyd, another Paramount contract player who later became a star of B Westerns playing the legendary screen cowboy Hopalong Cassidy.

8. William's character was based on an actual New York City attorney, William J. Fallon Jr., who allegedly resorted to any tactic, no matter how outrageous, to get his underworld clients off. The subject of a 1931 biography, *The Great Mouthpiece*, written by crime reporter Gene Fowler and published by Grosset & Dunlap, Fallon's batting average was without peer. He defended mob clients in more than one hundred homicide cases alone, and he never lost any. His legendary clients included, among many notable gangsters of the age, Nicky Arnstein, the racketeer husband of Ziegfeld Follies comedienne Fannie Brice, whose stormy romance was the subject of the 1975 musical *Funny Lady*, starring Barbra Streisand as Brice and Omar Sharif as Arnstein.

CHAPTER 3

1. Ironically, James Cagney would give an excellent performance as the real-life Lon Chaney in Universal's powerful and affecting biography of the silent star, 1957's *The Man of a Thousand Faces*.

2. Josef von Sternberg, *Fun in a Chinese Laundry* (New York: Macmillan, 1965), 40.

3. The scheme involves rousing thousands of the city's disgruntled foreign laborers ("Reds") to armed insurrection so that the police and the army must combine forces to stop them—during which Chaney and his men will move in and loot the city's treasury.

4. *Outside the Law* not only reunited Chaney with Browning but also with Priscilla Dean. She was fast becoming a popular fixture in Universal gangster films, having starred in two other underworld dramas for the studio, *The Wild Cat of Paris* (1918) and *Pretty Smooth* (1919), during the same period.

5. At one point, Black Mike even snarls the phrase "You dirty rat" via an inter-title. This phrase, of course, would later become most associated with Cagney.

6. The casting of Nolan was interesting, as the actress, much like her character, had escaped a scandalous past to seek a new life, although for very different reasons. As a rising star of the Ziegfield Follies in the mid–1920s named Imogen Wilson ("the most dazzling flower in the Ziegfeld hot-house," according to the press), the attractive blonde had become involved in a love affair with the Follies's top funnyman, the married Frank Tinney, who apparently had a fondness for beating the young woman up during their frequent liaisons. Following a particularly brutal slugfest, Wilson finally decided she'd had enough and called the police. News of the scandalous affair filled the headlines. Tinney's career was destroyed; Wilson was fired from the Follies, and she made her way to Hollywood to pick up her life, acting in the movies—under the pseudonym Mary Nolan.

7. A now-forgotten opera singer of the Roaring Twenties who had formed her own movie company to produce pictures as vehicles for herself. Her moderately successful career as a silent-era film star didn't extend into the talkie era, however. She retired from the movies in the late 1930s and made only one screen appearance after that, a cameo in the 1961 rocker *Hey, Let's Twist*. She died in 1982.

CHAPTER 4

1. *Underworld* was prepared by another director, Arthur Rosson, who was fired by the studio after the first day of shooting, and replaced by Sternberg. The cause of Rosson's

dismissal is unclear. Allegedly, it was because of excessive drinking, but this is unsubstantiated.

2. Josef von Sternberg, *Fun in a Chinese Laundry* (New York: Macmillan, 1965), 215.

3. Ibid., 216.

4. Three more would follow: *His Girl Friday* (1940), *The Front Page* (1974), and *Switching Channels* (1988).

5. Osgood Perkins, the father of *Psycho* star Anthony Perkins, played Burns, and Lee Tracy, who would go on to play a number of insolent, motor-mouthed reporters in sound films, played Johnson in the original Broadway production. The elder Perkins would also play a significant role in the film of Hecht's script *Scarface*.

6. Ironically, Hecht's last film, the 1964 James Bond spoof *Casino Royale*, would, like his first, not bear his name in the credits, either, as he died before completing the script.

7. The gangland territories run by the Italian and Irish mobs, respectively, in Chicago of the Roaring Twenties.

8. An arcane term derived from a nineteenth-century lower-class British colloquialism that today means "mugging" someone for their money and valuables.

9. This burst of America-first pride was a response to the widely held view at the time, even in America, that European films, especially those made by the innovative German directors F. W. Murnau, Ernst Lubitsch, Fritz Lang, and E. A. Dupont, outshined those of their American colleagues in technical virtuosity and artistic merit. Believing America's dominance of the young medium to be slipping, the heads of the major studios launched their own form of Lend Lease in reverse, luring these foreign talents to Hollywood, just as the conditions in Europe that would lead to World War II began stirring these artists to seek greener pastures. With his Germanic name, especially the "von," Sternberg was able to capitalize on this prevailing attitude in Hollywood toward European filmmakers and to use it to his advantage.

10. Herman G. Weinberg, *Josef von Sternberg: A Critical Study of the Great Director* (New York: E. P. Dutton, 1967), 39.

11. Ibid., 48.

Chapter 5

1. Previously filmed in 1918 under the same title, directed by James Kirkwood and starring Catherine Calvert, the wife of playwright Paul Armstrong, in the role played by Mary Astor in the 1928 version. This earlier film adaptation is presumed lost.

2. Lang's film was quite effectively remade in 1951 by director Joseph Losey and producer Seymour Nebenzal (an expatriate like Lang who, in fact, had produced the Lang original). The same title was used, but the locale was shifted to Los Angeles. David Wayne plays the serial killer hunted by the cops and the underworld.

3. The other entries in the series were *Undercover Doctor* (1939), also directed by Louis King and featuring J. Carrol Naish; *Parole Fixer* (1940), directed by Robert Florey; and *Queen of the Mob* (1940), directed by James P. Hogan and featuring Naish as well as James Cagney's sister, Jeanne.

4. Patrick McGilligan, *Robert Altman: Jumping Off a Cliff* (New York: St. Martin's Press, 1989), 369–370.

5. Loosely remade and updated by Tamra Davis as *Guncrazy* (1992), starring Drew Barrymore in the Cummins role and James LeGros in the part played by John Dall.

6. In 1960, producer William Faris also cranked out another low-budget gangster movie about the murderous matriarch called *Ma Barker's Killer Brood*, which appears as if it might have been culled from the Ma Barker episode of the TV series, but this doesn't seem to be the case. The series episode dealing with Ma Barker had already been cut into *Guns Don't* Argue and featured a wholly different cast from that appearing in *Ma Barker's Killer Brood*.

7. The technique of incorporating slow motion in scenes of violence was by no means an innovation of *Bonnie and Clyde*. John Ford had employed it briefly for an action scene in his 1948 western *Fort Apache*, and Akira Kurosawa had used it several times in his masterpiece *Seven Samurai* (1954). After *Bonnie and Clyde*, however, the technique became an action movie staple.

8. Newman and Benton's script, which the film adheres to quite closely for the most part, ends much less explicitly. The writers' intention was to show Bonnie and Clyde frozen in time via snapshots of them taken seconds before their death as gunfire fills the soundtrack. This freeze-frame technique was very much in the style of the French New Wave.

9. Phone conversation with the author.

10. Writer-director Quentin Tarantino snatched and used this same "what's in it that everyone wants so badly" device, changing it to a glowing suitcase for his ode to *Kiss Me Deadly* and movie pulp fiction in general titled, appropriately enough, *Pulp Fiction* (1994). The movie-savvy Tarantino also borrowed from Stanley Kubrick's *The Killing*, Phil Karlson's *Kansas City Confidential* (1952), and from *White Heat* (1949) for his first film, the gangster/heist movie *Reservoir Dogs* (1992), where Michael Madsen's droopy-eyed psychopath is a virtual clone of the sniper played by Timothy Carey in the Kubrick film, and the time-shifting structure of the picture is borrowed from the Kubrick film as well. The colorful fake names the crooks give each other to conceal their identities from one another mimics the masks the mastermind (Preston Foster) of the heist makes himself and his confederates wear to keep each other from knowing who they are in *Kansas City Confidential*. And crook Harvey Keitel's anguished response of a wounded animal upon discovering that a member of the gang he has trusted implicitly is an undercover cop inescapably calls to mind James Cagney's similar breakdown as Cody Jarrett in *White Heat*.

11. Stuart Byron, "Robert Aldrich Interviewed," *Film Comment* 13 (March– April 1977):52.

CHAPTER 6

1. Although the burly Bancroft's boss of bosses in Sternberg's *Thunderbolt* is not suggestive of Capone either, except in the broadest sense, there is an amusing reference in that film to Capone's real-life failure to send "Bugs" Moran a fatal St. Valentine's Day greeting when Bancroft emphatically denies a crime he's being accused of with the quip: "I make it a point never to kill any Morans."

2. Despite his "someone you wouldn't want to meet in a dark alley" looks, Louis Wolheim was by all accounts a sweet-natured, well-educated, and erudite gentleman. A

Cornell University graduate and former teacher of mathematics before turning to acting, his most memorable screen role was that of the brutish-looking but kind-hearted and paternal Sergeant Katczinsky in director Lewis Milestone's WWI epic *All Quiet on the Western Front* (1930). His career as one of Hollywood's most in-demand character actors ended the following year, however, when he died of cancer at age fifty.

3. Kevin Brownlow, *Behind the Mask of Innocence* (New York: Alfred A. Knopf, 1990), 210.

4. Mervyn Leroy, with Dick Kleiner, *Mervyn LeRoy: Take One* (New York: Hawthorn Books, 1974).

5. Among them, the 1951 remake of *The Racket*, which Burnett adapted from Bartlett Cormack's play in collaboration with coscreenwriter William Wister Haines.

6. John Huston, *An Open Book* (New York: Alfred A. Knopf, 1980), 78.

7. Robert Stack, with Mark Evans, *Straight Shooting* (New York: Macmillan, 1980), 221–222.

8. "The Untouchables" finally reappeared as a new series in January 1993 on the independent Fox Television Network. The Jimmy Stewart–like Tom Amandes played Eliot Ness and William Forsythe played Capone. A Native American (played by Michael Horse) was added to the now multiethnic team of crime fighters as well. The hour-long series ran for two seasons, forty-two episodes, and closed up shop in May 1994.

9. Roger Corman, with Jim Jerome, *How I Made a Hundred Movies in Hollywood and Never Lost a Dime* (New York: Delta, 1990), 126.

10. Brett McCormick, "Fred Williamson: The Hammer Strikes," *Psychotronic Video* 10 (Summer 1991):25. Apparently, the Hammer must not have heard of the gangster movies with all-black casts for all-black audiences such as *Easy Street* (1930), *Underworld* (1937), *Gangsters on the Loose* (1937), and *Gang War* (1940), featuring such actors as Lorenzo Tucker, whom fans called "The Black Valentino," or Ralph Cooper ("The Bronze Bogart"), and made by such pioneer black filmmakers as Oscar Micheaux.

CHAPTER 8

1. Tully's novel was filmed in 1928 by director William A. Wellman under that title, starring Richard Arlen and Louise Brooks.

2. The grapefruit scene is based on an actual incident co-scenarist John Bright heard about as a crime reporter in Chicago involving gangster Hymie Weiss, who allegedly smacked his moll in the kisser one morning with an omelet.

3. One of his best performances in a career full of them—as well as one of his most engaging characters, here more gangster-like than gangster—Robinson's overreaching high-stakes gambler Nick, who gets taken early on by some more experienced pros, is the flip side of the character Robinson would play almost thirty-five years later in *The Cincinnati Kid* (1965), where Steve McQueen's variation on Nick gets in over his head in an all-or-nothing game of cards one-on-one with Robinson's experienced old pro.

4. Murray Schumach, *The Face on the Cutting Room Floor* (New York: William Morrow, 1964), 172.

5. Ibid., 173.

6. A well-known newspaper columnist and crime reporter of the pre–World War II years, Mark Hellinger became an associate producer at Warner Brothers in the 1940s; his credits include the trucker movie *They Drive by Night* (1940), where George Raft finally got to play the good guy who got the girl; the Edward G. Robinson gangster comedy *Brother Orchid* (1940); and Raoul Walsh's *High Sierra* (1941). In 1945, he moved over to Universal to produce *The Killers* (1946), a considerably embellished adaptation of Ernest Hemingway's terse tale of a mob hit, and two other crime films, the prison drama *Brute Force* (1947) and the police drama *The Naked City* (1948), which inspired the later TV series of the same name. His career as producer of some of the best gangster and crime films of the war years proved short-lived, however, when he died suddenly of heart failure in 1947 at age forty-four.

7. Doug Warren, with James Cagney, *Cagney* (New York: St. Martin's Press, 1983), 172.

8. For most of his administration of the FBI, J. Edgar Hoover even denied the existence of organized crime (i.e., the "Mafia"). Not until the Kennedy administration, when Robert F. Kennedy became U.S. Attorney General, was the full force of the Justice Department finally committed to waging war against the mob. And not until 1963, when Joe Valachi, a low-level hit man similar to Al Pacino's character in *Donnie Brasco,* testified before the McClellan committee about the activities of the mob (which Valachi had joined in 1929), did Hoover finally own up to the fact that—yes, Virginia—there really was such a thing as organized crime. Valachi provided Hoover a way out, though, by referring to the mob as La Cosa Nostra ("Our Thing"); Hoover allegedly responded that of course the FBI had known about *that* mob, and had been on its tail for years.

9. Remade in 1958 and again in 1995, first as a Western, *The Fiend Who Walked the West*, co-starring future Paramount studio chief and independent producer Robert Evans as the grinning psychopath of the title played by Widmark in the gangland-set original. However, unlike Widmark, whose strong debut performance in *Kiss of Death* served to launch his long and distinguished screen career, Evans's hilariously awful, it-must-be-seen-to-be-truly-believed performance was his swansong working in front of the camera. In director Barbet Schroeder's loose remake of *Kiss of Death* (1995), actor Nicolas Cage potently expresses the sadism of the Udo character (renamed Little Junior Brown), but misses exposing the joy and thrill of it exhibited by Widmark's thug, and his progenitor, the Cagney gangster.

10. First published in Great Britain in 1934 as *Murder on the Orient Express* and in America as *Murder on the Calais Coach.*

11. Stuart M. Kaminsky, *Don Siegel: Director* (New York: Curtis Books, 1973), 124.

12. Actor-turned-actor/director Clint Eastwood acknowledged Don Siegel and Sergio Leone as his film school by dedicating his Oscar-winning 1991 Western *Unforgiven* to them.

13. The studio's less violent *See How They Run*, a chase melodrama, made media history by becoming the first broadcast made-for-TV movie (NBC, October 1964). Siegel still holds second-place honors as director of the next made-for-TV movie to air on the NBC network (November 1964): *The Hanged Man*, a remake of the 1947 gangster film *Ride the Pink Horse*. Siegel's *The Killers* (1964) has since aired on television as well, but it was never broadcast on NBC or any other of the Big Three networks.

14. Not to be confused with the 1955 thriller of the same name, also produced by Universal, about a group of plane crash survivors trying to recover a stash of money from the wrecked plane.

15. The older sister of actor Marlon Brando.

16. Remade in 1999 as *Payback* starring a miscast Mel Gibson in the Lee Marvin role.

17. Pseudonym of best-selling novelist Donald E. Westlake.

18. Mike Hodges's *Get Carter,* based on the novel *Jack's Return Home* by Ted Lewis, was in fact remade twice, the first time in 1972 as part of the "blaxploitation" cycle. Titled *Hit Man*, it starred Bernie Casey in the Caine/Stallone role and Pam Grier.

CHAPTER 9

1. Clifford McCarty, *The Complete Films of Humphrey Bogart* (Secaucus, N.J.: Citadel Press, 1975), 6.

2. Remade in 1945 as *Escape in the Desert* as a B film by director Edward A. Blatt with Philip Dorn substituting for Leslie Howard, Helmut Dantine substituting for Bogart, and escaped Nazi prisoners on the run who take over a hotel in the American Southwest substituting for gangsters.

3. Raoul Walsh, *Each Man in His Time* (New York: Farrar, Straus, and Giroux, 1974), 308.

4. Hayes cowrote the screenplay for the 1990 *Desperate Hours*, an updated and very loose—and considerably inferior—remake of the 1955 film as well. It was directed by Michael Cimino and starred Mickey Rourke and Anthony Hopkins in the Bogart and March roles, respectively.

5. Jan Herman, *A Talent for Trouble* (New York: G. P. Putnam's Sons, 1995), 359.

6. Remade in 1957 as *Short Cut to Hell* with newcomer (who went nowhere) Robert Ivers in the Ladd role. The film was directed by James Cagney, his first and only turn behind the camera.

7. Michael Pye and Lynda Myles, *The Movie Brats* (New York: Holt, Rinehart and Winston, 1979), 180.

8. Ibid., 180.

9. Remade in 1994 from the same Walter Hill screenplay (revised by Amy Holden Jones) based on Thompson's novel by New Zealander Roger Donaldson, starring Alec Baldwin and Kim Basinger in the McQueen, McGraw roles.

CHAPTER 10

1. Robert Culp, "Sam Peckinpah, the Storyteller and *The Wild Bunch:* An Appreciation." *Entertainment World 2* (January 1970):8–12.

2. Michael Sragow, "Screenwriter Jay Cocks and Director Martin Scorsese Thought Big When They Hatched Their Ideas for *Gangs of New York.*" *The Baltimore Sun,* 1 January 2003.

3. The head of a Mafia "family" who is responsible for a group of "soldiers" charged with carrying out his orders; short for "capodecina."

4. A synonym for the "syndicate" used interchangeably with other synonyms, such as the "organization" and the "outfit."

5. Largely because of a falling out between the star and studio chief Jack L. Warner over Bogart's bad-mouthing of this picture in particular and the scripts the studio was offering him in general.

6. Scorsese later hired Irving Lerner (a successful editor before turning director) to be supervising editor of his lavish noir tribute to the Hollywood musical, *New York, New York* (1977). Lerner died before the film was released.

CHAPTER 11

1. Ironically, the president of one of these pressure groups, the Italian-American Civil Rights League, was Joe Colombo, head of the Profaci crime family. While the film was still in production, he was gunned down on the orders of mob kingpin Carlo Gambino, allegedly for drawing too much attention to the Mafia with his antidefamation activities. Colombo survived the hit but lived in a vegetative state until his death in 1978.

2. Robert De Niro has also tested for a role in *The Godfather*—as Sonny, the part that went to James Caan.

3. Mob slang term for old-style Mafiosi.

EPILOGUE

1. Siegel henchman Mickey Cohen took over West Coast operations for the mob. This story is touched upon in Curtis Hanson's superb *L.A. Confidential* (1997), a highly recommended neo-noir that is only peripherally, and fleetingly, a gangster picture as well.

2. The full details of this escapade in Siegel's life are even more like a movie—in fact, a cartoon—and are worth going into. According to accounts, Siegel actually went to Italy to carry out his quixotic scheme on the pretense of selling Mussolini a new kind of explosive device. But the device failed to work during a tryout. Mussolini passed on it, and the disappointed Siegel scurried back to Hollywood.

Selected Bibliography

American Institute Catalog of Motion Pictures Produced in the United States, Feature Films, 1921–1930. New York: R. R. Bowker, 1971.

Anderson, Robert G. *Faces, Forms, Films: The Artistry of Lon Chaney*. New York: A. S. Barnes & Co., 1971.

Barnes, Margaret Anne. *The Tragedy and Triumph of Phenix City, Alabama*. Macon, Ga.: Mercer University Press, 1998.

Baxter, John. *The Gangster Film*. New York: A. S. Barnes & Co., 1970.

_____. *Kubrick: A Biography*. New York: Carroll & Graf Publishers, 1997.

Behn, Noel. *Big Stick-Up at Brink's*. New York: G. P. Putnam's Sons, 1977.

Bergen, Ronald. *The United Artists Story*. New York: Crown, 1986.

Bernstein, Matthew. *Walter Wanger: Hollywood Independent*. Berkeley: University of California Press, 1994.

Biskind, Peter. *Easy Rider, Raging Bulls*. New York: Simon & Schuster, 1998.

Bogdanovich, Peter. *Allan Dwan: The Last Pioneer*. New York: Praeger Publishers, 1971.

_____. *Who the Devil Made It?* New York: Alfred A. Knopf, 1997.

Brownlow, Kevin. *Behind the Mask of Innocence*. New York: Alfred A. Knopf, 1990.

Ciment, Michel. *Kazan on Kazan*. New York: Viking Press, 1974.

Corman, Roger (with Jim Jerome). *How I Made A Hundred Movies in Hollywood and Never Lost a Dime*. New York: Delta, 1990.

Dickens, Homer. *The Complete Films of James Cagney*. Secaucus, N.J.: Citadel Press, 1972, 1989.

Eames, John Douglas. *The MGM Story*. New York: Crown, 1979.

_____. *The Paramount Story*. New York: Crown, 1985.

Eisenschitz, Bernard. *Nicholas Ray: An American Journey*. London: Faber and Faber, 1993.

Fido, Martin. *The Chronicle of Crime*. London: Sevenoaks Books, 2003.

Frayling, Christopher. *Sergio Leone: Something to Do with Death*. London: Faber and Faber, 2000.

Gish, Lillian (with Ann Pinchot). *The Movies, Mr. Griffith & Me*. Upper Saddle River, N.J.: Prentice-Hall, 1969.

Hanke, Ken. *Early Talkies from Hollywood*. Jefferson, N.C.: McFarland, 1993.

Hecht, Ben. *A Child of the Century*. New York: Simon & Schuster, 1954.

Henderson, Robert M. *D. W. Griffith: His Life and Work*. New York: Oxford University Press, 1972.

_____. *D. W. Griffith: The Years at Biograph*. New York: Farrar, Straus and Giroux, 1970.

Herman, Jan. *A Talent for Trouble: The Life of Hollywood's Most Acclaimed Director, William Wyler*. New York: G. P. Putnam's Sons, 1995.

Hirschhorn, Clive. *The Columbia Story*. New York: Crown, 1989.

_____. *The Universal Story*. New York: Crown, 1983.

_____. *The Warner Bros. Story*. New York: Crown, 1979.

Huston, John. *An Open Book*. New York: Alfred A. Knopf, 1980.

Jewell, Richard B., and Vernon Harbin. *The RKO Story*. New York: Arlington House, 1982.

Kaminsky, Stuart M. *Don Siegel: Director*. New York: Curtis Books, 1973.

Kazan, Elia. *A Life*. New York: Alfred A. Knopf, 1988.

Kildare, Owen. *My Mamie Rose: The Story of My Regeneration*. New York: Baker & Taylor Company, 1903.

Lally, Kevin. *Wilder Times: The Life of Billy Wilder*. New York: Henry Holt, 1996.

LeRoy, Mervyn (with Dick Kleiner). *Mervyn LeRoy: Take One*. New York: Hawthorn Books, 1974.

LoBrutto, Vincent. *Stanley Kubrick: A Biography*. New York: Donald I. Fine, 1997.

Marill, Alvin H. *The Complete Films of Edward G. Robinson*. Secaucus, N.J.: Citadel Press, 1990.

McArthur, Colin. *Underworld U.S.A.* New York: Viking Press, 1972.

McCabe, John. *Cagney*. New York: Random House, 1995.

McCarthy, Todd. *Howard Hawks: The Grey Fox of Hollywood*. New York: Grove Press, 1997.

McCarty, Clifford. *The Complete Films of Humphrey Bogart*. Secaucus, N.J.: Citadel Press, 1975.

McGill, Frank N. *McGill's Survey of Cinema, Silent Films*. Englewood Cliffs, N.J.: Salem Press, 1982 (3 vols).

McGilligan, Patrick. *Robert Altman: Jumping Off a Cliff*. New York: St. Martin's Press, 1989.

_____. *The Nature of the Beast: Fritz Lang, a Biography*. New York: St. Martin's Press, 1997.

Miller, Don. *"B" Movies*. New York: Curtis Books, 1973.

Parish, James Robert, and Michael R. Pitts. *The Great Gangster Pictures*. Metuchen, N.J.,: Scarecrow Press, 1976, 1987 (2 vols).

Phillips, Gene D., and Rodney Hill. *The Encyclopedia of Stanley Kubrick*. New York: Checkmark Books, 2002.

Pye, Michael, and Lynda Myles. *The Movie Brats*. New York: Holt, Rinehart and Winston, 1979.

Quinlan, David. *The Illustrated Guide to Film Directors*. Totowa, N.J.: Barnes & Noble Books, 1983.

Robinson, Edward G. (with Leonard Spigelgass). *All My Yesterdays: An Autobiography*. New York: Hawthorn Books, 1973.

Rosenthal, Stuart, and Judith M. Kass. *Tod Browning and Don Siegel*. New York: A. S. Barnes & Co., 1975.

Sann, Paul. *The Lawless Decade*. New York: Crown, 1957.

Sarris, Andrew. *The American Cinema*. New York: E. P. Dutton, 1968.

Schickel, Richard. *D. W. Griffith: An American Life*. New York: Simon & Schuster, 1984.

Schulberg, Budd. *Moving Pictures: Memories of a Hollywood Prince*. New York: Stein & Day, 1981.

Schumach, Murray. *The Face on the Cutting Room Floor*. New York: William Morrow, 1964.

Schumacher, Michael. *Francis Ford Coppola: A Filmmaker's Life*. New York: Crown, 1999.

Segaloff, Nat. *Hurricane Billy: The Stormy Life and Films of William Friedkin*. New York: William Morrow, 1990.

Shipman, David. *The Story of Cinema*. New York: St. Martin's Press, 1982.

Siegel, Don. *A Siegel Film: An Autobiography*. London: Faber and Faber, 1993.

Sifakis, Carl. *The Encyclopedia of American Crime*. New York: Facts on File, 1982.

Sikov, Ed. *On Sunset Boulevard: The Life and Times of Billy Wilder*. New York: Hyperion, 1998.

Skal, David J., and Elias Savada. *Dark Carnival: The Secret World of Tod Browning*. New York: Anchor Books, 1995.

Stack, Robert (with Mark Evans). *Straight Shooting*. New York: Macmillan, 1980.

Sternberg, Josef von. *Fun in a Chinese Laundry: An Autobiography*. New York: Macmillan, 1965.

Thomas, Tony, and Aubrey Solomon. *The Films of 20ᵗʰ Century-Fox*. Secaucus, N.J.: Citadel Press, 1985.

Turkus, Burton, and Sid Feder. *Murder Inc.: The Story of the Syndicate*. New York: Farrar, Straus and Young, 1951.

Walsh, Raoul. *Each Man in His Time*. New York: Farrar, Straus and Giroux, 1974.

Warren, Doug (with James Cagney). *Cagney*. New York: St. Martin's Press, 1983.

Weinberg, Herman G. *Josef von Sternberg: A Critical Study of the Great Film Director*. New York: E. P. Dutton, 1967.

Wood, Robin. *Arthur Penn*. London: Studio Vista, 1967.

Index

About the Author

An adjunct professor of cinema in the Department of Theatre at the University at Albany (State University of New York), John McCarty is the author of more than twenty books about films, filmmakers, and the entertainment industry. In addition, he is the supervising writer and codirector of *The Fearmakers: Screen Masters of Suspense and Terror* (1995), a video documentary series produced by Group II Entertainment based on his 1994 book of the same name.

Born in Albany, New York, in 1944, McCarty attended Boston University, where he graduated with a degree in communications (broadcasting and film). A former Peace Corps volunteer, he has worked in broadcasting and as a copywriter for General Electric Company. He published his first book in 1978 and became a full-time author in 1983.

His affection for the horror film genre (and fascination with what was happening to it) led to his writing the cult classic *Splatter Movies: Breaking the Last Taboo of the Screen* (1984). It was followed by the companion volumes *John McCarty's Official Splatter Movie Guide 1* and *2* (1989, 1992).

Some of his other books about the world of movies include: *Hammer Films* (2002), *The Films of Mel Gibson* (1998), *Movie Psychos and Madmen* (1993), *Thrillers* (1992), *The Modern Horror Film* (1990), *The Complete Films of John Huston* (1992), and *Alfred Hitchcock Presents* (1985). His 1990 novel *Deadly Resurrection,* recommended for a Bram Stoker Award by the Horror Writers of America, was republished in 2000 under the new title *Atavar Speaks.*

In addition, John McCarty has collaborated on a number of books with leading experts in their fields, among them Julie Morgenstern's *New York Times* best-selling *Organizing from the Inside Out*, Ed Slott's *The Retirement Savings Time Bomb . . . And How to Defuse It* (Viking, 2003)—an Amazon.com and Barnes & Noble.com "Hot 100" seller—and public speaking guru Ivy Naistadt's *Speak Without Fear: A Total System for Becoming a Natural, Confident Communicator* (HarperCollins, 2004).

He lives in upstate New York with his wife Cheryl and their four cats.